For Bob

Child and Adolescent Psychotherapy

Child and Adolescent Psychotherapy

Process and Integration

Robert M. Leve
University of Hartford

Allyn and Bacon
Boston • London • Toronto • Sydney • Tokyo • Singapore

A Simon & Schuster Company
Needham Heights, Massachusetts 02194

Library of Congress Cataloging-in-Publication Data

Leve, Robert M.
Child and adolescent psychotherapy: process and integration/ Robert M. Leve.
p. cm.
Includes bibliographical references and index.
ISBN 0-205-14907-3
1. Child psychotherapy. 2. Adolescent psychotherapy. I. Title.
RJ504.L466 1994
618.92'8914—dc20 94-6275
CIP

Printed in the United States of America
10 9 8 7 6 5 4 3 2 1 98 97 96 95 94

To my loving daughters Lori and Mari,
respected scholars and beautiful women.

CONTENTS

Preface

Since the time I first began reading "serious" books, I've seldom read prefaces, and, as time went on, I noticed that I was not alone. I believe few people read prefaces because they are peripheral to the books's topic, being mainly a discourse on why the book was written with some thank you's thrown in, and most people want to plunge right into the meat of the topic. Also, prefaces usually aren't very interesting. Nevertheless, a preface is an author's privilege. Even at the cost of wasting a page or two, I will claim mine.

I began writing this book because I believed I had some ideas that would be helpful, but as the book took shape I came to realize two facts: first, this is a very presumptuous and egotistical attitude, and, second, whatever useful ideas I did have were dwarfed by what I didn't know. Nevertheless, I continued and the result you now hold in your hands. I persevered in my writing because in doing so I was also learning more than I ever imagined; that was what kept me going and became the main motivation for the book's completion.

Years ago, when I started training as a therapist, I was both naive and incredibly ignorant of even the most basic information. After a semester of floundering in profound confusion, I couldn't stand the barely concealed panic any longer. One afternoon, utterly overwhelmed and lost, I walked into my major advisor's office and said, "Dr. Pumroy, what is psychotherapy all about? I don't know what I'm supposed to do." Don Pumroy looked rather amazed, thought for a minute, and then answered, "I don't think anyone ever asked me that before." He paused for another minute, then said, "I guess the main thing is to bring your client to figure out what's wrong and then help them find a way to make it better. Yes, that's it in a nutshell, and the hardest part is to figure out what's wrong in a way they can understand, because if you do that the rest usually falls into place." I still think that is the best explanation I have ever heard. Knowing that, you perhaps can realize why I feel I'm being presumptuous writing this book. Whatever ideas I present in the remainder of the book are only elaborations of Don Pumroy's answer.

I do have many people to thank for their help in writing this book. Even though many years have passed I still remember Mr. Wheatcroft, my instructor in freshman English composition. He taught me to write and encouraged me. I also remember how much I learned in my child psychotherapy seminar during two wonderful postdoctoral years at Judge Baker Guidance Center and Children's Hospital, Boston. Irv Hurwitz and Joe Lord gave the most clear and comprehensive therapy seminar I have ever experienced, and I suspect I am in their debt for more of my ideas than I realize. As my primary supervisor, Irv Hurwitz's clinical brilliance was both intimidating and a joy. My other therapy supervisor, Dick Brodie, taught me the pragmatic parts of psychotherapy and how to enjoy the children I treated. Sadly, he is gone, and we all miss his laughter.

Pam Hogen, a friend and colleague, served, early on, as a cogent mirror against which to evaluate my ideas, and she provided the initial encouragement to begin this difficult and daunting task. Some of the more poignant examples are taken from her work. Joe Fitzpatrick, another colleague and friend, allowed me to use some of his case material as examples. I'm terribly proud that I contributed to Joe's clinical training as he has the rare inner strength to work with terminally ill children and our world desperately needs people like Joe. Some of my present students, Neil Metzner and Brian Quail, have been collaborators in our work on the relationship between diagnosis and treatment and their important contributions can be seen in chapter two. Brian also was very helpful in offering cogent criticisms of my writing and in providing a critical editing. Carolyn Steigler also was a great help in correcting some of my worst grammatical blunders, and her smile and pleasant ways were a wonderful addition to my office. The editorial staff at Allyn and Bacon were very helpful in guiding me through the complexities of the publishing process, especially Mylan Jaixen, my editor. He kept me on task and remained a source of encouragement even after I missed promised deadlines. Sue Hutchinson was helpful fielding my phone calls and answering my naive questions. Dr. Sally Moore-Pollock of Hutchinson and Associates provided me with a needed and useful critique of the manuscript. Linda Olender was a constant and silent source of encouragement and often put aside her own activities when I needed to focus my full attentions to this work. She has the gift of creating beauty all about her and those she loves. I am grateful for the help of John Goethe, who indirectly made it possible for me to finish this work. More importantly, he helped me to learn what can not be put into words.

This is a book about children, and we all know the importance of play in the life of a child. I believe that play is also important to adults, and my play is racing bicycles and flying sailplanes. I'm sure that my play helped provide the necessary pleasurable distraction needed to maintain my motivation for writing on a difficult and abstract subject. I hope that anyone reading this book also loves to play, because in addition to keeping us sane it gives us a joy in life. More than that, adults who can play better understand the children they treat.

I suppose this is the place to explain some of the idiosyncracies of my writing. I often write in the first person rather than following the more academically traditional third person. I do this because it is personal and therapy, or any work with children, is a very personal endeavor. I'll also confess that I feel more comfortable with an informal writing style. You will notice that I have chosen to use both male and female gender pronouns throughout the book. My way of solving the gender pronoun problem was to alternate the use of male and female pronouns in my chapters. This seemed to me a way of avoiding the predominant (if traditional) use of male pronouns and avoiding the awkwardness of using neuter pronouns. After a few pages I found this writing style quite comfortable, and I hope it is not disconcerting to the reader.

Having finished my explanations and thank you's I hope that my ideas contribute to helping you, as a therapist, help children. Ultimately, that's the only purpose of this book and what these years of work have been all about.

About the Author

Robert M. Leve received his doctorate in clinical psychology from the University of Maryland and completed a postdoctoral fellowship at the Judge Baker Guidance Center and Children's Hospital in Boston. As Associate Professor and Director of Dissertation Research at the Graduate Institute of Professional Psychology of the University of Hartford, he teaches courses in child and adolescent treatment and psychopathology. His most recent research activities focus on using an enhanced diagnostic system to predict the best match between type of therapy and the individual child. As a practicing clinical child psychologist, he treats children and adolescents through his clinical and consultative practice in Hartford, Connecticut. His major clinical interests are the pragmatics of integrating diverse treatment modalities and the process of developing individualized protocols for children.

Section I

What Psychotherapists Need to Know and What They Ought to Know

In the three chapters of this section we will cover the material that is needed for a proper grounding and understanding of the psychotherapeutic process with children and adolescents. As any experienced therapist knows, a pragmatic knowledge of therapeutic techniques and personality theory is not enough to be an effective psychotherapist with children. Such pragmatic knowledge must rest on basic theoretical underpinnings that ought to include the following:

1. A firm grounding in the basic theory of all the many kinds of treatments.
2. An ability to understand the psychological background of the child and his or her family.
3. Knowledge of the meaning of the child's symptoms and how they relate to the process of diagnosis.
4. An ability to understand the relationships between diagnosis and treatment.
5. An understanding of the assumptions that underlie the particular methods of treatment.

At the present time there are many kinds of treatments from which to choose, and there is a tendency for therapists to specialize in one technique or theory or school to the exclusion of others. Often practitioners will call themselves behavior therapists or cognitive therapists or family therapists. Sometimes, even these titles are too general, for although someone calls himself or herself a family therapist, he or she tends toward only one type of family therapy. Perhaps they are "structured" family therapists, as conceived by Salvador Minuchin, or "cognitive" therapists, according to Aaron Beck's ideas. While this may be satisfying to a therapist because it provides a person with a strong professional identity and resolves a great deal of the ambiguity inherent in the very complex and often confusing choices that must be faced in psychotherapy, this narrowing of focus and skills will limit potential effectiveness.

Of course no therapist can be all things to all children, but knowing the basic ideas underlying all forms of therapy not only allows a therapist to be more flexible in using whatever techniques a child needs, but it enables the therapist to know when he or she is not the best therapist for a child and then to make a sound referral. All too often the needs of a child are reinterpreted and redefined to fit the therapists way of doing therapy and this does not give a child the best possible care.

The topic of diagnosis is equally important, and although it is too large an issue to be discussed adequately in this book, it is also too important to ignore in a study of psychotherapy. Before a therapist can make a sound decision on the type of treatment a child needs, he must understand the background and symptomatology of the child and family. As a result, I have chosen to discuss what I feel are the most important aspects of the diagnostic process, especially the relationship between diagnosis and treatment. This is often a confusing issue because there are so many dimensions to both treatment and diagnosis. However, a therapist needs to understand the often confusing connection between them.

Lastly, I firmly believe that a therapist needs to understand the assumptions that underlie the psychological treatments used. Every type of psychotherapy is based on specific assumptions about such things as the values of the culture the child lives in, how children change, what are the important events in a child's life, who are the important people in a child's life, what kind of psychological theories best describe the development of personality and intellect, and many other basic aspects of children and childhood. Just as the type of mathematics we use depends on our assumptions of the universe, the type of treatment that is used will depend on assumptions about the universe of children. Few therapists ever take the time to identify or understand the basic assumptions that underlie what they do. Yet this knowledge allows a therapist to better understand what she is actually doing. It also helps when making therapeutic decisions, especially at those times when the usual theory or technique doesn't seem applicable. Of course, every therapist ought to construct and understand the assumptions that are basic to the type of treatment they use.

1

The Process of Psychological Change

Psychotherapy and Change

Perhaps this title is redundant because the process of psychotherapy implies that some sort of change is going to occur (hopefully, but not always, as every experienced child psychotherapist knows). In some form or another therapists talk about three different aspects of change.

Behavioral Change

This refers to actual changes in the way a child behaves or acts. It is what children do, especially in relation to the other people or objects within their life space. This is what we would see if we were able to watch the child go about in daily life, although as therapists we seldom see much of a child in everyday life. For the most part we see them in the confines of a very artificial and contrived situation, the therapist's office. Since behavior is an objective phenomenon, it can be easily observed and with some effort measured. Thus, we can compare a child's previous behavior with later behavior and assess whether a change has occurred. This is commonly used as a criteria in psychotherapy research.

Cognitive Change

Psychological theorists and researchers have provided us with many definitions of "cognitive," but we will avoid this valuable, but overwhelming subject by only dealing with cognitive change in psychotherapy. Here it refers to a child's ability to understand himself and the environment. To do this a child must be able to use logic. This sounds simple enough, but we need to know what we mean by the words understanding and logic.

In terms of a psychotherapeutic process, logic is the ability to identify what is important and what is unimportant. For example, if a ten-year-old boy yells back at his mother when she tells the child to stop beating on his younger brother, the boy needs to understand which aspects of this situation are important and which are irrelevant. The fact that his brother called him a name five minutes earlier may be important, whereas the fact that his brother drank a glass of milk is not. The fact that the mother has been yelling at both boys all day long is important, whereas the mailman delivering the mail is not. Almost all children can understand such simple relationships, but when children have a limited ability to see these logical connections between events, then they are seriously impaired in their ability to participate in certain forms of psychotherapy.

Understanding is the ability to relate a new event to an older one. When a child is faced with a new person, situation, concept, or emotion, that "thing" is unfamiliar, and the child tries to understand it by comparing it to some other experience that is familiar. If the youngster sees similarities between the two experiences then the child begins to understand it because it is like something else that is already understood.

Sometimes the comparison is a good one and the two events are in fact very similar. In this case, the new experience is no longer strange. Sometimes the two experiences are not similar and the child automatically seeks out another previous experience and makes another comparison. This is usually satisfying to the child; it is so rudimentary a process that children and adults do it continuously. Sometimes a child compares the new experience to an older one and believes they are similar when in fact they are different. Then the child is mistaken, but holds on to the belief because it makes the new experience seem familiar. As time goes on and the child has more new experiences he or she may come to see that the two experiences were not similar and will correct the initial understanding. Like the use of logic, the process of understanding is such a basic human process that without it an individual is seriously impaired.

All children organize their cognitive world differently and a therapist must try to understand the way each particular child does so in order to bring about the needed cognitive changes. Therapists bring about these cognitive changes by helping a child recognize misunderstandings and improve logical thinking.

Emotional Changes

Emotional changes are changes in the comfort, happiness, and satisfaction of a child. They are crucial to psychotherapy. Unless children "feel" good about an experience, they are unlikely to change the way they are. Forcing them to change is a painful and difficult process and any such changes will be temporary. Emotions are very hard to define. They are internal states that seem to be very powerful, but they can not be directly observed. In spite of that, people have little difficulty identifying what they mean when terms such as sad, angry, and happy are used, and other people seem to understand them quite well. The problem is that although we can see emotional behavior, we can not see emotions. When we try to use words to describe how we feel, they do not seem to fit and are inadequate to capture the power of the feelings. Perhaps emotions are so individual that the only way we can understand another person is to feel those very emotions ourselves.

A classic dilemma of therapists is that in trying to talk about feelings they must use words and sentences which by their very nature are inadequate and only partially communicate what the therapist and patient are feeling. Most experienced therapists find that emotions are better talked about not by using words per se but by relating common situations that both understand. Somehow the situation brings forth a recollection of the emotions better than words.

Of course separating children into behavioral, cognitive, and emotional parts is artificial. Children are single, unitary beings and do not function in three different ways. They simply act, live, and interact as one and we divide them into three different aspects because it simplifies them. As therapists, we have trouble understanding the totality of a child's functioning so we divide it into parts that can be better understood. It helps us to understand what is a very complex phenomenon, but it also can be misleading because we may think only about one aspect of the child's functioning to the exclusion of the others. We also may forget that each of these aspects is so intimately related that a change in one will almost always result in a change in the other. When children begin to understand something differently, they begin to behave differently and begin to feel differently. Similarly, when they begin to change the way they feel, they may begin to behave differently and may change their understanding of a situation.

The classical separation of people and children into these three aspects is probably a consequence of the way our Western culture has developed its psychological concepts over the course of many centuries. It is also a product of our language, which has changed to reflect the culture. We know that in other cultures these separations are not made or are not made in the same way. Nevertheless, to understand children to the fullest extent we need to remember that children do not see themselves as divided into conceptual parts, but as one thing, themselves. Unless we strive to remember that fact we are likely to become too simplistic in our treatment and are likely to ignore the important interrelationships between the cognitive, behavioral, and emotional aspects of a child.

How Children Change

How to bring about changes in children is what psychotherapy is all about, and there are many points of view on how to accomplish this. As a result there are many different theories and types of treatments. Sometimes therapists can become so immersed in the theoretical world they lose track of the fact that psychotherapy is only one way of changing a child's behavior—and, in the overall scheme of the world, a relatively unimportant one.

Most changes in children occur naturally as the result of changes in their life circumstances. A close friend moves away and they seek out new friends. They get older, move into a different academic track in school and their self concept changes. They enter junior high school and become less dependent on their parents. These and many other changes are made constantly and are so frequent that they are not even noticed. Even when a child lives in a relatively stable environment, there are constant changes occurring as the result of brain maturation and physiological growth. In a sense children are always in a mini-evolution. Changes occur in their life space and they adjust to the change.

Most changes occur in a nonremarkable and harmonious fashion, but this is not always the case. Sometimes changes are forced upon a child, and there are different consequences to forced changes as opposed to syntonic changes. Either within a psychotherapeutic setting or outside of it, forced changes are difficult. Children react to being forced to do anything they do not like, and so attempting to force a child to change usually causes a great deal of pain and anguish both for the child and the adult. As a result, it may change the relationship between them. Almost always they dislike each other for some period of time. Often the child will dig in his heels and simply refuse to submit, and many children are stubborn enough to carry this through. If the child does submit in the end, the change may be felt as foreign and will only be temporary, or last as long as the adult keeps up the pressure. The most common result is that there is an increase in emotional behavior because the child may feel angry and even depressed.

Trying to force changes on a child is seldom done in psychotherapy, with the exception at times of Operant Behavior Modification. Usually, the therapist does not have enough control of the child's environment to successfully force a change. Besides, such an attempt normally has a devastating effect on the therapist-child relationship. That is why therapeutic changes are usually syntonic changes and occur because the child either consciously or unconsciously accepts a new way of acting or thinking. Syntonic changes are often different from the usual child-adult relationship wherein the lower-status child is often forced to accept what the adult desires.

Why do children change their ways in therapy when they have steadfastly refused to do so before? There are many complex reasons for this, but the most important is that the therapist creates a warm, trusting relationship with the child so that the child feels safe enough to consider alternatives ways of thinking and acting. The emotional security of such relationship with the therapist provides the child with a sense of safety and allows the child to risk trying new ways of behaving and feeling. Of course the therapist-child relationship is not always warm and happy. Often it must be angry or unhappy and some children may feel the need to test it at times. In spite of this, a therapist must strive for a warm and trusting relationship with a child or teenager in order to bring about positive changes in the child's life. It is very easy to use the term "warm and trusting relationship," but more difficult to build and maintain such a relationship. To a great extent that is what much of the remainder of this book is about.

A Profusion of Treatments

> *"Psychotherapy no longer needs a prophet from the mountains to bring down from exalted heights a message of the true and correct way of doing psychotherapy" (Beitman, 1987).*

This statement reflects the attitude many scholars have toward the recent proliferation of treatments. Many would go further by saying that we no longer need any new treatments. Only thirty or so years ago the situation was drastically different. Then, there were basically only two schools of psychotherapy, Psychoanalysis, or some variation from it, and Carl Rogers's "client-centered" therapy. Some innovative therapists were just beginning to experiment with behavioral cognitive and family therapies, but most therapists belonged to one or the other of these two schools, and there was little overlap between them. Now the situation is quite different because the late 1960s and 1970s have produced well over a hundred wholly new and diverse schools of therapy, with many variations within those schools. For the most part we are fortunate to have these new and effective methods of treatment available, for they enable us to treat a wider range of disordered behaviors and to have treatments for specific to specific problems.

The easiest way to describe and conceptualize these different methods of psychotherapy is in terms of their differences. It is simple to think about the ways in which Operant Behavior Therapy differs from William Glaser's reality therapy, but that is only half the picture. Knowledge of similarities between treatment methods is even more important. However, seeing the similarities between treatments is a difficult intellectual process. People always are better able to grasp differences than similarities.

There are a number of psychotherapies used with children (Johnson, Rasbury, & Siegel, 1986) and I have listed these in appendix A along with their distinctive characteristics. This listing certainly is not exhaustive, but it does cover the major schools most readers are familiar with and should be sufficiently illustrative of the major trends in the field of child treatment.

People love lists and categorizations because they simplify the complex. Any list of therapies categorizes them, but hides the fact that there are as many therapies as there are therapists. I don't mean that as a cliché, but as something to think about. The very nature of the work requires a therapist to bring himself into it, and, just as people differ, so will treatments. Barry Nierenberg, a good friend of mine has a clever way of describing this (Barry Nierenberg, 1988). Barry Nierenberg believes that everyone does a unique brand of therapy, so he simply refers to Bob-therapy (mine), Barry-therapy (his), or Pam-therapy (another friend). We all do similar kinds of treatment, but his way captures the fact that as each therapist is different, so each provides a different psychotherapy.

The Difference Between Child and Adult Psychotherapies

The treatment of children is not adult treatment scaled down to a child's level. It is a qualitatively different process. In a sense we will be discussing this idea throughout the remainder of the book, but we need to identify some of the differences at this point.

First, the criteria of treatment is different. Adults, with the help of their therapist, set their own goals, but this isn't true for children, especially young children. Usually, it is the parents, with the help of the therapist, who set these goals, and the child has little say in it. In fact, the child may not like the goals at all and their desires are seldom met in the short run. For example, a twelve-year-old may be quite happy tormenting his younger brother and have no desire to stop this cruelty. Hopefully, the goals the parents and therapist set are best for the child in the long run, and the child will come to realize that.

Of course, assuming that parents and therapist know what is best means the child is in a relatively powerless position and no one, not even children, accepts this easily. That is one reason why children, especially at the beginning of treatment, are more likely to fight the therapist's attempts to bring about change. Why should they want to change themselves according to someone else's criteria?

Another difference is that children do not usually choose to come to see a therapist. They are brought by their parents, often against their wishes. Sometimes they are against therapy because they sense they will be coerced into changes they do not want to make; sometimes they react to the social stigma of having to see the "shrink;" and sometimes they just do not like the strange environment of therapy, and make no mistake about it, therapy is a strange and unusual situation for children.

At times, children do ask to see a therapist, but while it is not a rare occurrence, neither is it frequent. Teenagers are more likely to seek out a psychotherapist than younger children, perhaps because they are more sophisticated and know of the existence of people called therapists. Sometimes, they are more accepting of therapy because, as teenagers, they are more likely to be able to set the goals of their treatment. However, even most teenagers need the help, permission, and financial support of their parents.

Since children do not seek treatment by themselves and are not able to set their own goals in psychotherapy, they do not have or take on the same sense of responsibility for their treatment as do adults. Thus, they may not have the same overt motivation toward change. Even when they are quite unhappy they may not feel any great motivation to change the way things are. Often (as with many of us adults) the security of a familiar anguish is preferable to the unknown.

Of course, there are also important cognitive and intellectual differences between children and adults that significantly affect their treatment. Adults need a cognitive framework within which to organize their ideas, and it is through this cognitive mediational process that they bring about behavioral and emotional changes. Children, especially young children, do not have that same kind of hierarchical thinking (Piaget, 1951). They deal with particulars, and behavioral and emotional changes occur in a less verbal fashion. This cognitive difference has important implications for the process of child psychotherapy, and we will discuss this topic at some length in later chapters.

This difference in thinking means the therapist will not be able to use the familiar verbal processes that he or she uses with adult friends and colleagues. As therapists, we need to learn to converse differently with children because they think differently. That is not easy to learn, especially with young children. Adults speak to each other and assume (correctly for the most part) that we are understood. When someone does not understand, they are likely to say, "I don't understand what you mean." Children often do not understand what we are saying, but they seldom tell us. They usually just give us a confused nod of acceptance or do not say anything.

These are some of the more obvious ways in which psychotherapy is different with children than it is with adults. There are other more subtle differences, but these will emerge as we cover other more specific topics in later chapters.

Family Therapies

Including family therapies with individual therapies may seem a bit like mixing apples and oranges, but even though they look different, we better not forget that they are both fruit: They taste good and life would be less interesting if we only ate one or the other. Many therapists see themselves as family therapists per se and they often feel that it is a superior technique to individual therapies. This is because they understand that dysfunctional children are the result of family difficulties and carry the symptoms of the entire family. Establishing a new therapy by discrediting existing ones is a common occurrence in the history of psychological treatment and has occurred with behavior therapy, the cognitive therapies, and many of the newer psychodynamic therapies. However, it is simply a stage in the history of any new treatment. Now that family therapy has a well-established place in the world of treatments, this simplistic attitude has begun to change. In spite of the present differences between individual and family treatments, any competent child therapist needs to at least be familiar with both techniques.

Although family therapists often use therapeutic techniques and a theoretical basis that is different from individual treatment, family therapies also seem to divide themselves along behavioral, cognitive, and psychodynamic lines. There are a great number of family therapies, but we will review the four that have wide acceptance in child treatment. These treatments and their characteristics are listed in appendix B.

Principles Common to All Psychotherapies

"Psychotherapy is merely conversation."

Most psychotherapists would take offense at this statement, complaining that it is too simple and overlooks too many complexities of human interaction. They may be correct, but from a purely structural perspective, that is all psychotherapy is. We may prefer to think of psychotherapy in more grandiose terms, but in actuality it usually is a verbal interaction between two or more people. Before we overemphasize its unimportance, we need to remember that conversation and human interactions must be terribly important or we humans would not do them so often. We also need to remember that most emotional, behavioral, and cognitive changes in children take place as the result of some sort of interaction with other people, and conversation or verbal interactions are the catalyst for most of these changes. It is difficult to imagine a child making a significant change without the involvement of another person. Infants learn to smile more when their mothers coo and smile back. Toddlers learn to stay away from electric plugs when their mothers say, "No." Teenagers usually learn to drink beer with their friends, and they usually talk while they do it.

Sometimes children fail to develop normal behaviors or develop behaviors that are unpleasant and cause them and others to be unhappy. Then the important people around them try to change such a situation. To do so they use conversation or some sort of verbal interaction. Most of the time this works and life goes on. Sometimes, it does not work, and that is when we use the special kind of conversation called psychotherapy.

There are many differences between ordinary conversations and psychotherapy. Some of these differences are obvious. Conversations take place in the home, school, or other places familiar to the child while psychotherapy takes place in a strange office, hospital, or clinic. Conversations involve familiar people, such as parents, teachers, or friends, while psychotherapy involves strangers who often have titles. Of course most ordinary conversations are free, but there is usually a direct financial cost to psychotherapy. There are other differences, but these are enough to demonstrate the unusual quality of this special conversation.

We already have seen that these special conversations, take on many forms, but there are certain principles common to all. The unswerving emphasis on these principles constitutes the main difference between psychotherapy and ordinary conversation. Jerome Frank and Judd Marmor (1978) believe that all treatments have these four common aspects.

1. Close Relationship. All treatments strive for a close, trusting relationship between therapist and child.
2. Emotional Release. Therapists encourage the children they are treating to release and express their feelings.
3. Cognitive and Experiential Learning. Either directly or indirectly, therapists try to teach children different and more adaptive ways of behaving.
4. Practice. At some point therapists encourage children to use their new ways of thinking, behaving, and feeling in their everyday activities.

Unfortunately, these similarities between treatments tend to be large and global; usually too global to be applicable to specific situations. Paradoxically, we may be able to get a better idea of the useful similarities among psychotherapies by seeing on what dimensions they differ. If we can order different treatments on important dimensions then we will see not only to what extent treatments differ, but also to what extent they are similar. This kind of information will let us know if two treatments are similar enough to be used with the same child without causing therapeutic chaos.

How Therapies Differ and How They Are the Same

There are many dimensions that can be utilized to analyze psychotherapies. I will cover the ones that seem important to me, but other therapists are likely to organize psychotherapies on different dimensions. Also, this will not be a complete and exhaustive discussion of the topic. I only hope to show some of the important similarities and differences and how they may affect the eclectic use of different treatments. To make pragmatic decisions concerning a coordinated use of more than one therapy in an actual treatment situation requires the knowledge of many idiosyncratic patient, therapist, and environmental factors, which are impossible to consider in any theoretical discussion.

In an effort to organize and understand what goes on in psychotherapy we can divide it into content, or what is talked about and dealt with, and the process, or the psychological techniques that are used. In this book, section II deals with process and section III discusses content.

Most therapies postulate theories of personality or theories of learning and these are a crucial part of that treatment. The personality theory underlying the therapy usually determines the content discussed because that tells the therapist what issues are important. Unfortunately, psychotherapies differ a great deal in terms of their underlying personality or developmental theories; so much so that at the present time theorists usually differ in trying to logically arrange them on one dimension. Some therapies postulate personality theories, others learning theories, and even others are directly based on theories of development. Even within these categories there is little relationship. For example, "client-centered" therapy puts forth a personality theory based on a person's need for self-enhancement; psychoanalysis is based on ideas of psychosexual development; and object relations treatment is based on the early relationship between the self and other objects. These theories are so different that I hesitate to try to organize them in some logical fashion on a unitary dimension.

Fortunately, the theory that underlies a particular psychotherapy affects the therapist much more than it does the child. Theories are cognitive structures that help therapists organize their thoughts and decide what is important enough to discuss in therapy sessions. Children never have to deal with theories directly, but only in so far as it affects their therapist.

In respect to process variables the situation is less confusing. These can be organized on unitary dimensions with only "a bit" of stretching to make them fit. There are eight dimensions that I find helpful in emphasizing the similarities and differences between types of psychotherapy processes. These are as follows.

The Characteristics of Psychotherapies

Goals of Treatment

All treatments attempt to achieve certain goals or kinds of changes in a child. On one end of this dimension, behavioral treatments usually seek to change specific maladaptive symptoms. Examples might be self-stimulatory behaviors, hitting a classmate, bedwetting, and phobias about going to school.

Cognitive treatments attempt to change children across broader dimensions. They attempt to change the cognitions and mediating thoughts that determine the symptoms. By changing these underlying cognitions they assume that the specific symptoms will also change in a positive way. The symptoms usually are more general, such as not completing schoolwork, arguing with parents, and being depressed.

Some psychodynamic therapies, such as classical psychoanalysis, psychoanalytically oriented psychotherapy, ego psychology, and object relations treatment, try to provide the child with a subtle form of emotional insight into the causes of his or her emotional difficulties. This is the primary goal of treatment, although psychodynamic therapists usually assume that changes in emotional understanding will also result in specific symptom changes. The particular kind of emotional insight will be determined by the personality theory underlying that form of treatment.

Psychodynamic treatments, such as client-centered psychotherapy, existential psychotherapy, Adlerian psychotherapy, and Gestalt psychotherapy, also are concerned with emotional insights and also assume there will be an accompanying remission of symptoms. However, these treatments attempt to provide the child with a changed philosophy of life that raises the child to a different level of consciousness. In this respect they are similar in that they believe that psychotherapy should have a positive effect on a child's ethics, social responsibility, and general philosophy of life.

As you can see each kind of treatment has its own goals and these differ from one to another. Not only do the goals differ, but the entire process of goal setting differs. Behavioral therapies mandate that the therapist must be rigorous and definitive in setting specific goals. There is little room for ambiguity in this process. Goals to be achieved must be identified at the beginning of treatment and any changes or deviations must also be specified. For example, in operant behavior therapy, an undesired behavior is identified, defined, and often measured; elimination of that behavior is the specific goal of treatment.

On the opposite extreme are existential and client-centered psychotherapies. These treatments do not place such an emphasis on goal setting; and therapists do not feel a need to identify clearly defined goals at the beginning of treatment. This procedure is congruent with the basic philosophy behind these treatments, since in large part the child assumes control of the course of treatment and deciding upon the goals of treatment may be a part of the therapeutic process. At the beginning of treatment few children have such insight into themselves and their difficulties that they are able to be rigorous and specific about what they want to accomplish in treatment. If they did they probably would not need a therapist. Thus, goals usually are not clearly defined in these therapeutic methods, and the procedure of goal-setting is not emphasized. Often the procedure is ignored or spoken of casually and informally.

Whatever the form of treatment used, parents often define the goals of treatment in their initial discussions with the therapist. They usually tell the therapist what they are worried about or what they think is wrong with their son or daughter and to the extent that they define their child's problems. They also are implicitly setting the goals to be accomplished. Of course, a therapist needs to be part of this process and may redefine or reinterpret the parents' understanding of the child's problems. In this way the therapist affects this implicit goal-setting.

The question of setting goals with the child is a complex one and needs to be different for each child. Irrespective of the type of treatment used, there may be advantages or disadvantages to identifying the goals of treatment in the initial sessions. Some children make better progress when they know what they are trying to accomplish and when goals are made explicit. Other children are not interested: They may do better taking each session as it comes, without an overall future goal to direct therapy sessions. A therapist must make that decision at the beginning of treatment. There are no hard and fast guidelines. If the decision is not dictated by the type of psychotherapy that is used, it must be based on the therapist's knowledge of the child, therapeutic experience, and a good bit of clinical intuition.

Of course, child treatment is affected by the larger culture, and changes in our way of life have had a distinct effect on whether or not therapists are rigorous in delineating therapeutic goals at the beginning of treatment. We live in an increasingly bureaucratic and systematized world. Third-party insurance demands and peer reviews have taken away some of the independence of child therapists. These new factors in our culture emphasize systems, bottomlines, and objectives, and they often demand that child treatment conform to their criteria under the guise of cost-effectiveness or cost-containment. To some extent, therapists are pressured by these outside influences and often must modify their treatment to conform with these new factors. Usually, insurance companies or professional review groups demand that therapists have definite goals for their patients, even if this kind of specificity is not congruent with the type of therapy being used or the therapeutic needs of children or their parents. Often the goals that are demanded are too simplistic to be useful in an actual therapy situation. At the present time, this cultural trend is becoming steadily more pervasive. As the trend continues, therapists will need to be aware that the goals demanded by outside agencies are usually quite different than the goals that are useful within a therapeutic session. The two must not be confused.

Length of Treatment

Discussing the length of treatment is somewhat inexact because in every therapy the number of sessions depends on such things as the initial problems, the motivation of the child, skill of the therapist, and many other factors. However, there are general tendencies within each type of treatment. As a rule, behavior therapies are short-term treatments; but depending on the type of behavioral treatment and the particular behaviors needing modification, the actual number may vary greatly. Actually, the word sessions is often inapplicable to operant behavior modification since the retraining may go on continuously until the child reaches a certain criteria of positive behaviors. Respondent techniques, such as desensitization and flooding, are also short-term, but the mean number of sessions at some treatment centers is as high as 50.

Cognitive therapies, such as rational-emotive therapy, strive to be "short-term" treatments and usually are, but here, too, the mean number of sessions will depend on the particular patient and symptoms. The number of sessions in Donald Michenbaum's and Phillip Kendall's techniques is defined at the beginning of treatment, and child and therapist seldom meet more than twenty times. Aaron Beck advises limiting the number of therapy sessions in his treatment to twenty.

With few exceptions, the psychodynamic treatments are long-term, and child and therapist may meet once a week for a year, or even much longer. However, the time is variable and many children are successfully treated in a much shorter time. There is little difference between the psychodynamic treatments per se in accepted length of treatment. Usually, the number of sessions is determined by the progress of treatment and the needs of the child. Adlerian psychotherapy is an exception and advocates that treatment be both short-term and time-limited. There are a number of well-accepted and popular short-term and time-limited versions of psychodynamic treatments. These attempt to drastically shorten therapy. In these methods, the therapist is usually more directive and confrontative.

Time Orientation

All therapies vary in the time focus of treatment. In some therapies, the therapist and child tend to discuss and deal with present issues and problems, while in others they talk about what happened in the recent or distant past. The orientation of therapeutic techniques also can be seen as emphasizing the past, present, or future.

All behavioral therapies are strongly present and future-oriented. Both operant and respondent therapists use techniques that deal with present symptoms. They try to modify these symptoms to bring about a change, and although they hope these changes last for long periods of time, their methods are designed for the immediate future. An operant therapist hopes that a reinforcement schedule or an arrangement of Discriminant Stimuli (SD's) will be so powerful that the child will rapidly change his disordered behavior. Similarly, in flooding, the therapist dealing with immediate symptoms will look for a rapid decrease in a phobia.

Cognitive therapies also have a present and immediate future orientation, but they tend to have a greater concern with past events. To some extent, knowledge of how a dysfunctional way of thinking originated or how the child has functioned is helpful in designing or modifying cognitive techniques appropriate to the particular child. However, these treatments do not extend far into the past or focus on early events in the child's life.

As a group, psychodynamic therapies are strongly concerned with past events in a child's life; and since they are very verbal treatments, these past events may become a common topic of discussion. Of course, this is determined to a great extent by the age of the child. Therapy with young children deals more with the recent past, since their memories are not well developed, and they tend to be present oriented. Older children and adolescents do not have these cognitive limitations. Although many psychodynamic treatments use play techniques, the content of the play usually deals with issues from the child's past life. How far back in time a therapist tries to focus therapeutic discussions depends less on the particular type of psychotherapy then on the cognitive abilities of a child and the nature of his emotional problems.

Existential treatments in general and Glaser's reality therapy specifically are the exceptions in that they are more present oriented than the other psychodynamic psychotherapies. However, even these treatments are flexible and will focus on past issues depending on their idiosyncratic importance.

Depth of Therapist-Child Relationship

The relationship between the therapist and child is an important factor that differentiates methods of treatment. All treatments require some degree of relationship because caring adults can hardly try to help children without some kind of personal feelings growing up between them. However, because of the length of treatment, the techniques used, and the kind of personality theory underlying the therapy, this relationship varies a great deal.

Operant methods do not emphasize a close relationship since the therapist only tries to modify specific behaviors with rewards and punishments and spends little time learning about the child through conversation. In most of the respondent conditioning methods, such as desensitization and flooding, the therapist does learn about the child's fears and concerns and a warm relationship can arise. However, since treatment is so brief and task-oriented, the relationship tends to be positive, but not deep or long lasting.

A somewhat closer relationship usually arises with the cognitive treatment because treatments last longer and the technique is not as task-oriented as the behavioral methods. Cognitive therapists rely more on conversational modes, both to learn needed information about the child and to communicate the cognitive restructuring. However, establishing a deep relationship is not an important part of the therapy, and in some treatments it is actively avoided.

Almost all of the psychodynamic psychotherapies foster and utilize a deep and intense therapist-child relationship as an integral part of the treatment, and there are important similarities among them in the kind of relationship that is established. Psychoanalysis, psychoanalytically oriented treatment, ego psychology, Adlerian therapy and object relations therapy are similar in that the therapist fosters a strong relationship so that the child can express feelings concerning parents, siblings, or other important people in his or her life through feelings toward the therapist. The therapist is careful to control this relationship so it does not become so strong that it interferes with the therapeutic process. Therapists must also understand and control their own feelings toward a child for the same reasons.

In client-centered therapy the therapist is not as concerned with limiting the therapist-child relationship. Rather, the therapist must identify with the child and experience a deep "unconditional positive regard" for the child. Existential therapists are similar in that they strive for an "authentic" relationship with their patients and avoid trying to manipulate the deep feelings between therapist and child.

The therapist-child relationship in Gestalt therapy is intense and empathic, but different. Here the therapist is confrontative, and by continually pointing out the dysfunctional "games" the child uses, the therapist occupies a superior position to the child.

As can be seen, almost all the psychodynamic treatments strive for a deep and intense relationship; however, there are important differences between them. Therapists who attempt to switch from one mode of psychodynamic therapy to another must prepare the child for such a transition, because the deep relationship that is established makes the child especially sensitive to even minor relationship changes. That might result in a child who is likely to be hurt, confused, and upset.

Catharsis

Catharsis is the Greek word for purging or cleansing, but one interpretation maintains that it comes from the Greek word *katheiro,* which means "to rid the land of monsters" (Chatwin, 1987). In psychotherapy, catharsis refers to an intense expression of deep emotions (perhaps emotional monsters), which allows a child to feel better. A related concept used in psychotherapy is "corrective emotional experience." In this therapeutic technique, the child does not purge his emotions, but has an experience that corrects a prior maladaptive emotional reaction. For example, a child who has experienced rejection from important adults in life may feel depressed and ashamed. The therapist may correct this negative experience by developing a genuine love and respect for the child, which in turn allows the child to have different and better self feelings.

Cathartic experiences are seldom used in behavioral or cognitive treatments where the emphasis is on overt behavior or cognitive patterns and the therapist-child relationship is solution oriented. In these treatments the therapist usually avoids open expression of emotions, as that kind of behavior interferes with the treatment.

Cathartic expressions of emotions are commonly encouraged in most psychodynamic therapies. This gives the child a chance to express painful feelings in a helpful and supportive environment. Differences between treatments are more related to which emotions are focused upon than the process the therapist uses to encourage a child to express that emotion.

There are differences in the use of corrective emotional experiences. Although most psychodynamic therapies frequently use this technique, Adlerian, Gestalt, and Existential therapists tend to be more openly supportive or directly confrontative. Therapists of these orientations are more openly expressive of their own feelings in their efforts to provide a child with an emotional experience that would correct the child's maladaptive emotional reaction.

Therapeutic Control

Treatments differ in the extent in which the therapist controls the therapeutic process. In some treatments the therapist assumes total control and the child is simply a passive agent who follows the therapist's directions. In other therapies the child is allowed free reign in deciding what will be discussed and when, and the therapist assumes little direct say in the direction of treatment.

Operant behavior therapy gives the child almost no say in the therapeutic process. The therapist decides what behaviors are problems and then what particular behavioral methods should be employed to modify those behaviors. The basis of the treatment process is that the therapist assumes control over the child's environment and as the reward and punishment aspects of the environment change, the child will also change.

Modeling is similar in that the therapist defines the behaviors to be modified, and what particular modeling technique will be used. The child then simply participates in the therapist's program.

Most of the respondent behavior therapies allow the child to define the dysfunctional behavior. For example, in flooding or systematic desensitization the child defines the phobias and anxieties that trouble him or her. However, the child has little say in what process will be used and the therapeutic process requires the child to follow the therapist's direction in visualizing certain images. In hypnosis or the relaxation process of treatment, the child is again a passive agent that follows the therapist's specific directions.

Of the cognitive treatments, Michenbaum's "self speech" and Kendell's "self-instruction training" are the most rigid in assuming therapist control. Most of the time the therapist defines the problem behaviors and sets up a program for groups of children who have the same symptoms. The children follow the lead of the therapist by learning the words and phrases that will mediate their behavior. As Kendall has modified his treatment, he increasingly allows children more freedom in digressing from the therapeutic program.

In rational-emotive treatment and Aaron Beck's cognitive learning therapy, the therapist is very directive and often tells the child what to do. Usually the therapist is confrontative and often gives the child homework and exercises. In spite of the directive nature of these treatments, the child is an active participant in the treatment process and sometimes the youngster's ideas will influence the direction of treatment. Also, the child defines what the problems are, although the therapist is free to reinterpret what the child says.

In general, the psychodynamic psychotherapies allow a greater child participation in the control and direction of the treatment process, but there are important differences between treatments in this respect. For example, Adlerian psychotherapy allows the child a great deal of freedom in what is discussed and when. It is somewhat more directive in that the therapist relies heavily on interpretations and gives the child direct feedback concerning emotional strengths and weaknesses.

Like classical psychoanalysis, ego analytic, and object relations therapists, Adlerian therapists are directive in that they are more interested in conversation topics related to a particular personality theory. Adlerian therapists tend to focus on issues involving inferiority and superiority while ego analytic and psychoanalytic therapists are more attentive to issues that are related to those personality theories. Being more attentive to certain topics than others gives the child a direct message concerning what should be talked about. Because psychoanalytically oriented psychotherapy is not as closely wedded to personality theory, the therapist is not as subtly directive in influencing the course of therapy.

Client-centered, Gestalt and existential psychotherapies are not as closely connected to a particular theory of personality as the other psychodynamic treatments, and to that extent they do not focus the content of therapy sessions along particular theoretical issues. For example, an Adlerian therapist is likely to be highly sensitive to discussions about feelings of inferiority and a lack of self confidence and is likely to encourage the child to continue talking about these topics. As compared to other types of therapies, client-centered, Gestalt, and existential therapists do not give the child this kind of selective attention, which serves to reinforce a child for discussing certain issues and ignoring others. Rather, they encourage the child to choose what will be discussed.

Existential and Gestalt therapists tend to be more confrontative than client-centered therapists, and this often will pressure a child to discuss a troublesome problem he may be avoiding. Client-centered treatment differs in that the therapist believes a child needs free rein to choose the course of what happens in treatment. Usually, if a child does not wish to discuss a particular topic the therapist thinks is important, the therapist will not be confrontative and will put only minimal pressure on the child. This goes along with the belief that the client-centered therapist is only a catalyst to help a child use his natural inclination toward self-actualization.

The dimension of therapeutic control is important in determining the degree of generalization from treatment. Those treatments that tend to assume strong therapist control may not generalize to nontherapy situations as well as those that allow the child greater freedom in deciding the course of treatment.

Factors to Consider in Choosing the Appropriate Treatment

Cognitive Ability

A child's cognitive ability is an important factor to consider in choosing a treatment. By cognitive ability I do not mean intelligence, which covers a host of intellectual abilities such as knowledge, memory, and other skills that may not be directly relevant to how well a child can participate in therapy. I refer more to a child's ability to understand relationships between and within situations and to grasp cause and effect. These skills are crucial in certain kinds of psychotherapies and a therapist must know which treatments demand better cognitive abilities than others.

Cognitive ability is not a crucial factor in most of the behavioral treatments. Here the procedures are very structured and under the control of the therapist. Since the child is being conditioned to merely participate in the therapeutic process, they do not need to understand complex connections about past situations or relationships and then generalize this understanding to new situations. Many operant behavior therapies are excellent treatments for intellectually impaired children and are commonly used in retraining the retarded. This makes sense, since the theoretical techniques that underlie these treatments were developed using simple experimental animals such as white rats and pigeons.

Although bright children are intellectually able to participate in behavioral treatments, some therapists find they become bored or frustrated by the lack of freedom and intellectual challenge. Some do not like the fact that they have little or no say in what happens. This is especially true with operant behavior modification, where some children find that concrete rewards are not motivating.

It is also a problem with systematic desensitization because children may become bored going through relaxation hierarchies which seem to be inherently less interesting than the talking and listening characteristic of most verbal therapies. As in operant methods, they have little choice in the plan of their treatment—I have had children interrupt the continuity of treatment, saying, "Could we do this later because I want to tell you some things that happened."

Depending on the particular treatment, the cognitive psychotherapies may or may not require a reasonably high cognitive level to be effective. In rational-emotive treatment, children need to understand the intricacies of their own maladaptive thinking and to be able to follow the therapist when he points out certain concepts. This requires a reasonably good ability to understand cause and effect relationships. This same intellectual level is also needed to benefit from Beck's cognitive learning therapy. Michenbaum's and Kendall's methods are more structured and the child is only required to follow the therapists instructions, so these treatments do not require the same high cognitive ability.

Psychodynamic treatments are intellectually more difficult for children because they are required to deal with the concept of time in understanding how their past behavior and experiences may relate to what they are doing in the present and what they will do in the future. They also need to gain insight into complex human behavior, their own and that of others, and they need to be able to grasp often complex cause and effect connections. This is very difficult for intellectually impaired children and generally brighter children will do better with this process. However, do not think that psychodynamic treatments are ruled out for children who do not have superior intellects. In that situation a good therapist is often able to modify the treatment so that these children can also benefit.

As you can see from the preceding discussion, the relationship between cognitive level and treatment should be considered, but it is not exact. It only indicates a general trend. An important factor related to cognitive level is age. Since children become intellectually more able as they grow, there is an increasing probability that older children will benefit from a more complex treatment and little ones from behavioral methods.

Environmental Demands

The environment that a child lives in is an important determinant of the kind of treatment he or she will receive. For example, some children by the nature of their problems require extraordinary measures in their treatment. Sometimes, this means that they need to be removed from their home and placed in a special institution that is better able to handle them. In these situations some form of operant behavior modification is often needed because it quickly brings a child's disordered behavior under control.

For example, an autistic child living in a group home may have self-stimulatory atavistic behaviors that are life threatening. If not controlled, the child may head-bang to the point of fracturing his skull or scratch himself opening up serious flesh lesions. These can be controlled using some form of operant punishment procedure, a desired treatment under such circumstances.

Operant behavior modification procedures often are used to train retarded children in special school settings. This is an effective way to teach them useful social, vocational, and independent living skills. This kind of treatment is not only efficient in this kind of training, but it can be taught to relatively inexperienced staff members.

Normal classrooms will utilize a combination of treatments to deal with a disruptive child. The demands of a classroom are such that a teacher must avoid overt disruptions. Often some form of reinforcement procedure is effective in controlling classroom outbursts while the child may also receive some form of cognitive or psychodynamic treatment outside of school.

The environmental demands of a school-phobic child often dictate that many kinds of treatment be used. Avoiding any prolonged school absence is crucial in these situations, and operant reinforcement and punishment procedures are often needed. Also, systematic desensitization may be a quick way of helping the child control overwhelming fears, and in the long run some form of family or psychodynamic treatment may be required to help the child overcome the other less specific problems that are usually part of this problem.

Socio-Economic Considerations

Psychological treatments are by their very nature labor intensive and expensive, and the economic resources of the family often determines the kind of treatment used. Generally, the greater the economic resources of the family, the more likely they will opt for a long-term psychodynamic treatment, although this is only a general tendency.

Third-party insurance payments have become an important variable in recent years and are likely to become more important in the future. If the family belongs to an HMO that only pays for the first ten sessions, they are more likely to seek out a therapist who does some form of short-term treatment or the therapist they choose will select a technique that is short-term. If their policy pays 50 percent or 80 percent for an indefinite period, then chances are that treatment is likely to be long-term psychodynamic. I have known of situations whe re children were hospitalized even though they could be better treated as outpatients simply because the insurance covered hospitalization, but not outpatient treatment. Third-party payments are a recent and important development that introduce large and complex problems into child treatment which are far beyond the scope of this short discussion. However, it is yet another factor, not directly connected to a child's emotional problems, that will affect the choice of treatment.

Symptoms and Emotional Problems

The kind of symptoms a child presents ought to be the most important factor in determining the choice of treatment, and, in fact, it is a crucial aspect. However, things are never as simple as they seem. Symptoms are the overt manifestations of a child's emotional problems, and to a greater or lesser extent they do mirror those problems. Unfortunately, there is seldom a perfect relationship between a child's overt symptoms and the complex emotional difficulties that produce the disordered and dysfunctional behavior that we call symptoms. In many cases children with the same symptoms may have very different problems and often children with very different emotional problems develop the same symptoms. Another complexity is that therapists often do not agree with each other in assessing a child's problems, and if therapists disagree on their assessment of a problem then they are likely to prescribe different treatments to treat the child. There are many reasons for this unreliability in diagnosis. Therapists use different theories which lead them to different conclusions. Some focus more on symptoms, some more on underlying problems. Perhaps the crux of the problem is that human beings of all kinds just do not seem to agree on anything as complex as another human being.

In spite of these and other difficulties (and at the risk of being redundant), there is little doubt that a child's symptoms and emotional problems ought to be the most important determinant of the kind of treatment that is utilized. This relationship between emotional problems and treatment is so important that we will devote the entire next chapter to that topic. At this point we need to realize that it is a complex topic, but one that is crucial to child treatment.

2

Diagnosis and Treatment

In the preceding chapter we discussed the importance of the child's emotional problems in determining that child's treatment. However, we blithely ignored the difficulties a therapist faces in accurately determining just what that child's emotional problems are. In this chapter we will try to understand how a therapist goes about diagnosing a child's problems and how very difficult that process is. There are many reasons for using diagnosis and we will discuss some of these later in this chapter, but primarily we will concern ourselves with that aspect of diagnosis that relates to treatment. From a perfectly practical point of view that is the most important use of diagnosis. Diagnosis by itself does not help children overcome their emotional difficulties, only treatment does that, and to the extent that a diagnosis makes treatment more effective then it is useful in a child's life.

There are many other important aspects of child psychopathology, but they go beyond the scope of a text that attempts to deal primarily with the treatment of children. Issues concerning etiology, taxonomy, and development are just a few of the important topics child therapists should be aware of, and I strongly recommend books such as Thomas Ollendick and Michael Hersen's (1993) *Handbook of Child and Adolescent Assessment* and Thomas Achenbach's (1992) *Developmental Psychopathology,* both of which are excellent sources of information on a very complex topic.

The History of the Diagnosis of Children

Diagnosis, in one form or another, has had a long history. Perhaps as soon as our half-human ancestors began to notice each other they began to categorize each other. Even medical diagnosis is quite old; and back then an inaccurate diagnosis had unfortunate consequences. During the Reformation in Europe and in Colonial New England, emotionally disturbed individuals were often misdiagnosed as witches, and the consequences were terrible. Glicklich (1951) reports that children were diagnosed as enuretic as early as 1550 B.C., and since one of the treatments for enuresis was to have the unfortunate youngster drink wine mixed with hair shaved from a rabbit's scrotum, I imagine misdiagnosed children were not very pleased to be the victim of their doctor's error. (I doubt that correctly diagnosed children were wild about the treatment either.)

Our modern diagnostic system resulted from the work of Emil Kraepelin in the last decades of the 1800s. He organized the slowly accumulating ideas of nineteenth century psychiatry into one system and continued to revise this throughout his life. Unfortunately, he never included separate categories for children. In those days children were not as important as adults and everyone assumed that they were born wild and disordered creatures who had to be trained and molded if they were to become normal adults. Thus, adults assumed that normal children were abnormal if not strictly controlled, so no diagnostic system was needed. This attitude was also reflected in the fact that children were not treated, but trained. Concern with a child's happiness and parental understanding are parental attitudes that have become common only during the twentieth century. Before that children were bent to the will of their parents by punishment and fear. Beatings by both parents and teachers (for those fortunate children who attended school) were common, and some of the early laws in our country allowed and encouraged parents to use harsh punishments on their children. One Colonial law allowed a father to kill a child if the child cursed or hit him. During the eighteenth and nineteenth century children in England and France were taken to see dead bodies and public executions to instill fear in them. Given these attitudes we would not expect such cultures to develop humane and enlightened treatments for their children, and in fact treatment methods for adults were developed decades before methods were found to treat children.

Attempts at systematic diagnosis in recent times began with the publication of the first *Diagnostic and Statistical Manual* (DSM-I) of the American Psychiatric Association in 1952 (American Psychiatric Association, 1952). Unfortunately, it retained many of the medical biases and theoretical inaccuracies of Kraepelin's original work including his disregard for children. In fact, it included only two categories about children, "Adjustment Reaction" and "Childhood Schizophrenia." The second edition in 1968, DSM-II, was much improved in that it attempted to be more comprehensive and included more child categories. The latest revisions, DSM-III, and DSM-III-R, have numerous categories of child and adolescent disorders (American Psychiatric Association, 1968; American Psychiatric Association, 1980; American Psychiatric Association, 1987). Unfortunately, there is still a great deal of dissatisfaction with this system and some very serious problems (Rutter & Shaffer, 1980).

First, the reliability for adult diagnosis seems to be better than for children and adolescents (Rutter & Shaffer, 1980). Second, recent revisions were only partially based on research findings (Quay & Werry, 1986). Third, the overall agreement between clinicians on these categories is not high (Quay & Werry, 1986). And last, and perhaps most serious, the DSM revisions do not seem to be improving reliability (Mattison, R., Cantwell, D., & Russell, A.T., 1979) (Rutter & Shaffer, 1980).

By the early 1960s, many child clinicians were displeased with the inaccuracies in this system and the overall neglect of children, and as a result other diagnostic systems were proposed. The first of these came from the Group for the Advancement of Psychiatry, sometimes referred to as GAP (GAP, 1966). In 1966 they proposed a diagnostic system that tried to break from the traditional medical model by making their definitions as operational as possible and including categories derived from developmental psychology. This system had ten major categories and sub-categories under these. The major categories are as follows:

1. Healthy Responses
2. Reactive Disorders
3. Developmental Deviations
4. Psychoneurotic Disorders
5. Personality Disorders
6. Psychotic Disorders
7. Psychophysiologic Disorders
8. Brain Syndromes
9. Mental Retardation

An unusual aspect of this system is that it includes a category of normal responses to developmental and environmental crises, called healthy responses. Many clinicians liked this system because it included diagnoses related to familiar dynamic personality theory which they used in their treatment. Unfortunately, studies on the reliability of this system appear to be no better than the mediocre reliabilities for DSM III (Quay, 1986).

The World Health Organization has also proposed a diagnostic system for children (Quay, 1986). Based on four major dimensions;

Psychiatric Syndromes
Level of Intellectual Functioning
Biological Factors
Psychological and Social Factors

This system has the advantage of removing intelligence from the psychiatric dimensions and seems to have somewhat higher reliabilities than the GAP or DSM systems (Rutter, Lebovici, Eisenberg, Sneznevskij, Sadoun, Brooke, and Lin, 1969) (Rutter, Shaffer, & Shepard, 1975).

There are a number of other child diagnostic systems based on multivariate approaches which use high-speed computers and the sophisticated statistical procedures of factor and cluster analysis (Achenbach & Edelbrock, 1978; Quay, 1979). These procedures usually analyze the responses of children and adults to sophisticated checklists which measure many aspects of normal and abnormal child behaviors. They have the highest reliabilities of any of the systems, but at this point, in spite of their possible advantages, neither the GAP, the WHO, or the multivariate systems have gained a great deal of popular support among psychotherapists. This may be because most therapists do not feel that putting the children they treat into categories is an essential or helpful part of the treatment process. Usually, they do this when it is demanded by outside influences such as insurance companies or HMOs, and these bureaucratic institutions almost always demand the use of DSM-III.

The most recent edition of the DSM series is called the DSM-III-R and is a further revision of the DSM-III manual. It is similar to the DSM-III system and retains many of its disadvantages. There is little evidence to show that reliability has been improved, and many psychotherapists dislike its heavy emphasis on obvious physical and behavioral symptoms and its relative disregard for psychodynamic factors (Rapoport & Ismond, 1990). I personally find that the new system does not cover the universe of disordered child symptoms adequately, and I am often not able to find a category that adequately describes a child, or I find that the child could be diagnosed in three or four categories, none of which describe that child very well. Also, some categories are quite broad, such as anxiety disorders, and others are very narrow, such as tic disorders, yet they are both Axis I classifications.

DSM-III-R includes eight major categories (Axis I). These are as follows:

Disruptive Behavior Disorders
Anxiety Disorders of Childhood and Adolescence
Eating Disorders
Gender Identity Disorders
Tic Disorders
Elimination Disorders
Speech Disorders not elsewhere classified
Other Disorders of Infancy, Childhood, or Adolescence
There are also three Axis II classifications:
Mental Retardation
Pervasive Developmental Disorders
Specific Developmental Disorders

By reading the titles of these categories you can easily see that they overemphasize categorizing symptoms and are not terribly helpful in providing new information or understanding that would aid in the psychotherapeutic treatment of children because the same symptom can reflect many different kinds of emotional, familial, cognitive, and interpersonal conflicts. A therapist needs to have information about these conflicts themselves not just about symptoms. While knowledge of a child's symptoms is of importance to a therapist, it is only of limited help in psychotherapy. A system that is meaningfully organized and with categorized information about familial and interpersonal conflicts would be of greater use. The GAP system reflects that kind of classification better than DSM-III-R, but we have already mentioned that reliabilities of both systems are low.

Requirements of a Diagnostic System

Any system of categorizing emotionally disturbed children has two main requirements: reliability and validity. Both are extensive topics of great complexity, so we will limit our discussion to the aspects of these topics that have direct relevance to diagnosis and the treatment of children.

Reliability of a diagnostic system is of crucial importance. It tells us whether the system is consistent, and obviously we can not have a system that works on one occasion and not on another. Estimating reliability is complex both in terms of theory and statistics, and there are many kinds of reliabilities. The two that are most important for our purposes are interrater and rate-rerate reliability.

Interrater reliability means that two or more diagnosticians should agree with one another. In other words, the systems should allow a child to receive the same diagnosis from different practitioners.

Rate-rerate means that the diagnosis ought to be stable over time. A child given a diagnosis at one time should be given the same diagnosis four weeks or four months later (assuming that the child has not changed, and children usually do not undergo great changes in short periods of time).

Both of these kinds of reliabilities are crucial for a diagnostic system. Clinicians ought to agree with one another about a child, and when they give a child a particular diagnosis they should not be changing their minds a week later. This ought not to happen when using a good diagnostic system; the fact that the DSM-III and DSM-III-R interrater reliabilities are low definitely compromises their usefulness.

The second important requirement is the validity of the system, but validity applied to diagnosis has a different meaning than it does in psychological testing. In psychological testing, the main requirement of a valid test is predictive validity. When a test has predictive validity it predicts a criteria. For example, the SAT predicts how well a student will perform at college, or an MMPI profile predicts a person's psychological problems. In this case the SAT and MMPI are clearly the tests, and school performance and psychological problems are clearly the criteria.

However, the concepts of prediction are not as clear cut when applied to diagnostic systems. Placing a child in a particular diagnostic category does not predict how well or poorly he will do at various tasks, such as schoolwork, maintaining friendships, or getting along with adults. In a very imprecise way it may predict certain behaviors. For example, we know that children who are diagnosed as retarded will need special schooling, but we hardly need a diagnostic system to tell us that. We know that children with conduct disorders are not likely to get along smoothly with adults, but that is true of many other categories. A diagnosis of developmental articulation disorder or identity disorder does not indicate that such children will have disruptive behavior, but to our dismay we may find that some of them are disruptive. All in all, we know that diagnostic systems are not good predictors and in most situations they are not useful in making decisions about children.

Construct validity, another principle of psychological testing, might better apply to evaluating a diagnostic system. This is a rather abstract and complex concept that indicates the theoretical logic of a diagnostic system. For example, if the theoretical underpinnings of a personality theory assume that anorexia is related to the adolescent female personality, then five-year-old boys should not fit into that diagnosis. If autism is assumed to begin in the first year of life, then we should not diagnose sixteen-year-olds as having just developed autism. An encompassing diagnostic system ought to have independent categories, so it would not have good construct validity if a child could easily fit into four or five different categories.

Unfortunately, there is no agreed upon standard for construct validity. Each clinician and theorist could have an opinion on the adequacy of a particular diagnostic system in terms of its construct validity. In fact, since each personality theory is different, each would have different constructs and a different kind of construct validity. That means that we would need many diagnostic systems—one for each personality theory—and that would lead to a very confusing state of affairs. Certainly, there would be very little communication or agreement among therapists.

At present, the construct validity of systems such as DSM III-R have not been adequately researched, and a deeper analysis of the topic is needed.

The Purpose of Diagnosis

Even more basic than reliability or validity is the purpose of a diagnosis. Why and how we use a diagnostic system is crucial to the kind of diagnostic system we choose. We can identify six different uses for a diagnostic system.

Using diagnosis as a way of simplifying our data is its most obvious purpose. In this way it serves as a kind of shorthand, an attempt to summarize the many behaviors that describe a child in just a few words. From a statistical point of view, diagnosis is a kind of rough-hewn factor analysis. Instead of writing a long narrative description of a child, we simply give that child a diagnosis and let that describe the youngster. This shorthand-like procedure has some value, but such a summarization introduces problems. Things as complex as children can not really be described by the few words of a diagnostic label. Neither do they fit perfectly into a few discrete categories, and when we try to do that we introduce more inaccuracies and a good degree of unreliability into our work.

A second use of the diagnostic process is classification. As we noted before, diagnostic categories summarize information. But they leave out many details, and this may distort an accurate description of a child. So long as we are not leaving out important details or introducing too many inaccuracies, this kind of categorization may be useful. It certainly makes complex beings like children seem simpler, and we prefer simplicity to complexity. Besides, people like things to be orderly and putting things in categories may satisfy our sense of intellectual neatness. Whatever the reason, we like to classify children.

A third purpose is explanation and understanding. When we place a child in a diagnostic category, we are inherently saying that he is similar to certain other children. That makes an idiosyncratic and perhaps confusing child somewhat less confusing . Now we can say he or she is like some other youngsters we have known and perhaps treated. By relating the child to other familiar children we may better understand the child; he or she seems more familiar. We might even decide to use the same type of treatment on the newly diagnosed child, if that was successful with the first child. Of course, we pay a price for this understanding. In our efforts to see similarities, we may miss the individuality and unique aspects of that child.

A fourth reason has to do with third-party payments. Insurance companies believe that claims should not be paid unless the child is certified as emotionally disturbed or psychologically impaired in some fashion. I suppose they are concerned that hordes of normal children will want psychotherapy and flood the mental health system, emptying the insurance treasuries. The accepted way of certifying the child is to assign a diagnosis. This satisfies the procedures and allows a child's parents to be reimbursed or the therapist to be paid for the treatment.

The fifth purpose is prognosis. When a child is given a diagnosis, it often predicts the youngster's prognosis, that is, whether she will overcome her emotional problems, to what extent she will overcome the problems, and how long it will take. At least that is how a diagnostic system ought to work. To some extent the DSM-III-R diagnostic system does predict a child's prognosis, but it is not very precise, and in many situations it is blatantly inaccurate. Unfortunately, a diagnostic system by itself seems to be too crude a summation of a child to develop much accuracy in prognosis, and most psychotherapists rely on other factors, such as family support, ability of the child to form a close relationship, environmental tolerance of disordered behavior, and so on.

The sixth and last purpose of diagnosis relates to choice of treatment. It is this purpose that is the one that we will focus on because it is the most useful to a therapist.

Diagnosis as a Predictor of Treatment

In chapter one we touched on the issue of choice of treatment and agreed that the kind of diagnosis a child receives ought to determine the type of treatment used. This is sometimes referred to as "dispositional diagnosis." Simple logic indicates that if a diagnosis separates children into different categories on the basis of differences in symptoms, conflicts, and environments, then children with different diagnosis will need different treatments. When used in this way a diagnosis is very important. However, we know that diagnosis is not always used to determine the type of treatment a child will receive. Too often treatment is determined by the therapist's preference, orientation, the expectations of parents, the culture or subculture that the child lives in, or administrative decisions associated with a particular clinic or hospital. These factors are not related to the child's emotional problems, and in a perfect therapeutic world would not be part of a diagnosis or choice of treatment.

Although a formal diagnostic procedure ought to be helpful in deciding what type of treatment is appropriate, in actuality it is seldom very useful. That is because most diagnostic systems strive for a comprehensive description of a child; but a comprehensive description usually is not predictive of treatment. All diagnostic methods usually assume a stable underlying personality, but this, too, is not usually useful in predicting what treatment methods will be best for a child. There are even other aspects of children that may be interesting or important for other purposes, but they too may be irrelevant to choice of treatment.

For example, the severity of a child's symptoms or the amount of anguish or pain he or she experiences is not a good predictor of the type of treatment needed, at least not after the first few sessions. Similarly, the duration of the emotional problems is not a good indication of what type of treatment to use.

In this discussion we are only interested in those aspects of diagnosis that interact with treatment. Unfortunately, DSM III-R, the most commonly used diagnostic method, usually is not very helpful in this respect. Although, it includes a wide range of symptoms, conflicts, needs, and other variables associated with a child, it usually does not focus on those aspects of a child that interact with treatment procedures. In this sense DSM III-R is comprehensive, but does not identify those aspects of children that will tell us what kind of treatment to use.

To develop a dispositional diagnostic system we must discard most of the traditional notions underlying the common diagnostic system. First, we need to shift our focus away from a comprehensive interpersonal survey of the child and restrict ourselves only to those aspects of the child that indicate success within a certain treatment. Second, we must broaden the diagnostic procedure beyond the child to include aspects of the child's overall environment, since such variables are useful in deciding which treatment is best. Third, we need to discard the idea that diagnosis should be based on the child's stable underlying personality. We have already discussed how a child changes either through treatment or due to spontaneous environmental causes, and the type of treatment will need to change as the child's needs change. If a child undergoes a behavioral or personality change, then we need a new diagnosis, especially as this new diagnosis may indicate that a new type of treatment is needed.

In developing this kind of pragmatic dispositional diagnostic system, we have divided treatment methods into three general categories for ease of organization: behavioral, cognitive, and psychodynamic as listed in Appendix A. These are further broken into the following subcategories:

Behavioral Treatments

1. Operant behavior modification
2. Respondent behavior therapy

   Systematic desensitization
   Emotive imagery
   Flooding

3. Modeling

Cognitive Treatments

1. Programmed cognitive therapies

   Meichenbaum's self-speech
   Kendall's self-instruction

2. Nonprogrammed cognitive therapies

   Beck's cognitive therapy
   Ellis's rational-emotive therapy

Psychodynamic Treatments

1. Therapist directed treatments

    Classical psychoanalysis
    Ego psychoanalysis
    Adlerian analysis
    Object-relations therapy
    Psychoanalytically oriented psychotherapy

2. Child directed treatments

    Gestalt therapy
    Existential therapy
    Humanistic therapy
    Rogers's person-centered therapy

This is not meant to be an exhaustive list, but therapists can include other treatments by matching them to the general category and subcategory in this system. In a rather imprecise way, the list follows the general dimension of therapeutic structure in that it goes from the most structured to least structured treatments.

The other side of a dispositional diagnostic system is finding the factors that predict which treatment is likely to be effective. This system includes a number of nontraditional variables and is divided into three overall categories. These are:

1. Cognitive variables
2. Environmental variables
3. Social-emotional variables

These three categories comprise a different type of diagnostic system than that used in the DSM-III-R or any of the more traditional methods because the underlying organization is different. The sub-variables encompassed under the three general categories are important predictors in deciding which type of treatment will be effective. Since this is a new, speculative, and somewhat untested diagnostic system, it is presented in an experimental form and likely needs a great deal of revision. The variables that I and my students have identified seem to work when they were used with the child clients in our clinical settings, but there may be other variables that have not yet been identified or other ways of refining or reformulating these variables that will be more precise or reflect a more useful organization.

Many of the categories are broad and lack the precision that is usually desired in defining a diagnostic variable. To some extent this is purposeful because these broad variables are familiar concepts and practicing therapists may find them easier to use. Hopefully, the system will develop more precise definitions as it is used, and certainly each therapist will begin to redefine these variables or develop others that are more applicable for their particular therapy setting and patients. This system of diagnosis may need to be modified depending upon the groups of children treated or the type of clinical setting. There are five variables under each of these categories and they are as follows:

Cognitive

1. Adequacy of causal reasoning.
2. Social-emotional reality testing.
3. Generating creative therapeutic ideas and solutions.
4. Attention span.
5. Moral reasoning.

Environmental

1. Availability of finances.
2. Peer influences.
3. Adult tolerance of symptoms.
4. School cooperation.
5. Parental motivation and support of treatment.

Social-emotional

1. Ability to form and maintain close relationships.
2. Ability to identify feelings.
3. Expression of emotions.
4. Internal versus external expression of symptoms.
5. Internal versus external locus of control.

Cognitive Variables

This category of variables does not refer to the general concept of intelligence, which includes breadth of knowledge and school dependent learning, but rather to the Piagetian idea that there are certain basic cognitive skills essential to thinking and an accurate understanding of life situations. These skills are based on the development of fundamental logic, and if a child has not developed these important logical skills, they will not possess the cognitive stability needed to participate in certain types of treatment. Generally, the psychodynamic therapies require this basic logic, whereas behavioristic treatments do not. In the case of most behavioral therapies, the underlying logic is provided by the therapist who then attempts to train a child to use the logical solutions developed by the behavior therapist. Cognitive behavior therapists may also provide the fundamental logic underlying treatment issues, but they usually take on the additional goal of training a child to use fundamental logic. When different therapies are viewed in this way, the contentious arguments over which treatment is best becomes meaningless. Since children have different cognitive deficiencies, they require different therapies; and because the different types of treatment require different cognitive skills, these variables become important in predicting which types of treatment will be effective with particular children.

Table 2.1 summarizes the relationship between the types of treatment and the five cognitive sub-variables. Classifying a child on each of these cognitive factors will indicate which therapies are appropriate. For example, children with poor causal reasoning will not do well in psychodynamic types of treatment. The reasons underlying these charts will be explained in the overall discussion of each factor.

1. *Adequacy of Causal Reasoning*. Causal reasoning is a developmental skill that usually begins within the first two years of life during the sensori-motor phase of development. Children whose causal reasoning is inadequate will have difficulty grasping relationships in general and especially relationships between people. This makes for chaotic social interactions since they often misperceive social situations. This cognitive defect is often referred to as schizoid or borderline thinking. I prefer the term adequacy of causal reasoning as it is more descriptive. There are two important therapeutic difficulties that result from this kind of dysfunctional thinking.

First, these children are not able to discover or tease out the causes of problems in their everyday life. They will not understand why they are fighting with a particular teacher or why their father acts remote and uncommunicative. A normal child may not understand these situations and feel the teacher is picking on him or believe that he is to blame for his father's isolation. Once the child overcomes this emotional confusion as a result of treatment, he or she can begin to understand the complexity of the reasons involved in complex interactions. An inability to use adequate causal reasoning is a cognitive skill, but it is greatly influenced by intense emotions. The reasoning level of all children and adults regresses to a developmentally earlier level under the stress of emotions such as fear and anger, and children may often regress to the simplistic thinking of a preoperational child. Children who have adequate causal reasoning usually can avoid such regressive thinking when helped by a therapist, and they can recover their thinking when the stress disappears. Such a recovery may not occur in children whose thinking is impaired. These children may never be able to fully understand such situations.

TABLE 2.1 Cognitive Factors

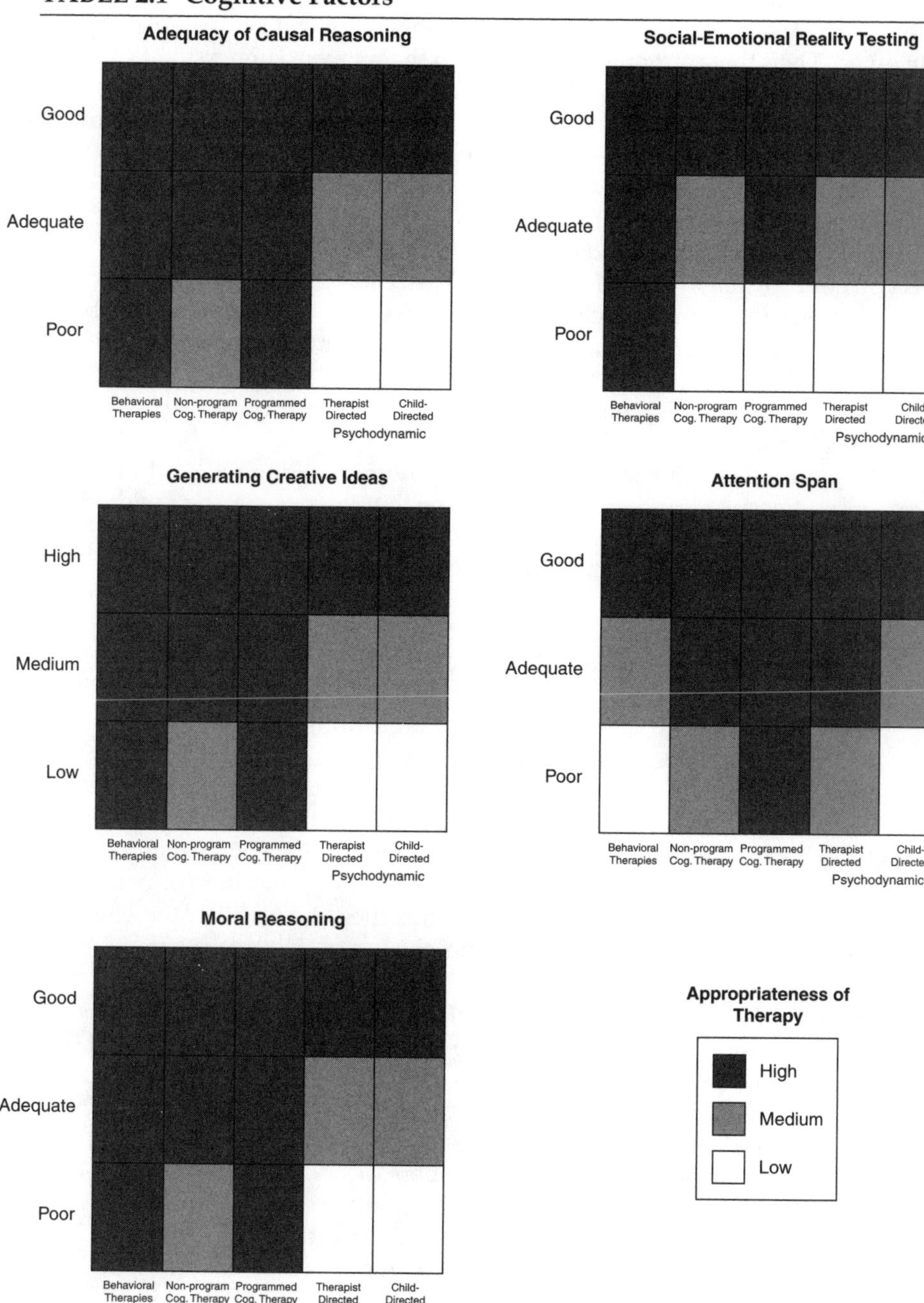

The second therapeutic difficulty is that if these impaired children do gain some insights at one point in time, such knowledge will be unstable and not retained. Their therapist may be able to lead them toward understanding some of causes of these complex situations, but since these insights are heavily dependent upon the therapist's intervention, the child cannot reason them out at a later time. Thus, when such explanations are forgotten, the child cannot recover them through his own efforts.

Cause and effect thinking is needed in most of the psychodynamic psychotherapies since some kind of insightful understanding is part of the process, if not a primary goal of treatment. Existential, psychoanalytic, ego-oriented, object relations, and client-centered treatment rely on the child being able to discover and understand cause and effect relationships at the developmental level appropriate to the child's age. Many of the social issues discussed in psychodynamic treatments are abstract. Understanding the causal connections is often difficult.

Cognitive behavior treatments do not require as high a level of causal reasoning because the therapist is more active in training the child; either explaining the important causal relationships or bypassing complex explanations by giving the child simpler behavioral instructions.

In most of the behavioral treatments, causal reasoning is not an important part of treatment because the therapist is chiefly concerned with training specific behaviors without the child needing to understand the underlying reasons for such training.

Notice that this variable operates in a nonsymmetrical fashion. By that I mean that if a child does not have good causal reasoning, the psychodynamic treatments will not be appropriate; but if the child does have adequate causal reasoning, all treatments, including cognitive and behavioral treatments, ought to be appropriate. The choice of treatment depends on many factors, causal reasoning being only one, and if some form of cognitive or behavioral therapy seems appropriate for other reasons then the fact that the child has good causal reasoning will not contradict the use of that treatment.

2. *Social-Emotional Reality Testing.* Reality testing is an old therapeutic term which refers to a person's ability to recognize the realistic nature of their thoughts. Since psychotherapy focuses on the social-emotional issues in a child's life, children must have the ability to distinguish relevant from irrelevant thoughts, ideas, and behaviors in respect to their own emotional reactions and their relationships with family members, peers, teachers, and other significant people in their life. Different situations necessitate different behaviors, and children need to judge which behaviors are appropriate for each situation. To do this they must be able to sense subtle and complex social-emotional cues so that even when the obvious structure of a situation is similar, they can choose appropriate behavior patterns.

For example, the usual competitive behaviors of playing a computer game with a friend will require a very different pattern of behaviors if the friend has lost the last three games. Then, more compassionate and sensitive words and actions are called for, and should occur in a spontaneous fashion, often without the compassionate child being aware of the change in his behavior. Children who do not sense the changed circumstances and gloat over their success are likely to lose friends and end up socially isolated.

Social-emotional reality testing allows children and adolescents to separate fantasy from reality. Although they may engage in momentary wild flights of fantasy and daydreams, they can easily come back to reality. This ability to regress into fantasy yet recover when necessary is important in many forms of psychodynamic therapies. Many treatments encourage children to regress to experience emotional conflicts, thus gaining the needed emotional information to solve their psychological difficulties. However, regression does not mean deterioration, and children have to be able to recover with a sound assessment of reality.

Good social-emotional reality testing is necessary for most of the psychodynamic treatments. It is also helpful in cognitive treatments since cognitive training is best done when children have not deteriorated into fantasy and the therapist does not have to cope with regressive behavior. The structured training techniques of modeling and operant behavioral methods do not require good reality testing, and since the inherent environmental control of these treatments minimizes behavioral deterioration they are more appropriate with children whose social-emotional reality testing is flawed.

3. *Generating creative therapeutic ideas and solutions.* Psychological treatment involves changing present dysfunctional thoughts, emotions, and behaviors so that they are more adaptive. In order to do this, children must develop new, more adaptive ways, and this is usually done with greater or lesser help from the therapist. One part of the therapeutic process is problem-solving and here the child, after recognizing his or her problems, needs to find solutions. Good reality testing and causal reasoning are essential in problem-solving, but at some stage the child must generate new ideas to replace the older dysfunctional ones. In other words, after asking the right questions the child needs to find answers. With emotional problems, these answers are often not cognitive solutions but emotional solutions in which the child finds a new perspective or sees new alternatives that previously could not be accepted.

The therapist usually is an active agent in helping to develop new ideas and find new solutions to emotional problems, but the best ideas and solutions normally are generated by the child. These are more syntonic to the child's thinking and will be easier to integrate into the child's life. Certainly child-generated ideas will be better accepted than those developed by the therapist.

Children differ in their ability to creative new therapeutic ideas. Some can better see and understand new aspects of their situation, and this allows them to find more alternatives. Maybe they can see other perspectives which result in their ideas being more relevant to a particular problem. However they do it, there is a difference in the ability of children to find and use creative therapeutic solutions, and different forms of treatment are needed for those children who cannot generate successful solutions to their therapeutic problems.

Finding new adaptive behaviors is an essential part of every form of psychological treatment, but treatments differ in how this is done. Operant behavior therapists provide children with new adaptive behaviors, and the focus of treatment is training a child, through reinforcement, to learn these new behaviors. Sometimes behavioral therapists are criticized because they focus more on eliminating behaviors than on the development of newer, more adaptive ones. Since respondent behavioral treatments, such as systematic desensitization and flooding, also focus on the elimination of symptoms, these techniques do not require children to be able to develop creative new therapeutic solutions to problems.

Most cognitive treatments try to develop new adaptive behavior patterns, but usually these are developed by the therapist and the child is not an important part of the process. As a result the child does not need to be proficient in generating creative therapeutic ideas and solutions.

Most psychodynamic therapies rely on the child to develop the creative ideas and solutions to the questions raised by treatment, although the therapist actively serves to facilitate this process. With younger children or children who have difficulty with this process, the therapist takes on the major responsibility for this aspect of treatment, although psychotherapy will be more effective if children are able to generate such ideas on their own. Because this is a needed skill in most psychodynamic therapies, children who are unable to generate creative therapeutic ideas and solutions are not good candidates for these treatments. This variable, like the preceding ones, is nonsymmetrical in that children who can generate such ideas can do well in any type of treatment, but children with limitations in this ability will have better success in cognitive or behavioral treatments.

4. *Attention span.* Children differ in the length of time they can attend to a task and the depth of their concentration. Children identified as having "attention deficit disorder" will be at the low end of this ability, while other children will show an extraordinary degree of concentration. Aside from these child differences, each type of treatment requires different attentional levels and differ in their ability to engage a child's concentration. For example, play therapy has an attractiveness for some children that would not be true for a verbal type of treatment. Similarly, some treatments, such as Kendall's self-instruction, are programmed with sequential tasks that are interesting to children and hold their attention. Operant behavior treatment tends to use techniques that are so controlling of the child's environment that it overrides a child's poor attention span. A token economy, for example, forces a child to pay attention to the reinforcers. If the treatment fails to do this, the treatment procedure will be changed to ensure that the child is paying attention.

Many of the psychodynamic therapies require a great deal of concentration for long periods of time, since they ask a child to deal with verbal material of a very abstract and complex nature. Thus, children who have a poor attention span will not do well in these treatments, even if the treatment process is modified to include play activities and other activities designed to increase the attractiveness of that psychodynamic therapy.

The preceding three variables tended to follow a fairly constant linear trend from behavioral therapies through cognitive techniques to psychodynamic treatments. However, this variable does not follow such a regular trend because the actual techniques differ. Thus, a psychodynamic treatment such as client-centered therapy may not be effective with a child who has a poor attention span because of its heavy verbal demands, while another psychodynamic treatment, psychoanalytically oriented psychotherapy, might be very successful because it can better utilize play as a therapeutic technique.

5. *Moral reasoning.* The term moral reasoning refers to the cognitive ability of children to understand moral concepts as opposed to morality, which refers to a child's actual behavior. That is, whether the child acts according to moral principles. Jean Piaget was the first to make this crucial distinction and to identify moral reasoning as an intellectual process with definite developmental stages (Piaget & Inhelder, 1969). According to Piaget's theory, moral reasoning develops in a fixed sequence and is related to a child's age; the older the child the better his or her moral reasoning ability. Although Piaget gives approximate ages for the development of certain moral reasoning stages, not all children master these levels at the usual ages and some children may be significantly retarded in their moral development.

Moral reasoning is an important variable in dispositional diagnosis because moral behavior is a crucial aspect of a child's life and an important focus in many treatments. Morality and related concepts like fairness, an understanding of intent, and the use of rules are crucial to all relationships. In one way or another all treatments deal with morality. If children have not developed the cognitive skills associated with moral reasoning, they will not be appropriate candidates for certain types of therapies because they will not have the skills to understand how to behave in an ethical way toward others. Most of the psychodynamic therapies, such as psychoanalytically oriented psychotherapy, Adlerian therapy, existential and Gestalt treatment, and others, require sound moral reasoning because they try to facilitate morality through verbal discussion, especially of social situations.

Cognitive treatments do not require as good an understanding since they attempt to train a child to behave in a moral manner in specific situations.

Adequate moral reasoning in not crucial to operant behavior therapy since it uses shaping and powerful reinforcements to create and maintain very specific behaviors in very specific situations.

Environmental Variables

Since traditional diagnostic methods are based on personality theory and symptom constellations, they look within the individual for the information used in formulating a diagnosis, but a disposition-based diagnosis need not be limited in the information it uses. Any variable that predicts differential success among treatments ought to be included when choosing one type of treatment over another. By definition environmental variables are outside of the child, but since they exert an influence on every child's life they not only need to be included, they can be crucial to the success or failure of a treatment. Most of the five variables included in this category are associated with a child's family, peers, school, or other institutions that closely affect his or her life. Table 2.2 shows the relationship between the five environmental sub-variables and various treatment modalities.

1. *Availability of finances.* Psychological treatment requires a great deal of time and effort by well-trained therapists who have invested many years in their training. Because psychological treatment requires such intensive efforts, it is financially expensive, and families have differing financial resources to expend on treatment. For the most part, behavioral and cognitive therapies are less expensive because they are short-term treatments lasting a few weeks or months, whereas many, but not all, the psychodynamic therapies are long-term and may last a year or longer. Of course this is a very general assessment and can differ depending on the particular problems of the child. For example, because autistic children are so impaired, their treatment can be lengthy and involve inpatient facilities or special schools. This will be a costly type of behavioral treatment.

Third-party payments, either from insurance companies or as state or federal monies, will alleviate the families' financial burden. But they often only pay a portion of the treatment expenses, and a large portion often falls on the child's family. Therapists must consider this factor in their choice of treatment. There is little sense in recommending long-term treatment if the family will have to terminate treatment in the middle of it. In that situation, a therapist

TABLE 2.2 Environmental Factors

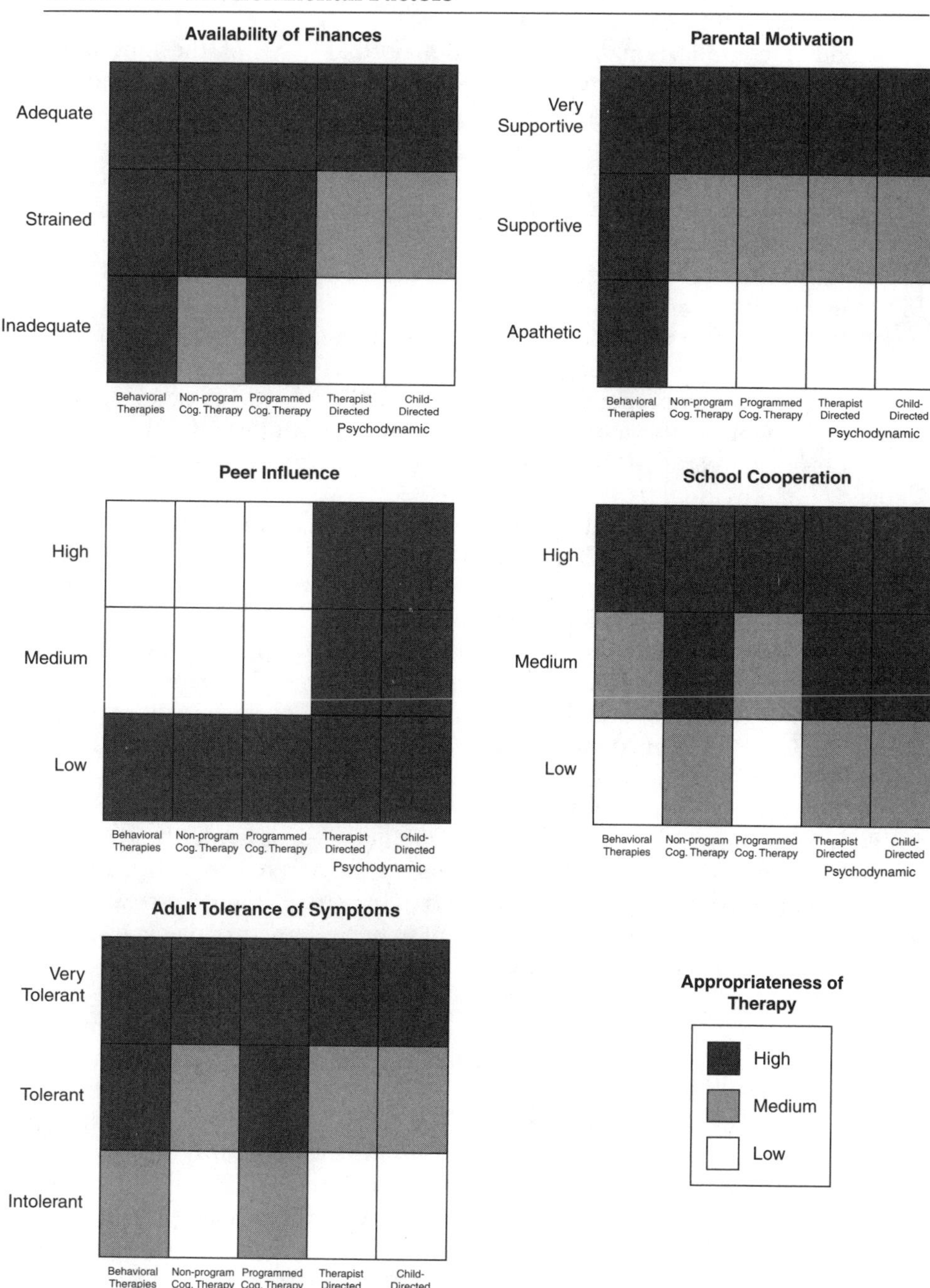

may need to recommend a shorter treatment that can be completed within the time span allowed by the families' resources.

Another complication in this situation is that most of the long-term psychodynamic therapies involve once-a-week meetings, whereas shorter behavioral treatments often require a number of meetings each week. This means the cost will be high for the short period of time that the child is being treated. Although these may be sensitive issues to discuss with parents, the therapist needs to know such things before recommending any treatment.

2. *Parental motivation and support of treatment.* This variable is related both to the consistency and intensity of the family's desire for treatment. Treatments that last a year or longer dictate that the parents maintain their enthusiasm for treatment over a long period of time. This means that parents will be willing to transport themselves and their child to weekly sessions and endure the financial burdens involved. This requires both a belief in the benefit and necessity of treatment. Of course, motivation for treatment is complex and depends on individual parents.

Some parents are motivated to involve their child in treatment, but avoid their own direct involvement. They are happy to take their child to a therapist, but aside from occasional parent-therapist meetings they leave treatment to the therapist and child. If this pattern of motivation cannot be changed, then the therapist may want to recommend an individualized form of treatment that places minimal demands on the parents or has minimal demands initially, but over time gives the therapist an opportunity to engage the parents in direct treatment. In this circumstance many psychodynamic treatments would be appropriate because they focus on individual child sessions.

Other parents want direct therapeutic contact and the preferred treatment might be some form of family therapy, a combination of individual and family meetings, operant behavioral treatment where the parents are trained to be the behavior modifiers, or some other form of parent-intensive treatment. Parental motivation is especially important in behavioral treatments because the parent is a crucial agent in modeling, monitoring behavioral changes, and giving rewards according to the correct contingencies. Parental support may also affect cognitive treatments. If parents are giving confusing or contradictory messages to their child, this will conflict with the logical and consistent training that is occurring in therapy.

Yet other parents have little motivation for treatment in any form and in this situation the therapist will need to recommend a therapy that will be short-term and demand little from the parents. Of course the therapist will need to try to increase the parents' motivation, but if this is not possible, the child is usually better off obtaining some treatment even if it does not meet his or her complete needs. In this case a short-term treatment that requires little parental involvement is best. Actually, the topic of parental motivation is a complex one and becomes an important part of the treatment plan. Choosing a treatment to meet the parents' needs is only one solution to the problem. Other approaches already have been discussed and will be covered in later chapters.

Another consideration is the location of the treatment since that directly affects parental involvement. Many forms of treatment, such as operant behavior therapy and Kendall's self-instruction, tend to be administered within a school or institution and only require parental permission, but little effort or motivation from parents.

3. *Peer influence.* Many children are very dependent on the support and approval of their friends, especially during the adolescent years, and any therapy that conflicts with the opinions, accepted behaviors, and values of a peer group will face difficulties in bringing about therapeutic change. There are two general ways to get around this problem. First, we could choose a treatment that so controls the child's environment that it overrides any peer influences, or, second, we could choose a treatment that avoids conflict with peer values. Therapies that directly conflict with peer values are the ones that will have the greatest difficulty.

Many of the psychodynamic therapies, including client-centered or humanistic treatment, tend not to conflict with peer values because they are nonconfrontative forms of treatment. They allow the child or adolescent a strong voice in selecting the issues that are dealt with in therapy. Thus, treatment can center on issues that do not directly affect peer relationships. Often psychodynamic therapists will initially avoid confronting peer influences. They may wish to wait until the client-therapist relationship is more secure before introducing such topics, or they may want to wait until the child or teenager recognizes such problems and brings them up. Discussing peer issues is easier when it comes about through the child's choice.

Certain cognitive treatments that emphasize the acceptance of adult social values may be most affected because they often conflict with peer values. For example, rational-emotive psychotherapy with its confrontation of the child's thinking and its emphasis on the logic of long-term reality is likely to be difficult with adolescents who have strong ties to the short-term acting out of their friends. Similarly, children whose aggressive or chaotic classroom behavior is supported by their classmates are not likely to go along with a Michenbaum or Kendall type of treatment.

Operant behavior modification techniques often conflict with peer values when the therapist attempts to condition adult-sanctioned behaviors in a child or teenager. For example, other classmates may tolerate or encourage disruptive class behaviors such as making jokes or not doing homework. Teenage friends may encourage getting drunk and doing drugs at weekend parties, and even become resentful if a friend begins to avoid such get-togethers.

Depending on the peer groups' values and activities, therapeutic attempts to extinguish such behaviors will be more difficult if attempts run counter to the expectations of friends. But these efforts can be successful when the therapist has contingencies and reinforcers that are powerful enough to control the child. In some behavioral programs the child is removed from peers and placed in a new social situation that is supportive of the therapeutic changes. Inpatient programs which remove the children from his home, school, and community use this approach.

Some respondent conditioning techniques, such as systematic desensitization or implosion, do not confront peer value systems because they deal with phobias and fears, symptoms that are usually hidden from peers. Even when a child's peers are aware of the problem their values do not conflict with treatment.

4. *School cooperation.* We have already discussed how school performance and adjustment are intimately interwoven into every aspect of a child's life. Usually, school difficulties are a direct focus of treatment because most psychological problems affect school adjustment. But even when school difficulties are not a therapeutic focus, cooperation of teachers and administrators can be an important influence on treatment because certain forms of treatment require the support of the child's school. In some cases school-based input is indirect in that it may monitor the child's behavior or give a therapist needed feedback. In other cases the school needs to become an integral part of treatment. Obviously, a school's motivation and ability to provide such support will determine whether certain types of treatments will be successful.

A school's ability to aid in a therapeutic process is dependent on many factors, including the adequacy of staff resources, the psychological sophistication of the staff, and whether school officials believe that the type of treatment will be helpful. Usually, problems that directly affect classroom behavior and academic performance will increase staff motivation because any positive changes will make their work easier. Of course, the most important people in this process are the teachers or staff members who work directly with children. They are the people who know what is happening with a child and will actually carry out any therapeutic interventions. Their motivation and cooperation is the most crucial. Although knowledge of psychological treatment methods and principles is helpful, I have found that it is not essential. Experienced teachers know their children well and if a therapist can explain logically what needs to be done, then the child's teacher can understand what is needed and, using his or her individualized knowledge of the child, can usually implement an effective treatment procedure.

Certain behavioral treatments are heavily dependent on adequate cooperation with school staff. Many operant interventions are actually carried out in the classroom, which obviously requires the cooperation of the teacher. Even operant interventions initiated outside the classroom may require teacher encouragement or in-class reinforcement if the new behavior is to be generalized to the school setting. Often, behavioral changes need to be maintained and this requires that the teacher modify the usual classroom rules and procedures to build in environmental reinforcers.

Modeling procedures usually require the same kind of close school cooperation as operant behavioral methods. Respondent behavioral techniques, such as systematic desensitization and flooding, are exceptions in that they can be carried out relatively independent of school aid.

Many cognitive techniques also depend on close school cooperation if they are to be carried out successfully. Therapies such as those of Kendall and Michenbaum often target disruptive classroom behaviors and are carried out within the school. This necessitates close coordination with teachers. Here, too, the positive changes may need to be maintained through special attention on the part of the teachers.

Most psychodynamic treatments occur outside the school and can be carried out independent of the child's classroom. If the focus of the intervention deals with family or interpersonal issues separate from school, then little or no teacher coordination will be needed. When the focus does involve school behaviors or school-related activities, then teacher consultations and modification of certain classroom activities and rules may be helpful, or even crucial to the child's progress.

Nevertheless, compared to behavioral or cognitive treatments, the school's role is often ancillary to therapy because the dynamic treatment methods themselves can be carried out without input from the school and vice-versa. This is unfortunate because good school-therapist coordination can be helpful. In many cases this does not occur because of the difficulties in maintaining close contact between busy professionals located in two different institutions. Another reason is that the basic orientations of school and the dynamic therapist are quite diverse and therapeutic methods usually do not easily translate into specific classroom procedures.

5. *Adult tolerance of symptoms.* Children and adolescents are surrounded by adults, usually parents and teachers, who make the major decisions in their lives. Such decisions can have a crucial impact on psychological treatment. These adults differ in their ability to tolerate the consequences of the child's emotional difficulties. Some parents may be so upset by the perceived stigma of having a child with emotional problems that they will avoid treatment as a way of denying such a disgrace.

Adults not only differ in their ability to tolerate dysfunctional behavior, but their tolerance differs according to the particular symptoms and child. Some cannot tolerate overt aggression, especially if the child is disrespectful.

Others are more sensitive to a child's sadness and distress. Often, their intolerance of a symptom is related to their own difficulties and sensitivities.

Usually, adults have the most difficult time with aggressive acting-out behaviors because it is such a direct and obvious challenge to their authority. However, this varies from one adult to another. Teachers are especially sensitive to disruptive children because it also interferes with learning. Of course the individual personality of the child is crucial, because the misbehavior of one child may drive a teacher to distraction while similar behavior from another child will be easily handled. If teachers like a child they can often keep the child within their class, but if they dislike the youngster, that individual will go to a time-out room or be kicked out of class completely. Often whether a child remains in a school or is sent to a special school depends on the tolerance of the school staff as much as on the child's problems.

Children whose problems are more passive and who tend to withdraw are generally easier to tolerate and so parents, teachers, and other adults are likely to have more patience with such children. These children will often be overlooked and may not receive the treatment they need. Most adults are reasonably tolerant of fears and phobias unless, like with school phobia, they interfere with the child's life. However, if the child's symptom has a special significance for the adult or if they have had a similar fear they may become very upset and unable to tolerate the child's problem.

In some situations parents or teachers may be unable to cope with one kind of symptom and yet be able to tolerate another equally dysfunctional behavior. For example, one family had little difficulty coping with their teenage daughter's violent arguments and her refusal to do any work in school. They seemed only mildly upset when she failed every class in spite of the severe implications for her future. However, they became quite upset and forced her to leave home when she engaged in some age appropriate and relatively innocuous sexual behaviors. This family could tolerate aggression and failure, but not the embarrassment of sexual acting out.

An adult's tolerance of a child's symptoms impacts on treatment in a number of ways. Generally, the more intolerant the adult, the more they will opt for an intrusive treatment that either removes the child or quickly controls the disturbing symptom. This obviously affects the time available for treatment. Parents who feel unable to cope with their child's disruptive symptoms may precipitate a crisis by seeking quick and drastic solutions, such as residential treatment for younger children or forcing adolescents to leave home. Sometimes, they may become discouraged and remove the child from treatment. To avoid such drastic steps, any treatment of choice would need to be a short-term therapy that has a high probability of alleviating the child's symptoms in a short time span. Most of the psychodynamic treatments tend to be long-term, and these treatments could be used only if parents and teachers can put up with the child's disturbed behavior during the lengthy course of therapy. As a group, the behavioral treatments tend to be short-term and so these might be the best form of treatment in that situation.

In some cases a short-term treatment might not be the best overall choice, considering all aspects of the child's difficulties. But given the significant adult's inability to cope with the child, such a treatment may be necessary. One solution would be to start treatment with a short-term approach, hoping to quickly alleviate the child's more intolerable behaviors, and then change to the more appropriate long-term model.

Another solution is for a therapist to try to increase the parent or teacher's tolerance of the child. Sometimes this can be done by providing treatment in some form for the parents. Perhaps family therapy may be needed or increasing the amount of parent-therapist meetings. Talking and meeting with teachers can be very helpful. When parents and teachers have the feeling they are not alone and that someone is listening to their problems, they often are much better able to cope with a child. Just the perception that they have some support from the therapist can make a real difference.

An important factor to consider is how directly a treatment targets specific symptoms. Many of the psychodynamic treatments, such as classical psychoanalysis, existential, and humanistic psychotherapy, do not focus on symptom change but on underlying conflicts that the therapist believes are causal to the child's difficulties. This indirect approach means that symptomatic change may be slow in occurring. Sometimes, allowing symptoms to persist for some period of time may be therapeutically desireable since it can make the child aware of more serious underlying difficulties, or they can better see the impact they are having on others.

Most behavioral and cognitive treatments are more symptom focused, and the goal of therapy is to eliminate problematic symptoms. Behavioral treatments, such as operant behavior modification, flooding, systematic desensitization, and modeling, immediately target specific behaviors to be changed, and these therapies may be likely to give adults needed relief so they can tolerate a child's behavior.

Often, when adults are unable to tolerate a child's symptoms they may react to the child in a destructive way and increase the problem. Often they will increase the pressure on the therapist to "show some results." They may also increase their demands on the child when he or she is unable to meet such demands. This will not only slow therapeutic progress, but may create serious obstacles for the child-therapist relationship. Sometimes the inability of important adults to cope with a child's symptoms may become so intense that little progress can be made because the focus of treatment shifts to dealing with the demands and difficulties of the adults.

As already mentioned, the ability of adults to tolerate a child's symptoms will have a major impact on the choice of treatment, and generally the less adults can cope with emotional difficulties, the more a therapist needs to chose a treatment that provides immediate symptomatic relief.

Social-Emotional Variables

Social-emotional variables are those factors associated with the characterological aspects of the child. This refers to such things as how deeply the child feels emotions, the form by which these emotions are expressed, and how well the child can identify and understand feelings. Children also differ in their ability to control their emotions which will have an important effect on adults and peers. Even at very early ages, children have developed certain emotional traits that will have a profound effect on their ability to utilize treatment. Such factors as the ability to control emotions are important to consider when choosing the type of treatment most appropriate for a child.

Obviously, a child's social life is crucial to his or her happiness and overall functioning. Since emotional reactions underlie most of our social relationships, these two factors are closely related. All therapies require some minimal form of social contact, but they differ widely in the social relationships demanded of therapist and child. Thus a child's ability to initiate and maintain a relationship is an important variable in choosing an appropriate treatment. Table 2.3 indicates the relationship between the social-emotional sub-variables and types of treatment.

1. *The ability to form and maintain a close relationship.* We have already mentioned that psychological treatment in any form requires social interaction, but there are vast differences in the social intimacy and trust demanded of the many therapies. Of course, close social intimacy may occur between therapist and child in any form of treatment simply as a result of natural caring and frequent meetings, but the difference is that some psychotherapies require a close relationship or even intimacy for success while others can be effective without it. The somewhat dated term "transference" associated with psychoanalytic therapies is just one example of the emotional intimacy between therapist and child. Most psychodynamic therapists would maintain that the deeper the therapeutic relationship, the more effective the treatment.

Generally speaking, social intimacy is not necessary for success with operant and respondent behavioral methods, and since these treatments are often short-term, such closeness usually does not occur. Cognitive therapies, especially those that are confrontative, require a openness about thoughts and activities so that the therapist can deal with such things as negative thoughts and illogical behavior. Such openness concerning daily activities and thinking is quite different from an emotional closeness. Also, cognitive therapies do not require a closeness on the part of the therapist toward the child or teenager,

TABLE 2.3 Social Emotional Factors

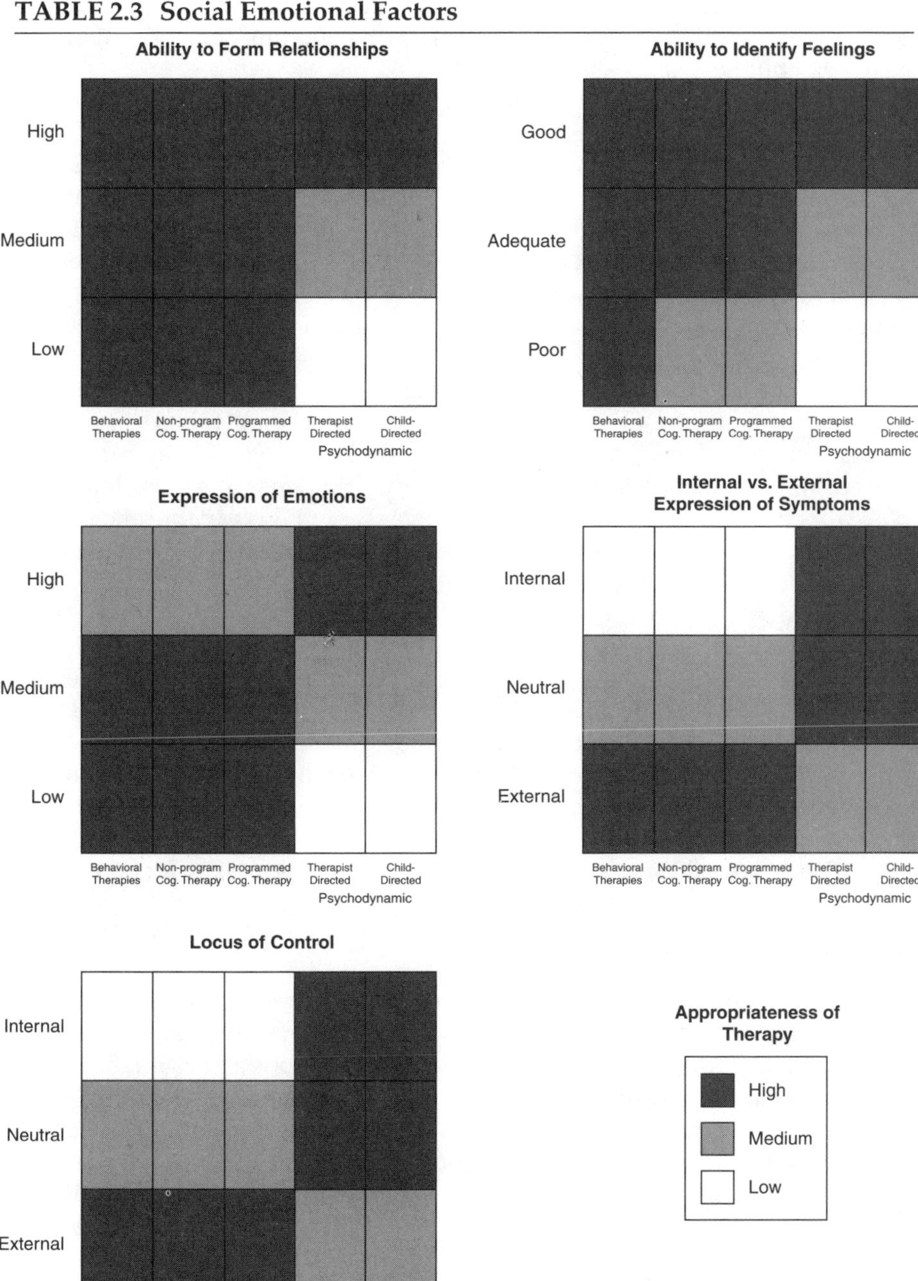

and in fact such closeness may interfere with the needed objectivity. Thus, in order for a cognitive therapy to be successful, a child must have the ability to be open about herself and her life.

Some kind of trust and emotional closeness is required in almost all forms of psychodynamic psychotherapies, and usually this closeness is a central part of the treatment. The therapeutic relationship between child and therapist is so central to psychodynamic treatment that we will devote an entire chapter to that topic, while many other authors have devoted entire books. Not only should such a therapeutic closeness exist, but it needs to deepen and be maintained over the course of treatment. Most theories underlying psychodynamic treatment predict that to the extent that such closeness does not develop the therapy will not be successful.

Although an emotional closeness is needed for effective psychodynamic treatment, sometimes such treatments can be used when a child seems unable to form emotional ties. Some children have the ability, but it is repressed for one reason or another. Other children can learn this closeness over the course of treatment. As long as the therapist believes the child is capable of developing the needed trust and emotional closeness, some form of psychodynamic therapy can be successful.

A child's ability for emotional closeness can be assessed by looking at the kind of relationships the child has with adults and peers. Does the child have friends? Do they have one or a few best friends? Listen for what they do together and the emotional tone the child uses to describe their time together. Certainly, the closeness of the family and how affectionate they are is an important indication of emotional closeness. Most important, look for intensity of feelings, even in anger: Children who have intense emotions are often capable of closeness in time. Another factor is how the child behaves when upset. Does the child seek comfort from others or do they pull away? All these situations are indications of a child's ability to form the kind of relationships needed in treatment.

2. *The ability to identify feelings.* The ability to identify and differentiate different emotions and feelings is crucial to many types of psychotherapies. Identifying a feeling means that the child is able to put a verbal label on an emotion or can intuitively separate one emotion from another. Sometimes this is done by associating an emotion with a certain person, situation, or relationship. The child also needs to see the consistency in his or her emotions over time with the same person or situation, or from one person or situation to another. In addition to identifying their own feelings, children need to be able to do the same with other people. In many forms of therapy children need to also understand the emotional reactions of parents, siblings, and peers.

If a child cannot identify and differentiate one emotion from another they often become confused and overwhelmed. This is detrimental to all types of treatment because when a child is overwhelmed and confused, they do not learn well and such a state is antithetical to the emotionally based problem-solving used in most forms of treatment. Such a child will have little insight into his behavior. Without such insight, he will be handicapped in developing emotional controls or behavioral strategies and will tend not to seek out or use help from others.

Children who cannot identify feelings in themselves and others become confused and need a structured treatment in which the therapist provides the insight and understanding. In behavioral treatments this is imposed by the therapist through powerful behavioral contingencies. Even a child who is too overwhelmed and confused to understand the intricacies of their feelings and behaviors has only to cooperate with the therapist's plan.

When children are more skilled in this ability they can utilize a cognitive or psychodynamic form of intervention. Cognitive treatments are more structured and often provide the child with verbal instructions and therapeutic guidelines for developing the needed emotional or cognitive insights. This type of treatment can be appropriate for children who have only partially developed the ability to differentiate between feelings and who will be somewhat confused but not overwhelmed.

Most of the psychodynamic treatments require a child to be able to reason and learn about their emotions, and this means that the child must not be emotionally confused. Of course, most psychodynamic treatments are complex and the better a child can differentiate their emotions, the better they develop insights into themselves. Thus, children ought to have this skill to be able to do well in psychodynamic treatments.

3. *Expression of emotions.* The expression of emotions can occur in so many diverse ways that one has difficulty discussing this topic as if it were a single issue. Most therapists, however, would agree that certain children are quite able to express their emotions while others are very constricted. In some cases the therapist might question whether or not a child even experiences certain emotions. We have already discussed the primary emotions of sadness, fear, and anger, and there are many ways these can be openly expressed in terms of activity level. Perhaps the most active is some sort of temper tantrum, a naked physical attack on another child, or hysterical sobbing. A more passive expression would be some kind of verbal complaint in which the child describes their feelings to another person. In the most extreme situation the child would seem flat and entirely devoid of emotions.

The manner in which children express their emotions has important implications for choosing the type of therapy appropriate for that child. Psychodynamic treatments place a heavy emphasis on emotional expression since emotions are an important focus of treatment, and in some therapies emotional expression is the primary therapeutic communication process.

Whether emotions are expressed through play, discussed by recounting extratherapeutic experiences, or symbolically acted out through a transference relationship, they are a major part of psychodynamic psychotherapy. As a result, children who are emotionally constricted will not be good candidates for this type of treatment. Of course, we must distinguish between those children who are capable of emotional expression, but are inhibited for certain reasons, and those children who are constitutionally unable to express emotions. The former group may in time become able to utilize a form of psychodynamic treatment whereas the latter will be better off with another kind of treatment.

Emotional constriction is not as serious a problem for cognitive and behavioral treatments because these therapies do not emphasize the expression of emotions as a goal of treatment nor do they utilize emotional expression as part of the therapeutic process. In fact, when control of excessive or maladaptive emotions is a goal of treatment, these treatments can be very effective.

4. *Internal versus external expression of symptoms.* Of all the variables in this category, I think this is the least able to predict the appropriate type of treatment. It is included, however, because it does have some predictive ability. Perhaps when refined, it will be a useful consideration. Internal expression of symptoms are those that are painful or troubling to the child, while external expression of symptoms includes those symptoms which are disturbing to other people. For example, depression or guilt is a symptom that is upsetting and debilitating to an individual whereas verbal or physical attacks are upsetting to others. Of course, these are not completely independent. Guilty children may cause a great deal of anguish to their parents and a child who physically attacks another may be frightened and ultimately depressed.

Although various types of treatment may be successful with either type of child, there is a tendency for the behavioral treatments to be more successful with children who express their problems in a way that is disturbing to others. Such symptoms are very specific, easily identified, and difficult for the child to deny, and behavioral treatments work well with such symptoms. Systematic desensitization is very effective with specific phobias; modeling is most successful with observable behaviors, and operant behavior modification goes best when there are specific discriminative stimuli.

Cognitive treatments also tend to be more effective with definitive symptoms as the illogical nature of such obvious behaviors can be more easily understood, and usually symptoms directed against others are more public and observable.

Most psychodynamic treatments can be effective with either category of symptom although this varies with the particular psychotherapy. The intensive, long-term, verbal nature of these treatments allows the therapist an opportunity to help the child identify even nonspecific symptoms such as sadness or generalized anxiety. At the same time, psychodynamic treatments can be equally effective in treating more specific symptoms, such as physical or verbal aggression, defiance of authority, and overt panic attacks.

5. *Locus of control.* Locus of control is a concept which refers to whether individuals believe they have control of their life or whether they are controlled by their environment. When children have an overall belief that they are the most important influence in their life they will have an optimistic attitude and are more likely to believe they can change as a result of treatment. Conversely, when they believe they are at the mercy of the forces around them, they are likely to be pessimistic about the future and more likely to have serious doubts about whether psychotherapy can be helpful.

Children who have an outer-directed locus of control usually do not do as well in psychodynamic therapies because, as a group, such treatments place the responsibility on the client and the therapist allows and encourages the child to direct the therapy. Outer-directed children may be reluctant to take such responsibility because they will not see themselves as an important agent of change. They may believe their efforts are futile compared to what the outside world does to them. If outer directed children are put in a psychodynamic psychotherapy the main task of the therapist is to change their attitude and make them see they can genuinely affect their own lives. The therapist usually takes an active role in encouraging such children to try to assert themselves, hoping they will meet with success and be reinforced by their efforts. After dealing with the child's external locus of control, the therapist can then move on to other emotional problems.

Children with an external locus of control are usually better candidates for cognitive or behavioral treatments. They will be more content with the therapist directing and having responsibility for their treatment.

Children who have an internal locus of control usually do better in psychodynamic therapy because they believe they are the most important factor in changing their life; thus they want to take responsibility and control of their treatment. They are unlikely to do as well in cognitive treatments, and especially behavioral treatments, because they will fight the orientation toward therapist control and responsibility.

Summary

As we have already mentioned, this dispositional diagnostic system is imprecise and some of the variables will need to be redefined. Nevertheless, it is a first attempt at using a diagnostic system specifically designed to predict the most appropriate type of treatment for each child. Such a system should be used not only at the beginning of treatment, but throughout the entire course of therapy. Because children change during the course of treatment, they often need a new treatment approach and this system ought to be a helpful guide in predicting the appropriateness of the new approach.

One obvious difficulty with such a system is the fact that there are fifteen variables to take into account, and they may differ from one another in their predictions for treatment. This is to be expected since these variables reflect three different areas of a child's life. In devising this system we tried to find areas and variables that were independent of each other. Thus, there is little reason to think that the families' availability of finances and a child's causal reasoning would predict the same type of treatment. Similarly, there is no reason to expect that a child's ability to express emotions would be closely related to the degree of cooperation provided by his or her school.

There obviously will be some amount of disagreement in the type of treatment predicted by these variables. Unfortunately, the system does not have the precision needed to generate a formula with appropriate weights that would calculate an overall prediction of the best therapy to use. In fact, this dispositional diagnostic system is not designed to be used in such a precise and actuarial way. Rather, it is a rough guide designed to make therapists aware of important variables in selecting an appropriate treatment. In this way, a therapist can use his or her own clinical judgment, utilizing knowledge of their own client population and clinical setting, to decide which variables are more important than others. Then they can find a way to combine the information to arrive at a thoughtful and accurate treatment decision. Hopefully, being aware of which aspects of a child's life are important to treatment will help therapists design a therapeutic program that is appropriate to the child's needs both at the beginning and at any given point throughout the course of treatment.

3

The Blending of Treatments

Treatments and Therapists

Obviously, therapists differ in their theoretical beliefs. As we have already seen there are many theories of personality and psychopathology, and therapists group themselves across these theories. Some of us even try to adhere to more than one and call ourselves eclectic or multimodal.

Aside from theoretical differences, there are personality differences among all people, and therapists are no exceptions. Any attempt to discuss all of the personality differences between therapists would take volumes and would still miss the most important point. Each of us must learn the nuances of our own personalities and how that affects our own choices of the treatments we use and therefore affects the children we are treating. Knowing one's personality and how it affects our therapeutic work is a process that comes after a great deal of experience. It is greatly helped by insightful supervision with very experienced therapists. Many therapists also go through their own therapy which helps them understand themselves, which makes them better able to see how they affect their child patients. I might briefly mention a few therapist characteristics that have been found to be important.

First, therapists differ in activity level. Some of us need to be more active than others. We may not feel comfortable unless something is always happening or there is continual talking. Others are more comfortable with a passive role in which there may be long pauses or silences. This type of therapist may not need to feel that therapeutic progress is continuous.

Related to this is a therapist's need for control. Some therapists are not comfortable unless they are in firm control of the course of therapy. They need to be directly involved in bringing about decisions and feelings that they always know what is happening in therapy. Other therapists are able to tolerate the ambiguity of not always knowing what is happening. They are content to allow therapy to proceed on its own course or to let the child determine the activities and content of treatment.

Both the therapist's activity level and need to have control of treatment are likely to determine which kind of psychotherapy that therapist is likely to be comfortable, which also will affect the type of treatment received by the parents and children. Without trying to ferret out the nuances of this process, I think therapist's with a strong need to control are more likely to be comfortable with an operant behavior therapy. Therapists with a high activity need will tend to choose a confrontative treatment like rational-emotive therapy. Many of the psychoanalytic and client-centered treatments require a very patient therapist who can be comfortable having little direct control of the therapeutic process.

The above examples are only elementary observations of generalized trends. People are so multifaceted and complex that we cannot develop a simple personality-therapy cookbook that will predict what kind of therapy is going to be best for what therapist. Too bad the world is not that simple or we might easily develop a "Therapist Choice Questionnaire" for students to take before entering professional training. It would save them a good deal of anguish and searching. Fortunately, that searching and the accompanying anguish are probably valuable learning experiences and are a crucial part of becoming a therapist. Therapists do not know the true value of their methods unless they have tried and rejected others. Hopefully in this process they learn to respect and see the value in the therapeutic methods they have rejected. Hopefully, too, they have not rejected those methods because they are useless but because that method did not fit well with their cognitive, emotional, and personal style.

We also need to be aware of those therapist characteristics that affect the child's or more likely the parent's choice of a therapist. Obvious factors such as age, race, and appearance have an impact on what therapist a child or the parents will choose. Some parents may expect to see a professional looking middle-aged therapist dressed in a conservative dress or a suit and tie. They may not have confidence in a therapist who is younger than they are. However, a male, high school sophomore with a drug problem may initially have a more positive reaction to a bearded, blue-jeaned therapist in his mid-twenties than to the therapist the parents preferred. These factors tend to be more important in the beginning of therapy and decrease or disappear as time goes on and the more significant factors associated with the therapist's personality begin to emerge.

Another influence on what therapy a child receives is the kind of training the therapist has received. Often due to historical accident (such as which graduate school accepted us or which one we could afford or which one was convenient), we end up receiving psychotherapeutic training that slants us in one direction or another. Many of us were relatively naïve when we were accepted to the universities and internships that provided our training. Seldom do student-therapists learn all therapeutic orientations and then make a studied, rational choice of the one they prefer. They usually take on or are profoundly influenced by the professors and supervisors of their training institutions. As a group, clinical social workers, psychiatrists, clinical psychologists, and child therapists differ from each other in professional orientation and to some extent that reflects the different training each has received. I am pleased to see that these differences seem to be disappearing in recent years as each group is more open in accepting the knowledge of the other.

What Therapy for What Child

I suppose that in the most logical of worlds, treatments would be based on the needs of children, and, to a limited extent, this does happen, but only to a limited extent. Unfortunately, many, if not most therapeutic choices are made according to therapist preference, parental inexperience, institutional dogma, or just plain happenstance. You may disagree, thinking that I overstate the situation, but consider that most parents chose a therapist for their child or teenager based on recommendations from friends, relatives, teachers, neighbors, or their family doctor, none of whom know much about the therapeutic orientation of the therapist they recommend. If they take their child to a clinic or hospital, that institution is likely to have a theoretical bias that differentiates it from other institutions. Depending on whose caseload is full or open, among other bureaucratic factors, a child or the family will be assigned to a therapist with a particular therapeutic allegiance. Even these situations may vary depending on what part of the country they live in, because different areas have abundant or scarce mental health facilities.

Of course we live in an imperfect world, but still, it is hard to escape a simple logic:

> *Treatment should be chosen based on the particular emotional problems and needs of a child.*

Unfortunately, this simple logical statement is not so easy to carry out. One problem is that in order to chose an appropriate treatment we must have an accurate idea of what the problems and needs are. In other words, we must have a good initial diagnosis. As we saw in chapter two, all of the present diagnostic systems are to some extent unreliable and imprecise. Even when we achieve an accurate diagnosis based on the initial information, we may later learn additional information which changes the initial assessment of the child's problems. Of course, children are not static objects but developing beings, and they are constantly changing in different ways. Some of these changes will not affect their therapeutic needs; others will have a profound effect. The type of treatment appropriate at one time may become inappropriate or inefficient at a later time. As children change, either through normal development or through improvements due to treatment, another therapy or therapeutic technique may be needed.

The notion that an exact diagnosis predicts a particular treatment is called the medical model. Many therapists feel, with good reason, that the medical model is not applicable to emotionally disturbed children and psychotherapeutic treatment. Without going into all the details of this argument, we agree that a system that works well in physiology and medicine may not apply to psychological difficulties. First of all, psychological and psychiatric diagnosis is inexact and has nowhere near the precision of medical diagnosis. A good medical diagnosis predicts a particular drug or surgical procedure, but the precision of this system does not exist in the treatment of emotional problems. In medicine there is a galaxy of different treatments from which to choose. That, too, is not the case in psychotherapy.

Another important difference between medicine and psychotherapy is that in medicine the personality of the physician, the theoretical beliefs, and the doctor-patient relationship does not affect treatment to the extent that it does in psychological treatments. In psychotherapy these factors are crucial. These problems ought to be obvious to any thinking individual once he or she realizes that the two situations are so different. Medicine deals with the structure of an individual, psychology deals with the function.

Now that we have acknowledged the problems with a medical model, we also ought not to throw out the baby with the bath water. Therapists can be more helpful if they relate the method of treatment to the child's emotional problems. We may never develop an exact formula for this because psychotherapeutic treatment is a complex mixture of science and art, and the effectiveness of treatment depends on the relationship between child and therapist. But we should not allow theoretical identity or personal bias to determine the choice of treatment.

The Complexities of Children Demand a Complex of Treatments

At the present time the field of psychotherapy is facing a difficult, double-horned dilemma.

Dilemma number 1: If children are complex and different (and they are) then different children need different treatments.

Dilemma number 2: The emotional problems of any one child are often complex and diverse. Few children are so homogeneous that one type of treatment will suffice for all their needs. Also, children change due to therapeutic progress or normal development, so a child often needs different techniques during the course of treatment.

Unfortunately, many therapists are limited to one psychotherapy or system of psychotherapy and use that with all the children that come their way. Sometimes they may refer a child when they realize that a particular child's problems are inappropriate for their technique. More often they redefine the child's problems so that they seem appropriate to what the therapist has to offer. Very few therapists are so familiar and so competent with every psychotherapy that they can provide the most appropriate treatment for every child.

As we will see there are some very good reasons for this situation. Systems of psychotherapy tend to interact with a therapist's personality, and just as a therapist cannot chameleon-like grow and shed new personalities, so they cannot take on and discard psychotherapies. Certain therapies "fit" them, and they are probably most effective with those techniques. Besides, it takes a great deal of time and experience to learn and become competent with a treatment modality. Some research shows that there is an interaction between certain aspects of a therapist's personality and the type of treatment he or she uses (Wolberg, 1982). As a group, cognitive therapists are more verbally active than other therapists, and are more directive and questioning in their interactions with patients. Behavior therapists also are verbally active, but tend more toward direct teaching and encouragement of their patients. Psychodynamic therapists tend to be more passive and lead their patients in more indirect ways. We can't be sure that these differences don't reflect the demands of the various treatment techniques, but to some extent they likely indicate personality differences among therapists that led them to select their particular mode of treatment.

Most therapists believe they modify their treatment techniques to fit their patients, but this may not always be true. Hans Strupp (1981) found that most therapists usually overestimate how much they accommodate their techniques to their patients. There is little doubt that allegiance to a particular therapy has some definite benefits, but some researchers have found that treatment effectiveness is related not so much to which treatment a therapist uses, but whether or not the therapist is consistent in following the techniques and philosophy of that treatment (Luborsky et al, 1983) (Shaw, 1983). The crux of this finding may indicate that following the techniques and philosophy help guide a therapist and avoid therapist confusion. Perhaps it provides the therapist with a stable and understandable way to organize the complexity of information about a child. Faith in the system is also likely to give the therapist confidence in her work and will heighten her expectations of a "cure." However, it does not indicate that a therapist should only subscribe to one form of treatment. So long as the therapist is consistent in following a therapeutic philosophy, then there is little evidence to show that she is limited to only one technique or that she can use more than one technique. The key is internal consistency, avoiding therapeutic confusion, and conveying confidence and positive expectations.

The more interesting aspect of the Luborsky and Shaw studies is that one technique seems to be no more effective than another. A cogent explanation of this phenomenon is offered by Lewis Wolberg (1982), who speculates that although different treatments focus on different aspects of a child's emotional problems, the effect of the treatment may generalize to seemingly untreated problems because symptoms at different levels may be closely related and dependant on each other. In other words, when a behavior therapist focuses on desensitizing an anxiety-ridden child, she not only affects fears and anxieties, but also may increase the child's peer relationships or resolve certain unconscious developmental conflicts because these are related to and affected by the child's anxiety level. Similarly, a psychoanalytic therapist who focuses on a child's early psychosexual conflicts may positively affect a child's ability to handle anxiety and may better the child's peer relationships.

Hopefully, there is a beneficial compromise between providing for the varied therapeutic needs of children and asking therapists to be all things to all children. The crux of that compromise is that therapists need to become more flexible in their treatment. Psychotherapeutic treatment of children has grown beyond the inflexibility of a therapist having only one way of treating all their patients.

Many theorists are pessimistic. They see little sign that therapists are beginning to use therapies other than the one they adhere to, and they do not believe that there will be a general reconciliation of the different forms of psychotherapy (Zeig, 1987). While such pessimism may be an accurate reflection of today's situation, it need not predict the future. The field of psychotherapeutic treatment of children can change. If we believe that we can change the behavior of children for the better, why should we not believe that we can change ourselves? Certainly there are difficulties in combining and melding multiple kinds of treatments, but by understanding the difficulties we will be better able to bring this about.

James Prochaska (1984) has a useful system that helps organize the confusion inherent in the attempt to use multiple forms of treatment by therapists. He divides therapists into four types.

1. *Dualistic therapists:* These therapists believe there is a one correct form of therapy and that all others are in error. They are what Prochaska calls the "true believers," and they can be found in any system of psychotherapy.

2. *Multiplistic therapists:* These therapists accept that there is uncertainty concerning which treatment is best, but believe this will be resolved in the future. At that time we will "know" which treatment is best. They hope it will be the one they are using.

3. *Ethical therapists:* Ethical therapists choose a form of treatment based on their sense of personal ethics. These therapists may accept other methods as equally useful and valid, but commit to one system because its values are "better for humanity." Ethical therapists then attempt to master and improve that system as best they can.

4. *Relativistic therapists:* These are eclectic therapists who believe no one therapy is correct. They believe that a therapy is relative to the situation. Some believe the choice of therapy should be determined by the child's symptoms; others believe it should be determined by the child's personality; while even others think it should be decided relative to the therapist's personality. Currently, there are few hard and fast rules to tell us which therapy is best in which situation, and that might be different for each relativistic therapist anyhow. Therefore, choice of treatment is made individually by each therapist on the basis of that individual's clinical knowledge.

A more positive view of this problem is offered by Wolberg (1982). Looking at the common elements among therapy systems, he believes that all therapists emphasize one of three areas: therapist-patient relationships, reward-punishment, or cognitive restructuring. To some extent a therapist will touch on all these elements in the course of treatment, and the real difference between them is only on the emphasis. Viewed in this way, an eclectic approach to treatment is only a matter of emphasis, meaning all therapists have the possibility to use many forms of treatment.

Recent trends seem to indicate that as a group therapists are becoming more eclectic in their work. John Norcross (1986) found that 30 percent to 40 percent of all therapists describe themselves as eclectic and Norcross and J. D. Guy (1989) found that eclectic therapists tend to be older and more experienced. These findings support the notion that therapists are beginning to realize that different children need different kinds of treatments, and that they must provide whatever treatment is required. Perhaps we are beginning to move away from the egocentric notion that our one form of treatment is good for every child.

In the beginning of this discussion we said that there are two aspects of this problem. First, a therapist must have appropriate treatments for many kinds of children, and, second, he must have appropriate techniques to deal with the differing and changing problems of the same child. The first situation requires a therapist to comfortably and competently use many disparate, conceptually different treatments. This demands flexibility and a broad base of knowledge on the part of the therapist.

The second problem is more complex because it requires a therapist to combine different therapies with the same child. When treating an emotionally disturbed child one cannot go about mixing therapies or therapeutic styles willy-nilly and assume that such extreme eclecticism will work. That is why a competent therapist needs to know the similarities and differences between psychotherapies. Different kinds of therapies must be integrated in a way that will be effective in helping children overcome their emotional problems, and this raises new problems. Such a blending of treatments must feel harmonious to a child and that is often difficult to accomplish. Children become familiar with a certain therapeutic style and can be upset with therapeutic changes they perceive as discordant and confusing behavior on the part of their therapist.

There are certain obvious principles that must be followed when attempting to use more than one therapeutic method with a child. First, having theoretical and pragmatic knowledge over the entire spectrum of treatments better enables a therapist to choose the most appropriate treatment. Unfortunately, almost no one can be experienced with all forms of treatments. You can, however, develop a working theoretical knowledge of all forms of psychotherapy or, at the very least, a general concept of the overall systems that underlie the many forms of treatment. If nothing else, this reflects an openness to other approaches, which is needed. Unfortunately, some therapists reject other forms of treatment because, by putting down the others, they build up their own.

Secondly, therapists must have a sound working knowledge of the kinds of therapies they are thinking of using. Therapists can not just be familiar with their own method and then decide, "Well, this other method looks simple enough. I think I'll give it a try and see if it works."

Thirdly, combining treatment methods adds an extra complexity to the treatment process. You not only use two forms of treatment, but there is an important transition process. How a therapist goes about the transition from one technique to another is crucial, and it must be integrated so that both therapist and child feel a minimal sense of disruption. To do this well, a therapist must know the similarities and differences between various types of treatments. Differences, because they will alert a therapist to potential difficulties in combining treatments; and similarities, because they will enable a therapist to blend them together in a synchronous fashion. Both are important to know when combining treatments.

Perhaps meld or blend are better words to describe this process than combine. Combining treatments indicates that one method simply follows another whereas when we blend treatments we show an awareness of how harmoniously they go together. Any therapist needs to think out the consequences of the particular blend of therapy that he attempts.

For example, trying to combine client-centered or humanistic therapy with operant behavior modification is potentially disruptive. In the first type of treatment, the therapist allows the patient a great deal of control concerning what issues are to be dealt with, and the child has responsibility for the consequences of what he or she chooses to do. In most forms of operant behavior modification, the therapist assumes a greater degree of control of treatment and arranges behavioral consequences for the child. Even when done in a gentle and sensitive way, this approach is disparate from humanistic and person-centered treatments. Most children will be confused by such an abrupt change in the therapeutic relationship and the restriction of their freedom in the therapy session. They might even have a severe emotional reaction to such an abrupt change and become furious with their therapist. The child-therapist relationship might be destroyed to the point where the child becomes noncooperative or attempts to terminate treatment.

These two types of treatment seem to be polar extremes, and some therapists would maintain they cannot be blended. However, they have some common elements, and for the sake of the example, we will try. First, the therapist must prepare the child ahead of time by explaining why such a change is needed and how it will be of benefit. The therapist might say something like, "We've gotten to the point where you understand what you are doing, but you need help stopping it. There is something else we can do that might be helpful, but it's very different from the way we've been doing things."

What the therapist says will depend on the previous therapist-child experiences, but the main thing is to tell the child to expect things to be different. Also, the therapist is not forcing the behavior modification on the child but is giving the child a choice. By doing so he is enlisting the child's cooperation. Perhaps the key to a successful transition in this situation is modifying the operant procedure by avoiding any strident imposition of severe behavioral consequences.

A helpful step would be to allow the child to participate in setting up the behavioral contingencies and consequences. This is commensurate with the tone of the earlier client-centered sessions. In this way the child will feel that he still has some control over treatment. Whatever the particular details of the therapeutic strategy, the therapist needs to be careful to preserve the stability of the original therapist-child relationship.

The above example highlights how a therapist might consider the implications of the differences between therapies, but we also need to see how knowing similarities between treatments determines how a therapist plans out a treatment strategy.

Perhaps a therapist is referred an eleven-year-old child who has few friends, is generally unhappy, and has great difficulty controlling him or herself in a classroom. The therapist might choose to start treatment by using Kendall's self-instruction training to help the child with disruptive school behavior, and then turn to psychoanalytically oriented play therapy to deal with the peer problems and the general unhappiness.

In assessing the similarities between the methods the therapist would realize the following. Both methods are task-oriented in that they provide things for the child to do. In Kendall's method the tasks are structured and chosen by the therapist, while the play therapy activities are chosen by the child and are likely to be more spontaneous. This transition may be an easy one if the therapist goes from self-instruction training to psychoanalytically oriented treatment, as most children will have little trouble dealing with the increased freedom of choosing their tasks. There may be more difficulty if the therapist tries to reverse the order of the treatments.

Although both treatments strive for a positive and close relationship between child and therapist, trying to move from psychoanalytically oriented treatment to Kendall's self-instruction training is likely to be more difficult. One factor is that as treatment progresses in psychoanalytically oriented treatment, the relationship may become more intense and likely more regressive. Although reasonable self-control within the session is necessary, the therapist will tolerate and encourage more outward expressions of emotional behavior and fantasy play. At this point moving to Kendall's treatment method would require more self-control within the session, and this runs counter to what the child is accustomed to. This type of blending also involves a change in the therapeutic relationship.

Another difficulty is the change in treatment that occurs over time. Although both treatments are initially reality-oriented and centered on the child's present life, Kendall's self-instruction training remains so, while after many sessions psychoanalytically oriented treatment often begins to deal with issues from the child's past. Trying to move toward Kendall's present-oriented methods at this point might be confusing and feel disruptive to the child.

There are two important differences between the methods that also need to be taken into account. Kendall's methods do not foster a cathartic emotional release. It will occur more as psychoanalytically oriented psychotherapy progresses. If the child has been using therapy in this way, then switching to self-instruction training may be very frustrating. They may still need the emotional release, but that will interfere with the programmed timetable of self-instruction training.

If children need to have this kind of emotional release, the therapist is faced with two solutions. He may try to drastically modify the self-instruction methods to allow the child to have the needed cathartic experiences. However, this may be impossible to do. Kendall's methods are not designed for these kinds of behaviors, and the therapist's work does not foster that kind of experience. Trying to integrate cathartic release within a programmed type of treatment also may destroy the beneficial and essential aspects of the treatment.

Another, and perhaps better, solution is to begin treatment with the self-instruction procedures and then utilize psychoanalytically oriented play therapy. At that point the child and therapist will have developed a good relationship and the child is likely to feel more secure with the therapist. As the self-instructional treatment ends, their time together will be less programmed and the therapeutic relationship can become closer and more trusting. At this point the child is more likely to gradually become more open to the therapist and experience cathartic emotional releases.

There is a second important difference between the two treatments. In Kendall's treatment the child is taught self-control words that are signals and is taught steps to follow in solving a problem. This is provided by the therapist in a clear and unambiguous fashion. In psychoanalytically oriented psychotherapy the therapist does not give the child solutions to emotional difficulties, but provides an environment in which the child finds solutions. In this situation the therapist may have to ease the transition by gently telling the child something like, "I think we've accomplished a lot by working together over the past few weeks. For one thing you've learned to control yourself better in school. I tried to give you a lot of help in solving that problem, but now I'd like to let you find your own way of solving problems. I'll help you, but you know yourself better than I do, and I think things might go better if you tried to find the answers." I offer the preceding imaginary conversation only as a rough-hewn example of what needs to be done. Most likely, such a transition would take place over a period of time with many and more subtle conversations. Of course, the subtlety of such conversations is determined by the therapist's intimate knowledge of each child's idiosyncratic personality.

Therapeutic Styles and Blending Treatments

In the preceding section we discussed blending complete and intact methods of psychotherapy and the discussion centered on how complete therapies could be blended by taking their similarities and differences into account. As we have already said, this is a very difficult thing to do. Most therapists have an allegiance to a particular system of psychotherapy which is part of their therapeutic style. Even if they believed that blending treatments was a desirable thing, they might be unable to do it. To effectively use a new and unfamiliar treatment means that the therapist would have to adapt a new set of concepts and change their usual way of thinking and that is not easy. To be effective, a therapist also needs to feel comfortable with a type of treatment and trying to blend a familiar treatment with a strange one usually is not a comforting thing to do.

Most therapists can understand a child through more than one theoretical framework, but I doubt that anyone is able to effectively understand a child through every theoretical system. Of course, a therapist may know the principles and concepts of a particular psychotherapy in an academic sense, but that is very different from being able to use those concepts to understand the complex nuances of a child's life and then generate an effective treatment. To do that the therapist must be able to think and conceptualize the child's problems within the theoretical framework of that psychotherapy. To be able to do this with many systems of psychotherapy is difficult.

I suppose most therapists blend treatments not by using two completely diverse psychotherapies, but by incorporating useful elements of some other technique into their particular style or usual form of treatment. This is an easier transition. In this way a therapist can retain the familiar conceptual understanding they have about a child, and certainly a therapist must have some coherent way of understanding a child if he is to provide effective treatment.

Perhaps this method of blending techniques from a diverse psychotherapy within the framework of a familiar psychotherapy is best seen through the following example.

> For about a year I treated a fourteen-year-old girl who came to me because she was having a very difficult time with her parents and her friends. She was very angry with her parents, who she felt were constantly after her about the things she did wrong. There were constant fights when she disobeyed them by violating curfews and not doing her schoolwork. She felt her parents did not trust her, had never trusted her, and as a result she defied them. Although she had a good number of friends, she was always insecure with them, feeling she could not really trust them. She often put them through tests to reassure herself that their friendship was genuine.
>
> The crux of my treatment was psychoanalytically oriented psychotherapy in which we explored her feelings concerning parents and friends. For the most part the therapeutic relationship between us was close and positive, although she was slow to believe that I would respect therapeutic confidentiality. Much of my work involved leading her into emotional insights concerning the way in which her parents responded to her. My reactions to much of what she said gave her corrective emotional experiences and helped to change her impulsive reactions. Around the end of the first year she had made good progress in starting to trust her friends and getting along better with her parents.
>
> Throughout her life she had had a very close and loving relationship with her grandparents, who she felt were more loving and trusting than her parents. Sadly, her grandfather developed terminal cancer and this became a major focus in therapy. At this time I felt that the psychoanalytically oriented treatment was not the most appropriate treatment. I began to include some principles of Existential Treatment in our work together, even though I do not consider myself an accomplished existential therapist and would have difficulty attempting to change my way of

understanding this young girl from my psychoanalytically oriented framework.

The main reason for this transition was the unchangeable reality of her grandfather's death. He would die within a few months and she had to accept this fact. Nothing she could do would change that and an existential acceptance of this painful event was the best solution to this tragedy.

Since both forms of treatment are psychodynamic, there were enough similarities to make for a smooth transition. Our therapeutic relationship remained essentially the same. However, I became somewhat more forceful in having her confront her problems and did not make as much of an effort to provide insight into the causes of her difficulties. By helping her to confront her grandfather's death and not helping her to find a solution to this sadness, she was forced to come to grips with her inescapable helplessness and a realization that she needed to find her own answers, which she did.

Unfortunately, I recall another case where my ineptitude in trying to blend two forms of therapy resulted in a good bit of anger, irrevocable damage to the therapeutic relationship, and a premature termination of treatment.

Mike was an eight-year-old who had attention deficit disorder, serious peer difficulties, and very poor school performance. He was terribly sensitive to failure and became angry at the slightest reminder of his problems. We had formed a good therapeutic relationship and he eagerly awaited our play therapy sessions. After seven months of treatment, I became frustrated with our progress and decided to change from our psychodynamically oriented play therapy to a cognitive programmatic treatment based on Kendall's work. Unfortunately, after reaching this decision I simply went ahead with the change. I did not do a good job explaining the reasons for the change, and I did not ask his permission nor use a slow transition over the course of two or three sessions. I simply began one session by saying that we would be doing some different things and plunged ahead. At first he was quite excited at the prospect of earning rewards, but by the second session he became increasingly unhappy and was complaining that he didn't like these new games. The crux of the problem was that even the slightest failure was too difficult for him to accept. Unless he always earned a reward, he became angry and depressed. I persisted, trying to cajole him into participating, but finally gave up when he became very angry and resisted coming to our sessions. At this point I tried to resume our original psychodynamic play therapy, but I had irrevocably damaged the therapeutic relationship and two months later his parents terminated treatment.

There is little doubt in my mind that I was insensitive to the magnitude of the transition that I expected from this youngster, and I had not cogently thought out the difficulties from his point of view. I had not protected him from his reaction to failure and the new therapeutic technique brought this out in a way that he could not handle.

Attempting to "import" techniques and concepts from other therapies and use them within one's own familiar therapeutic system has both advantages and disadvantages. One benefit is that it gives therapists a greater sense of familiarity and comfort because they are working within the overall confines of their own system. Most likely, they can better conceptualize and understand the child they are treating. It is also an excellent way to broaden a therapist's knowledge and experience. When therapists attempt to integrate unfamiliar techniques from other systems of psychotherapy, they learn not only the particular technique, but begin to acquire a greater knowledge and familiarity of the other system of therapy. In addition, the therapist learns to use the new system and its techniques in a pragmatic "hands on" way, which is likely superior to an academic understanding. Through this kind of learning, they will eventually be able to understand the child within that new system.

However, we must also consider some of the problems. Often it is difficult to take just one technique or aspect of an overall system without the other parts. It may not work in isolation. It may need to be used along with the other techniques and concepts of that overall treatment. Also, therapists must be sure that the borrowed technique fits with the system they are using. Often times there are theoretical incompatibilities between certain techniques. An obvious example is that the behavioral technique of punishment is incompatible with a humanistic system of psychotherapy.

Just as important as theoretical incompatibilities is the fit with the therapist's personality and values. There is little point in trying to use a technique that seems morally offensive, and therapists cannot use a technique that is at variance with their usual way of doing things. The rational-emotive therapist who has a strong need to be active and assertive in therapy may have difficulty trying to allow a child to feel his or her own helplessness and insignificance, even when the therapist feels the child needs to experience that aspect of existential psychotherapy. Similarly, there may be some therapists who feel it is morally wrong to coerce children into certain behaviors and there is little point in their trying to use therapeutic techniques from certain kinds of behavioral therapies.

I do not underestimate the complexity of trying to either blend two kinds of psychotherapies or to blend a diverse therapeutic technique within one's familiar system of treatment. This is especially difficult since there has been little research in this area. (Actually, it is an area of such complexity that I think the shared experiences of therapists may be more helpful than objective research studies.) But, rather than becoming frightened by the hodgepodge of therapeutic choices and decisions involved in such blending, I would encourage therapists to try it whenever they feel it will be helpful to a child. We will never learn how to blend treatments unless we attempt it. We must expect to make mistakes, but a sensitive therapist will see those mistakes and then return to the pre-existing treatment or try a new and better blend. I think that most therapists are sensitive enough to read the reactions of the children they are treating. Besides, many children will bluntly or subtly inform their therapist when they are confused or unhappy. Luckily, psychotherapy is not like neurological surgery. Mistakes can be changed and good therapists are always doing this within their own theoretical and psychotherapeutic systems.

Obstacles to Integrating Therapies

Perhaps the main obstacle thwarting integration of treatments is the fact that each school of therapy gives different explanations for the cause of emotional problems, and in offering their own explanation they disallow any others. Usually each school offers one or at most a few causal determinants that assumes coverage of the entire psychological universe, and de facto reject a multideterministic approach that incorporates other theories. Related to this is the fact that each school has its own unique language, which makes it difficult for adherents of one school to speak to one another and understand the ideas of a different school. This, too, constitutes a formidable obstacle for integration. As a result each school develops techniques and procedures designed to ameliorate its self-defined emotional problems, and these factors lead to confusion and sometimes contentious misunderstandings.

For example, some psychoanalytic schools would explain childhood autism in terms of unemotional mothering and interruptions in the oral stage of development. They would offer long-term psychoanalytic sessions oriented toward basic relationship and transference issues. A behavioral school would offer defective early learning as the explanation and prescribe strict operant conditioning methods and modeling which attempt to teach the child such basic skills as speech and self-care. The humanistic school would likely not become involved with such a child, as the symptoms and psychological problems fall outside of the universe of their explanatory concepts and they have no treatment techniques to fit this situation. The unfortunate result is that the explanations of each school preclude the other and hinder integration. In reality, a combination of operant conditioning and an appropriately modified, but intense relational therapy is often used successfully in treating autistic children.

Of course, when a skilled therapist of a particular school gains success in treating a child, that reinforces the belief that the school's explanation and treatment were the "correct" ones. Since most psychological interventions, regardless of theoretical orientation or school, are successful, the "correctness" of a school is confirmed frequently, and so the question of whether another treatment might be just as or more effective is ignored. The more likely explanation is one that we have already discussed. Emotional problems exist and interact on many levels and even a narrow treatment focus on one level is likely to produce beneficial changes across the larger universe of personality functioning. In other words, the use of operant procedures designed to teach basic verbal and emotional skills is likely to also yield changes in an autistic child's ability to relate to others. Similarly, a treatment designed to produce improvements in the child's interpersonal relationships is also likely to yield positive changes in basic skills, such as speech and self-care.

Transtheoretical Analysis

Two of the most prolific and cogent innovators in the development of eclectic techniques are James Prochaska and Carlo DiClemente (Prochaska, 1984, Prochaska & DiClemente, 1984, Prochaska & DiClemente, 1986). They have developed a system of integrating psychotherapies which they call "Transtheoretical Analysis" and which they and their colleagues have used successfully with adult patients. They assume that different types of treatments are needed at different stages of treatment and their system attempts to provide guidelines in knowing when and under what circumstances a particular treatment can be successfully used. The central idea of this system is that treatment unfolds in a set sequence through four distinct stages. These are precontemplation, contemplation, action, and maintenance, and they identify specific therapies and therapeutic techniques that are used with each stage. Briefly, precontemplation is a time when patients become aware that they have a problem, begin to see the disadvantages of their difficulties, and confront their psychological defenses. Contemplation is the stage when patients try to understand their emotional difficulties and reevaluate themselves. The action stage is when patients go through the process of actually changing their problematic thoughts, feelings, and behaviors, and in maintenance patients work on maintaining the gains they have made. Although some clients may enter the therapeutic process at a more advanced stage than others, and may rapidly pass through a stage, the sequence of going from precontemplation to maintenance is invariant.

The advantage of this interesting system is that it provides definite guidelines for a therapist to follow and places all patients in the same theoretical framework. For example, patients in the contemplation stage are most open to techniques such as consciousness-raising, bibliotherapy and other educationally based techniques. During the action stage, patients are most likely to benefit from techniques that bring about behavioral change, such as counter-conditioning and stimulus control. Although the system is not definitively prescriptive, Prochaska and DiClemente advocate that a therapist follow a systematic sequence, as opposed to an individualized approach, tailored to the idiosyncratic characteristics and environment of the patient. They believe this is less confusing and likely to provide a therapist with a more understandable use of eclecticism. Obviously, each therapist will need to chose his own style; however, I prefer the more individual-oriented approach, even if that has fewer guidelines and is the more difficult to use. Perhaps the major difficulty with the system is that while it seems to indicate which treatment might be useful at certain stages in treatment, it does not show how to make the transition from one type of treatment to another. Also, the four stages seem more applicable to an adult model and may not be as advantageous in describing the sequence of child treatment. Whatever the preference of a therapist, this is an interesting approach to integrative treatment and contains many thoughtful and innovative ideas.

The Importance of Therapy Integration with Children

Therapeutic eclecticism is a growing trend among therapists of all disciplines, and is probably a more important therapeutic skill in working with children than with adults. There are many reasons for this. Children need a wider spectrum of treatments for many reasons. Most adults tend to define the focus of their treatment, and they concentrate on those problems which are causing them psychological pain or emotional anguish. Children seldom define the focus of therapy, and although parents usually give a therapist a good description of their child's difficulties, they, too, usually aren't specific as to what symptoms and problems they want focused on. This allows a child therapist more latitude in determining the therapeutic focus, and with a wider spectrum of problems the therapist may need a wider spectrum of treatments.

For the most part, child therapists deal with and must be concerned with wider life dimensions than adult therapists. Most individual adult therapists spend their time with the patient and focus on disturbing symptoms and emotional conflicts as defined by that patient. Child therapists focus on these internal difficulties, but they must also be concerned with the child's interaction with school and parents. This, too, necessitates a broader range of treatments. For example, in treating an angry youngster who is a behavior problem at school, a therapist may use a psychodynamic approach to explore and help the child understand his anger. But the therapist may also need to use some kind of behavioral treatment to help the child control his classroom outbursts.

Unlike adults, children are constantly going through developmental changes, and so their emotional problems change or at least take on different forms that are more appropriate to the new developmental level. The symptoms and conflicts of an elementary school child are quite different from those of a junior high student, and these can be vastly different from the peer determined problems of a high school student. Seldom does a child therapist treat a child who stays in one developmental stage through the course of treatment. In one of my recent cases, I found myself treating a thirteen-year-old boy whose major characteristics were his lack of social relationships and deep anger. Because he was functioning at the emotional level of a nine-year-old, his anger was symbolic, inhibited, and never expressed openly. Only ten months later he had matured to the emotional level of an early teenager and the changes were dramatic. He now had become part of a semi-delinquent group of boys and had been suspended from school for hitting another student with a rather large board. Although the underlying problem and angry feelings were the same, I used a psychoanalytically oriented therapy to explore the earlier difficulties, but the overt anger and school difficulties required cognitive-behavioral self-control techniques in addition to the psychoanalytic approach. This kind of rapid emotional maturation is not uncommon in children and certainly indicates that child therapists need to be more familiar with therapeutic integration than their adult counterparts.

4

Guidelines for Integrating Psychotherapies

The Considerations for Integration

There are two basic tasks every therapist must confront in using different treatments with the same child. The first, and perhaps the easier task, is choosing the correct treatment for a particular problem and at a particular time. Most therapists familiar with a broad range of treatments will have little difficulty making appropriate choices. The more difficult task involves the transition from one therapy to another. As we have already discussed, this is a complex issue and one which requires a great deal of therapeutic skill and sensitive knowledge of the child one is treating.

In this section we will discuss the guidelines for such transitions; however, I feel a good bit of trepidation and insecurity in writing such guidelines for a number of reasons. First, there has been little direct work in this area and so I do not have the benefit of other therapist's ideas against which to evaluate my own. Many authors, such as Arnold Lazarus, James Prochaska, Larry Beutler, and John Norcross, to mention a few, have written very comprehensive and cogent ideas on therapeutic eclecticism, but with the exception of a 1982 article by Lewis Wolberg there has been little written on the actual methods of integrating diverse treatments. Secondly, the existing research mainly focuses on adults not children, and certainly the integration of therapies with children is quite different from that of adults for many reasons, which we shall discuss. Lastly, the ideas that I will present in this section have not stood the test of time or incisive research. They are ideas that have grown out of my own clinical work and that of my students, and as a result these ideas are presented as guidelines, not infallible rules, and need to be understood in that light.

Appropriateness

The first guideline ought to be obvious. Whatever treatments are chosen to be blended need to be appropriate to the child, and some forms of treatment are inappropriate for certain problems and children. For example, it's useless to use systematic desensitization with an acting-out, conduct-disordered twelve-year-old boy. Desensitization attempts to reduce feelings of anxiety and such a child would not typically be troubled by anxiety anyway. If fact, the child might be better off if he remained worried about his disruptive acting out.

Because certain therapeutic techniques are more effective with certain emotional difficulties, a therapist needs to identify specific emotional problems in order to choose the appropriate treatment technique. Knowing that a treatment should be appropriate to a child is obvious. The greater difficulty lies in knowing which treatment is appropriate. The key to this is establishing a differential diagnosis which will identify the problems that must be dealt with. As we discussed in the first chapter, the traditional diagnostic procedures, such as DSM-IIIR, are not particularly helpful in generating a differential diagnosis that predicts the appropriateness of particular treatments. Hopefully, the dispositional diagnostic system will be more useful, and this can be used at any stage of treatment. Although a diagnostic system can be helpful, I believe a therapist's idiosyncratic knowledge of a child is likely to be more accurate. Usually by the third or forth session a competent therapist has separated out the individual difficulties of a child, and will have a good notion of what treatments are likely to be effective with what problems.

Common Factors Determine Integration

A useful indication as to how well therapies will integrate is to look at the extent of their common factors. Obviously, treatments that are more similar in their basic structures ought to be easier to integrate. However, psychotherapeutic treatments can be analyzed on many different dimensions, and any listing of common factors will differ according to which dimension is emphasized. In his article on the similarities and differences among therapies, Wolberg (1982) suggests three factors that all therapies may have in common. These are the therapeutic relationship, the extent of rewards and punishments, and the emphasis on cognitive restructuring. Comparing treatments on these three factors is simple enough and perhaps gives a rather rough-edged, but useful, indication as to similarities.

A more detailed and sophisticated list of the change factors in treatment was offered by Lisa Grencavage & John Norcross (1990). They list the following sixteen factors:

1. Opportunity for catharsis.
2. Acquisition and practice of new behaviors.
3. Provision of rationale (psychological insight).
4. Foster insight/awareness.
5. Emotional and interpersonal learning.
6. Feedback/reality testing.
7. Suggestion.
8. Success and mastery experiences.
9. Persuasion.
10. Placebo effect.
11. Identification with the therapist.
12. Contingency management.
13. Tension reduction.
14. Therapist modeling.
15. Desensitization.
16. Education/information provision.

The list follows a descending order from factors that are shared by many psychotherapies to those that are relatively unique to only a few forms of treatment. For example, catharsis is commonly used by many forms of treatment, whereas desensitization and education are factors used only by a few. Comparing two therapies on this list or a similar one will give a therapist some indication as to their common factors and techniques, and to the extent that they share common factors they are likely to be easier to integrate. Of course, looking at common factors gives only a rough indication of how successful a blending will be because it only looks at the relationships between treatments, which is only one variable to consider. Obviously, we must take the individual child's characteristics into account as well as the all important child-therapist relationship.

Blending Must Fit the Flow of Treatment and the Progress of the Child

Any attempt to introduce a divergent therapeutic technique must fit with the ongoing flow of treatment. If a therapist has decided upon a central theoretical approach, switching to a treatment that is very different will be difficult. For example, when a therapist is involved in an approach that emphasizes warmth and empathy, the therapist cannot easily switch to a structured, confrontative, and demanding approach like rational-emotive therapy or cognitive restructuring. Therapists who do switch from an empathic therapy to a confrontative treatment must try to be confrontative in a warm and gentle way. Of course, the problem is that a warm and gentle type of rational-emotive therapy and cognitive restructuring may be totally ineffective. Generally, a therapist should not interrupt the flow and continuity of treatment without a compelling reason, and the following example should illustrate that point.

> I had been treating a seventeen-year-old girl for about four months during which time our discussions centered on her anger at her father and her difficulties with boyfriends. This was a very useful topic as it revealed how her father raised powerful feelings of insecurity within her. Then, during two consecutive sessions, she reported that she had begun to hyperventilate. After a short discussion I learned that the hyperventilation was the result of feelings of panic that she was unable to control.
>
> At this point I was tempted to use systematic desensitization or some other respondent behavioral technique to help her control the anxiety and hyperventilation. However, I choose not to do this for a number of reasons. The most important was that we were making excellent progress through our psychodynamic discussions about her father and I did not want to interrupt that to use a completely different type of therapy. I was concerned that if we took off in a different therapeutic direction for a number of sessions we would not get back to the discussion about her father or if we did it would have a different emotional intensity.
>
> Another problem was the difference between the two treatments in terms of the therapeutic relationship. Using systematic desensitization meant that I would have to take control of the direction of therapy and I believed this would have been confusing to her, to say nothing of the change in structure which would have required us to begin making hierarchies and using structured relaxation techniques. Also, I believed that the insecurity concerning her father was related to the her recent panic attacks and to alleviate the feelings of panic might lessen her motivation to deal with the difficult problems about her father. Lastly, I hoped that her panic attacks and the resulting hyperventilation might be temporary and disappear as therapy continued. Fortunately, I guessed correctly and both the hyperventilation and panic attacks began to disappear within a month. If they had persisted I likely would have attempted to try a respondent behavioral technique, but hopefully, I would have been able to wait until we had finished dealing with the essential emotional issues concerning her father.

Preparing a Child for a New Treatment

Children must be prepared for any blending of treatments because they will sense the change in therapeutic activities and in the therapist's reactions. In order to prepare the child for such changes therapists must try to anticipate how this will feel to the child. The best way to do this is to try to take the child's point of view. In this way the therapist can assess whether or not the change from one form of treatment to another will cause difficulty. If the shift will be marked, then the therapist may need to tell the child that things will change, how they will change, and explain the reasons for it. In this situation it is best to obtain the child's agreement if at all possible. Hopefully, giving a child a truthful explanation on a level they can understand will convince the child. Sometimes that is not possible, but even if the therapist decides to utilize a new type of treatment without the child's approval, the blending will go better for the therapist having been open and truthful.

Of course the greater the change, or the child's perception of the change, the more intensive and time-consuming the preparation. If the change between treatments is not very striking or the transition will be very gradual, then the child is not likely to notice any difference. In that case the child will not need any overt preparation and the therapist need not say anything. Nevertheless, the therapist will need to be alert to signs that the child finds the transition difficult.

Sometimes the transition from one treatment to another is smooth because changes the child has made in treatment naturally prepare him for another type of therapy. In other words, the success of the previous therapy necessitates a new form of treatment. In this situation, the child often understands that the transition is beneficial and that the therapist is being attentive to his progress and newly emerging needs. He is likely to be pleased by the therapist's sensitivity and desires the new integration. The following case study is an example of such a situation.

> I had been treating a twelve-year-old boy named Alan who was referred because of his violent temper outbursts against his parents, his lack of friends, and his frequent depression. Alan was terribly resistant to seeing me and often refused to come into our sessions. I quickly learned that the root of his intense anger was his father's need to control and intrude into every part of his son's life. This situation was especially frustrating because the father intruded in a calm and seemingly helpful way and then became very depressed when he was accused of controlling his son. Needless to say Alan felt as if he had no freedom and no escape from his father.
>
> The first six months of therapy were spent trying to deal with and control Alan's angry outbursts at me. Most of that time I used two forms

of treatment concurrently. In a psychodynamic sense he had the cathartic release of the angry explosions and when he was drained by the outpouring of his anger, I utilized a cognitive, reality-oriented approach in which I attempted to have him realize the consequences of his outbursts. Of course, I did place limits on his outbursts for fear they would injure me and consequently frighten him. During this time I purposely held back on any interpretations and did not try to link his anger with his father.

As we began to form a close relationship (although it was still far from being a pleasant one), Alan had less of these outbursts. Now he began to complain about his father and how angry he was at him. At this point I was able to move fully into a psychoanalytically oriented type of treatment. We then tended to deal with present issues of his anger at both parents for forcing him into decisions he did not like, chores he did not want to do, and not getting him things that he did want. I tried to provide a corrective emotional experience by listening and accepting his complaints without trying to control him, either by telling him when he was being unreasonable or giving him solutions. This was an easy transition because he wanted less interference of any kind in his life and I was moving from an intrusive treatment where I pointed out the consequences of his temper tantrums to a nondemanding listening and acceptance of his feelings.

As we continued, Alan became aware of his unreasonable demands, even though I did not challenge them directly. Just by listening to himself and not feeling as if he had to defend his unreasonable thoughts he began to change.

During this phase of his treatment, Alan became less depressed and began to form some close friendships with other boys. His general anger at the world and the excessive outbursts for the most part went away, but he still had to deal with his father's repressive control. His father had been in individual treatment for a number of years, but still was unable to give up his need to control everyone in his family. Since his father was obviously unable to change, Alan needed to somehow come to grips with this situation.

At this point our relationship had become very close (and positive) and I decided that a humanistic kind of treatment was more appropriate to his present problems and to our relationship. He was also now fourteen and had a greater intellectual maturity, which allowed him less egocentrism in seeing his problems. Now he was much better able to see what problems were of his making and which were outside of his control. Here, too, the transition was quite natural and required no overt action on my part. At this point I slowly allowed him to take all the responsibility for treatment. I simply tried to be as authentic as I could in my reactions to what he chose to talk about. In this way I allowed him to seek his own understanding of his father's compulsive need to control him and how to deal with it. He still experienced a great deal of frustration with his father, but now he understood what he could and could not do about the situation. He came to see that it was an ongoing problem that he would have to cope with as long as he lived at home, but he also realized that his reactions were only connected to his father. He no longer assumed the rest of the world would act the way his father did and therefore he did not need to react with an angry outburst to appropriate demands.

Changing the Child-Therapist Relationship

If we accept the premise that a therapeutic relationship is the central and most crucial aspect of any treatment, then any change in this factor will likely have the greatest impact on the child, and any attempts to integrate treatments will have to consider how a new technique or therapy will affect the existing therapeutic relationship. This is true of all therapies, including very structured behavioral methods. Whatever the therapy, the child-therapist relationship will be the most difficult to change and will bring the most patient resistance. Generally, the greater the change in the therapeutic relationship, the greater the danger that the blending will fail. To avoid such a potential failure the therapist will have to make a concerted effort to try to keep the relationship the same or at least minimize any differences. Knowing that one must make an effort is the easy part. The hard part is knowing what to do.

Since a child-therapist relationship can differ on many dimensions, such as authority, permissiveness, activity level, warmth, etc., a therapist needs to think about which dimensions might be affected by a relational change. Perhaps a therapist needs to ask, "How will this feel to the child? Is the child reasonably flexible in his relationships with others? What kind of behaviors will likely emerge as a result of a change in the therapeutic relationship? What are the most important emotional aspects of our relationship?" These and other questions may give some indication as to how a child will react to a new form of treatment.

Every therapist gives children a certain proportion of reinforcements. Usually these are verbal and in the form of praising the child or agreeing with him. Children quickly become accustomed to this and will find any changes in this part of the therapist's behavior disconcerting. The obvious implication is that when trying to change to a different form of treatment, a therapist ought to try to keep the proportion and amount of reinforcements approximately the same.

Related to this is the degree of understanding and sympathy shown by the therapist, and this, too, should not be decreased. Even if the child cannot express the fact that he is upset by his therapist not being as sympathetic and supportive, this is still likely to interfere with therapeutic progress and to significantly interfere with the therapeutic relationship. The obvious implication is that therapists will have great difficulty trying to change to a form of treatment that requires less overt understanding and support, whereas therapists can switch to a form of treatment which requires them to become more overtly understanding and empathic as this will not be as upsetting to the child. As a general rule (but only general as there are great differences among individual therapists), the psychodynamic and humanistic therapies generate more support and understanding on the part of the therapist than behavioral and cognitive therapies, and once again this indicates that switching from psychodynamic therapies to cognitive and behavior therapies will involve greater difficulty than the reverse. Since cognitive and behavioral treatments are more structured than psychodynamic treatments, a good overall rule of integration is to go from structured to nonstructured treatments.

The fact that therapist's personalities are relatively stable will mitigate potential relationship difficulties. Even when we use different treatment technique the essential and often subtle aspects of our personality remain the same. So even when changing to a new form of treatment, the therapeutic relationship will tend to remain the same. In fact, most therapists consciously or unconsciously choose forms of treatment that feel comfortable. They may have difficulty changing to a new treatment that does not "fit" them. We must also consider the difference between a therapist's actual behavior and her basic personality. When changing to a new treatment, the behavior may be different, but the child may be reassured by the fact that the underlying personality is the same.

Changing Therapist-Child Verbal Activity

Some kind of verbal activity is characteristic of all treatments and must be considered when attempting to change to a new form of treatment. However, to adequately understand this concept we need to clearly distinguish between the verbal activity of a session and the verbal content. Even though they are similar, they have different implications for blending. Verbal activity refers to the extent and tone of child-therapist interactions: how much the child talks as compared to the therapist; who initiates conversation; the extent of spontaneous talking, such as free association; and the overall verbal structure of a session. This is quite different from verbal content, which refers to what is talked about. Since they are different, we will discuss them as separate topics.

Generally, children find it easier to progress from therapies that are verbally focused and structured to those that are spontaneous and use free association. This is so because at the beginning of therapy children easily accept that adults determine the content and focus of their verbal interactions. Since children see therapists as being like their parents and teachers they have little difficulty in allowing a therapist to provide the verbal focus to their sessions. Obviously this varies with the individual child and certainly some children will want more spontaneous and egalitarian conversations with adults. Generally the less structured the therapy situation, the more the child will look to adults to "carry" the conversation, and since the beginning of some therapies is very unstructured, that is a time when a therapist needs to talk more than the child. Of course, this phenomenon is somewhat age-related and older children, especially adolescents, are more self-directed and may verbally plunge into their sessions, having little difficulty talking.

As children become more familiar with therapy and their therapist, they will naturally relax and become more spontaneous. As a result they will better tolerate less-focused verbal content in their sessions and will more easily begin to generate a free associational type of verbal content. At this point they may object if the therapist wants to talk more in their sessions. This process can reverse itself if therapy focuses on a new symptom or problem. When faced with a new difficulty the child may become confused, not know in what direction he or she ought to go, and again turn to the therapist to lead them. Now the therapist will need to adopt a more directive and verbally active type of interaction.

In summary, the therapist should be more verbally active at the beginning of treatment and allow the child to talk more as treatment proceeds. When the child is confused by new symptoms and problems, the therapist may again need to increase her verbal activity. This progression suggests that therapists need to be wary of shifting to a new form of treatment once a child has become comfortable with a more spontaneous and self-directed verbal style in treatment. They may see such a change as an unwarranted intrusion on their freedom. This indicates that therapists will have an easier time blending from a therapy that requires a good bit of therapist verbal activity to one that allows more verbal activity from the child. If attempting to blend treatments that result in increased therapist verbal activity, the therapist may want to tell the child why she is switching treatments, that now she will talk more, and she would like to have the child's permission for such a change. The therapist might suggest that the child give it a try to see if it is OK. The child may refuse and these requests may not help, but at least it gives the youngster a choice and preserves the sense of freedom provided by the earlier treatment.

Changing the Verbal Content of Sessions

Different schools of psychotherapy focus on different therapeutic content. This fact is one of the most recognizable differences between schools. Cognitive therapists direct their attention to contemporaneous life conflicts as a way of exposing illogical thinking. Anxiety symptoms are the content in systematic desensitization. Person-centered therapists focus on the feelings behind verbalizations. Classical Freudian analysts direct their attention to past life experiences centered around Oedipal or anal issues. We could go on, but the point is that the content of treatment does differ from one form of treatment to the other.

In spite of the importance of content to therapeutic schools and therapeutic theory, surprisingly, it is not likely to be a significant obstacle when blending treatments. Children usually can change easily from one content area to another. For the most part children are relatively naïve in respect to what they should be discussing in a session, and unless touching upon a sensitive or traumatic area, they seem to easily follow our lead. Also, therapists have many ways to guide sessions into areas we feel are important, and these efforts are usually successful. We can ask direct and forceful questions, we can give the youngster special attention when an identified topic is mentioned, or we can manipulate play materials that are likely to bring about the desired discussion. So long as the therapist is attentive to what the child is saying and the areas discussed are not sensitive, we should have little trouble getting a youngster to switch to a different content area. This kind of change is easy because it follows a natural progression in treatment. Usually, therapists will switch to a different form of treatment because new problems and conflicts have emerged or the child has moved into a new stage of therapy. However, by virtue of the fact that the problems are new and different, children are likely to generate a new and different content. If so, the change will be a very natural progression, and one that is likely to be so harmonious that it will not be noticed by the child.

Another reason children easily switch from one kind of verbal content to another is that the verbal content of a session is of greater importance to the therapist than the child. It is a variable that guides the therapist, not the child. Different psychodynamic therapies stress different issues as being important causal factors of emotional difficulties. Some identify inferiority, others inadequate mother-child bonding. The list goes on. A therapist will focus the verbal content around these issues because they are important to her cognitive understanding of the child and his problems, however the child does not know this and usually doesn't care. To the child what is talked about is either pleasant or unpleasant, interesting or boring, comfortable or frightening, depending on the topic.

Children are often reluctant to deal with certain content areas because of personal sensitivities and fears, but this is an all too common therapeutic problem and occurs with most if not all types of treatment. If a new form of treatment dictates a problem area painful for the child, then the attempt to change to a new form of treatment obviously will be difficult. However, the problem is not due to the therapeutic technique or to integration, but rather to the therapist asking the child to do what is too difficult at that point in treatment.

Demand Characteristics of Therapy and Integration

Therapists have a perhaps subtle, but nevertheless definite power over the children they treat. A therapeutic relationship is marked by certain demands in the form of expectations. Consciously or unconsciously, children are encouraged to meet these expectations. All therapies, even the most undemanding, expect children to cooperate in some fashion, but the character of this therapist-child interaction varies with the particular treatment used. For example, in operant behavior modification a child is expected to follow direct instructions from the therapist and go along with the behavioral contingencies. In therapeutic modeling, the child is expected to attend to the model and modeling situation, but little else. In Kendall's self-speech, the child is expected to do what the therapists asks by going along with the lessons. In psychoanalysis, the child is expected to play or converse about conflicts and emotional traumas, but the analytic therapist puts few demands on the child in choosing therapy activities or the verbal content of the sessions. Each therapy allows the child differing degrees of freedom and acceptance. Changing from one set of expectations to another can create difficulties, and must be done with care. As a general rule therapists have more success blending from treatments with greater therapist power-and-demand characteristics to treatments that allow the child more freedom and make less demands. Since structured therapies, such as operant behavior modification, have the greatest therapist-demand characteristics, therapists are likely to have an easier time changing from structured therapies to unstructured therapies than the reverse.

The reason for this is that most people, including children, dislike having their perceived freedoms taken away. At the beginning of treatment children do not have definite expectations about therapy. It is a new experience and they tend to accept what the therapist demands of them. During the initial therapy sessions expectations begin to form and these are based on the therapeutic model utilized. If the therapist starts with a psychodynamic model that has moderate demand characteristics, the child will likely accept this situation. If the therapist begins to assume a higher demand profile, as would be expected in more structured treatments, the child is likely to be angry at the loss of freedom inherent in this particular blend of treatments. Thus trying to impose a behavioral contract or a punishment schedule within the context of a psychodynamic approach is likely to result in confusion and resentment. Perhaps a more realistic situation is when a therapist attempts to use demands that are incompatible with a previous form of treatment. For example, a therapist may pressure a child to confront a phobic object or face a past repressed traumatic episode. These kinds of demands, even when done subtly, are not likely to be compatible with most forms of psychodynamic therapies and children are likely to perceive the therapists as no longer being kind and understanding. Such techniques can be blended into psychodynamic treatments, but it must be done slowly, with careful understandable explanations, and careful monitoring of the child's reactions.

If treatment is begun with a restrictive and structured type of therapy, then the child will not expect to have much freedom of choice in the activities, content, or direction of treatment. Then moving to another technique that gives the child more freedom will not upset the child and, in fact, may be pleasing.

As a rule therapists tend to deal with debilitating symptoms first. So, in a normal sequence of blending, they move from structured to unstructured treatments. That pattern occurs because children enter therapy with symptoms that require immediate attention, but their problems moderate as treatment continues. Symptoms such as violent temper tantrums, refusing to attend school, physically attacking other children and teachers, severe anorexia, and serious delinquency, by their very nature, demand attention. They need to be controlled quickly. The more structured techniques, such as token systems, behavioral contracts, response cost, systematic desensitization, and Kendall and Michenbaum's cognitive approaches, are ideal for this purpose. They tend to provide a quick change in symptoms, and they are better suited to cope with these kinds of behavioral problems. Once these immediate problems are alleviated, then a therapist might begin using other less structured psychotherapies that are better suited to less symptom-specific problems. The following example should illustrate how this progression takes place.

> Betsy was a seven-year-old whose hyperactivity was so severe that she needed to be hospitalized for two-and-a-half months. Her hyperactive behavior was so pervasive and she was so disruptive to the residential unit staff that the nurses and aides were driven to distraction by this seven-year-old perpetual motion machine. Her therapist found that, aside from other family problems, this youngster was used to being yelled at constantly by everyone from teachers to parents. However, the immediate problem was to get control of her disruptive, hyperactive behavior.
>
> The therapist started by using operant techniques to keep her in the therapy room and sitting down. To do this she pasted tiny green dot stickers on her arm for even minimally controlling herself. When she earned five of the green dots she could get a "real" picture type sticker of her choice. This quickly controlled much of her behavior in the therapy sessions. Then the therapist began using a technique from Kendall's

self-instruction therapy. Her therapist taught her Kendall's seven steps to control herself. Within a few weeks the child was able to repeat the self-control instructions to herself and she was better able to control herself on the unit.

Now that Betsy was able to control herself, her therapist decided to use a reality-oriented psychodynamic treatment that focused on her feelings about being constantly yelled at. The therapist felt that Betsy needed to be prepared for this change in therapy, and so when she was ready to stop the self-instructional therapy she told Betsy that they were going to do something different, but very important. She sympathized with Betsy and told her that she imagined she was often unhappy being constantly yelled at. Betsy then poured out her unhappiness about this, often crying and telling her therapist how hard it was. This led to talking about her feeling that no one liked her and many of the other unhappy feelings that she had never had a chance to tell because the adults around her were always dealing with her hyperactive disruptions. Betsy left the hospital improved enough to return to school, and she and her therapist continued in a psychoanalytically oriented psychotherapy on an outpatient basis.

Obviously, her therapist needed to start with a structured form of treatment and was able to blend to a nonstructured form of treatment very easily. It would have been foolhardy to begin with a psychodynamic treatment and then try to blend in operant behavior modification or Kendall's self-instructional training. Betsy hardly had the self-control to stay in the room, let alone talk with her therapist and participate in a psychodynamic form of treatment. In addition, Betsy would not have had an easy transition trying to adjust to the structure of operant and cognitive techniques after experiencing the freedom and lack of demands associated with a psychodynamic type of psychotherapy.

Time Dimensions and Integration

Time dimensions are different for each type of psychotherapy. Some, like classical analysis, may focus on the distant past. Others, such as systematic desensitization or cognitive therapies, focus on the present, while still others, such humanistic psychotherapy or Adlerian analysis, can focus on both the past and present. Usually, children are able to change time dimensions with little difficulty, although they will have less problem in going from a psychotherapy with a past-time emphasis to one that emphasizes the present. When children are open enough to talk about their difficulties, they seem to be able to switch from past to present without even noticing. This kind of shift is common in the psychodynamic psychotherapies. Often the bulk of the middle sessions is spent dealing with events from the child's past and later sessions deal with how the youngster can learn to cope with these traumas in his present life. The earlier example of Alan illustrates this well. Alan had to come to grips with a host of early life experiences centering on his father's need to control his family, but the later sessions dealt with how he might cope with his father in their present day-to-day interactions.

Children have a more difficult time switching from a treatment with a present-time orientation to a past-time orientation because past events are often traumatic and children will have a tendency to avoid them. Trying to integrate psychotherapies that transition from a present orientation to the past is possible, but the therapist needs to be aware that the child may resist this kind of an integration.

Another, more general difficulty in changing from one time dimension to another is the fact that children and adults differ in their ability to understand and use time concepts (Piaget, 1969). Adults, therapists included, have little difficulty relating past events to the present and understanding the implications that arise from this. Children, depending on their age, may have much greater difficulty doing this. They tend to keep their time dimensions separate and may not be able to see how the trauma of past life events can affect their present emotional adjustment. Therapists must realize that although they can tolerate the change in time dimensions as a result of switching treatments, the child they are treating may be much less able to do this. The resulting confusion may seriously disrupt progress.

New Treatments Must Fit a Therapist's Style and Ethics

If a therapist attempts to use a type of therapy that is uncomfortable and incongruent with her personality, this discontinuity is likely to be sensed by the child and the attempt at integration may fail. I suppose this situation is unlikely to occur because therapists typically avoid using treatment methods that do not fit them; however, this is an important guideline because it is likely to have a devastating and perhaps irremedial effect on treatment. A child can easily sense that his therapist is uncomfortable and this will be confusing and certainly unproductive for therapeutic progress. If this causes the child to reject the therapist, then the therapeutic relationship may be destroyed and therapy may be ended.

I like to think that as the result of my early therapeutic training, I am comfortable with a wide spectrum of psychotherapies. Personally, I have little difficulty in accepting and integrating therapies ranging from operant to humanistic techniques. However, I do have strong stylistic preferences concerning gentle versus stern interactions with the children I treat, and as a result I find that I have difficulty using any cognitive techniques that are direct and confrontative. Even when I know that such a technique may be useful I am still reluctant to use it because it makes me uncomfortable. I'm aware that this is a limitation in my therapeutic skill, but I believe that I am better off acknowledging this deficiency and facing it. If I unknowingly tried to use strong confrontative techniques, I doubt that I could integrate this to benefit the children I treat.

Therapeutic Goals Determine a Plan of Integration

Obviously planning any therapy integration at the beginning of treatment is quite helpful as it allows the therapist to sequence therapeutic techniques in a way that will be harmoniously accepted by the child. Whenever possible this should be attempted according to a cogent overall plan of treatment. In that way a therapist can begin using a treatment that is likely to blend well into the succeeding treatment. However, we seldom can anticipate all of a child's needs at the beginning of treatment because we are lacking the complete and robust knowledge of the child that typifies the middle sessions of treatment. I suppose that even if we do not know all we need to about the future course of a youngster's treatment, we can try to plan ahead by anticipating expected needs, symptoms, and problems or by beginning treatment with a form of therapy that will allow for a smooth transition to another form of treatment. In many of the preceding guidelines we have seen that, as a general rule, transitions are easier going when from structured to unstructured treatment. If in doubt, a therapist might err on the side of choosing a more structured form of treatment.

As therapy continues, the task of planning ahead becomes easier because the therapist now knows the child and can make a more accurate guess as to how the child will respond to the integration of a new technique. However, even at a later stage of treatment and with detailed knowledge of a child, integration can be difficult if the therapist is only responding to immediate needs that arise in treatment. A much better response is to always plan ahead. If the therapist plans ahead, then the therapy or therapeutic technique presently being used can be modified to fit with the proposed new technique. This is a much better procedure than just hoping that the child will accept the new form of treatment or trying to change the new treatment so it fits with former methods. Planning ahead allows a therapist to modify both the present therapy technique and the proposed new technique, and this allows for a much easier transition and ultimately a more successful therapeutic integration.

Obviously, planning therapy integrations ahead of time is beneficial, and the more knowledge one has of the child and his response to a previous form of treatment, the easier such planning will be. One crucial aspect in formulating a plan of integration is the knowledge and agreement on the goals of treatment. Such agreement can either be explicit or informal, depending on the style of the therapist and needs of the child. Goals to a great extent determine the type of treatment utilized, and if a therapist and child are in basic agreement on the goals of treatment, then they are more likely to agree on the methods. This kind of agreement means integration is likely to be a smoother process. Although some time may elapse before a therapist has a thorough knowledge of a youngster, he usually has a general sense of what the goals of therapy ought to be after the first two or three sessions, and this can be used to formulate a general plan for integration. Thus, even at the beginning of therapy, a therapist can be preparing an atmosphere that will support the blending of one or more new therapeutic techniques. Obviously, such a preliminary plan may have to be modified and made more precise, but even a general plan will help in determining the sequence of integration.

The following case example illustrates how having even a general sense of therapeutic goals allows a therapist to develop a plan of integration.

> Evan, a high school sophomore, began seeing me after he and two friends were arrested for breaking in to the local school bus garage and stealing road flares, which they then proceeded to set off near the town municipal building. Needless to say neighbors reported the unusual nighttime festivities and they were arrested. During the first two sessions I learned the following: 1. That there had been other delinquent pranks, but he had not been caught; 2. That he avoided his mother because "she tries to run my life"; 3. He got along better with his father, "because I don't see much of him"; 4. His grades were just passing in spite of very high intelligence test scores; 5. His parents expected him to go to an Ivy League college; 6. That he wanted to join the Army Special Forces; 7. That he felt very insecure and had little self-esteem.
>
> Knowing just this information I was able to formulate the following goals:
>
> 1. He needed to learn to control his impulsive delinquent behavior.
> 2. He needed to understand why his grades were so poor and whether or not he wanted to try for better grades.
> 3. We needed to explore the reality to his feeling that his mother controlled him.
> 4. Why was his father unavailable and what effect had this had on his past and present life?
> 5. Was his desire to join the Army an attempt to escape from the pressures and expectations of his family?
> 6. What were his expectations of himself and his own plans for the future?

I have listed these goals in the sequence with which I planned to deal with them, knowing of course that they were not completely separate from each other and so one would likely overlap with another. Following this sequence I decided that learning to control his impulsive delinquent behavior would be best dealt with in a cognitive-behavioral framework so that he could see the consequences of his behavior. The issues around his poor grades could also be handled through cognitive techniques, although here we would need to do some general psychodynamic questioning about his academic motivation. This would be a rather focused kind of technique in which I would likely need to lead him to question his feelings about his grades and his motivation.

When we began to talk about his mother's control over his life I would likely not need to lead this kind of therapeutic discussion, as his anger would provide all the motivation he needed. Sensing that he was upset over his father's unavailability (he was a high-level executive who was often away and when he was at home he was preoccupied with his work and career) I knew that I would have to provide a sense of safety and trust in order for Evan to come to grips with such painful questions as, "Does my father really care about me?", Why doesn't he show it?", "What is wrong with me that he doesn't care enough to spend time with me?", and "Am I likable at all, to anyone?" These issues seemed to lend themselves best to an Adlerian form of psychotherapy (but not psychoanalysis) in which he could look at his feelings of inadequacy and how they related to his father. The last issues would also be best dealt with by allowing him to take the lead in a self-explorative type of treatment, but modified existential techniques would be useful in helping him explore his self-expectations and his ultimate relationship with his family.

In laying out such an overall therapeutic plan I was able to go from structured to less structured forms of treatments, and I was able to anticipate transitions from one type of therapy to another. This allowed me to change or modify the treatments I was using to fit this young man, and I was able to plan ahead for any anticipated difficulties. I certainly don't present this example as the best way to treat Evan. Other therapists are likely to have other and equally effective treatments, however this example shows how a treatment plan can be very helpful in blending treatments.

Sequence and Timing Are Crucial to Integration

Once a therapist has an idea of the problems to be treated, she has to not only decide on which treatments will be useful, but also the sequence and timing in which these treatments will be used. In discussing some of the previous guidelines we have already touched on the importance of proper sequence in blending treatments and the difficulties associated with this. In addition to these ideas, there are three others which can be useful in the sequencing of treatments. First, the most seriously debilitating symptoms should be dealt with first. Second, the therapist must think about which treatment technique ought to come before some other. Third, the therapist must decide which problems must be resolved in order to get to others. Being aware of these three issues will help a therapist choose a useful sequence in treatment.

In addition to finding an appropriate sequence, a therapist must also choose the proper timing for integrating one treatment with another. I suppose the most basic question for a therapist to reflect upon is "Why now?" What are the factors associated with the child and his social environment that indicate a change in therapy technique is timely? Have new symptoms emerged that require a blending to another technique? Most important, has therapeutic progress reached the point that the child is ready for a new form of therapy? These questions may seem simple in the abstract, but they require a thorough knowledge of the child at any given time and a sound sense of therapeutic judgment.

Perhaps the best general rule in respect to the timing of integration is to go slow. Abrupt changes in treatment are more likely to be distressing to a child, and if a therapist introduces a new procedure slowly, she can more easily monitor the child's reaction and modify aspects of the integration or even decide to terminate it if it isn't working. Another advantage of integrating treatments slowly is that the change is likely to be less obvious to the child and may not be noticed at all. A general indication as to the rate of change a therapist can elect is the number of common factors inherent in the two treatment modalities. The more they have in common, the less the child will perceive a change and so the transition can occur at a faster pace.

Placing Cognitive Boundaries Around Disparate Techniques

There are times when therapists must attempt to integrate two therapeutic techniques that are vastly different, which presents unique problems for both therapist and child. Even though a therapist would never voluntarily plan such a difficult integration, it can be necessitated by life situations that are beyond the therapist's control. Sometimes it is precipitated by a new and unanticipated development in the course of ongoing therapy. For example, I had been treating a fourth-grader for more than a year when I learned a well-kept family secret. His seemingly mild-mannered father occasionally flew into rages and physically abused my patient. Obviously, this necessitated a drastic change in our therapy. This can be seen in the following example whereby the therapist had little choice but to suddenly change the course of treatment.

> Larry was a sixteen-year-old I had been treating for severe learning difficulties, few social skills, no close friends, and longstanding diffuse anxiety symptoms. I had been treating him for about a year using a combination of psychoeducational and psychodynamic techniques designed to help him deal with his school difficulties and confront his poor self-esteem and lack of confidence. One positive experience was his involvement in the local volunteer fire department in which he was a very active junior member. More than that, he took his departmental responsibilities very seriously and became the most motivated and active junior member. Treatment was progressing well when his frantic parents called me to say that Larry had been arrested for arson and calling in false fire alarms. These were very serious incidents, and he faced the real risk of going to prison. In spite of this threat, he again turned in another false alarm only a week after his earlier arrest. Obviously, I needed to protect the local community from harm and Larry from calling in another false alarm or starting another fire, which would result in his facing even more serious court charges. I found I had little choice but to suddenly and drastically change the focus of treatment, and at this point I adopted an intrusive cognitive-behavioral approach that emphasized the consequences of being sent to prison. In addition, I increased the frequency of our family sessions in order to enlist his parents and two older sisters in helping him control his impulsive need to call in more false alarms. The urgency of the situation demanded a new form of treatment and although I realized that a sudden change from a patient-directed psychodynamic approach to an authoritarian cognitive-behavioral treatment would be difficult, I had little choice but to do this to protect Larry.

In these situations, the therapist seems to be faced with an insoluble dilemma. Either continue with an inadequate treatment for the present problem, or risk a precipitous change to a new therapy that is likely to disrupt treatment because the child is unprepared and is likely to be upset when the therapist changes their relationship. Coping with such a situation may be difficult, but is not impossible. The therapist can still prepare the child for the change, but this is done quickly (within the next session) and as part of a crisis-intervention procedure. From a theoretical perspective, the therapist must cognitively isolate the new procedure using verbal boundaries. In other words, the therapist must tell the child that because of the crisis (hopefully, the child agrees that a crisis has occurred) they are going to try something very different from what they had been doing. At this point, giving the new technique a name is useful because it helps the child clearly differentiate between the two treatments. By cognitively isolating the new technique within verbal boundaries, the therapist is cutting down on the child's confusion and providing a logical understanding for what might seem arbitrary behavior on the part of the therapist.

In the previous example, I told Larry that in order to save him from going to jail, we needed to do things very differently and I was going to seem harsh and demanding at times, but that was necessary, at least for a while. I called what we would be doing "arson-consequences therapy" because he needed to recognize the dangerous reality of what he had done and understand the consequences he faced. Although he was uncomfortable with my new role, he understood that we were going to be doing something different and was agreeable.

Usually a therapeutic crisis carries an urgency that changes the characteristics of therapy so that it is easier to integrate a new and disparate therapeutic procedure. Often the child and his parents are so upset and anxious they give up their earlier expectations about therapy and the therapeutic relationship. They usually become more dependent on the therapist and this allows the therapist to become more authoritarian and directive. In a sense they realize that things need to change and so they are not only more accepting of changes initiated by the therapist, but often they look to the therapist to do this. Of course, this is most pronounced at the time of the crisis, so any treatment changes should be done immediately.

In my experience there is often a time limit within which one can use a new and disparate technique, because as the fear and emotion of the crisis wane, the child looks to going back to the previous and more comfortable treatment. This usually occurs slowly, but after a time children begin to resist the new form of treatment and in all sorts of ways try to reestablish the previous therapeutic relationship. Often this occurs before the crisis is completely resolved and a therapist may have to use a good bit of persuasion to stay with the new treatment.

Preparing Parents and Other Adults for Treatment Changes

Since children live in a complex environment that includes many other people they too must be included in the overall therapeutic strategy whenever a therapist contemplates changing or blending to another type of treatment. Parents and teachers are the adults most likely affected by such changes and usually they need to be informed, although this depends on the therapist's judgment. Obviously, when a therapeutic change requires parents and teachers to deal with the child differently, they must be informed and prepared for the change. If they are likely to detect changes in the child as the result of the integration of a new treatment, they probably ought to be prepared so they are not surprised and confused by such changes. As we have already said, whether and which significant adults are told and how they are told ultimately depends on the therapist's judgment.

Usually, a rational explanation of the therapeutic plan, well-explained, and encouraging questions is a sufficient type of preparation. However, a therapist needs to be careful to avoid giving an overly complex and technical narration. Usually, a simple logical explanation that emphasizes the changes they should expect in the child and how to handle problems associated with the change should be more than sufficient. Sometimes, a change in treatments may require more or a different kind of cooperation from parents. Since different treatments require different parental involvement, parents and teachers will need to know that not only will the child be different, they will have to provide a different kind of therapeutic support.

Individual Characteristics Transcend any Guidelines

Now that we have discussed this long list of guidelines by which therapies can be usefully blended, we need to be aware of a danger. These guidelines are helpful ways by which we simplify a very complex task, and make no mistake, integrating psychotherapies is a very complex task. However, like any theory, guidelines only provide a theoretical structure to our thoughts; it is a kind of technology of therapy. Like any technology or product of science, it is helpful, but the real art in psychotherapy is in knowing the individual characteristics of a particular child and using that knowledge to bring about a cogent and helpful blending of treatments. Knowing an individual child allows us to predict how that child will respond to a new therapeutic approach. Such knowledge of a child's idiosyncracies indicates the potential problems as well as the benefits of a therapeutic integration and enables us to carry out a blending that meets the child's needs. Ultimately, knowing how an individual child will interact with a new form of psychotherapy is more important than knowing how this psychotherapy will interact with another. The former tells us how a specific child will respond; the latter tells us how groups of children tend to respond.

Blending Individual and Family Therapy

I hope you have not been overwhelmed by the complexities of blending different types of individual therapies because we also need to discuss the additional complexities of blending individual and family treatments. As I mentioned earlier in this chapter, many family therapists originally rejected individual methods of child treatment, saying they were too narrow in scope and needed to include the family. Now there is a greater tolerance of other treatments. Stuart Sugarman (1986), a family therapist, has written that the literature of the past decade demonstrates not only a peace treaty between family therapy and other perspectives, but a strong tendency toward integration.

In studying this situation, Sugarman concludes that there are certain individual and family psychotherapies, such as psychoanalysis and structured and strategic family therapies, that are "purist" and focus on either individual or family to the exclusion of the other. However, there are others, such as object relations therapy and Murray Bowen's family therapy, that tolerate integration and at times oscillate back and forth between the two perspectives. Some family theorists, such as Jay Haley, Virginia Satir and Carl Whittaker, have always integrated their techniques with individual treatment methods.

Perhaps we can better understand the problems involved in blending family and individual therapies if we take a different perspective. Putting aside the many theoretical and technique differences between family and individual treatment, there is one central way in which they differ. In family therapy, the emphasis is on an individual's (or many individual's) relationship with other people; especially important other people such as parents, children, or spouses. In individual therapy, the emphasis is on the problems that exist within an individual. But, as any experienced therapist knows, both of these emphases are too narrow. It would be a very unusual individual therapist who did not believe that the relationship a child has with other important people was very important, and an equally unusual family therapist who ignored difficulties within the family members they were treating.

The major difference between family and individual therapy is the way each carries out intervention. Family therapists carry out their interventions with all the important people (the entire family) present at the therapy session. Their therapeutic thinking is based on the concept of the family as a unit rather than a group of individuals. This arrangement has some obvious advantages. Having everyone together enables the therapist to see more and so develop a more accurate perspective than the biased report of one person. The therapist can deal with interpersonal problems in the here and now as they occur. In addition, more people can be treated at one time. However, having so many people present can be a disadvantage as it vastly in creases both the complexity of the situation and the amount of information with which to deal. This may be taxing and even overwhelming for the therapist and the family members. Also, the interactions can be so powerful that conflicts within individuals are not given adequate attention.

In individual therapy, the situation is simpler, but the therapist only gets one, often very biased, perception. The therapist is better able to deal with conflicts within the child, but difficulties in relations among family members are hampered by the fact that the child may not mention these. Thus, the therapist may miss important therapeutic information and only see events through the child's perspective. This limits the therapist's opportunities to deal with here-and-now family interactions.

Seen from this perspective there is no one "best" type of therapy. Each is a mountaintop from which to view a valley: The scenery is the same, only the perspective is different. Each has certain advantages, and few experienced therapists, either individual or family, would ignore obvious problems even if such problems did not fall within the mainstream of their method of treatment. For example, once an individual therapist was aware of a parent-child problem, he or she would attend to that either within his individual sessions with the child or by meeting with the child's parents. Similarly, a family therapist faced with a severe interpersonal problem of one family member would find a way of dealing with that problem. They might work on the problem in the family session or they might meet individually with the child or parent.

The main point is that both types of therapists will find a way to deal with any serious problem that arises. The real question is whether one approach is more efficient than the other, given the particular child, family, therapist, constellation of problems, and the interaction between all of these factors. This is a difficult question to answer, especially in the abstract. We might utilize the obvious and simplistic guideline of using family therapy when the central problem concerns that families' relationships, and individual therapy when the problems are within the child. However, such a guideline is very general and subject to great differences in interpretation. The decision on which mode of therapy to use can be better determined when the specifics of child, family, therapist, and conflicts are known. Even then there is likely to be vast disagreements and biases along the lines of the therapist's identity.

A better solution may be to blend these two modes of treatment when it seems appropriate. Stuart Sugarman is brave enough to offer some general rules of thumb for when to integrate family and individual therapy. He lists four indications:

1. Does it appear that different modalities would help significantly with different therapeutic goals in different levels (e.g., social versus psychological)?
2. Does it appear that a given modality is either not helpful or of limited usefulness without the additional modality?
3. Is there significant motivation on the part of the patient system to combine modalities?

4. Are the modalities synergistic, enhancing one another?

Stuart Sugarman (1986) also gives three contraindications for blending individual and family treatment.

1. The epistemological foundations of the various modalities are often based on contradictory assumptions. The goal of clinical work is to provide a coherent, cognitive ordering of the world; however, combining modalities can at times confuse the patient.
2. The additional time and money involved in combined therapy may be unnecessary. A single modality is often powerful enough to accomplish what is therapeutically necessary.
3. Different modalities can dilute the potential commitment to each separate therapeutic involvement. To the extent that the concept of psychic energy has meaning, combined therapy could divide this energy so that not enough is available to accomplish therapeutic work.

Perhaps these ideas can be used as a rough sort of guide until the field of psychological treatment matures and provides more definitive indications.

SECTION II

The Process of Psychotherapy

Process is a difficult word to define when used in connection with psychotherapy because it summarizes so many individual behaviors, emotions, and interactions between a therapist and a child. The first thing to remember about process is that it is a verb as well as a noun. As a verb, "to process" means action, movement, dynamic change. Psychotherapeutic process really refers to the "how" of psychotherapy. How does a child change? How does the therapist bring about changes? How does the special relationship between therapist and child affect each of them? These are a few of the questions therapists intuitively act upon in their treatment of a child.

Process also refers to what the therapist does. To a certain extent this is determined by the theoretical system the therapist uses, but we must be sure to understand that what a therapist does and what he believes may be related but are often quite different. Theoretical beliefs organize the psychotherapy for the therapist, but do not directly affect a child. However, what the therapist does is directly experienced by a child.

Certainly, process refers to how the child reacts, feels, and thinks during a psychotherapy session. This psychological activity is the crux of treatment and determines whether children will overcome their emotional problems and in what way those problems will be overcome.

Lastly, process implies a continuity, a pattern over time. In this sense process refers to how psychotherapy changes or remains stable over the course of the entire treatment. In all therapies there should be a logical process followed by a therapist, a pattern that remains stable enough that the child does not become confused or overwhelmed, yet changes as a child's needs change.

The chapters in this section attempt to describe this process of psychotherapeutic treatment. They focus on changes and how a therapist brings about beneficial changes in a child. The first two chapters deals with the stages of change. How therapist and child begin to engage with each other, how they identify problems, how they begin to understand the implication of the problems, and how they strive for a better adjustment. It also discusses how a child comes to question maladaptive behaviors and feelings, and how a therapist helps a child do this. The second chapter discusses the role of emotions in this questioning process and the difficulty in dealing with emotional questions. The last chapter deals with the obstacles a therapist and child must face in order to carry out this difficult and painful questioning. There are many difficulties, ranging from the child's reluctance to question his present ways to therapist-child differences, which hamper the child's desire to delve into an unknown and potentially painful experience.

5

Stages of the Heuristic Process in Child Psychotherapy

The Stages of Psychotherapy

In a general sense, any process of psychotherapy can be broken into certain basic stages. Of course, the analysis of an incredibly complex interaction between two people into discrete stages is a terrible simplification and usually is a better description of the way a therapist would like things to be than the way they really are. The complexities of human behavior are so varied they only fit imperfectly into ready-made stages. Likewise, therapy does not proceed in a rigid fashion like the movements of a baroque symphony. Depending on the child and the therapist, it goes backward and forward according to its own idiosyncratic schedule. Different stages will overlap one another, and sometimes we might see evidence of two or more stages within the same therapy session. Generally, there is a time sequence to the stages of psychotherapy. For example, engagement between therapist and child, the first stage in psychotherapy, is carried out during the initial sessions, but sometimes engagement will continue through later stages and even continue to deepen late in treatment.

So long as we realize these imperfections of setting psychotherapy into sequential stages, such a simplification can be useful. The advantage is that it helps us to understand a confusing series of therapeutic interactions that might otherwise overwhelm us with its very complexity, and that allows us to better use our therapeutic systems to help the children we treat.

Another problem with setting the psychotherapeutic treatment of children into stages is that it can be done in many different ways according to the many different forms of treatment, and our understanding of the children we treat will be different according to the particular dimension or system we choose to use. For example, the stages of operant behavior modification will be different than for Adlerian psychotherapy. In an operant form of therapy, the therapist and child need little time to engage with one another since the relationship is not an important part of the process. Similarly, identification of the problem is not an important stage of operant treatment since it is defined by the therapist at the beginning of treatment and the child usually is not included in this process. Thus, the stages we use to analyze psychotherapy will differ according to the theoretical system with which we adhere.

Although the stages that we will discuss in this section cannot be so robust as to apply to all forms of treatments and theoretical approaches, they are general enough to apply to the great majority of child psychotherapies. Certain stages will have a greater or lesser importance depending upon the treatment, but this conceptualization of stages will apply to all psychotherapies that rely on a meaningful therapist-child relationship.

Engagement

The first stage in any treatment is engagement, the process by which the child and therapist begin to form a close and trusting relationship. By outward appearances the process ought to be very simple. The therapist reaches out in a warm, friendly way to the child, and the child responds. It is often this simple, but do not count on it. There are so many factors that affect the child-therapist engagement process that we can only briefly mention some at this point, but we will discuss the complexities of this process in greater detail throughout the book. Even though engagement is only the starting point of treatment, it is crucial, because if there is no engagement, there is no treatment.

Unlike adults, children usually do not seek out a therapist on their own. Parents (or parent surrogates) are almost always intimately involved in the process. Some adolescents are able to do this, but even when adolescents do find a therapist, their parents almost always have some therapist contact. This means a child therapist must engage with both parents and child, and often the therapist may need to have an equally intense involvement with the child's parents, especially if family therapy is an important part of the treatment or when there are frequent therapist-parent meetings.

Engagement with parents is different from that with children or adolescents. Parents need to come away from the initial meetings with a feeling that the therapist is competent and understands their problems. To this extent, respect for and confidence in the therapist is an important part of therapist-parent engagement. If parents do not have this basic foundation, they are likely to discontinue therapy or seek out another therapist. Beyond confidence and respect, parents ought to feel they can speak freely and easily with the therapist. There are many different ways therapists bring about these reactions in parents. These methods depend on the theoretical beliefs and personality of the therapist, but no matter how the therapist creates these initial feelings, they are essential.

Relational Engagement

There are three aspects to engagement with children or adolescents. The first centers around the relationship between child and therapist. As soon as child and therapist begin to react to each other in a way that is different than the usual semi-formal child-adult interactions, then relational engagement has begun. There are some very important distinctions between casual child-adult contacts and relational engagement. The usual social context is modified by the fact that to some extent the child realizes the therapist is a special and important person, and there is a special purpose to their meetings. The purpose is to change the child, but usually a child cannot sense this clearly. Children sense an emotional reaction in themselves. Sometimes they are anxious, sometimes they are angry, and often they are both.

A competent therapist will sense their feelings and react. The therapist may try to put the child at ease through what she says or does, and hopefully the child's feelings change in reaction to the therapist. This occurs in both positive and negative ways. The child may feel anxious and the therapist may do something to put the child at ease. When the child and therapist generate feelings in the other and they react to those feelings, then this is the point at which relational engagement has begun. This can occur in many ways. The therapist may think, "This is a neat kid, I like her." Or the therapist may feel that although the child is acting tough she is scared, and intuitively the therapist may try to put the child at ease. A frightened child may sense that the therapist likes her and begin to feel more secure. The child may relax and talk more with the therapist. Perhaps at the end of the session the child might say, "When am I going to see you again." Initial feelings are often positive, but they can be negative, and either indicates that relational engagement has begun. The important point is that an emotional reactivity has occurred.

> I once saw a ten-year-old boy who refused to come to my office and finally was carried there by his father. To emphasize his refusal to participate, he promptly zippered his jacket up over his head and stayed that way for the first four sessions. He was both terribly angry and terribly frightened. Needless to say he refused to talk to me. In this blatant effort to ignore me he was showing many intense feelings and creating many feelings in me (confusion, embarrassment, frustration, and sympathy, just to mention a few). In spite of the fact that we had

not even seen what the other looked like (his head was hidden in his jacket), we had begun to engage because each of us was reacting emotionally to the other.

Therapeutic Engagement

A second and higher form of engagement could be called therapeutic engagement because it is connected with therapeutic change. This occurs when the therapist and child go beyond expressing and reacting to their reciprocal feelings. Now both use the relationship to move the child toward therapeutic change. This can occur in many different ways. Perhaps disruptive symptoms which are easier to ignore in a casual relationship become more obvious in the closer therapeutic relationship. Perhaps the child comes to better trust the therapist and begins to unburden her fears and worries. Perhaps the newfound closeness leads the child to assume that the therapist will banish her unhappiness or change the child's overbearing parents and she feels disappointed when this does not happen. Perhaps the child simply becomes angry and frustrated when the therapist does not do what she wants. All of these situations and others force a child to feel or recognize her emotional problems and that is a crucial first step toward change.

Structural Engagement

The third aspect of engagement establishes the structure of therapy sessions and is called structural engagement. As with the other forms of engagement, this is different for each child and therapist. Sometimes the therapist must directly describe the limits and procedures of therapy sessions. At other times the therapist may not need to say anything because the child will intuitively discern the structure from the ongoing interaction of the session. Usually, the therapist does something in between . However this is done, the child needs to come away from the first session with some understanding of when and how long she will meet with you, why she is coming to see you, what kinds of things you will do, what things are not permitted, and the role and limits of confidentiality. Usually, these are not fully understood in one session and a therapist must be alert for misperceptions and be ready to correct them. Obviously, the way sessions are structured depends on the age of the child, since very young children will take a longer time to fully understand the structure and meaning of psychotherapy sessions. This structuring is important because it tells the child what to expect and so minimizes any feelings of uncertainty. This probably increases the likelihood that children and their parents will remain in treatment since they better understand the rules of therapy.

Engagement in Behavioral Treatments

Engagement of some sort must occur in every type of psychotherapy. The kind of engagement we have been discussing is characteristic of psychodynamic or cognitive treatments, but engagement is also a part of behavioral treatments. Of course, the engagement process in behavior therapy is different in some important ways. The theory underlying this treatment implicitly places limits on the child-therapist relationship and it has little of the reciprocal flexibility characteristic of other treatments. Since the therapist controls what happens in therapy by arraigning positive and negative consequences, she is concerned more with the child's environment than with the child. The child may have emotional reactions to the therapist or what the therapist does, but the therapist does not respond or responds in a controlled and stylized fashion. Once a desensitization procedure has begun, the child's overt expression of feelings toward the therapist will interfere with the progress of treatment. Similarly, once an operant program has been set up by the therapist and the contingencies decided upon, emotional reactions by the child are detrimental and often will be ignored by the therapist.

Relational engagement and therapeutic engagement are severely curtailed in behavioral therapies; however, structural engagement is important as the child needs to understand and behave in accordance with the structure of the therapy. To the extent that the child violates the therapeutic procedures, the effectiveness of behavioral treatments will be diminished.

Identification of Problems

Of course a child's problems have to be identified. If a child or his therapist does not know what the problems are, how can they do something about them? This statement is obvious, but it still underemphasizes the importance and difficulty of this stage. The difficulty lies in bringing the child to identify emotional problems. Therapists armed with theoretical knowledge and diagnostic skills usually have little problem, but the situation is quite different for children in a number of ways. They do not have the therapist's psychological sophistication, or the ability to see themselves from another person's perspective. Also, most children try to avoid their problems and feelings or are simply unaware of them. They can be experts at denying even the most obvious feelings. Identifying a child's problems is the crux of treatment in most psychodynamic and cognitive psychotherapies and a significant aspect of even behavioral therapies. However, if this step is carried out correctly, then the rest of the treatment process will follow easily.

Every therapist spends a great deal of his or her time (and no small amount of frustration) dealing with this aspect of therapy and trying to point out to a child how that child feels. I remember one unhappy seventh grade boy moping around my office. When I commented on how sad he seemed, he ignored me. When I commented on it again, he denied it, and when I foolishly commented on his sadness a third time, he got angry. Then I told him that he seemed very angry at me and he denied that, too.

Even when children can recognize the serious distress and turmoil they feel, they are usually unaware of the conflicts that are behind their pain. The fact that children do not understand the relationship between their feelings of anger, fear, sadness, anxiety, warmth, security, and happiness, and the situations that bring forth these feelings is a central problem of treatment. Certainly, a major goal of treatment is for the child to understand how, when, and why the distressing feelings are related to situations and people in that child's environment. Only then can the child begin to bring about a beneficial change.

Emotionally troubled children always have these feelings, and they usually have little insight into the cause of either their happy or unhappy feelings. Therapists, of course, are primarily concerned with a child's unhappy feelings. Most children experience their unhappy feelings directly. They become frustrated and lash out at a parent. They become angry and have a temper tantrum. They become deeply hurt when rejected by classmates and friends. They become depressed and try to punish themselves by destroying a favorite model or toy. Sometimes they feel so wretched that they try to destroy themselves. However it is felt, these children experience their pain.

For other children the feelings come indirectly. Usually they vent their unhappiness on others. They may be parent-killers who drive their parents up a wall and cannot be controlled by adults. They may be rebellious adolescents who abuse drugs or alcohol. They may seem to enjoy beating up other children or hurting their pets. But, even these children experience their unhappy feelings eventually. Even when they seem to enjoy their acting out for that moment, they eventually experience the uselessness and emptiness of their actions. Of course, at some point they have to face the punishment and rejection of their parents and the other important people that they have abused.

The crucial importance of identifying and recognizing problems is that it forces a child to do something. Once the child knows a problem exists, he must make a choice. The child can make a maladaptive choice and decide to continue to ignore the problem and do nothing. But, he also has other, more adaptive alternatives, and can choose one of these. The child can try to understand the relationship between the unhappy feelings and the situations that cause them. He can try to be aware of how these behaviors affect other people. The youngster can try to understand how he is affected by their own emotional reactions. He can try to recognize how certain feelings bring on other feelings. In the pragmatic, idiosyncratically complex world of a child there are innumerable alternatives to be understood, but in most psychotherapies, what the child does is less important than the fact that recognition of a problem forces him to do something.

Of course this is a very basic description of a very complex psychological process. In reality, a child must first come to realize that he has certain feelings that are disturbing or behaviors that disturb others. Then the child must become aware of what these feelings and behaviors are, how intensely they are felt, and how disturbing they are to other people. This is a crucial first step, but often the child needs to also identify the conflicts and situations that bring about the upsetting feelings and undesirable behaviors.

Perhaps that task sounds simple, but usually it is anything but simple because few children want to face the things that upset them. Their natural instincts are to avoid, deny, ignore, and do anything but try to understand what they fear. Some children even try to avoid this by withholding information from their therapist. They fear the therapist will use such information to come to their own recognition of the child's problems, and that, too, is frightening to the child.

The most important tool the therapist has in overcoming this fear is the relationship with the child. As a result of therapist-child engagement, a therapeutic relationship develops and the child begins to trust the therapist. As a result of this trust and a sense of confidence in the therapist, the child feels cared for and protected. Within this sense of safety the child can begin to explore and face the feelings, conflicts, and behaviors that are upsetting, or can allow the therapist to subtly lead them in this direction.

In most kinds of dynamic psychotherapies, this is a delicate and sensitive process, but in some forms of treatment, the therapist will use direct confrontation, deliberate interpretation, or persuasion. Even when these rigorous methods are utilized, the child still must feel enough safety and comfort to face the problems that he is unable to face alone. If not, therapy will be distorted and progress will be minimal.

Correct Realization of Problems

Identifying a child's problems is a crucial stage in psychotherapy, but that alone is not enough. The child must come to correctly understand these problems, and this is another important stage in treatment. Emotional conflicts are uniquely different for each individual child. When we say a child is depressed, that word brings to mind a category of logically related behaviors that apply to many children, but for each depressed youngster, depression is different. The sadness is unique, the people she acts sad with are unique, their reactions to the child are unique, the situations she is sad within are unique. I could go on in even greater detail for any individual child and her idiosyncratic environment.

The main point is that each child needs to find her own understanding of a problem. The problem needs to be understood within her own cognitive structure, and based on and integrated within aspects of her own life. This is a complex process which needs to be repeated over and over again. Initially, the child, with the therapists help, forms imprecise understandings that are then rejected in favor of more refined realizations. This is done over and over again before the child comes to formulate feelings, conflicts, and problems in a way that allows her to achieve a better adjustment.

In a sense, both therapist and child go through this process because the therapist is also constantly reformulating the understanding of the child's problems so that he can then use this more accurate understanding to help the child in treatment. This sophisticated procedure emphasizes the similarities among children, but the therapist's job may be the more difficult one because after he understands a problem in a way that is meaningful, the therapist then must reformulate it in a way that is helpful to the child. This is the crux of the therapist's problem. Even when the therapist has a good understanding of the child's emotional difficulties, he cannot just explain it to the child. Even if the therapist avoided too theoretical and psychodynamic an explanation, the child would likely not understand such an explanation for a whole host of reasons. The child might not want to hear it; he might be unable to understand an explanation based on the intricacies of adult thinking; or the therapist might not explain it in a way that reflects the idiosyncracies of the child's life.

Actually, the therapist's task is not to explain what he has understood to the child, but to help the child come to his own understanding. To the extent that the therapist has a good grasp of the child's difficulties, that will help in this process, but the therapist cannot give the explanation to the child. The therapist must help the child seek it through his own insights and through trial and errors. Often therapists attempt to explain a child's problems in a commonsense fashion that is in harmony with the child's thinking, and such an explanation can be helpful. But no matter how sophisticated and sensitive the explanation, the child must ultimately reformulate it into his own individual understanding.

The preceding discussion describes the stages of problem identification and problem reformulation from the point of view of most psychodynamic psychotherapies. These stages apply to other forms of treatment, but they differ in certain ways. In operant behavior modification the child has a minor role in identifying and reformulating problems. The therapist identifies the problem and reformulations are also done by the therapist using information obtained from the child and others in his immediate environment. In systematic desensitization and other forms of respondent behavior modification, the therapist and child work on defining the problems together, but the therapist has a very active role in guiding the process. Ultimately, it is the therapist who is responsible for the hierarchy of problems generated.

In some forms of cognitive behavior therapy the therapist has a very direct role in defining the child's problems, but in others the child has an equal voice in this process. It depends on the type of theory underlying the treatment. However, once the psychological problems have been identified, the therapist plans, sets up, and guides the treatment program. This means that the stage of correcting and reformulating the initial problems is not an important part of cognitive behavioral treatments, at least not for the child.

In behavioral or cognitive treatments, a child's problems are clearly defined as objective behaviors, such as self-destructive head-banging, smoking pot, uncontrolled self-stimulation, overactive classroom behavior, or agoraphobia. The fact that the problems are so objectively identified by the environment, and the therapist is very directive in these kinds of treatments, dictates that the child usually has only a minor role in these stages of treatment. Theoretically, they are still integral stages in the therapeutic process, but in this case the work falls to the therapist. If the therapist does not do an adequate job of identifying and refining the child's problems, then the therapy will be less effective.

Understanding the Implications of a Problem

In this stage a child comes to understand how a problem affects her life. Conceptually this stage involves an understanding of cause-and-effect relationships and consequences. The following case is an example of this concept.

> A seven-year-old I was treating suddenly became afraid of going out to play with the other children on his street. As a therapist I realized there were many consequences that might result from this behavior. For example, his friends might start to reject him, since he was avoiding them. Likely, they would stop going to his house and asking for him, and he would lose his usual place in their street games. As the other children began to ignore him, he might avoid them even more. As a result, he would be spending much more time in the house watching TV and playing with solitary kinds of toys. He would also be spending more time with his mother, talking with her, and generally demanding more of her time. This would begin to increasingly irritate his mother, and they would begin to fight. As a result, his mother might try to avoid him or send him outside. As he senses her rejection, he is likely to become more dependent on her and this vicious cycle was going to require my therapeutic attention.

For the most part there is a definite difference in the way a therapist sees the consequences of emotional problems and the way a child sees them, and therapists need to be aware of the difference. Therapists will understand the consequences in theoretical terms related to the assumptions and concepts of the personality theory that underlies their form of treatment. Children do not think this way. They will be more aware of specific, pragmatic situations that result from their problems. Of course there are differences among children that need to be recognized. An active problem, such as a flying into uncontrollable fits of rage, will bring very direct, immediate, and harsh consequences. Children are more likely to be aware of the consequences of such problems because they have such a heavy impact on their life. By contrast, the consequences associated with a passive problem, such as being excessively shy with classmates, are not as identifiable and do not have as dramatic or heavy-handed an impact on the child. That is not to say the consequences of that problem are any less important, but they are easier to avoid or ignore.

What the therapist does during this stage is determined by the type of psychotherapy being employed, the cognitive level of the child, the kinds of problems that the child is experiencing, and the particular implications of those problems. How the child becomes aware of the consequences of her emotional problems is a very important aspect of treatment. For example, therapists can either be very directive in pointing out the consequences and implications of a child's problems or the therapist can allow the child to discover this on her own.

In behavioral treatments the directiveness or nondirectiveness of the therapist is usually not an issue. This is because the emphasis is on training the child to behave to a certain criteria and most behavior therapists do not feel that the child's knowledge of the consequences of her problems is crucial to improvement. Rather, awareness of the consequences is important to the therapist because control of consequences is crucial in setting up the contingencies of behavioral treatment.

Most cognitive therapists are also very directive in pointing out the consequences of problem behavior. In treatments such as Ellis's rational-emotive therapy, or Michenbaum's or Beck's therapy, a primary task of the therapist is to directly point out the repetitively harmful consequences of the child's present behaviors.

In psychodynamic therapies, the therapist has a choice. Sometimes, he may be directive in pointing out consequences of a child's problems, but more likely the therapist prefers to subtly guide the child or allow the youngster to do this on his own. There are both advantages and disadvantages in allowing children to independently learn the implications their problems have on their life. Often the process takes longer and there is the risk that the child will not be able to understand the consequences of his problems. Often children will refuse to recognize these consequences. However, allowing children to do this on their own is in harmony with the normal ways children learn. In response, children may be more accepting since they discovered it by themselves.

Certainly, they will not have the feeling that it was forced on them by an authoritarian therapist, and so it should not be as damaging to the therapeutic relationship. Generally, when children discover problem consequences through their own efforts, they will better understand and probably can better generalize their understanding to other situations. Also, they will have learned an important life skill, which they can use for recognizing the implications of other problems.

Certainly, a child's cognitive level affects whether or not the therapist will be directive in pointing out consequences of a problem, because if a child is not intellectually able enough to understand or recognize cause-and-effect relationships, then the therapist needs to actively help in the process. Of course, sometimes children will not grasp the connection even when the therapist spends a good bit of effort in this, so there are times when even with the most directive approach, the child will not understand what the therapist is pointing out. More commonly the child will grasp the implications of a problem, but only imperfectly.

Perhaps the most important factor in this stage of treatment is the kind of problems and how directly the child is affected by the consequences. We have already discussed the fact that some problems have direct and immediate consequences that cannot be avoided, while the consequences of other problems are indirect. The therapist's role is different in each situation. In the first instance, the child is already aware of the consequences, so the therapist's task is to help the child realize all the implications of the problem. Often, the therapist may want to point out emotional reactions that the child has not yet recognized, and he might want to show the child how these problem consequences are occurring in other parts of the child's life. The following example shows how a therapist can help a child understand unrecognized problems.

> I once treated a very unhappy and angry teenage girl. She lived with her father and older sister and was bitterly angry at her father. She felt he did not really care for her because he did not buy her the things she wanted. In reality, her father was doing a good job raising and providing for his daughters considering their limited financial circumstances. The mother had left her family when my patient was five-years-old, and her sudden and unexpected departure resulted from her own serious psychological problems. Even though she lived close by and saw both girls once a week, she never told them why she left her family.
>
> Within a few sessions we began to talk about her mother, and soon the powerful feelings of confusion and sadness about her mother's absence began to overwhelm her and she spent session after session crying uncontrollably. This continued month after month and often she was racked by her childlike sobbing as soon as she entered my office. This deep sadness and depression were the obvious consequences of her

mother's abandonment, and there was little need for me to point this out to her. However, the anger she felt toward her mother was displaced onto her father because he was the safer target. She knew that he would not leave her no matter how angry she was, whereas she did not have this same feeling of security with her mother. For many sessions she refused to recognize this and only toward the end of therapy was she able to understand and accept that many of her feelings toward her father were the result of her anger at her mother.

When the consequences of emotional problems do not have a direct impact on the child, the therapist's role will be to help the child recognize such consequences. This is a more difficult task because environmental pressures are not supporting the therapists efforts. Often the therapist must be very patient and wait until environmental pressures change and become more obvious, or until the youngster becomes more sensitive to his or her difficulties. Again, a case example can show this therapeutic difficulty.

I am presently treating a high school senior who has purposely isolated himself from his classmates. He has only one off and on friendship, he sits alone in the cafeteria and lounge area, and he has assiduously cultivated an appearance that sets him apart from every group in the school. As part of this "I don't care about anything" image, he seldom did his homework. The many negative consequences of such a lifestyle are obvious, but for session after session he maintained that this image was exactly what he wanted. Realizing the futility of directly confronting him about this, I patiently waited.

By the middle of the school year his grades had dropped to the point that they threatened his acceptance at colleges, and for the first time I saw that he was beginning to worry. The next session, in an uncertain tone, he told me that he had received a score of twelve on a math test. In the past he had seemed proud of his poor grades and seemed to want my approval for thwarting the academic establishment. This time I quietly said, "You're worried, aren't you? I know you don't like to get good grades, but this is a real disaster."

For the first time he was able to listen as I pointed out the many self-defeating consequences that went along with his proud isolation. We talked about his low grades being part of his anti-establishment image, and while that image pleased him, it was costing him a chance at a decent college. We talked about his being an excellent basketball player, yet he could not try out for the varsity because that would have forced him to be part of a close-knit team. We spoke about his quitting the cross-country ski team in his freshman year because the team members were a cliquish group and he would have had to go to their parties and get-togethers. All these things and others were direct or indirect consequences of his nonconformist image.

This young man had been able to ignore these consequences for three-and a half years of high school and many therapy sessions. Finally, the combination of some environmental pressure and my accepting attitude opened his eyes to the implications of what he was doing. His mother had been trying for years to get him to see some of these things, to no avail. In previous sessions I had gently tried, but he was not ready. His problems had not had enough of a direct impact to make him aware of the implications of his behavior.

Generally, when the consequences of a problem do not directly affect a child, therapy will be more difficult and last longer. This is especially true when the consequences of a child's emotional problems affect others and have only an indirect impact in the child's life. When a child continually bullies his or her sibling, it is the sibling who suffers the consequences. If the parents do not punish the child in some way, he will not feel the effects of his cruel behavior. In this situation, the therapist must find a way to make the child aware of what he is doing; however, this is easier to say than do.

Change

Changing oneself to a better adjustment is the last stage in the therapeutic process. It is the logical result of the preceding stages, and if the therapist and child have been diligent in carrying out the earlier tasks, then this one falls easily into place. In this stage, the child gives up his maladaptive behavior patterns and substitutes new and better ones. If we view psychotherapy strictly in terms of behavior, then this stage will be very important. Those therapies that emphasize behavior patterns as the criteria of treatment give greater emphasis to this stage in their work with children. For example, in operant behavior therapy, once the deviant behaviors have been identified, then the crux of treatment is the negative conditioning of those behaviors and the positive reinforcement of other behaviors. Similarly, once the fear causing situations have been identified in systematic desensitization or flooding, the main work of the therapist is to eliminate those fears and bring about new emotional reactions.

Even in many cognitive and psychodynamic psychotherapies, therapists help children by teaching them new ways to behave. In some cases they may model a new behavior, explain the logic behind it, or simply exhort a child to try it. For the most part these are also the usual methods that nonpsychotherapeutic agents use in getting children to change. Usually, a parent or teacher's attempts to change a child involve some form of informal operant behavior modification, which usually has been tried to exhaustion before a child arrives at the therapist's office. The main reason they work at this stage in psychotherapy is that the preceding stages have changed the child's cognitive and emotional reactions so that he can accept the new behavior patterns. Now the therapist is in harmony with the child. The new patterns are not viewed as an alien demand imposed from outside.

In many forms of dynamic psychotherapy, the emphasis is on cognitive, attitudinal, and emotional change, and the therapist does not believe that overt behavioral changes are a necessary part of treatment. Such therapists believe that once a child understands a problem and its social and emotional implications, his job is over. At this point the child is free to implement a change in behavior or not, according to his own values and wishes. By attempting to coerce a child to change, the therapist would be violating the ethics of treatment and destroying the effectiveness of the treatment process.

Often, this stage of treatment is a minor part of therapy because many children do not need any therapeutic help in changing their overall adjustment. By the time they have gone through the preceding stages, the changes they must make are obvious and they need no explanation or exhortation. Also, when the child has a firm understanding of a problem and is intellectually capable, then the child may be the best one to decide on what changes need to be made and how to bring about these changes. Therapeutic suggestions may be good from the therapist's point of view, but no therapist ever sees the world exactly the way a child does. Changes that are initiated by the child will be better integrated into the child's idiosyncratic way of doing and seeing things, and he is likely to feel a greater sense of commitment to its success.

Our discussion of stages in therapy has pointed out that psychotherapies differ according to the emphasis they place on particular stages. Most psychodynamic psychotherapies emphasize identification of emotional problems, and the therapist and child spend most of their time and effort on these phases of treatment. Cognitive treatments emphasize the implications and consequences of emotional problems and spend the bulk of their efforts in this part of treatment. Lastly, behavior therapies emphasize the change process and focus their efforts in this phase of treatment. These differing emphases are a consequence of the theoretical assumptions underlying each treatment and as the assumptions differ, so the phase of treatment they emphasize will differ.

In concluding our discussion of the stages of treatment, we must realize that stages are conceptual simplifications. They help therapists break treatment into smaller parts so they can be better understood. But a child sees things differently. Children experience one continuous, ongoing process. Also, psychotherapy is not a rigid, one-way process going from engagement to problem identification to problem implications and ending with change. At times children may try to change themselves before they fully understand a problem. They may struggle with the consequences of a problem before they have a clear realization of all of its aspects. Obviously, engagement is one aspect of a complex relationship that continually changes throughout treatment. Thus, the stages we discussed do not follow a perfectly rigid sequence, but will vary depending on the particular therapist and child.

Of course, children will be dealing with many emotional problems at the same time, and they will likely be in different stages of progress at the same time. Certainly, the work they do on one emotional problem may change them so that they may be better able to deal with other emotional difficulties. All of these factors make psychotherapy with children a very complex endeavor, but the more a therapist can understand that the child's experience does not follow the logical principles of treatment, the better they will help the children they are treating.

6

The Heuristic Process as the Basis of Psychotherapy

Choice and the Heuristic Process

In chapter one we saw that there are many differences between the various kinds of psychotherapies. We also discussed the similarities and saw that in many ways, diverse forms of treatment are in fact alike. Perhaps we might have expected to find more similarities than we did, since all treatments have the same overall goal, that of changing a child's behavior in a positive way. If all therapies have the same overall goal, then there ought to be one basic similarity in the process they use to achieve change, and that basic similarity is that in all therapies, children have a choice as to whether or not they will change. All psychotherapeutic treatments attempt to lead children to change and in some therapies, therapists believe they are forcing a child to change, but to some extent, no matter how minimal, children exercise a choice.

Certainly, in the psychodynamic and cognitive therapies children are given more freedom in this choice than in the behavioral treatments, but even in structured behavioral treatments they have a choice because they can refuse to participate in the desensitization procedure or the token economy. Even when they decide to go along with a harsh behavioral contingency they dislike, they are choosing that over outright rebellion and refusing treatment (which might bring even harsher contingencies upon them).

In psychodynamic and cognitive treatments, the therapist does not attempt to take on such strict control, and the child usually has a choice in what happens in therapy. When a child chooses to participate and even take on some of the responsibility for treatment, she is choosing to question the present ways of thinking, feeling, and acting in the hopes of finding a better and happier way for the future. It is this questioning that is the crux of treatment, because until a child begins to question, he cannot begin to change. Unless the child becomes unhappy with her present ways, there is little reason to look for or accept newer and more adaptive emotions and behaviors. This is the process that produces a disequilibrium in a child, that motivates a searching for something different.

In some form or another, psychotherapy encourages a child to question, and this questioning process is at the base of almost all treatment methods. English dictionaries refer to this questioning as "heuristic," and they define a heuristic process as "An educational method in which the student is stimulated to make his own investigations and discoveries." This definition identifies the tasks of both child and therapist. The child needs to question her present behaviors in order to discover new ones and the therapist should stimulate and encourage this questioning. Reduced to its basics, the process sounds quite simple, but when transformed into the activities and discussions of a therapy session, it is more complex.

In this process the therapist leads the child to wonder why she feels a certain way, why she reacted in a particular fashion, or why a certain situation happened the way it did. This leads the child to evaluate the utility of her thoughts, feelings, and behaviors. If the evaluation shows the child that the existing ways are dysfunctional or maladaptive, there is a natural human tendency to look for alternatives. While this seems easy to carry out, it is not. Children tend to hold on to what is familiar and safe, even if it is fraught with pain and problems. They are likely to resist this questioning for the very reason that it can be helpful. It leads to change, and they may be frightened, angry, or upset facing what is new and unknown.

Freedom to Reject Therapeutic Change

In order to help a child ask the difficult and frightening questions that are the essence of this heuristic process, the therapist must allow the child to reject any changes that come out of the self-questioning. The therapist should never pressure or try to force a child to accept a more adaptive way of behaving. Change is the unknown; it is a threat and may be a frightening experience. Children prefer what is familiar. Like Hamlet, they would rather "Bear the ills we now have rather than fly to others we know not of."

If children sense this pressure from their therapist, then they are likely to stop the self-questioning. This means that one of the assumptions of this heuristic process is that a child must have the freedom to hold to existing disturbed ways. While this may be frustrating to a therapist and fly in the face of what he knows is best for the child, it an essential aspect of treatment.

I also must point out that children almost never choose to hold on to a maladaptive lifestyle once they understand that they can choose a better one. If children have thoroughly questioned their problem behaviors and emotions and fully understand their implications, then they will usually choose an alternative set of behaviors and emotions. That is a natural human tendency. The essential point is that they must feel they can reject a choice if they choose to do so, and the therapist must be scrupulously honest in allowing them to do this. Of course, children are likely to reject an adaptive choice or change for quite some time. Questioning behaviors, feelings, thoughts, and a lifestyle one has had for years is not a quick or easy thing to do . The questioning of these things may be a lengthy process, but if the heuristic process can be carried to completion, a child almost always rejects the existing maladaptive ways and accepts the newer, more adaptive ways.

The main reason why a therapist should allow a child freedom to accept or reject positive adjustments is that the therapist ultimately has little choice in the matter. A child who does not wish to change can resist a therapist and ultimately prevail. Even if the therapist somehow forces or coerces the child to accept a change, that change will likely be flawed or incomplete because it is not in harmony with other aspects of the child's beliefs. The therapist's conception of a problem and its solution may also have excellent theoretical logic according to the therapist's conceptual framework, but it may not be understood by the child or congruent with the child's conceptual framework. Thus, forcing a choice on a child is likely to be at best an imperfect technique, since therapeutic coercion is antithetical to the heuristic process. It will hamper a child's freedom, and a sense of freedom is essential to fully explore all the ramifications of ones existing lifestyle.

There are other reasons for allowing a child the freedom to ultimately choose her own alternatives in therapy. Children enjoy this freedom to choose and it improves their motivation for treatment. They are also likely to have a more favorable attitude toward their therapist under these conditions, and perhaps they are less likely to interrupt treatment when their sessions become difficult.

The Difference Between Asking Questions and Stimulating a Questioning Attitude

There is one essential point in this process that must be understood. Using a heuristic process in psychotherapy does not mean that the therapist questions the child. In fact, though therapists need to do this at times, direct questioning of a child is not a good therapeutic technique and should be avoided if there is an alternative. The primary goal of psychotherapy is for the child to have a questioning attitude and to ask questions of himself. In a sense, the child needs to wonder, to be puzzled by what he is doing, thinking, or feeling, and when psychotherapy is at its best, the questioning is done by the child. The therapist's task is to stimulate the child to initiate and participate in this process.

In the nontherapeutic world of everyday living, the primary way of dealing with problems is to find solutions, but in the heuristic procedures of psychotherapy the emphasis is on the identification of problems. As we have already discussed, the primary assumption underlying this form of treatment is that once child and therapist fully identify a problem then the child will become motivated to solve it. Usually the best solutions are those generated by the child himself. This means that psychotherapy does not need to focus on problem-solving, but on questioning. When the child wonders about why he became furious with his father, or broke his favorite model, or felt sad without knowing why, then the child will struggle to find answers to these problems, and that is the crux of the heuristic therapeutic process.

Ideally, this process works best when one question leads to another. That is, when the answer to one question intuitively leads the child to ask a further question. The following case history illustrates the sequential questioning that occurred with a seventeen-year-old college student.

> The session began with the young woman saying she was furious at her father because, while complaining to her mother about an arguement with her roommate, father interrupted and blamed her for the disagreement. In the therapy session she angrily wondered why he did that when he knew it would make her angry. She answered her question by saying that her father always needed to be right. But if he disagreed with what she was saying, why did he not keep it to himself? She answered this question by saying that her opinions were not very important to him. Should her opinion of her roommate have been important? Yes! She knew her roommate far better than he did, and if that was the case why did she get so angry and upset at her father when he was the one who was wrong. At this point she realized that she was not only angry, she was sad that he was not more respectful of her opinions and her version of what had happened during the roommate argument. Why did he not think better of her, and why couldn't she demand that of him?

In this example, each question led to an answer which led to another question. This is the way that the heuristic process should proceed. At the end of her thinking she came to wonder why she had not demanded that her father respect her opinions, but this was not really the end. Hopefully, this answer would also have led to another question, and in this way she was beginning to understand both her father and her own reaction to him.

An important point to keep in mind is that she was asking herself questions within the specific context of the conversation about her roommate. As a therapist I might have been tempted to say something like, "You feel that your father doesn't respect you." However, this remark changes the level of her questioning so it is more global and abstract. It is typical of the theoretical way therapists think, but she was asking her questions within a specific context, and if I had interrupted with my more global comment I probably would have interfered with her own more effective questioning.

Sometimes therapists are tempted to ask questions designed to elicit solutions to the problem with which a child is struggling. While these kinds of questions can be helpful at times, it is likely to stop the child's own questioning process and the therapist needs to decide if that is the best thing to do. This can be seen in the following case.

> Alan was a thirteen-year-old who was constantly frustrated and hurt by his divorced father. The father would make an definite appointment to see Alan and then arrive a day or two late. My patient was able to complain to me and his mother, but never to his father. In one of our sessions he was talking about his father and the ridiculous excuses he gave. After listening for a while I ineptly asked, "How come you don't get angry at him and refuse to see him for a while?" Whether or not this question, which was designed to elicit the possibility of a solution, was a useful thing to say is not the issue. He was already talking about his father and his father's excuses and in doing so he was attempting to answer questions like, "What is my father like," "Are his excuses at all reasonable," "Does he really care about seeing me," and "Will he be late next time?" This self-questioning was more likely to help him understand his father than my question, which could only help him find a premature solution to a situation he still did not understand.

If the heuristic process is proceeding well, the therapist hardly has to ask any questions. She must simply encourage the child to continue this process in whatever way is successful and often this is to simply keep quiet.

Where Does the Heuristic Process Lead?

There ought to be some point in this process whereby questions stop leading to other questions, a time when the child has a sufficient understanding of the problem. At this point there ought to be answers and a self-knowledge that the child can use in bringing about useful change. Actually, there are two end points of the heuristic process.

The first is when the child, consciously or unconsciously, realizes that there is an answer to his problem and does something about it. This is a therapeutic form of the everyday problem-solving that we all do so often. Usually, this necessitates that the child change the way he is feeling, thinking, or acting. The previous example of Alan and his irresponsible father illustrates this situation. After doing a great deal of questioning about his father and their relationship, he decided that his father's excuses were "stupid lies" and if his father loved him, he ought to get there on time, or at least not a day or two late. The next session he said his father had again been late, but this time he had told his father that if he could not arrive on time, then he shouldn't come at all. In this case, the child's questioning had led to a series of changes. His anger was now openly expressed; he had developed the confidence to confront his father. He made the decision to do it, and did so without telling me he had found the solution.

There is a second end point to the heuristic process that involves an existential acceptance of those things that cannot be changed. This is a common situation for children, since they live relatively powerless lives and often confront situations which cannot be controlled or changed by their actions. For example, their father may be abusive and no matter what they do, their father will not change. Perhaps they are upset about having to go to a special education resource room for help, but the reality is that they do have learning disorder reading problems, and they need the special help. Maybe they are upset over their parents' impending divorce, but again, nothing they do can change it.

Children need to realize that these situations have no solution. Becoming aware of an unhappy reality is difficult and sad, but it is better than ignoring the situation or pretending that it does not exist. The heuristic process allows children to question all aspects of such situations and come to the realization that nothing can be done; the situation will not change and must be accepted. Obviously, this will be a difficult process. A child needs to question every aspect of such a problem before he comes to the inescapable conclusion that nothing can be done.

Coming to this realization is a more hopeful situation than it may seem. First, if the child correctly understands that the problem will not change and will not go away, then he has no choice but to accept it. This kind of acceptance is beneficial. Children need to learn this. This kind of acceptance is difficult, but adaptive, and such adaptations are the opposite of emotional disturbance. Children also may realize that while nothing can be done in the present, time passes and things can change. I have often treated children in this situation. Usually, they were being badly mistreated by a parent and the parent's own emotional problems were so entrenched that they were incapable of change. The only way to cope was for the child to first accept the painful reality of the situation and then realize that as he grew older, he would be less dependent on and involved with his parents. Eventually, he would leave home completely. By accepting the unchangeable reality of his parents' difficulties, he can come to see that although his parents are abusive, others are more rational and not abusive, that in time he has the possibility of a better life.

There is another positive aspect to an existential acceptance. Although problems cannot be changed and a child's life is dismal, the child may be able to change his emotional reaction. When nothing can be done, the best response of the child may be to de-intensify feelings and emotions. To whatever extent the child can do this, it can be helpful. Of course, he will still suffer when being mistreated or abused or ignored, but an existential acceptance that the situation cannot be changed is better than self-delusion, repression, or confused anguish.

The Pragmatics of the Heuristic Process

In the heuristic process, the therapist's task is to create a questioning or wondering attitude in the child. We need to discuss the pragmatics of how that is done. There is little doubt that therapists of every persuasion end up asking many questions of the children they are treating. It is probably the single most frequent type of therapeutic statement. However, the questioning process is quite different than therapeutic interrogation, and, as a general rule, a therapist does best to ask as few questions as possible. Relying heavily on questions has some definite implications for treatment (Weiner, 1975). It implies that the therapist is taking responsibility for what is going to be discussed in therapy, and that the child's task is only to answer the therapist's questions. Usually, children do not like to answer lots of questions and this may affect their acceptance of psychotherapy. Finally, it may imply that after the child has answered all the questions, the therapist will provide the answers.

A skilled therapist will create questions in the child through a host of methods. Much of the time they only need to be quiet and listen and let the child talk. In this way, a child will explore his thoughts and emotions and discover important questions. Usually, a therapist will want to guide the child's discussion by paying more attention to some topics than to others. This can be effectively done with nonintrusive responses, such as with "Really," or "Un-huh," or "That's very interesting." These statements communicate that a discussion or topic is important and encourages the child to discuss it in greater depth. Sometimes, a nonverbal gesture like leaning forward, nodding, or cocking one's head to one side may have the same effect.

There are so many simple and complex ways of bringing the child to question. Sometimes a surprised look will cause a child to question what he did or said. Sometimes the way the therapist plays a game will do it. I once spent a few sessions playing Monopoly with a very compulsive, inflexible fourteen-year-old whose game strategy was to never spend any money. I played with the better strategy of buying property when appropriate, and won every game. The continual losses prompted him to wonder why he was always losing, which led him to realize that his compulsive inflexible strategy was not a good one. The next question was why was he so compulsive when it stopped him from winning and enjoying the game. Every therapist will have different ways of helping a child use this questioning process. However it is done, they will need a large and creative repertoire of verbal and nonverbal statements to guide children to important questions.

Often a therapist can substitute a declarative statement for a question, and this is usually a more effective procedure. Research studies indicate that more experienced therapists tend to use declarative statements while less experienced therapists ask questions. Changing a direct question into a declarative statement is usually fairly simple. For example, I was trying to get an eleven-year-old boy to question his feelings about his parents never allowing him to eat junk food and forcing him to have dried fruit as a dinner dessert. I could have asked, "How do you like eating that for dessert." Instead I said, "I don't think you're very happy eating dried fruit every night."

The two responses are similar, but there are subtle differences. The question version asks for information and the child might answer by saying that he did not like it. That stops the conversation and I would be forced into asking another question. Continually coming up with questions is taxing and probably gives a child feelings of being on the spot, and that does not contribute to a smooth conversation. Also, it forces the therapist into taking on the responsibility of determining the direction of the questioning process. In this situation, the declarative version is more responsive to the child's feelings. It reflected his unhappiness at his parents' restrictions. It also focuses not so much on information, but on his emotions since I commented on his not being happy. Hopefully, this would induce him to express his feelings and makes him more aware of them. Finally, as a more open-ended statement, it is likely to elicit a longer and more thorough response, the kind that explores the issue.

The heuristic process is somewhat different, depending on the stage of treatment. Early in therapy, the therapist has not yet identified the important problems and so does not know what questions are pertinent. This is a time when the therapist may need to ask more direct questions because of the need to obtain information about the child and his life. Usually these questions tend to be more open-ended because open-ended questions solicit more information than simple yes and no queries. In spite of the need for information in those early sessions, a therapist must remember that the primary task is engagement and building a relationship with a child, and to the extent that questions detract from this, they need to be avoided.

Since the early sessions set the parameters of later therapy sessions, an over-reliance on direct questioning may lead the child to expect that this is the usual mode of therapeutic communication. Unfortunately, there is no firm formula or rule that tells a therapist the proportion of direct questions to other activities in the early sessions, any more than there are such simple guidelines for other aspects of child treatment. A competent therapist must grope for a balance depending on the individual child.

We need to remember that the lack of a therapeutic relationship in the beginning of therapy hampers the use of the heuristic process. In order to bring a child to deal with problems that are frightening or difficult to face, that child needs to have the feeling of security provided by a close, trusting relationship with a therapist. Since that has not been developed in the early sessions, a child will naturally be reluctant to jump into difficult problems. However, the child can deal with less emotional and less frightening problems, and the therapist can help a child use the questioning processes with these issues. Use of heuristic procedures early in therapy is beneficial as it sets a direction and orientation to the therapeutic process that will characterize later sessions.

Content Choices and the Heuristic Process

If a therapist's task is to bring a child to question and wonder about important problems, then he or she must identify those problems. That is, they must choose the content of their discussions so it leads to a thorough understanding of the relevant problems and their implications. The content of questions is chosen from an almost infinite number of topics which are then refined down to those topics that have emotional and behavioral importance to the child. A therapist starts treatment with a limited knowledge of the child, but this quickly expands as he or she becomes more familiar with the child, parents, school, friends, fun activities, community, and other aspects of the child's overall environment. The child may tell about past experiences, pleasant and traumatic. He may report dreams and fantasies that are important. The child therapist relationship will likely become part of the content of treatment. Questions will also be generated by the particular personality theory used by the therapist. All of these topics and more are screened through the therapist's theoretical system and experience. Important ones are used to generate questions for the heuristic process.

Although a therapist's theoretical system is helpful in generating and identifying questions, it may be limiting in that it slants the therapist toward a particular perspective of the child and may ignore other important questions. A therapist with a broad theoretical perspective will be able to integrate many personality theories into her understanding of a child and will have a broader base to generate questions. Not only will the therapist be able to cover more aspects of a problem, but likely will be better able to bring these into a child's awareness.

Refining Questions

Once the therapist and the child become aware that a question needs to be considered it must be refined to get to the important aspects of the question and to lead the child into considering other, more basic questions. This process is so dependent on the child, the therapist, the stage of treatment, and the idiosyncracies of the particular moment of therapy that there are few rules or guidelines that can be followed, but the process can be seen in the following example.

> A close friend was treating an eighteen-year-old college student who suffered a serious traumatic brain injury as a result of an auto accident and spent seven months in the hospital for medical treatment and rehabilitation. As the time for discharge approached, she faced a difficult problem. Before her accident she had fought constantly with her overbearing and controlling mother, and when she left home for college she selected a school hundreds of miles away. Now she was being discharged to her mother's care for further recuperation. In one of her final therapy sessions she said, "I don't know what I'll do having to leave Ithaca [the location of her college]. It's the only place I feel free. I'll die at home."
>
> There are many ways her therapist could have responded in order to get her to question her feelings and her situation, but I can discuss only a few.
>
> The most obvious one is to say something like, "You don't sound like you can do very much about it." This response focuses on problem-solving and leads her to question what, if anything, she can do about the situation. That could then lead her into thinking about whether she can do anything to help herself, and if so, what.
>
> A second statement would lead her to question her emotions and feelings about her mother. The therapist might say, "Going home sounds like it will be terrible." This focuses on how she feels and what her emotional reactions are to going home. This should make her more aware of how she feels in general about the situation and, specifically, how she feels about her mother. She might then question why she feels that way and that could lead into an in-depth discussion of her mother.
>
> A third approach might be to say, "I guess you think things are going to be really bad between you and your mother if you feel as if you are going to die at home." This should lead her to think about what happens when she and her mother are together. She might question why things go so badly and what part each of them plays in bringing it about. She is probably too emotional to develop a rational understanding of their relationship at this point, but this kind of questioning could start that process.

In another example, a sixteen-year-old patient of mine came to one session and told me that his car had been totaled. Evidently, he and some friends were partying in a local field the previous Friday night and one of the girls who did not have a driver's license asked if he would "teach her to drive." Although he was in the front seat, she lost control of the car and hit a tree. Fortunately, she was going slowly enough so that no one was hurt but fast enough to bend the frame and total the car. My patient did not want to admit to his parents that he had allowed the girl to drive the car, so he told them that he had been at the wheel and took a good bit of blame and the criticism about his poor driving in order to hide what had really happened. When we talked about this, he was obviously confused about what he should do and was looking to me for help.

At this point, I could have questioned many different aspects of the situation. Focusing on his fear of his parents finding out what had really happened, I could have said, "You're really scared about your parents finding out, aren't you?" Hopefully, this would have brought him to question his parents' reaction. Would they really have been angry at him? How angry? Would they get over it? Would he be able to tolerate their anger, their punishment, if any? Leading him to question his parents' anger and his reaction to it might be very helpful.

I could have focused on the morality of his lying to his parents by saying, "You don't feel very good about lying to your parents." I already knew he was troubled by having to lie to them—as he seldom did—and I hoped this response would lead him to think about his guilty feelings and whether he had really wanted to lie to them.

In the end I choose to talk about what I felt was most important to him. Were his parents going to find out and would he get caught? I did that because I felt he would be better able to question the other two issues if this one were resolved first. Discussing the reality of who would know what happened, would they tell other people, and would his parents hear about it enabled him to question, for the first time, the risks involved in what he had done. In the end it led naturally in to his questioning the other issues. (Ultimately, he never did tell his parents, but that was his choice and at that point he had a much better understanding of what he was doing and why.)

The preceding examples show how the heuristic process is used to explore issues in therapy, and it also shows the many choices the therapist and child have in deciding what topic they need to explore. A therapist needs to make those choices spontaneously based on an intuitive sense of the child's needs at that point in treatment. In making such choices, the therapist is selecting what she feels the child needs to become aware of, a choice greatly influenced by the personality theory of the therapist, the child's symptoms, problems, emotions, and a host of other factors.

Questions and Pseudoquestions

Often, what seems to be an important question in psychotherapy is in reality a "pseudoquestion." It is false in that it misses the real issues and often obscures them. These kinds of questions are often difficult to detect because they may sound as if they are important, but one of the tasks of a therapist is to see through such questions and expose the more important underlying questions. There are a number of ways in which pseudoquestions can masquerade as real questions. I will discuss some of the more important of these. Although the categories overlap to some extent, they can be a useful way to conceptualize the problem of pseudoquestions in treatment situations.

The first category of pseudoquestions involves a selective avoidance by a child. In this situation, a child chooses to discuss a less important question that is easier to talk about rather than a more important question that is more distressing. Sometimes the child may have a vague, foggy awareness of the more difficult issue, but usually he is unaware of the distress. This occurs often in psychotherapy and the following case of a third-grade boy illustrates such selective avoidance

> He came into one session very shocked and angry and proceeded to tell me about a classmate who had been really bad because he spoke back to the teacher and refused to do the homework that day. From the way he reported this incident, I could see he was upset, and his anger was out of proportion to what happened. There was no realistic reason that he should have felt so strongly about a classmate who was not a friend and who he did not even care about. I was tempted to focus our discussion on the classmate's behavior: Why did the child do that, what did the teacher do, and how was he punished? These issues covered the actual subject of the child's conversation, but in this case it would have missed the real issue.
>
> My patient was a very anxious boy who was afraid of his teacher. Seeing such outright defiance by his classmate frightened him. In his imagination he pictured himself being that rude to his teacher, and then was terrified by the thought of his teacher punishing him. Realizing that this was the real issue I did not ask about the classmate directly, but about the classmate's emotional reactions. I first asked if the boy was scared of the teacher, and how he reacted to her threats to send him to the principal's office. Then I was able to say, "Imagine if you had done that. What would have happened to you." At first he denied that he

would ever do that, and after I agreed with him, he felt reassured that he was not in danger of defying his teacher. Then he began to talk about how he would have felt if he were the other boy and told me how frightened he would have been.

This is a common situation in psychotherapy with children. The child is too frightened or upset to talk directly about a traumatic situation or event and so therapist and child talk about it indirectly. In this case, we talked about his own fears in terms of another child because that was less threatening to him. He experienced the same emotions, but in a safer, more indirect way. At different times during our talk I was tempted to ask him if he felt that way himself, but he was making better progress toward understanding and becoming aware of his fears in this indirect way, and more direct discussions could wait for a later session when he had overcome some of his fears.

A second type of pseudoquestion occurs when a child chooses to discuss an emotion which, although disturbing, is tolerable, rather than a more basic emotion that causes greater pain and anguish. The way this often emerges in a therapy session is that the child will say he is upset about one situation or circumstance, but in reality is upset by something else. In this way the youngster substitutes one emotion for another. Usually, this kind of pseudoquestion is difficult to detect because the expressed emotion is real and seems distrurbing to the child. To detect such a self-deception, the therapist must have a thorough knowledge of the child and his history. The following examples illustrate the deceptive aspect of this type of pseudoquestion.

One of my students was treating an eleven-year-old boy who was furious with his parents because they were so strict and did not do the things he wanted them to do. They forced him to attend religious school three times a week, did not let him go to McDonald's, restricted his television time to a half-hour daily, and refused his entreaties to take a family vacation to Disneyworld. As he saw it, his friends and classmates did get to do these things. The pseudo-issue was his anger at his parents because they were unfair and did not treat him as well as his friends were treated by their parents.

In reality the more important issue dealt with feelings he had about himself. He was a very guilt-ridden youngster who secretly believed that he had done something wrong and his parents mistreatment was the result of his being "bad." The more relevant questions this boy needed to consider had to do with such things as: "Was there something wrong with him that made his parents not love him?" "What had he done wrong?" "Had he in fact done anything wrong?" Realizing that these were the relevent issues, his therapist focused their sessions on these questions which helped him to understand his feelings and to question whether such feelings were appropriate.

After a few sessions he began to understand his own guilty feelings. As a result he was better able to question his angry feelings toward his parents. Now he was able to consider other things: "Were his parents angry at him?" "Were they really being unfair?" "Did they put these restrictions on him out of their own concern and parental love?" "Were such restrictions too strict and inappropriate?" "What caused his parents to treat him as they did?"

If his therapist had chosen to focus solely on the child's anger toward his parents, she would have missed the main issue and probably delayed his progress. Of course, they needed to talk about his anger at first. If they had not, the child might have felt his therapist was ignoring his feelings, However, by getting to the more basic concerns the child had about himself, the therapist avoided the pseudo-question and correctly focused on the important problem.

This next example shows an adolescent who is completely unaware of how he is substituting one emotion for another. Treatment is usually prolonged by this intransigent denial. Sean was a high school junior who was furious at his father for having divorced his mother and moved out of state. Session after session he gave me a "news report" about what his father had done or not done. Some of his typical complaints were: his father's child-support check was late; he had not called in three months and two weeks, which set a new record; he did call his mother but did not speak to Sean; or he had become involved with yet another girlfriend.

Obviously, Sean was terribly angry at his father, but he also felt deep sadness because he missed his father. He could not understand why his father had abandoned his family and rejected him. For Sean, the anger was a far safer and less painful emotion than the sadness and depression that were more basic. Expressing the anger was an active process and gave him some relief. Sadness was more difficult to cope with and so he avoided those feelings. Unfortunately, they existed and came out in other ways, such as his withdrawal from friends and his inability to maintain any motivation for schoolwork. Of course both emotions, anger and sadness, were appropriate given the situation, and he needed to deal with both. In his case, I had no choice but to first deal with his anger at his father, and I spent many sessions helping him to question his anger, to express it, and to understand its implications. However, this kind of questioning led him to see that he felt something more than anger. We began to talk about why he always reacted to his father's slights, and why he just did not write his father off. By wondering about these kinds of questions, he began to realize that he missed his father, and he became aware of the deep hurt that came from his father's rejection. When he began to recognize these emotions, he also began to question himself and his father. He wondered whether his sadness was warranted, given his father's blatant mistreatment. Didn't his father realize how badly he was hurting Sean? How could his father be such an unfeeling parent? Could he, Sean, ever hope to cope with such unhappiness? These were the kinds of questions that eventually led to a reluctant and painful acceptance of his father and the parent's divorce .

As a last example of pseudoquestions hiding relevant questions, I will describe how a terminally ill child tried to overfocus on a barely tolerable situation in order to escape facing his imminent, death, which was intolerable. In this instance, the child was aware of the more painful or difficult question, but refused to confront that question.

A close friend was treating a hospitalized eleven-year-old boy, who had lived through three episodes of a very virulent childhood cancer. As a result of powerful chemotherapy and radiation treatments, he had outlived his physicians' most pessimistic prognosis. However, the chemotherapy treatments had caused serious neurological lesions. His legs became paralyzed, he was confined to a wheelchair, and he had begun to lose strength in one arm. Of course, he was very depressed, as was his family.

At this point he was discharged from the hospital because his symptoms were in remission. However, three months later new tumors appeared and his physicians realized he was going to die. In spite of the hopelessness of his condition, his oncologist decided he needed more radiation treatments to cope with the terminal pain. When his mother told him his cancer had reappeared and he would need the radiation, he asked her if the treatments would help. She said, "They will help the pain go away." He thought for a moment, then asked, "Am I going to die?" She told him, "yes."

During his next therapy session he began to tell his therapist about the upcoming radiation treatments, and when she asked about it, he reassured her that it would not be too bad. When she asked if the treatments would help, he did not answer her question, but continued to describe the radiation treatments. Again she asked, but this time he fell silent. Then he took his head in his hands and began to shake. Tears came to his eyes as he slowly answered, "If it doesn't help I'll go puff." Feeling his fright and sadness, she asked, "Do you want to talk about that." He answered, "No, not now." Then, as if by mutual consent, they both changed the subject and began to talk about other things.

This child and his therapist knew that talking about his upcoming radiation treatments was tolerable, but talking about his death was not. Wisely, the therapist allowed the child the choice of avoiding the issue of his death. She did this for a number of reasons. First, the child needed to have the ultimate choice. If he did not, he would have avoided the intolerable topic anyway and disliked his therapist for trying to force him to do something he did not want to do. Second, this child knew he was dying. He was not so much hiding from that as he was saying, "This is too fearful for me to face now. I need some time to decide if I'm strong enough." He was also saying, "I can't do this all at once. I've admitted to both of us that I'm going to die and now I must pause before I take the next step; before I can allow you to help me understand my death."

"Why" Questions

When helping children with the heuristic process, there are certain questions that often fall into the category of pseudoquestions. I call these "why" questions because they begin with or contain the interrogative "why." Therapists are often tempted to ask questions that begin with "why" because they are simple and easy to ask. However, they are usually a poor question to ask for a number of reasons.

The problem is that "why" questions imply a single cause, one right answer, and there is seldom one cause or one factor that is responsible for something as complex as human behavior. "Why" questions are more appropriate to scientific investigations. Psychotherapy, on the other hand, is not a quasi-scientific analysis based on an accept-reject type of decision theory. It is a personal searching among the multitude of factors in a person's life. It is this searching that is most helpful to a child. Broad-based searching helps a child identify the many important problems that trouble her, and the many implications of these problems. Questions that use "what" and "how" as the interrogative are usually better questions than those using "why." "What" and "how" questions do not imply that there is only one answer. Rather, they push a child to wonder about many important aspects of her life, such as *how* she feels, *what* someone thinks of her, *what* makes her happy, and so on.

Reducing a child's problems to a simple cause-and-effect strategy leads a child to believe that therapy is an intellectual process, and she must "think" her way out of the emotional problems. That is one part of the psychotherapeutic process, but it leaves out the crucial nonverbal, emotional, and relational aspects of treatment. Even in cognitive behavior therapies, which put a heavier emphasis on the intellectual processes, the single cause-and-effect model will put limits on a child's alternatives and should be avoided.

Another difficulty with "why" questions is that because they imply a right answer, they tend to pressure children. There are few right or correct answers in psychotherapy, and these kinds of questions often make children feel as if they are "on the spot." Therapy proceeds best in a relaxed, spontaneous atmosphere. Under those conditions, children can freely search their thoughts and emotions, and spontaneous searching is a more effective psychotherapeutic endeavour than struggling to come up with a correct answer.

Even though "why" questions are not the best kinds of questions to use in therapy, they are a normal and frequent part of our everyday conversation. As such, therapists are likely to use them out of habit. So long as these kinds of questions do not dominate the therapist-child interaction, they are not harmful. Much of what a therapist does will not reflect perfect therapeutic technique, and the children we treat manage to improve in spite of our imperfect therapy. There are times when a "why" question may be useful because the therapist does not know what else to say. Even an imperfect question can keep the conversation alive until the therapist better understands the child and is able to ask a better question.

Using the Heuristic Process in Each Stage of Treatment

Since each stage of the psychotherapeutic process is different, the heuristic process will be used differently. It has greater applicability in certain stages than others and so therapists will emphasize it more in those stages.

During the early sessions, when the therapist focuses on engagement and forming a good relationship with a child, heuristic questioning will not be needed as much as in later stages. There are a number of reasons for this.

First, the emphasis in this phase of treatment is the relationship and that means the therapist needs to be spontaneous and exceptionally attentive to the child. The therapist will not want to withdraw her attention in order to think about the child's problems and how she can bring the child to reflect on questions about himself. It is too early for that kind of theorizing because the therapist does not know enough about the child to generate relevant self-questioning. Even if she did, therapist and child do not have a close and safe enough relationship for the child to be able to face potentially difficult questions.

The therapist needs to gather information about the child during this time. This is done in two ways. By naturally interacting with the youngster through a game, a model, or just spontaneous conversation about things the child is interested in, a therapist develops a good understanding of how a child reacts, feels, and thinks. That is how a therapist learns the more subtle and indirect ways of a child. Of course, a therapist needs to learn the more obvious aspects of the child. These are the situations, feelings, and reactions that the child is aware of and willing to talk about in conversations and discussions. To learn this aspect of a child, the therapist will want to ask the child direct questions. Such direct questions are information-seeking and not designed to lead a child to greater self-understanding. These questions are quite different from the types of questions used in the heuristic process.

Of course, no stage of psychotherapy is totally different from another stage. There is a great deal of overlap in terms of the procedures used, and the transition from one stage to another is gradual. To the extent that a child is able to tolerate heuristic questions early in therapy, then that technique can cautiously be utilized because it may speed therapeutic progress. However, there is no reason to hurry the course of treatment, since the results will be incomplete and inadequate. The crucial aspects of the engagement phase are concerned with the therapist-child relationship and that comes before the questioning process in overall importance.

In the "identification of problems phase," the heuristic process is useful as it helps a child discover emotional problems that he is unaware of or is reluctant to face. Given that a child has a safe and secure therapeutic relationship on which to rely, the child can be helped to question his behavior and wonder why he did what was done, thought what was thought, or felt what was felt. As each answer leads to another question, the child can discover what is troubling him. Self-questions in this phase of treatment will be more concerned with discovery and with leading the child to become aware of what kinds of things trouble him. Now, the therapist will have ideas of the content areas of the child's problems and she can try to help the child ask questions that lead to his discovery of these problems.

The heuristic process is just as useful in the next phase: "correct realization of a problem." As the child has developed insight into what problems are troubling, so he needs to realize the personal and idiosyncratic ways he is affected by these problems. The child needs to see, feel, and understand his problems in an individual way, through his own eyes and within his own individual cognitive structure. This is best learned through a personal self-questioning. The heuristic procedure in this stage should focus on individualizing questions so that the child sees the questions in terms of his own way of thinking. As the child becomes aware of his emotional difficulties, the child must be helped to understand these problems in his own way and not as the therapist understands them. Of course, both of these stages overlap because, as a child begins to develop a personal understanding of a problem, he is also discovering new problems.

As we said earlier, if the child has thoroughly worked out an individual understanding of the problems in the preceding two stages, then the next two stages, "realizing the implications of problems," and "changing one's behavior," will naturally follow. In these two stages the heuristic procedures can be useful, but they are not as crucial or used as often. At this point, the therapist may need to listen to the child reason out the many alternative implications of his or her problems, sometimes helping the child see implications the child may not realize. Here, too, the therapist is better off helping the child see the new implications through self-questions, rather than telling the child directly. When a therapist tells the child some unseen implication directly, then the child understands it through the therapist's emotional and conceptual framework. But when the therapist can lead the child to discover the implications of a problem through his own wondering and self-questioning, then the child will have a better understanding and the particular implications of the problems will have more significance and importance for the child.

Limitations of the Heuristic Process

In an earlier chapter we discussed the idea that treatments must be selected so as to be appropriate to a child's needs and concerns. Since children and their problems come in more shapes and sizes that we can count, there is no one psychotherapy that is so robust that it will be perfect for all children. This same limitation applies to the heuristic process in psychotherapy.

In order for the heuristic process to be useful, a child needs to question, wonder about his thoughts, feelings, behaviors, and any other important aspect of life. Obviously, children who are better able to do this will find this procedure more helpful. To the extent that a child is unable to question and wonder about important aspects of his life, this method will be less helpful.

A child's ability to self-question is dependent on several factors. Perhaps self-motivation is the most important. The more a child is self-motivated to overcome his difficulties, the more likely he will want to question and understand troublesome aspects of life. Related to motivation is the amount of "pain" the child feels. Generally, the more the child feels his distress, the more motivation he will have to find an escape from these emotional difficulties. Emotional pain often increases the child's motivation for change, and the child may become an eager participant in therapy. Unfortunately, some children may have an opposite reaction and try to avoid such distress through blatant denial or attempting to repress any awareness of problems. If a child responds in this way, he will not want to seek out questions or wonder about his emotional problems, and is likely to resist the therapist's attempts in this direction.

A child's symptoms also may hinder any attempts at self-questioning. Children may be too frightened to ask questions. A child's fears of the situations and feelings that underlie the problems may be so overwhelming that the child may shrink from any knowledge of emotional problems. For example, abused children often are afraid to explore their feelings about the abusing parent because they are frightened by their own negative feelings toward their parents. They may be afraid to learn that they hate their parents and reject them, because all children, even children with abusing parents, depend on their parents for their survival. It may be less frightening to deny their anger rather than face the fact that they would like to reject their parents and risk their parents' rejecting them. This may be too intolerable a situation for a young child to cope with.

Often children are too depressed and discouraged to use the heuristic process. If discouraged, they may feel that nothing will help, and they have no energy to go through a difficult and taxing self-questioning. The heuristic procedure is an active process and requires hard work from a child. Depressed children are usually inactive and may not have enough energy for such work. Angry children present a different problem, but one that can seriously interfere with the heuristic procedures. Quite often angry children do not want to cooperate with a therapist. They may have transferred anger from other important adults in their life and displaced it to a therapist. They may reject psychotherapy as a disagreeable intrusion into their time and activities, or there may be many other reasons, idiosyncratic to each particular child. Whatever the reason, uncooperative children will not allow a therapist to help them seek out questions about their life.

To a certain extent, cognitive level probably affects a child's ability to use the heuristic process. Asking self-questions is a creative process and requires the ability to detect and understand complex and abstract relationships. To best utilize the heuristic process, children need to have the cognitive flexibility to think of many factors in their attempts to answer questions. Highly motivated, bright youngsters require little help from their therapist in this process. Once they feel they can trust their therapist and have the security and self-confidence of a therapeutic relationship, they are likely to seek out questions spontaneously. They need only minimal therapeutic guidance to ask relevant and important questions. Children who do not have the same cognitive skills can utilize the heuristic procedure, but they may not be as facile in understanding relationships or in including the breadth of factors that are connected to emotional problems. They may not be able to generate the broad range of questions needed. The therapist may need to be more directive in guiding the child to consider relevant factors and in helping him see how one question leads to another. The heuristic process can even be successfully used with children of limited intelligence, so long as the therapist attentively guides the child in understanding the more complex aspects of the process.

Although intelligence and cognitive level can affect the heuristic process, it should not be given undue importance. The crux of the matter is whether a child has the ability to ask questions and find answers. To the extent that this is related to intelligence, it will have some importance. However, most children can and do spontaneously wonder about aspects of their life whatever their cognitive abilities, and if a child has this natural curiosity, then a therapist can help the child use the heuristic process. The therapist's ability to know when and how to help the child is just as important as the child's abilities.

This is only a brief summary of some of the factors that make the heuristic process difficult to use with certain children. In a later chapter we will discuss this in much greater detail and try to learn how a therapist can overcome these therapeutic obstacles. These problems are common to all types of treatment, and are serious obstacles to therapeutic progress. In another sense they are also opportunities because the very symptoms and personality traits that make a child resistant to the heuristic process are the grist of psychotherapy. To the extent that they hinder the therapeutic process, they become more difficult for a child to ignore.

For example, an angry child will be resistant to the heuristic process, but his anger is an important symptom and a key starting point to discovering the child's difficulties. This gives the therapist a good place to begin because the angrier the child becomes, the more obvious that anger becomes. With some sensitivity and subtlety (usually directly pointing out a negative emotion like anger only makes the child angrier and less able to self-question), the therapist can help the child become aware of the anger, even if the child can not give it up. Once the child realizes how he feels, he can hardly avoid wondering why he is so angry, and that is the first step in the heuristic process.

Perhaps we can best put the heuristic process in proper perspective by realizing that it is not a type of therapy or a distinct psychotherapeutic school based on a theory of personality. It does not deal with content and does not tell a therapist what issues are important. It is a very basic technique, a way of organizing interactions with a child that can be used with many different kinds of treatments.

Advantages of the Heuristic Process

Perhaps the most important advantage to using the heuristic process in psychotherapy is that it defines the roles and the tasks of therapist and child. This is especially important for a beginning therapist who is often unsure of what to do when immersed in the complexities of child psychotherapy. All therapists at some time or another become confused, and the heuristic process can give a therapist a focus and an overall goal that identifies where he is going. The goal is to bring children to wonder about what they are doing, thinking, and feeling, and to the extent that they are helping the child do that, then they are being therapeutic. They still have many choices to make about the content and timing of this questioning process, but even if the content is imperfectly chosen and the timing of when things are discussed imprecise, the heuristic process will eventually lead to the necessary therapeutic discussions and interactions.

The heuristic process also tells a therapist how to bring about therapeutic change in a child. Therapists often struggle with what issues need to be addressed in a therapy session and they often rely on one personality theory or another to identify these issues. Unfortunately, personality theories by their very nature try to explain and understand the behavior of all children, or all children in a particular culture. In other words they concern themselves with large groups of children, not individual children. If they describe and explain the behavior of many children, then we say they are good theories. The fact that there are so many personality theories and so much disagreement between them may indicate that they do not describe individual children very well. However, the task of a therapist is to understand one individual child or family, and since personality theories are not designed to focus on that one particular child or family, they may have a limited usefulness. A personality theory can give a therapist an overall orientation about a child or hints about what kinds of things to look for in understanding that child, but these can only be general guidelines and ultimately a competent therapist must understand the individual child she is treating.

In contrast to personality theories, which are very general and nonspecific, heuristic procedures are oriented toward discovering and understanding the individual aspects of a child. Children are relatively ignorant of personality theories, and their self-questioning will reflect their own individual feelings, thoughts, and concerns. To whatever extent the therapist can encourage and help a child engage in this therapeutic self-questioning, the psychotherapy will focus on the individuality of the child. Perhaps this is best illustrated through a clinical example.

> Dan, an-eleven-year old, was admitted as an inpatient to a children's treatment ward because he began stealing knives and hiding them under his pillow. In addition, he was frequently sadistic to his younger half-brother. He disliked his stepmother, constantly argued with and defied her, and purposely let his pet rat escape its cage as a way of frightening her. More seriously, he went into bouts of angry depression during which he would shout at both his father and stepmother telling them how miserable he was and how he deserved to die.
>
> Dan's natural mother had run off with his father's employer when Dan was three-years-old, and his overwhelmed and paternally inept father took care of Dan and his older brother by hiring a succession of women who lived in the home for periods ranging from three months to two years. One of these women moved in with her own daughter, who she openly favored, and when she left she took all of Dan's toys. Another was an older women who made it clear that she simply did not like children. When Dan was seven, his father remarried. His stepmother tried to "mother" him, but within a year she gave birth to Dan's brother, and much of her attention had to be focused on the baby.
>
> Dan's natural mother had not seen him for the first three years after she abandoned the family, but then she began to see both boys at infre-

quent intervals. When Dan was ten, she married a wealthy man, and when she did see him she showered Dan with expensive gifts. Dan's response was to idolize his absent mother and to hate his stepmother.

Relevant personality theories would correctly focus on the absence of a consistent early maternal figure during Dan's early years as the most important if not sole cause of his difficulties, but I doubt that any theory would be able to accurately predict Dan's particular problems and symptoms. Knowing that his difficulties were related to an absent maternal figure provided his therapist with an overall orientation concerning Dan's difficulties, but it did not tell her much about the specifics of treatment procedures.

Using the heuristic process, Dan's therapist led him to understand his difficulties in terms of the individual situations he was familiar with. Although there were many dimensions to his treatment, I will mention some that illustrate the progression of the heuristic process.

One topic that Dan was pleased to talk about was his pet rat. His therapist readily led him to wonder why he set his pet rat on his step-mother. Dan's answer was to discuss and reflect in his play his intense anger at his step-mother. The next self-questions focused on why he was angry with his step-mother, and this led to talking about what she did that made him angry. Next his therapist led him to wonder why she did those things, and, after trying to understand his stepmother, he came to question whether or not she loved him. In his answers, he came to realize that she did love him, and he spoke of the things she did for him, especially making him a special snack of Austrian pancakes with red current jam. This discussion led to the realization that his natural mother bought him special fast-food treats, but had never made any food that he liked. Now he began to question his mother's feelings about him, not in a general and abstract way, but rather in terms of specific things she did or said. He talked about phone conversations, a computer she gave him, not coming to his soccer games, and other details. This was Dan's way of wondering whether she loved him, but he never asked the question in that fashion, Rather, he faced it in terms of the things she did. Through many sessions he and his therapist dealt with the nuances of that question, and since it was too complex to have a yes-no answer, he answered it by coming to understand in what ways his mother did show her love, and in what ways it was inadequate. Despite some effort on his therapist's part, Dan never wondered why his mother had left her family. This was an issue of importance to his therapist, but not to Dan. He had already developed an understanding of his mother based on how she treated him at the present time, and their past was not an important concern to him. Of course, there were many other important aspects to their work together, but I have presented this brief vignette to illustrate the individually oriented aspect of the heuristic process.

I hope that this example illustrates that in the broadest sense, the role of the therapist in the heuristic process is that of a trusted teacher who gives a child the confidence to learn about himself. The therapist is not expected to provide answers or solve problems directly because the therapist's answers will not be as useful or as applicable to the child's situation. By helping the child ask his own questions, the child develops answers that are applicable to his own cognitive-developmental level, and these reflect the idiosyncracies of the individual child's life situation.

7

Emotional Aspects of Psychotherapeutic Treatment

The Role of Emotions in Psychotherapy

Emotions are at the core of almost all human experience and basic to all types of psychological treatment. But what are emotions? This may seem like an easy question, but it has occupied philosophers and psychologists since the time of Aristotle. Emotions are difficult to define and understand because by their very nature they are nonverbal. They are feelings, not concepts, ideas, or objects which can be accurately described by words. They are felt rather than spoken, and although we do have words that identify different feelings, we usually find this vocabulary imprecise and inadequate, especially when we attempt to tell someone else how we feel. Emotions are closely connected to overall bodily states, and we can understand emotions better from a clenched fist, a radiant smile, or body-wracking sobs than from an empty verbal description.

This imperfect relationship between words and emotions has enormous consequences for psychotherapy, and all forms of treatment have individual theories and techniques to overcome this problem. We have already pointed out that psychotherapy is a special form of conversation, and as such must to some extent rely on words. When therapists face problems that are emotional in nature, we must modify our verbal communication to accurately include emotions or find other nonverbal, emotionally based means of communication. This is true of adult treatment, but it is especially true of child treatment because there we have the added complication that young children are poor at using words. They do not have an adult's precise verbal skills, so communication in the area of emotions is especially flawed. A large part of this chapter will be an attempt to overcome this basic treatment problem with both children and adolescents.

We know that emotions are very powerful. At times they are so powerful they often override logic, reason, and even the desire for self-preservation. Intense anger, deep love, and profound sadness may in some circumstances bring us to voluntarily die in battle, sacrifice our lives for others, or take our own lives. The incredible power of emotions has a twofold importance for psychological treatment: It is both an ally in therapy, and the problem which makes therapy necessary.

As a positive force, emotional pain is what motivates people to enter treatment. Also, feelings alert people to things that disturb them, and so they help us identify specific psychological problems. Often identifying and confronting emotional problems produces a change in the nature of the emotions, and this change can result in new and more adaptive reactions. Sometimes, just confronting upsetting emotions can result in feelings of satisfaction. Thus emotions can produce a strong motivation for change, and this needs to be used as a therapeutic tool.

As a negative influence, emotions, in some form, are always a part of psychological difficulties. Adults usually seek help because they are unhappy, and parents bring in their children because they sense the child is unhappy. Even when children are referred because of chronic acting out, we usually find that feelings like anger or depression drive this kind of misbehavior. Thus for both children and adults, emotions are the basis of their problems.

Therapists of almost any persuasion agree that emotions are an important part of treatment, but, as we have seen, they are difficult to understand and even more difficult to use in treatment. They are, however, the most powerful treatment method that a therapist can use, and their importance necessitates that therapists need to try to understand emotions and how they are used in therapy, difficulties not withstanding.

Primary, Secondary Reactive, and Instrumental Emotions

There are many ways of categorizing emotions, but a simple system devised by Leslie Greenberg and Jeremy Safran (1987) seems to be especially helpful in psychotherapeutic treatment because it identifies what types of emotions are useful in psychotherapy and what kinds are negative and likely to create and maintain emotional difficulties. They identify three categories of emotions.

Primary Emotions

Primary emotions are the most basic feelings. They are the immediate, bodily sensed response to a situation or circumstance. Examples might be the flash of anger at an insult, the sadness on hearing of a friend's death, or the joy of seeing a close friend or lover after a long absence. These are adaptive responses to specific circumstances and are usually so powerful that we have no choice but to experience such emotions. We often experience these emotions as overwhelming and immediate. Even when they have occurred in the past, we feel as if they are happening in the present.

Anger, sadness, and fear are the primary emotions and experiencing these feelings is adaptive because it provides a child with motivational information and clarifies their thoughts. After children experience these kinds of emotions, they often feel better. For example, when a child experiences primary anger in a therapy session, she usually feels relieved. In addition, the child better understands why she is angry and how she can cope with the person or circumstance causing the angry feelings.

Experiencing sadness can also be adaptive. The cathartic expression of sadness through crying, even hysterical sobbing, often diminishes the sadness and leaves the child feeling cleansed. Feeling the sadness also helps the child correctly identify the source of the sadness and then the child is better able to find an adaptive solution.

Fear is a common childhood experience and although children typically avoid the fearful object or situation, experiencing such fear in tolerable doses can be helpful. When this is done in the safe confines of a therapy session, a child is likely to become less fearful and has the possibility of better understanding exactly what frightens her.

Usually, the expression of primary emotions is seen as positive by therapists, and they should try to facilitate such feelings. There are a number of benefits to helping a child become aware of these feelings. Aside from the benefits of a cathartic experience, children gain more information about themselves, providing both therapist and patient with more material for treatment. Children also learn that they can tolerate emotions, and that emotions need not be avoided. They see that expressing their anger will not drive people away, and experiencing pain may hurt, but will not kill.

Although, most primary emotions are positive and beneficial, some become maladaptive and must be treated. Many maladaptive emotions come about because a child learns an adaptive response to a pathological situation which becomes maladaptive in subsequent situations. For example, one of my patients withdrew from his schizoid mother because she would alternately be overly warm and caring toward him and at other times cold and critical. This boy's self-protective response was to become very angry at any sign of affection from her and try to shut her out of his emotional life. While this did give him some protection from her unpredictable behavior, such actions were not adaptive with other adults who did not act in such an emotionally chaotic way. In these situations, his constant angry outbursts in school and in my office were not helpful to him.

Another way in which children develop maladaptive primary emotions is when a normal emotion becomes associated with an inappropriate stimuli or social cue. Most young children are quite fearful of separation from their parents. This is a realistic fear which probably has had a long evolutionary history because children who become separated or are abandoned by caretaking adults will die. Often this fear of separation becomes linked to other cues, and, as a result, children develop phobic reactions to innocuous stimuli.

For example, a toddler overly sensitive to maternal separation may cry and become hysterical when her mother leaves the house. If the youngster notices that just before the mothers leaves a teenage babysitter arrives to take care of her, the toddler will begin to associate the sight of that teenager with the separation. As a result, the child may become hysterical at the sight of any teenager that enters the house. I experienced a similar situation when my oldest daughter was three-years-old. She had become very frightened by a rather gruesome Halloween mask worn by one of our neighbor's children. A few days after the incident, I mentioned to my wife that I was going to varnish the mast on my sailboat. Upon hearing this, Lori began to cry and say, "No mast, don't like mast." I could not understand why she was so frightened by a sailboat mast until I realized she thought I was saying "mask," and was reminded of our neighbor's Halloween mask.

Secondary Reactive Emotions

Secondary emotions are dysfunctional behaviors that are learned defensive reactions. They are attempts to avoid recognizing and coping with frightening and traumatic primary emotions. Usually, the secondary emotion is an attempt to cover over the primary emotion, screening it from conscious awareness and making it less disturbing. Unfortunately, the secondary emotion is not the real problem, but only a mask for the authentic feelings.

Secondary emotions can be very intense and upsetting, and often it is these feelings that bring the child into treatment. Usually, the child or parent believes these are primary emotions and, as such, are the authentic feelings creating the emotional problems. Secondary emotions can appear in the form of any of the many emotions humans experience: frustration, anger, annoyance, panic, hurt, despair, depression, hopelessness, among others. Often these feelings are difficult to identify as reactive emotions because they may seem like and be experienced as primary emotions. Greenberg and Safran (1987) state, "Anger, for example, can be a primary affective response to being violated or restrained, but it can also be a secondary reaction to underlying hurt, vulnerability, or fear. Similarly, sadness can be a deeply experienced sense of loss or pain, or it can be a secondary reaction to feelings of unexpressed or unrecognized anger or possibly fear."

Distinguishing between primary and secondary emotions can be difficult and often requires a great deal of clinical experience and sensitive intuition. Sometimes the therapist can tell a secondary emotional reaction by the fact that the child's attention can shift away from such a reaction more quickly than from a primary emotion. The best indicator is that the child is unable to work through such emotions and seem stuck with the feelings. That is because the emotion is secondary and the original feelings and problems are not worked on.

Usually, children will want to focus on reactive emotions because it continues their avoidance of the primary emotion. However, therapists need to avoid this because the repetitive expression of these feelings is not therapeutic and will not result in cathartic change. In this situation, the therapist must help the child become aware of the primary feelings and then focus on those feelings. Open expression of a blocked primary emotion is likely to result in a positive cathartic adaptation.

Sometimes, the reactive emotion is related to a negative self-concept. For example, a child may feel angry at the teacher when she gets failing grades. However, this is reactive anger, and the primary emotion is disappointment with her own efforts. Perhaps the child believes she is stupid or is frustrated by her inability to muster enough motivation for studying. A therapist must approach this situation in a somewhat different way. Before trying to make the child aware of the primary feeling of self-disappointment, he may need to reassure the child and protect the child from the strong feelings of failure. The therapist might focus on other adaptive emotions, which give the child a sense of reassurance and confidence. If this is not done, the child may avoid or refuse to acknowledge the primary feeling because it is too painful.

Instrumental Emotions

All emotions usually affect the other people in our lives. There is one category of emotions, though, whose main function is to change or manipulate our interpersonal environment because the expression of these emotions often results in some kind of positive payoff or interpersonal reward. Because of the operant nature of this class of feelings, Greenburg and Safran (1987) refer to them as "instrumental emotions." For the most part these kinds of emotions are learned early in life and become stable personality traits which are automatically expressed when the individual senses the right social cues. Usually, such emotions are designed to achieve some desired reaction from another person, but sometimes just expressing such emotions makes the individual feel more secure or provides her with a comforting sense of familiarity.

There are many kinds of instrumental emotions and many ways in which children use them. Children may act unhappy or even depressed to get the attention and concern of their parents. Every infant and toddler knows that crying is an effective way to get her parents' attention, but most of us develop other more appropriate communications as we grow older. However, for some children, crying may become a characterological unhappiness or even depression because this is an effective way of getting a desired emotional reaction. Often instrumental emotions are modeled from parents or other adults. In some families, depression is a way of life and the child quickly learns not to act happy when one of her parents is suffering. Of course, imitating the parent is very natural in such circumstances.

Using anger to manipulate others is a common emotional behavior. Sometimes children learn that their complaints will not be listened to until they have reached a certain level of anger. Some are not listened to until they have a full-blown temper tantrum. Whatever the nuances of the developmental process, children quickly learn that high levels of anger can be an effective way to feel powerful and get what they desire. Most children give up these maladaptive instrumental emotions in favor or more effective means. They learn that their parents do not react to excessive anger and that anger beyond a certain level results in punishment. Hopefully, they find other, more pleasant and effective ways to communicate needs, but for some children, especially those whose parents characteristically respond in inappropriate or emotionally disturbed ways, these feelings will become stable aspects of their personality.

Sometimes children manipulate with instrumental emotions. Guilt is a good example. A sixth grader I was treating would constantly disobey his parents overly strict rules about study time and sneak downstairs to watch television. He always felt guilty afterwards, but within a few days he would do the same thing again. I soon realized that his guilty feelings justified his actions and made him feel better. So long as he was guilty, he was reassuring himself that he was still sufficiently moral.

Usually, a therapist can identify instrumental emotions because they are feelings that have some sort of environmental payoff. When they are expressed the child gets some reaction from other people and then begins to feel better. Of course, a patient is not likely to want to give up such emotions because they work in the short term by obtaining a desired interpersonal response. The task of the therapist is to show the child that while such emotions sometimes are reinforcing, they have other unpleasant consequences, and, in the long, run they do not work.

Therapists should not try to encourage greater expression of instrumental feelings. Rather, they need to confront or interpret such emotions. However, these direct efforts usually are resisted by the child. A more subtle way to make the child aware of such feelings is to use the heuristic process and bring the child to question these feelings, especially their functional and operant aspects. Once the child understands the goal-oriented aspects of her emotions, she can then question whether there are more efficient and less distorted ways to get what she wants. This will lead the child to seek out alternate ways of obtaining her goals.

Another effective therapeutic technique is for the therapist to respond to such emotions in a neutral way. When the child expresses such feelings toward the therapist and the therapist does not go along with the emotions or does not challenge the child, she becomes confused. This hopefully leads her to think about the therapist's behavior and question her own.

Indicators of Emotional Conflicts

During every therapy session there is a continuous therapist-child interaction, and as part of that interaction the therapist is consciously and unconsciously making choices about what issues and techniques will be used. Every verbal and nonverbal interaction is designed to help the child understand and change dysfunctional emotions. However, before a therapist can initiate a treatment process to correct problematic emotional reactions, he must be able to identify those reactions and gain a reasonable understanding of them. Often this is not a simple task because, as we have seen, emotions are repressed from conscious awareness, overtly hidden from other people, distorted by outside circumstances and situations, and confused with other emotions. Yet therapists need to be aware of these emotional reactions if they are to develop effective overall treatment strategies and to modify their ongoing therapeutic interactions within a session. Detecting such emotional reactions requires a good bit of therapeutic experience, but there are certain signs that can alert a therapist to the presence of emotional conflict within children which therapists need to be aware of. The following is a list of such signs based in part on the work of Leslie Greenburg & Jeremy Safran (1987).

1. Children sometimes act as if they are reacting to some vague and undefined threat and a therapist may sense a self-protective attitude in the therapy session. They may be excessively reluctant to disclose relative harmless and innocuous information about themselves. Sometimes, they may seem reluctant to admit to an act or thought that fails to reach some excessively high self-standard. Usually, these children are attempting to avoid facing painful and disturbing emotions, and in their efforts to do so, they become fearful of disclosing any related information. Because they sense such emotional reactions to be threatening or painful, such a patient often seems tense and may have trouble making eye contact, clench their fists, or hold a rigid posture.

2. A common situation in treatment is the incomplete or unfinished expression of emotional reactions. Therapists must be alert for this problem. Often children may seem to work through an emotional crisis, but the experience is a bit too easy or ends too quickly. A child may even express the problematic emotion by crying or yelling, but often this is not enough and the memories and fantasies connected to the emotions will still remain to afflict the child.

> Quite some time ago I treated a 14-year-old boy whose father had died when he was ten. He was reluctant to talk about his father, but finally, during one of our early sessions, he told me about his father and the details of his death. Although he was appropriately sad, I had the feeling that we had not completely dealt with this traumatic occurrence. Through the next eight months we occasionally mentioned his father's death, but without a great deal of sadness.
>
> In the middle of one very ordinary session he began to recall the house he and his mother lived in when his father was alive (since then they had moved to a low-income apartment). Then he began to talk about his life before his father died. Slowly, as if he were there, idiosyncratic images of the time of his father's death came back to him. He recalled his mother calling the ambulance and telling him not to come upstairs. He remembered the flashing lights of the ambulance and men carrying his father out of the house. He could not recall who told him that his father had died, but he remembered his mother and unfamiliar relatives leaving him alone in the house when they left with the hearse to take his father to the cemetery. For the next two sessions I listened to these poignant, but profound memories, and only now was he was able to completely express his emotions about this sad event. Obviously, the initial session in which he told me of his father's death did not result in a complete therapeutic experience.

In this situation as in others the original expression of emotions was incomplete. Perhaps this occurs because the child still believes the feeling to be too dangerous for open expression. Some children believe that they will be overcome by the sadness or they will lose control of their anger and kill someone. Sometimes they just cannot let go of an old anger or hurt. Usually, an abstract cognitive description of a trauma does not lead to a complete expunging of the feelings, and usually the child will need to express the feelings in terms of the original situation. Often a complete therapeutic expression can be stimulated by a particular image or word. Of course the incomplete expression of emotions can occur with any emotion, such as anger or guilt, but it is especially common in feelings of sadness and grief.

3. Sometimes children seem to be focusing on an important emotional reaction, but in reality they are dealing with an unimportant aspect of their emotions. This is indicated when the child seems to go round and round on a subject, but never gets to her feelings. Another indication is when the child seems to lack involvement with the subject or becomes confused. This occurs because the child is focused around the subject and never gets to the essence of his feelings.

4. Another sign of dysfunctional emotional reactions is shown by conflicting emotional reactions to the same person or situation. A normal occurring example of this reaction is the toddler who is both fascinated and afraid of a circus clown or elephant in a zoo. A more pathological example is the child who lives in fear of an abusing parent, but still loves the parent. In a therapy session, children will show this splitting of emotions by making contradictory statements such as, "My dad gave me the car this weekend, but he just blew up at me when I was only ten minutes late." The word "but" is often an indicator of conflicted feelings.

Often conflicting emotions will be separated in some way. The child may choose to experience them at different times or one may be temporarily repressed. A therapist will need to be keenly aware of the sequence of the session to realize this.

5. Negative or self-critical statements are often a reliable sign of emotional conflict. Under emotional stress children are often very hard on themselves and are likely to become their own worst critics. They may even go to great lengths to devalue their efforts and accomplishments. These kinds of statements indicate that a child may be depressed and that there are maladaptive primary and secondary emotions that need to be addressed in treatment.

Parents, friends, or teachers may respond to such statements and the dysfunctional emotions behind them by trying to refute them or offering encouragement. They may argue, telling the child that she is competent or good-looking or athletic. They may remind the child of other accomplishments or times when they were successful. Some forms of cognitive treatment, such as those of Beck or Michenbaum, utilize encouragement in the form of positive self-statements, and they can be successful. However, such encouragement often only has a temporary effect or no effect and unless the basic emotional reactions are treated, the negative self-image is likely to remain.

The Therapist-Child Relationship Needed to Treat Dysfunctional Emotions

Open discussion and expression of emotional reactions are a difficult process for children for a number of reasons. Sometimes children are afraid of being ridiculed or not taken seriously for what they believe to be silly fears. They may withhold anger for fear of rejection or the guilt, especially if the anger is expressed toward parents or someone they are dependant upon. Adolescents may fear that if they express a strong feeling they will lose control and be overpowered by that feeling. Children may even avoid dealing with an emotion in therapy because they believe they will have to take some action that they want to avoid because it is painful or frightening.

We have already discussed some of the fears connected with this process. In addition to the fear and embarrassment directly related to the emotion, many children are uncomfortable with the open intimacy that naturally occurs when discussing the situations and circumstances associated with their emotions. In general, children feel vulnerable to criticism and rejection when they are asked to openly share their most personal thoughts and feelings.

In order to bring about a therapeutic treatment of affective problems, a therapist must create a certain atmosphere within their relationship. During their sessions, the child must feel safe from verbal attack and not pressured into disclosing embarrassing or sensitive feelings. The child should not feel the therapist is monitoring or recording her feelings, but rather that there is an open spontaneity to the session. Obviously, a child must not feel the therapist is judging what she is saying. To the contrary, a child ought to feel she is being protected by the therapist.

To create this atmosphere, the therapist must create a therapeutic alliance with the child, so that even if this is unspoken, both feel they are working together. They ought to have a therapeutic bond in the relationship, and we will discuss this in greater detail in a later chapter on therapist-child relationships. This therapeutic bond is necessary for the child to trust the therapist.

Along with protecting the child, the therapist must also help the child explore her emotions. This often is a delicate balancing act between confrontation and protection (actually confrontation is a poor choice of words as this process ought to be one of stimulating questions rather than confronting). However this is done, the therapist must be sure the process proceeds at a pace satisfactory to the child. There are even times when a therapist needs to slow the process to be sure that the child does not experience emotional reactions that will overwhelm and cause the child to refuse any further emotional exploration.

Techniques of Emotional Exploration

Most forms of psychotherapy include catharsis both as a healing technique and a therapeutic construct. Obviously, this is an important concept, but in spite of the collective importance given the term, it lacks specificity and, depending on how used, it usually refers to a number of patient activities and experiences. Generally, beginning therapists are trained that bringing about cathartic experiences is helpful, but they often need more specificity in knowing what to do.

Actually, catharsis, which emphasizes the experiencing of emotions, can be seen as one of three general areas which describe affective change. Another is insight, which refers to the discovery of new meaning to emotions, and the third is repression and similar psychological mechanisms which serve to keep emotional material out of conscious awareness.

In their work on emotions in treatment, Greenburg and Safran (1987) try to break these three general areas into specific and pragmatic treatment techniques which can be used with patients. They list four techniques of affective change which can be utilized in psychotherapy.

Acknowledging Emotions

We have already discussed the therapeutic effects of experiencing and expressing primary emotions, but often children are unaware of their feelings. Sometimes, such feelings are unacceptable to their self-concept, and sometimes they are too frightening. Whatever the reason, a therapist needs to help children acknowledge such emotions so that they can be directly expressed and the child can find a sense of relief. There are many ways to do this, depending on the child and the particular emotional reaction. These can range from the self-exploration of heuristic questioning to the direct confrontation of rational-emotive therapy.

In addition to the acknowledgement of their emotions, children also need to realize that emotions have what Greenburg & Safran (1987) call an "action tendency." This means that every emotion carries specific desires and wants, and a child must also recognize and experience this behavioral aspect of an emotion. This is important because most of the time just becoming aware of one's emotions is not enough. Children must fully experience the pain, the desires, the disappointments, and all the active aspects of an emotion in order to experience that emotion more fully. This is an important part of a therapist's work.

Emotional Arousal

Although awareness of emotions is an essential therapeutic process, it is not sufficient. To fully experience an emotional reaction, the emotion usually needs to be aroused and intensified. Through that process, the emotion is emphasized and the child is likely to experience the power of the emotion. This is what is usually referred to as a "catharsis".

Therapists can bring about increased arousal in many ways. They can be very direct and utilize imagery asking a child to form a mental picture of the emotional situation. For example, they can ask the child to picture a teacher yelling at her in front of the class when she does not have her homework. This would heighten many feelings, including a sense of embarrassment, fear of, and anger at the teacher. Such therapeutic imagery can be recollections of previous traumatic events or contrived situations.

Therapists can also encourage arousal by selective listening and focusing a patient's attention on certain events. A colleague who had treated a young man during the last year and a half of high school met with him again when he returned during his college Thanksgiving break. This very sensitive student told how lonely he had been and of missing his mother and sister while he was away (his mother was suffering from a potentially terminal form of cancer). Rather than being satisfied with this awareness of his loneliness, the therapist tried to deepen these feelings. This was done by first asking about his loneliness and then selectively listening as his patient told how every morning he used his calculator to subtract the date he arrived at school from the date of Christmas vacation to calculate how many days remained before he could go home. Then he calculated the percentage of time that had elapsed and the percentage of time remaining which he announced to his roommate. Listening to these and other activities helped him fully experience the sadness and worry of being separated from his mother.

Because emotional arousal is a technique that raises powerful feelings, a therapist must use this carefully and appropriately. This kind of emotional arousal can be overwhelming and should not be forced on an unwilling youngster. Obviously, timing is important, as a child must be ready to cope with such powerful feelings. Of course there are some children with borderline or schizoid thinking who cannot tolerate such intensification of their emotions. These children would only be frightened by such a technique and further withdraw from their feelings.

When done well, emotional arousal results in the emergence of new behaviors that are more adaptive and appropriate. The release of unresolved feelings allows clearer more flexible thinking and an ability to see new perspectives and alternatives. Now the child is better able to recognize other emotional reactions in herself, and may find a sense of happiness from the expression of sadness or a sense of satisfaction from the resolution of anger.

Taking Responsibility

Teaching children to take responsibility for their emotions is another effective technique for helping children. To do this, the child must come to see herself as the creator of the problematic emotion, rather the emotion being the result of some outside person or circumstance. Another way of saying this is that the child must own the emotion. Of course children are likely to see outside events as causing their emotional reaction, and to some extent they are correct. Certainly other people or circumstances do initiate emotional reactions, and to the child they are likely to associate the distressing feeling with the outside person or event. However, events are outside an individual, but the emotional reaction is the individual's response. To prove this point one only needs to remember that different people will have quite different emotional responses to the same event. Once a child realizes that the emotion is her individual response, then that child can see that her particular emotional reaction is self-determined, and, therefore she has the possibility of controlling that emotional response.

This technique is quite different from an intellectual explanation, which results in cognitive insight. Such explanations do not carry the same impact as an emotional understanding of a psychological event. While such intellectual explanations related to a patient's responsibility are an integral part of cognitive therapies, Greenberg and Safran (1987) maintain that in other forms of psychotherapy the treatment is more effective when it is emotionally based. They suggest that the intervention is most effective if done while the child is experiencing the emotion. In this way, any therapeutic discussion or symbolic play is more immediate and easier to understand. The child also can become aware of the process through which she is constructing the emotional reaction because she is experiencing that process at the very same time.

When emotional reactions have been present for some length of time they tend to become a stereotyped process that is initiated whenever the child detects a relevant cue. The technique of taking responsibility attempts to break that automatic reaction and allows a child to control her response. When children take responsibility for their emotional reactions, they realize they have the possibility of controlling the reaction and can choose what they will do. It is this sense of choice that allows children to transform their automatic emotional reaction.

> A colleague was treating a young college student who was caught up in this kind of automatic emotional reaction. She regularly told her mother about her dates because of her need to be close to her mother. However, her mother was a very intrusive woman and immediately began to interrogate her about intimate details of her sexual activities. Helpless in the face of her mother's persistence, she would reveal details of her sexual activities, but would also become irate and furious at her mother's intrusive questions. These interactions almost always ended in an ugly fight. Nevertheless, the pattern repeated itself over and over again in spite of the daughter's telling her mother to stay out of her life. In therapy, this young woman would become upset and constantly complained about her mother.
>
> Any astute therapist would realize that this young women's need for closeness was initiating the conflict, and if she simply stopped telling her mother about her dates she would not subject herself to such inappropriate intrusions. Her therapist was supportive and listened to her complaints about her mother, but she knew that providing her with

intellectual advice would do little to change her behavior. In this situation, the young woman needed to see herself as the creator of her angry emotional reaction and realize the implications of her actions when she was experiencing the intense anger at her mother. To do this, her therapist allowed her to become emotionally upset, and while experiencing this anger the therapist helped her to understand her own behavior and how that initiated the intrusive questions from her mother. This eventually allowed her to gain control of her resentful emotional reaction.

Reprocessing Incomplete Emotional Reactions

At times children form incomplete emotional reactions to traumatic situations, and this results in dysfunctional feelings. This comes about because the child finds herself in circumstances that result in a traumatic emotional reaction, but somehow this is not processed in the child's thoughts. Perhaps the child is frightened by the situation or her own emotional reaction. As a result, the situation is blocked or screened from conscious awareness. At some later time the child comes in contact with something that cues the emotion associated with the traumatic situation, and because the child has had an incomplete cognitive awareness of the experience, she feels the upsetting emotion without knowing why. Thus, the child has emotional sensations that are puzzling, confusing, and usually upsetting. They are confusing because there is no verbal representation to the upsetting emotion.

To deal with these kinds of emotional reactions, the therapist must help the child reconstruct the original situation and then, in the safety of the therapy session, reprocess the experience. The child needs to become aware of forgotten details, subjective feelings, and idiosyncratic reactions in the situation. This helps the youngster gain new perspectives that lead to a cognitive reorganization so that the full experience can come into awareness. Ultimately, the child can generate new response patterns instead of the confused emotional reactions of the past. This is best done by helping the child reflect on the original situation as if she was there. Sometimes imagery or connotative language are useful techniques to make the process more vivid.

Treating Dysfunctional Emotional Reactions Through the Heuristic Process

The heuristic process can be an effective way of implementing many of the techniques identified by Greenburg and Safran (1987), as well as being a separate therapeutic procedure in its own right. However, when dealing with emotions, the heuristic process must be modified in order to be appropriate to this nonverbal and complex form of behavior. Certainly, asking emotional questions which are nonverbal is very difficult for therapists who are comfortable and secure with words as a means of communication. But as emotions are nonverbal, so the therapist must utilize therapeutic means which do not depend on words. In these situations, questions must be felt, not asked. Even the term "emotional questions" seems inappropriate because questions imply a cognitive process. A better description of the therapist's actions might be creating successive emotional experiences. When done well, each emotional experience leads to another emotional experiences and eventually to an overall emotional understanding. Of course some emotional problems are readily communicated through words, and in that situation, therapists can use verbal means to bring a new awareness to a child which results in a positive change. Usually, this is easier for therapists since adults rely on verbal communication. Perhaps talking about emotions is most useful when the emotional situation is easily described and both child and therapist can easily undestand and communicate with one another. Generally, the older the child, the more a therapist can use this approach. It can most often be used with adolescents. The danger is that although the verbal communication may seem beneficial, such a discussion may not carry sufficient emotional power to produce needed emotional changes. Perhaps the crux of this issue is the theoretical orientation of the therapist, since cognitive therapists will more likely be verbal in dealing with emotional events, while psychodynamic therapists will try to focus on purely emotional responses. Of course the best approach is the one that best fits the child. The main point is that even when dealing with emotionally based difficulties, verbal communication is often needed and useful.

When the difficulties are primarily emotional, then the communication is best carried out through emotions. In some instances, a therapist attempts to bring about a behavior change or personality restructuring by using the emotional reaction that is the root of the difficulty. In other instances, the therapist might utilize a different, perhaps contrasting emotional reaction. The therapeutic use of emotions is a somewhat abstract, complex, and unfamiliar procedure, but the general rule is that a therapist should try to rely on the expression and manipulation of emotions, since this will have the strongest effect on a child. In this section we will discuss some of the different ways this is done. I ought to point out that while emotional questions between child and therapist are the most powerful and effective kind of communication, this is not always possible. Most therapy sessions cannot sustain such emotional intensity, and most of the time therapists have little choice but to use the usual verbal forms of communication. This is perfectly acceptable so long as the therapist continues to look for those opportunities in which emotional communication is more appropriate.

Stimulating Emotional Questions

When discussing emotional questions the term "stimulating" is more appropriate than the term "asking." Therapists are more effective if they are indirect in stimulating these kinds of questions and avoid asking direct questions. Since emotional situations are often frightening or embarrassing, a direct approach often results in avoidance of the issue or even downright refusal.

One of the best techniques is to guide the normal content of the session so that it focuses on emotional topics. This is done by inquiring into topics that are related to the emotional issues, or by the therapist showing greater interest or attention to those issues. This is a very simple technique, but very effective. By being selectively attentive to certain issues, the therapist naturally focuses the child toward thinking and talking about important emotional problems, and this is easily and subtly done by changing one's posture, using a more emphatic voice inflection, or making direct eye contact when the desired topic is mentioned. These techniques are useful in helping a child identify problematic emotional reactions and to intensify those emotions.

Another useful practice is to seek out other emotions that are dormant and not being expressed at the time. Often, these are contradictory or opposing to the expressed emotion. For example, a nine-year-old boy was angry at his mother because he felt she favored his seven-year-old brother. He felt that she took him to McDonald's more and insisted that they have the same bedtime in spite of the differences in their age. After being attentive to the child's complaints, his therapist also led him to question his positive feelings for his mother. Of course he loved his mother and was very jealous of her attention, and soon realized that was why he became so angry whenever she seemed to favor his brother.

In this situation, the therapist did not bring out the opposing emotion by directly asking questions or telling the child that he loved his mother. That would have probably been futile, since he was angry at her and complaining about her favoritism. Rather, the therapist nodded, agreeing that his mother was unfair. Finally, she said, "You must really hate her when she does that." This overstrong statement led him to say no, he did not hate her, and now his therapist asked, "Well, how do you feel?" From this point on she was able to listen to him describe both his negative and positive feelings, and with appropriate nods of agreement and other mainly nonverbal gestures, she was able to lead him into questioning both his loving and angry feelings.

Often one emotion will serve to hide another, and the heuristic process is useful in helping a child do this. Sometimes, these are secondary emotions which need to be reframed into primary emotions. In the preceding example, the nine-year-old boy was not only angry but also unhappy and feeling sad about his perceived treatment. He needed to become aware of those feelings. The therapist might have led him to his sadness by simply saying, "I think that you're not only angry, but also unhappy," or "Lots of time people are also unhappy when they're angry." A less direct approach might be to wait until he mentioned a specific incident, and then say, "Boy, I'd be mad, but I'd also be unhappy if she did that." An even less direct approach, but one equally effective, would be for his therapist to look sad and simply shake her head in sympathy.

Another effective way to bring out emotional questions is for the therapist to take on the emotion. This can be done by simply describing your own emotional reaction or what you think your emotional reaction might be. For example, one of my adolescent patients was told that a close friend of hers was killed in an automobile accident while driving drunk. She was very upset, and could not understand the senselessness of his death or the finality of the fact that she would never see him again. In an effort to help her to understand and accept this sadness, I told her that the hardest part of coping with my father's death was the realization that I would never see him again. For a long time I just could not seem to accept that fact, and I would sometimes catch myself wanting to tell him something or assuming he would arrive for a holiday visit. I did not so much talk about my father as about my feelings, and this sharing of our sadness helped her understand her feelings. Sometimes she would ask me how I felt, and seeing my emotional reactions helped her to continue to explore her own feelings.

Often a therapist can help a child deal with an emotional reaction by using her own genuine emotional response. Emotions are usually reciprocal in that seeing an emotional reaction in someone else can often bring out a similar or complementary emotional reaction in ourselves. This is easily seen in the following example of a therapist who spontaneously feels sad in reaction to her twelve-year-old patient's sadness.

> As the result of a parental divorce, a twelve-year-old girl lived with her father and seldom saw her mother. However, she idolized her mother and during the first session spoke of how much her mother loved her. She maintained this picture of her mother for a time, but slowly and reluctantly began to talk about ways in which her mother disappointed her. As she and her therapist spoke of her mother during one session, her profound sadness spilled out and suddenly she fell apart, sobbing uncontrollably. The raw sadness that came out was horrible to see; something like watching the terror of a small, lost child. Her therapist's first reaction was a look of shock at the intensity of her sadness. Then, as she felt the child's sadness, she simply said, "Oh Jen," and then fell silent.
>
> Although there were almost no words spoken, there was a very clear emotional communication. The look of shock on her therapist's face at seeing her uncontrollable sadness was a clear emotional commu-

> nication, as was the concern and empathy in her therapist's voice as she simply said, "Oh Jen." This was not a time for words or explanations, but for an immediate and spontaneous expression of how she felt. Her therapist's spontaneous look of shock stimulated her to wonder about her reaction and the depth of the feelings underlying them. Now she had some idea of the intensity of the many feelings of being left by her mother that she had been holding back for all these years. Her therapist's concern and silence at not knowing what to say told her that something was terribly wrong. Her idealized image of her mother, which she held to so desperately, could no longer hold back her sadness, and eventually, this would lead her to question this distorted view of her mother. In time, she came to question many of these feelings and beliefs about her mother, and found other feelings: feelings of sadness for all the happy times that she and her mother had missed, feelings of anger at her father for allowing her mother to leave, and even feelings of concern for her mother's lonely and empty life. In later sessions, she came to question these feelings, which led to many other questions concerning her family, and ultimately to a new understanding based on a more realistic assessment of her mother.

Another way a therapist can take on an emotion is to show the child your own reactions within a situation. A ten-year-old boy was referred because of his violent temper outbursts at home. His parents were divorced because of his father's uncontrollable temper outbursts in which he would verbally abuse his mother and the children. In his therapy sessions, this youngster was very reluctant to act angry in the slightest, and avoided any discussion of the topic.

During one session he and his therapist were building an intricate balsa airplane model, and his therapist became very frustrated when pieces of wood kept splitting apart. Rather than hide his anger, his therapist let out his feelings including a couple of "damns" and "This is driving me crazy," all said with emphasis, if not vehemence. The boy's reaction was to back off a few steps, and, with a fearful look, he carefully watched his therapist. Of course his therapist was appropriately angry, but unlike this youngster or his father, he did not blow up. All his anger was expressed with words, and in ten minutes the therapist was his usual self. This boy was astounded to see an angry reaction that was both appropriate and controlled, and he then began to tell how frightened he had been and what he thought his therapist might do if he "lost it." This led to a much broader discussion of how he and his father get mad and his feelings about being both angry and frightened.

Of course, therapists have to observe some cautions when showing their own emotions to a child. They must be certain that the emotional reaction will not be misinterpreted and that the child can tolerate such emotional expression. For example, the preceding example would be inappropriate and even destructive if the boy had become overwhelmed by his fear of the therapist's anger or if he thought that any open expression of anger was not permissible. In using this particular technique, therapists must be sure that the child does not have borderline reasoning or an psychopathic inability to control his or her impulses.

Another way to help children question their emotional reactions is to ask about the emotions that other people might be feeling. This can make them aware of emotions other than those they are feeling. By seeing and imagining how others are feeling, they can get a better perspective of their own feelings. This decreased emotional egocentrism can lead to a better understanding of their own emotional reactions and how their emotional reactions affect others. This technique sometimes is not effective with younger children because of their inherent cognitive egocentrism, but it is often effective with older children and adolescents. In the following example, I had hoped that the child I was treating would be able to see his own feelings through understanding the feelings of a friend.

> This twelve-year-old boy had managed to form a backyard rock band in spite of the fact that he had a difficult time getting along with other kids his age. One session he was very angry at the drummer, who had missed a practice, and he decided to throw him out of the band. He seemed unaware of the fact that originally he had wanted to be drummer, but had settled for playing bass. After talking about his anger at the drummer, I asked how he thought the drummer would feel when he found out that he had been bounced out. I also asked him to imagine what his reactions would be if he were the drummer. Although we talked about this for some time, he really did not seem to want to explore these feelings, and I am not sure that session was very productive. I believe, however, that the technique is useful, and I would think perhaps the way I did it was inept, or perhaps he just was not ready for that kind of intervention.

Since emotional reactions are difficult to question and explore, therapists need to be very sensitive in doing this. Certainly, telling a child that what he or she feels is bad is not helpful, since it usually results in the child clamming up and avoiding feelings. Even when such feelings are harmful to others or destructive to the child, an open expression of the feelings in treatment is the first step toward change, and any evaluation of the social consequences of the emotional reaction must come much later.

Also, therapists must not be too quick to reassure a child or tell him or her that everything will be all right. Therapists must allow children to feel their pain if they are going to make any therapeutic progress. Telling a child that everything will be all right or trying to make things better will tend to deintensify the emotion and make it less available for exploration. Why should children talk about their despair if they have been reassured by their therapist that all will be OK? Of course, reassuring children is a difficult natural tendency to fight. All of us have entered this work because we want to help children and cannot stand to see them suffer. Unfortunately, reassuring children too soon is short-sighted because it does not allow them to deal with their feelings and they do not learn their own ways of solving their emotional difficulties. Any reassurance must come after the dysfunctional emotions have been identified and fully expressed.

Therapeutic Reflection and Therapeutic Spontaneity

Emotions are a spontaneous form of human behavior that are usually an immediate reaction to a situation. If therapists are going to encourage emotional expression and exploration in children, then they must create and foster an atmosphere of spontaneity and natural interaction. The opposite of this kind of spontaneity is a reflective, thoughtful atmosphere wherein the therapeutic agenda is planned and issues are carefully evaluated. This kind of therapeutic environment is not appropriate when dealing with emotional issues. Unfortunately, this presents therapists with a dilemma.

All therapists use some kind of theoretical conceptual system to organize their thoughts and to understand their child patients. Since almost all theoretical systems are complex and highly cognitive, a therapist has to put no small amount of effort and attention into this process. In addition, a therapist needs to evaluate the child's activities and responses as they occur during a therapy session in order to understand what is happening. All these cognitive activities on the part of the therapist help to guide and facilitate the session.

Of course, all of this highly conceptual thinking detracts from the attention paid to the child and from the spontaneous atmosphere that facilitates therapeutic treatment of emotional issues. Children are less likely to freely express deep emotions when they sense that their therapist is somewhat distracted and tending to evaluate their very personal feelings and expressions. What is a therapist to do?

Unfortunately, there is no simple answer, but knowing the problem goes a long way toward finding the answer. Of course, each therapist must find his or her own answer, but all of us must come to some balance between therapeutic reflection and therapeutic spontaneity.

My answer is to err on the side of spontaneity. I prefer a very natural, age-appropriate kind of interaction with a child in which I try to talk and react without doing a great deal of analytic and evaluative thinking. I usually reserve this part of treatment for between session times when I am not distracted by the ongoing flow of a session and the pressure of fostering a natural kind of therapist-child interaction. There are, of course, many times during a therapy hour when I do analyze and evaluate the content of the session, but I tend to do this in a somewhat unconscious fashion. I think this kind of unconscious therapeutic awareness and analysis comes with therapeutic experience. A beginning therapist should not be frustrated or discouraged if she finds the process difficult.

One way to facilitate therapeutic spontaneity is to let the child direct the session, and I try to do this whenever possible. If the child is selecting the content, the session will tend to have a natural interactive quality and it is easier for me as a therapist to just follow along and be part of things. Of course, this is not always possible, for a host of reasons. Some children need their therapist to initiate important issues, some can't sustain their attention to important issues, and sometimes parental or school pressures require a specific and focused attention to certain problems.

A common mistake of beginning therapists (and experienced ones, as I sometimes catch myself doing it) is to try to force a discussion of therapist-generated problems when the child is not ready for that. This often comes out of the therapist's own insecurities. Therapists may feel guilty if they just play or chat with a child, believing that they are not doing their job. Sometimes, when there is a lack of progress in treatment, therapists become anxious or upset and try harder, which often results in forcing issues on the child. Sometimes, therapists just feel as if they are doing something wrong if they do not sound like therapists. That usually means they need to be talking about symptoms and interpersonal conflicts.

In fact, the therapist often needs to do exactly the opposite. When a therapy session seems to bog down or go poorly, the best thing to do is relax and try to enjoy the time with the child. This kind of child-therapist interaction is not a waste of time, but is usually productive. For one thing, it relaxes both child and therapist. The session may have been going poorly because one or both was anxious or uptight. If nothing else, this kind of relaxed, fun interaction will help deepen the therapist-child relationship, and, as we shall see in later chapters, that is a crucial part of therapeutic progress. It also makes therapy more enjoyable for both of them, and there is a great deal to be said for having fun, even in therapy sessions.

> I had a wonderful, if somewhat humbling example of this with a high school student I was treating. He was a youngster who had no friends because of his social immaturity, his poor self-image, and the fact that his interests were more that of an adult than a high school sophomore. He was reluctant to admit that he desperately wanted friends his own age, but he did. During one session I was trying to discuss his social isolation, but he thwarted my every attempt. Finally, he noticed the

laptop computer on my desk and began to ask questions about it. We discussed the computer for a while, and when he found out that I had an interactive computer game called "Hitchhiker's Guide to the Galaxy," he told me that he had used that game and asked if he could see it. After calling up the game, he insisted that I play it while he watched, since he was an expert. I was an absolute turkey at that particular game, having never even gotten out of the first room, which resulted in me and the rest of the planet being quickly destroyed by a Vulgon spaceship.

We spent a half hour with him laughing at my inept play and sarcastically offering me helpful hints, which did not stop the destruction of the Earth, me included, but did postpone it for a longer time than I had ever managed before. Near the end of the session he commented that his father would not be very happy to learn that we were wasting our time playing computer games. I responded that we seemed to be enjoying ourselves and I thought the time was well spent. He asked, "How so." I answered that usually I was the expert in our sessions, but for this session he was clearly the expert, and since he often doubted his self-confidence, that must have felt good to him. Our session ended talking about why he felt lousy about himself and how depressed he felt being ignored by all the other students in his high school. He clearly felt unhappy and embarrassed to admit that he was such a "reject," but expressing these emotions was very therapeutic for him. I doubt he would have been able to do that if not for the spontaneous activity of the computer game in which our roles were reversed. Being the expert to a "doctor" gave him some of the emotional strength to face his depressing situation.

This case study illustrates the advantages of flexibility and spontaneity on the part of a therapist. Often a rigid, excessively goal-oriented approach is not therapeutic; it constricts a child's behaviors and cognitive reactions and generates a stilted tone in the therapy session. Of course the degree of therapeutic spontaneity will be different for each child and how much is appropriate is an important decision the therapist must make.

8

Obstacles to the Therapeutic Process

By its very nature, psychotherapy is an optimistic endeavor. What could be better than helping children find a better and happier way to live? Unfortunately, it is inherently a difficult process because most children do not want to change to a happier and better life, and those who do still will have a deep-seated reluctance to change old familiar ways. Therapists view children in therapy as having symptoms that indicate emotional difficulties. To a therapist, a symptom is an aberration, but to a child a symptom is simply her way of thinking or acting. In short, it is just the way the child is, and since it is her ordinary behavior, the child seldom wants to change.

To children, symptoms are familiar, comfortable, and even logical ways to cope with their world. The idea that symptoms and emotional problems, in general, are logical ways of behaving may seem strange, but not from a child's point of view. To them, these symptoms are simply adjustments and compromises developed over time to survive in the youngster's idiosyncratic environment. Well-adjusted children may learn to share their toys with friends for a number of reasons. Their mother may have insisted, their teacher may have praised them, they may have learned that their friends will reciprocate, or a host of other reasons. Whatever the reason or reasons, this kind of sharing becomes familiar and natural.

The same process occurs with dysfunctional children, and their disturbed ways seem just as familiar and natural to them. The Spinabifida child walking with crutches may vehemently deny that she cannot play soccer because the pain of being different is too great. The learning disabled child who refuses to go for resource room help may not be able to face her inability to read. The socially inept child may find social isolation preferable to overwhelming and confusing peer interactions. Even the anorectic, facing a life-threatening blood electrolyte imbalance from weight loss, may find a schizoid-like distortion of her body image to be a satisfactory adjustment to overwhelming social and sexual fears.

All of these children have found their own solution to their world, and they perceive and believe their behavior to be perfectly logical. Even these simplistic examples do not begin to capture the psychological intricacies and self-deceptions that make such dysfunctional behaviors seem natural and familiar. Usually, disturbed children cannot see that such distorted behaviors, thoughts, and emotional reactions are poor solutions and short-sighted adjustments. They are not aware that in coping with one kind of pain they create other, more serious anguish; that what works at one age may cause many more problems later.

A most important point all therapists must grasp is that emotional symptoms are logical to children, and they will usually fight any attempts to change them. It is this unwillingness to change that gives rise to some of the most serious obstacles in psychotherapy.

Some children are reluctant to change because of what Irving Weiner (1975) calls "neurotic equilibrium." This describes the situation whereby other people adjust or even come to depend on the child's symptoms and emotional problems. A child may find these relationships very satisfying because they are predictable and ensure some sort of emotional contact. Perhaps the child's father finds some satisfaction in losing his temper in response to the child's misbehavior. Maybe being the class clown makes the child feel accepted, or at least tolerated. Perhaps the child needs to create family problems to distract her parents from their own marital difficulties. Whatever the reason, a child may sense that therapeutic progress will change these distorted relationships, ultimately alienating important people. Thus the child risks losing emotional gratification and even love. If the child is unhappy with the way she is, at least the child can count on how others will respond to her.

There are other kinds of therapeutic obstacles besides the child's own reluctance to change. Every child lives in an environment populated by important adults, and people such as parents and teachers can be a positive agent of change. They can also be serious impediments to treatment. All therapists must deal with parents, brothers and sisters, other family members, teachers, and all the other important people in a child's life. Many children find that their dysfunctional symptoms and disordered behaviors result in some sort of reward, and this "secondary gain" has long been recognized as a serious impediment to therapeutic progress.

Other therapeutic obstacles are the result of inherent communication problems between therapist and child. Every child therapist must be aware of the fact that the cognitive skills and conceptual beliefs of an adult are very different from the cognitive simplicity of an elementary school child, or even from the rapidly changing life of an adolescent. In this chapter we need to discuss the many obstacles to treatment, and how to deal with them.

Resistance to Change

We have already discussed the importance of emotions in the treatment of children, so it should come as no surprise to find that emotions also motivate many of the obstacles to psychotherapy. Emotions such as fear, anger, depression, and shame are important factors that cause children to avoid, or in many cases reject any efforts by the therapist. Of these emotions, fear is perhaps the most common obstacle to overcome.

Fear of Change

This is a very common resistance to treatment. Many theorists speculate that all fears are related to our earliest infantile fear of separation from our maternal caretaker, but whatever its origin, fear reactions are common and occur in many different forms. Usually, a child's reluctance to change in treatment is related to specific issues, and a therapist must identify and understand those issues if the child is to make any progress. Sometimes these therapeutic issues are easily seen; but at other times they are not readily apparent and treatment will be delayed in that area. There are so many different kinds of fear reactions, and they are expressed in such idiosyncratic ways, that we might even say there are as many types of fear reactions as there are children. As therapists, we can group such reactions into a few categories which identify the significant issues that must be dealt with in treatment.

Fear of Intellectual Incompetence

This is a common fear among children, since cognitive skill is so basic to our society. Schools not only emphasize and demand intellectual competence, they provide children with ways of evaluating themselves and comparing themselves to others in the form of grades. Obviously, children who do poorly in school are likely to be unhappy, have poor self-confidence and a poor self-image. The crux of the problem is the connection between poor cognitive skills and a poor self-concept. This is the issue that must be addressed in therapy because protecting one's self-concept will become an important obstacle to treatment. Children are usually relectant to face the pain arising from their belief that they are not as bright or talented as their peers, and so they will try to avoid confronting this reality. In the process, they may have developed many debilitating symptoms which will be difficult to deal with in treatment. The following examples show a few of the many ways a therapist can help a child confront her poor self image.

A colleague of mine treated a sixteen-year-old high school junior, Nancy, who was somewhat depressed and had rather precipitously rejected almost all of her friends. This effectively isolated her from everyone except one friend who was intellectually gifted, but who manipulated Nancy in a very domineering way. Throughout her school years, Nancy had been a marginal student who barely managed to stay on grade level in her work. At various times she was placed in remedial special education classes, but Nancy disliked these and often found ways to avoid going. In spite of her school difficulties, she maintained her desire to go on to college. As the work became more complex in her sophomore year, her school decided to increase the number of special education classes planned for her junior year.

It was at that point that Nancy rejected her friends and became depressed. In addition, she put a great deal of pressure on her parents to transfer her to a local parochial school, which they agreed to do, but also requested that she start seeing a therapist. In spite of her reluctance for treatment, she complied.

As you might expect, Nancy's reluctance for getting treatment was motivated by a fear of facing what she believed to be her intellectual incompetence. From her perspective she was afraid that she was "stupid," and she could not admit this to herself or allow her friends to think it. Needless to say, any direct attempts at bringing her to question these beliefs were thwarted. Interestingly, Nancy was able to admit to a very specific learning difficulty which she called an "auditory memory problem," a term she had picked up from one of her intellectual evaluations. This is an excellent illustration of how she was afraid of being "stupid" overall, but could accept a more limited deficit which did not have such global implications for her self-concept.

Since Nancy's depression and the self-destructive abandonment of her friends was a distorted attempt to cope with her poor self-concept, her therapist realized Nancy needed to face her "stupidity." She needed to ask herself many questions including whether she was stupid, in what ways was she "stupid," why she was "stupid," and a host of other related questions. The crux of her therapist's problem was that Nancy feared any change because she sensed that changing meant facing her intellectual incompetence, and that was too painful.

There are many therapeutic approaches a therapist could take with this girl, but in this situation her therapist followed two paths. First, he relied on their therapeutic relationship to give her the emotional strength to take risks with her poor self-esteem. As treatment progressed, Nancy developed an excellent relationship with her therapist, meaning that she trusted him and respected his judgment. Obviously, her therapist cared for Nancy and could see not only all of the wonderful human qualities we find in all children, but those qualities special and unique to Nancy. To her therapist, her learning problems were only one aspect of her being, and not a terribly important one in the overall scheme of things. Even if not directly spoken in words, Nancy could sense this "unqualified positive regard" or overall personal respect. Such basic respect gives an individual confidence, and with this "borrowed" confidence, Nancy was able to take risks. Timidly, fearfully, but inexorably she could allow herself to wonder about her school failures, her overall intelligence, and all the individual situations associated with this part of her life.

However, her therapist had to find an indirect path to her perceived lack of competence and that came through discussions about her domineering, intellectually gifted friend. Nancy would readily talk about this friend, complaining that she always had Nancy drive, went shopping at stores her friend liked, and basically did what her friend wanted. At first her therapist sympathetically listened to her complaints, but soon Nancy was wondering why she allowed herself to do these things. This led her to wonder about the differences between her friend and herself, and in turn, this led to talking about differences in their grades and overall intelligence. It was the start of a long process in which Nancy realistically questioned her competence in many areas relating to school and intelligence, and overcame this obstacle to her treatment.

Fear of Separation

Separation is a basic and common childhood fear, and most children will resist facing it if they can. Most forms of treatment "push" a child to confront such fears. The child; in turn, believes he is not strong enough to face such anxiety and thus is reluctant to try to change any existing symptoms. This is a common obstacle to therapy, and it is exacerbated by the fact that children are often embarressed by what they sense is immaturity on their part. The therapist's task in this situation is twofold. He must bring the child to confront the fear at a comfortable enough pace—a pace that will not panic the youngster—and he must provide the child with a sense of safety and security. In the following example, the therapist was able to use the safety of the therapeutic relationship as a means of helping to overcome a severe fear of separation.

Jon, a seventh grader, was an unhappy boy who readily complained to his parents about the many things they did that upset him. In spite of the fact that he was bored and unhappy at home, he tended to stay close to home rather than go off with friends and involve himself in the usual rough-and-tumble of afterschool play and sports. Even as a seventh grader he was reluctant to be independent. In therapy he was very happy to complain about his parents and his boredom, but was not willing to talk about his fear of being separated from his parents. This was not only embarrassing because seventh grade boys are not supposed to be babies, but it was also difficult to admit because that meant he ought to grow up and act in an age-appropriate way. In other words, admitting his problem implied change, and he was afraid of such a change. This was the obstacle to any progress in treatment.

His parents precipitated a crisis when they insisted that he go to an overnight camp for one month during the summer. This parental ultimatum presented Jon with a dilemma that was used to overcome his resistance in treatment. Jon habitually avoided talking about separation issues, but he could not avoid talking about the camp situation because he was so upset about it. In his therapy sessions, he coped with his dilemma by avoiding separation issues, but constantly complained about camp and his parents' cruelty. His therapist used his need to complain to lead him to consider certain questions related to separation.

This was done in a number of ways. First, they had to talk about the imminent horrors of camp life which deintensified some of his fears. They talked about using strange bathrooms, sleeping in one room with a group of other boys, getting poison ivy, not having a stocked refrigerator available for snacks, and other situations he disliked. Now, his therapist was able to bring what he would miss most about home, such as his bed, his computer, and his parents. This led him to realize all the familiar things he was tied to and how important they were to him, and then to question what made them so important and if they should have so much meaning that he could not do without them. They even questioned what life would be like if his parents went to camp and he stayed home. Of course all these discussions were focused on the central problem of his separation fears, but by starting out with a focus on the camp, they were able to avoid his initial resistance to his separation fears.

Fear of Social Maturity

Most children enjoy being with their peers, and from their preschool years on they seek out friends. They find that friends are fun in all sorts of ways, and they slowly learn the wide range of social behaviors that go along with peer interactions. Children who have not developed these skills early in life will have a difficult time because the social behaviors learned so easily at an early age come with great difficulty later on. The later a child tries to learn such skills, the greater the anxiety she feels.

Socially inept children face a difficult problem, and one that gets worse as they get older. The social skills that they must learn become more complex as they get older, and many children feel nervous, and even overwhelmed, at the thought of initiating peer contacts. Of course, there is reality to these fears because the rejection and humiliation suffered can leave emotional scars for many years. The fear of such rejection and the resulting avoidance of appropriate peer social contacts is often a difficult therapeutic obstacle when treating socially immature children.

> Josh, a high school freshman, is a good example of such a therapeutic resistance. In addition to many emotional problems, he was socially inept, had no friends, and little interest or ability in age-appropriate sports. Both of his divorced parents had problems being assertive with other people and were easily embarrassed. His mother, who Josh lived with, had one good friend, but apart from this friend she was socially reclusive. Although 48-years-old, she was so afraid of her parents' disapproval she never dated, afraid they would think she was being promiscuous.
>
> Josh thwarted all efforts on my part to talk about his lack of friends. Being a clever patient, he knew I hoped to discuss this issue, and he realized that the more we talked about this, the greater pressure he would feel to do something about it. Having no experience or knowledge about high school friendships, he doubted he could cope with the seemingly confident popular kids around him. As a result, any direct attempts on my part to discuss other students, social activities, sports, beer parties, or girls were effectively thwarted by his disinterested responses.
>
> I quickly gave up any direct attempts to discuss this and turned to other, less anxiety-causing issues. We spoke often of his frustration about his mother's overprotective ways, and his anger at his father who would continually show up hours and often days late for his visits. During these sessions, we developed a close relationship, and, as a result of my direct confrontations with his mother concerning her overprotective rules and his father concerning his chronic unreliability, Josh developed a firm trust in me.
>
> As often happens, Josh's fearfulness was too strong to be dealt with directly, but his newly developed interest in music was one of the indirect ways to circumvent his fear. Developing a social life involves more than direct socialization. At his age music is an integral part of socialization, and although his interests were in blues and old-time rock and roll, I knew this interest would eventually motivate him to share his excitement and satisfaction with others. Talking about his music did lead to discussions about what other kid's liked and how his tastes were different. Predictably, he criticized his peers for their poor musical taste. I agreed with him knowing he needed to be critical in his efforts to build up his own self-esteem. Eventually, this kind of discussion led to his

questioning other ways in which he was different from his high school peers and, ultimately, a critical analysis of his own reactions with them. After a time he began to realize that if he was to have friends to share his music (and by now other age-appropriate interests), he would have to change his attitudes. In reality, many of his critical attitudes were ways for him to cope with his fear of the other high school students. At present, he has begun to develop some friends with other low-prestige boys. I do not expect him to ever be part of a popular group (that is not important anyway), but now his fears are not keeping him from talking and asking himself questions about his social life or that of other students. Getting around this obstacle at least gives him the opportunity to decide what kind of social life, or lack of it, is possible.

Fear of Family Issues

There are any number of family problems that can result in therapeutic obstacles for children, and many children are fearful of discussing family problems with their therapist. Sometimes these may be very simplistic fears, almost like unconscious phobias and superstitions, and children are reluctant to talk openly about the family problem for fear it will come to pass. When children become furious with their parents, they may wish them dead, but they may be reluctant to discuss their anger in therapy for fear that if their angry thoughts are exposed, the parent may in fact die. In a similar vein, children may be very fearful of their parents fighting, yet they will not discuss the problem for fear that openly talking about this will cause their parents to divorce. This kind of superstitious human behavior is certainly illogical, but it is common in children, especially young or thought-disordered children.

Children are often fearful of bringing family difficulties into therapy as that is their way of protecting certain family members or family secrets. I once saw a yongster whose seemingly mild-mannered father would fly into rages and beat him, yet he hid this from me for more than seven months of weekly treatment. Most children are reluctant to bring family secrets into their therapy sessions because they are afraid to expose their family or themselves to the therapist. There are two powerful reasons for this reluctance. The first is a fear of being disloyal to the other family members, and then being rejected or punished for their disloyalty. In this situation, the ultimate fear is being expelled from the family, a very serious, perhaps even ultimate punishment. Secondly, children are afraid the family will disintegrate if they expose the hidden secrets. Here, too, the disintegration of the family will ultimately result in abandonment. In the face of these intense fears, therapists must expect that children will be loath to bring family problems into their sessions.

One way for a therapist to cope with such fears is to build a sound sense of therapeutic trust with the child so they then feel secure and protected enough to openly work on family issues. Another way is for the therapist to discuss the issue in an indirect fashion, thus helping the child deal with the fears, but not in terms of her own family. In this technique, the therapist might discuss parental abuse in the abstract, or have the child talk about a friend whose mother was mean and slapped the friend around. In terms of divorce, the therapist and child might talk about a classmate whose parents were divorced. These indirect approaches often allow the child to open up and soon talk about her own family difficulties.

> Harold was a sixth-grader whose parents had a nonmarriage in that, although they lived in the same house, they seldom spent time together and had almost no intimacy. In spite of their virulent dislike of one another, the parents seldom fought openly, but the arguments were bitter when they did. For the most part, a quiet silence characterized their marriage. Harold's mother was planning on divorcing her husband, "When the time is right," and so the entire family existed in this tenuous relationship in which nothing was directly said, but a family disintegration was imminent.
>
> Harold rarely mentioned his parents' difficulties, but on one occasion he told his mother that if she and his father divorced he would choose to live with his father because his father would need someone more than she would. Although the imminent divorce was only one of the issues dealt with in treatment, it presented a serious obstacle to treatment. Like his parents, Harold avoided any discussion of his parents' problems in therapy. Despite many efforts on his therapist's part to bring this out in the open, Harold acted as if everything were perfectly fine at home. Harold's therapist realized that Harold needed to deal with this problem as it was one of the reasons behind his angry outbursts at teachers and friends and his poor school motivation. Aside from the obvious trauma that all children suffer during a divorce, Harold was very confused. His statement about where he would live was not only a way of protecting his father, but it was also a way of solving a common problem of children in divorce. Who will he live with, and what would happen to him? In a way this was also Harold's problem, despite his attempt to hold on to some stability in the face of the disintegration of his family. His therapist wanted to discuss this problem so that Harold could explore his fears and prepare himself for whatever might occur. However, attempts to talk directly about divorce were easily avoided as Harold acted surprised and said his parents were fine since they did not fight.
>
> Realizing that direct confrontations could not break through such denial, his therapist had to find more patient approaches. Rather than dealing with his parents directly, the therapist dealt with other issues of

loss and separation. They talked about friends' parents who were divorced, the recent death of a friend's father, and a friend who had moved to a different state, always focusing on the feelings of the people involved and how they eventually coped.

Harold's comment about protecting his father indicated that his sense of security was threatened. His therapist knew Harold needed a kind of overall reassurance that there would always be someone to care for him. One of the ways his therapist did that was to reassure Harold that he would always be available to help with these kinds of problems. As they continued, the therapeutic relationship deepened. This, too, reassured Harold that he could rely on emotional relationships in his life.

The preceding four situations are only a few among the many different ways in which a child's fears will present serious therapeutic obstacles. Sometimes these fears will encompass many areas of a child's life and be very debilitating. But often they will be limited and specific to an isolated incident.

I was in the process of termination with a twelve-year-old that I had been seeing for more than a year when he told me that before he went to bed every night he had a ritual in which he checked under his bed and in his closet for dead bodies. Asked why he had never mentioned this, he said he was too embarrassed and it did not seem very important. At first he could not remember why he carried out the nightly ritual, but finally he recalled that it started five years before, shortly after his uncle died. Further talking revealed that he had been very curious about how bodies decomposed in a coffin, but this thought also terrified him. Eventually, he remembered he had been worried that his uncle's decomposed body was in his room, so he had to check before he could go to sleep. As you might expect, he gave up this phobic ritual shortly after our discussion.

This youngster could not bring up this isolated fear until the end of treatment for two reasons. First, he was embarrassed to tell me, and second, he was afraid that he might have to give up the reassuring ritual. Since it did not interfere with the other, more important issues in treatment, there was little pressure for this to emerge. Near the end of treatment, our relationship was so secure that he could risk his embarrassment, and he was strong enough to give up his ritual.

Activity Level as an Obstacle

Psychotherapy requires a certain optimum range in activity level, and children who deviate from this range present inherent difficulties. Low activity level is a serious obstacle in treating adults because depressed adults are often so lethargic they have little or no energy for treatment. The problem is not as common with children because children rarely suffer from an overt depression. In fact, it is so rare that DSM-III-R does not have a category for childhood depression. Typically, children handle depressive feelings in different ways, usually through acting out or poor school work.

Depression in children can affect treatment. Even when their overall activity level is high, these children have difficulty concentrating or even staying with a topic for any length of time. Such children cannot seem to sustain or focus their energy in treatment, which is similar to their inability to sustain motivation in school. They will often complain about coming to therapy and look for excuses to miss sessions.

In addition to depression, some children seem to have a characterologically low activity level. They may have a passive approach to life and lack the energy and assertiveness desired for most forms of psychotherapeutic treatment. Coping with this therapeutic obstacle is difficult because there is no therapeutic issue which, when resolved, will increase a child's activity level. Many therapists use attractive play activities to cope with this problem and better engage the child. Another strategy is to allow time to intensify positive aspects of the child-therapist relationship, which tends to engage the child more because the child is more likely to follow the therapist's lead. Usually, the therapist has to become more active with these children to compensate for their own inactivity. Often this involves modifying treatment toward some form of cognitive-behavior therapy, such as that of Beck or Michenbaum.

A more common problem is the high activity level experienced by children with hyperactivity, attention deficit disorder, or poor object relations. These are children who seem to be all over the therapy room, difficult to control, and almost impossible to focus on a therapeutic problem. If the focus of therapy is the hyperactive behavior, then Kendall's or Michenbaum's cognitive behavioral approach might be helpful. If there are other serious therapeutic issues to be dealt with, the therapist might begin with these treatments and then move to more psychodynamic methods as the child develops better self-control. Even when using a psychodynamic approach, the therapist will need to be more active and directive.

Treatment Noncompliance

Not complying or refusing treatment are common problems for child therapists due to the very nature of child treatment. Most adults choose to enter treatment, whereas adults, most commonly parents or school authorities, make that choice for children. Children typically live under the thumb of adults, and to a greater or lesser extent they fight this control. In fact, one of the most important tasks of growing up is to become independent, which means getting out from under parental control. This task becomes even more important during the transition stage we call adolescence. At that time, escaping parental control can take on the appearance of a battle royal, as many parents and teenagers know. Because of these very normal tendencies, children often will fight their therapist because they, too, are adults, and because they believe their therapist is another extension of parental control.

Characterological Refusal of Treatment

Aside from these normal tendencies to refuse treatment, there are other factors related to emotional difficulties that result in children refusing treatment. Most emotionally disturbed children do not refuse or try to thwart treatment, but some do. These children can be difficult to deal with because they have such a deep-seated characterological anger.

These children have many ways of showing their resistance to therapy. They may refuse to leave their parent's car or the waiting room. When in the therapy room they may refuse to talk or interact, just giving minimal yes-no answers to their therapist's questions. Some children may even become overtly angry, yelling and arguing about how they do not need to come to therapy and how they hate you, their therapist, because you are forcing them to be there. Children with such direct and persistently angry reactions to treatment cannot control their aggressive impulses, which often indicates that their reality testing and logical reasoning may be flawed. They may not be able to tolerate the close emotional relationship in psychotherapy. They may fear they will become too dependent, or have any number of other distorted reasons for their actions that have little basis in reality. Usually, there is some deep-seated fear motivating such aggression, but in these situations the aggressive reaction is so pervasive that the child only senses the anger, not the fear.

There is no getting around the fact that these children are difficult. Having had parents carry their child to my office screaming how much they hate me to a crowded waiting room is not soothing to my ego. Even worse is trying to engage a nonresponsive child who cleverly thwarts my every attempt at therapy. Of course, there is no one solution to dealing with such children. Since the reasons for hostility are different for each child, each one needs a slightly different approach. However, there are some general guidelines that are useful.

First, the therapist must realize that he is not the cause of the refusal and anger. It is the child's problem and an integral part of the reason she is in treatment. If the therapist has a personal reaction to the anger, this will only maintain it and potentially give the child a way to manipulate the therapist.

Second, overtly angry children can be successfully treated while they are angry, even if they remain angry throughout the course of treatment. Their anger is therapeutic material, "grist for the therapeutic mill," and can be effectively used as part of treatment. From my experience (and that of many colleagues), I have found that children who are initially angry and who stubbornly refuse treatment seem to have just as good a prognosis as cooperative children.

Third, because this kind of anger is characterological, the therapist must be patient. These are deep-seated emotions not likely to be given up easily nor to disappear as the result of some "magic" therapeutic intervention or new technique. Usually, therapists have an easier time dealing with children who are openly angry because, in spite of their negative behavior, they are responding to their therapist. Even children who refuse to talk at all are not too difficult to handle as they usually cannot keep that up for more than a few sessions. The hardest to deal with are the passively angry children who do not initiate anything and who only give minimal answers to their therapist's attempts at conversation or play. These children refuse to wonder about themselves or question their own behavior. Yet even these children can be effectively helped if the therapist is patient and refuses to succumb to the child's rejection. A child can sense when her therapist cares enough not to give up, and this realization cuts through anger. Hopefully, in time the child will participate in treatment.

Lastly, therapists need to gently but directly confront the child with the reasons why she needs treatment, despite her efforts to deny the situation. Since many of these children have somewhat flawed reality testing and defects in logical thinking, hearing a realistic description of their problems will help correct their erroneous attempts at denial. Of course, this will take time, and they will likely argue and deny what their therapist says. Even then, they need to hear the reality of their situation. In doing this, the therapist must be sensitive and not "bash" the child with a harsh assessment. For example, when telling this to a twelve-year-old who is in trouble at school for beating up other kids, a therapist should not emphasize the fact that the child is being cruel and nasty to her classmates. Instead, the therapist could talk about how such behavior gets teachers and other kids angry, which is why she gets in trouble. Spelling out the consequences and reactions is easier to hear and helps correct the child's distorted understanding.

Transference Related Resistance

Certain kinds of resistance to treatment are related to different aspects of the treatment process itself, and these need to be considered when treating children. Resistance can sometimes arise as a result of the positive and negative feelings that come out of the therapeutic relationship or transference reaction. This can occur in two different ways. Children often have positive feelings toward their therapist, but sometimes they begin to idealize the therapist and are desperate to be liked. As a result, they become oversensitive to the therapist's opinion, and they begin to censor what they say, making sure they do not say anything that would result in their therapist disliking or thinking less of them. Perhaps the child might even embellish what she says in order to attract more interest or approval. The end result presents an obstacle to treatment in that it impedes communication and the child is less able to analyze and question his or her own feelings and behaviors.

A more common reaction occurs when a child becomes disappointed with her therapist as the result of a negative transference. Perhaps the child wants more attention or closeness than the therapist can provide. Whatever the reason, a child in these circumstances is likely to become frustrated, depressed, and angry. Sometimes children will express their angry feelings directly, attacking the therapist with insults as a disguised way of saying they are cold and ungiving. This usually is not much of a therapeutic obstacle, since dealing with such direct anger is therapeutic in itself. These transference feelings often are simply another manifestation of the child's original problems.

Typically, resistances motivated by transference reactions are not expressed through direct anger. Most often children act out their depression by becoming sullen and silent, punishing the therapist in a more passive way. This is an effective way of punishing people, and it has an added advantage: Because the anger is silent and indirect, the child can easily deny his feelings. In this situation, the therapist cannot go along with the silent anger but must bring these feelings out in the open. In addition, the disappointment and hurt of the transference feelings need to be addressed rather than focusing only on the anger.

Resistance to Being a Patient

Another factor motivating refusal of treatment in children is what Weiner (1975) calls "resistance to patienthood." This refers to the stigmatizing effect of treatment. This is an important factor because children, especially preadolescent children, are sensitive to criticism from their peers. Many feel they will be teased or embarrassed if others find out they are seeing a "shrink." Children with poor self-esteem are especially sensitive because they often feel that needing therapy indicates they are even more inadequate and worthless than before. As a result, they try to refuse treatment to preserve their fragile self-esteem.

The most important way to treat this problem is to address the lack of confidence in therapy. Sometimes the therapist may need to directly explain that accepting treatment is not an indication of weakness but the opposite, because an individual must be strong to admit they need help. Also, strength is required to face the difficulties in psychotherapy, and they will become even stronger as a result of their treatment.

They also need to know that their participation in psychotherapy is confidential, that they have control over who has knowledge of their treatment. This topic will be covered in greater depth in a later chapter, but this ought to be arranged and told to the child in the very first session. This is sometimes a problem, as certain professions and certain states do not have legal confidentiality. Of course, the location of treatment is a factor. Children who are seen in a private office can maintain confidentiality of treatment, whereas children who are seen in their school building or another public area cannot realistically count on anonymity.

Normal Adolescent Resistance

Adolescents often present a kind of treatment refusal that is associated with their age and stage. They often skip appointments or show up late. Usually, this is not a real refusal of treatment, but age-appropriate and shows a normal desire for independence. Part of the problem is that adolescents are too old to have their appointments monitored by their parents, but many are not organized enough to keep track of these on their own. Typically, adolescents tend to be egocentric and so concerned with friends and social activities they simply do not keep track of responsibilities, appointments among them. This does not mean therapists should ignore the problem. However, a therapist must distinguish between those teenagers overtly refusing treatment for emotional reasons and those exhibiting the "emptyheadedness" of adolescence.

Resistance Due to Secondary Gain

Secondary gain is an old therapeutic term referring to the rewards and gratifications gained as a result of particular symptoms or emotional disturbance. This creates a problem for therapists because such rewards and gratifications motivate children to maintain their emotional problems. The benefits can occur in many ways. Adults may be more sympathetic, give less responsibilities, or even excuse inappropriate behavior because the child is "ill." Secondary gain seldom results in the development of new symptoms, but does cause a child to hold on to the existing symptoms. For example, the panicked crying of a school-phobic child is often reinforced when a parent allows the child to miss school that day. Some children become nauseous or develop an upset stomach to achieve the same end. Any symptom that can be reinforcing to the child will serve to become a part of the secondary gain situation.

I once treated an eleven-year-old boy who flew into fits of violent rage when he did not get his way with his mother. As soon as his anger escalated to a point that she feared he would be uncontrollable, she gave in, allowing him to take his older sister's things, buying him toys, and giving in to a host of other demands. Because of her own personality and family background, she could not tolerate his open expression of anger. Needless to say, treating this youngster was hindered because his rage served to give him all sorts of rewards and privileges that he could not otherwise obtain.

Sometimes this kind of secondary gain can become part of a disturbed symbiotic relationship with one or both parents. For example, a colleague told me about a ten-year-old boy who he humorously described as suffering from "Cinderella Syndromes." He had few friends, was a scapegoat by classmates because of his immature behavior, and did poorly in school, which he disliked. His mother, feeling sorry for him, allowed him to be dependent on her. She was oversympathetic at the slightest unhappiness, and even permitted him to sleep in her bed. However, she became depressed at times and used her son to cope with her own depression. When she had little energy she would stay in bed and have him wash the floors and iron the family's clothes. At other times she would go on impulsive shopping sprees in which she would take him out of school so he could carry her packages. In this case, the secondary gain of allowing him to be dependent on her was a price for his taking over when she became depressed and dysfunctional. Obviously, when this kind of secondary gain is enmeshed in parental and family dynamics, it will be much more difficult to treat.

Although the therapeutic resistance due to secondary gain can be a serious problem in treatment, it usually is not maintained over long periods of time. With most people, there is a limit to how long they enjoy being dependent and cared for, because accepting such dependence means giving up feelings of responsibility and independence. With children, secondary gain is even more time-limited for two reasons. First, since children are in the process of constant developmental change, their symptoms and needs change. What was a gratifying dependence at one developmental stage is rejected at a later stage. Secondly, most types of secondary gain are counter to normal development and children feel this pressure from their environment. For example, children love to miss a few days of school, but they sense that missing weeks of class is too great a violation of society's rules and they do not do that. Even high school students who hate classes, teachers, and everything connected with school do not try to get suspended (at least not forever). They have an uneasy feeling about such a flagrant violation, and realize it is not normal. Even very dependent children cannot continue to sleep in their parents' bed or cling to transitional objects beyond a certain age because the realization of their inappropriate behavior begins to outweigh the dependent gratification.

Obstacles from Outside the Therapy Session

There are a multiplicity of factors involved in the complex matrix of a psychotherapy session, and many of these are independent of the therapist-child relationship and ongoing psychotherapeutic discussions. These can include anything or anyone that exerts a significant influence on the child or the therapist's life. A therapist must be alert to assess how these outside factors can create therapeutic obstacles. The three most important influences in a child's environment are parents, school, and peers, and we need to discuss the many ways in which obstacles can arise from each of these categories. Of course, these are only descriptive categorizations and we need to be aware that grandparents and parental guardians can present the identical therapeutic obstacles as can the staff of a school or authoritarian institution.

Therapeutic Obstacles Created by Parents

Since this section is going to highlight many of the negative influences associated with parents, we must remember that most parents exert a positive influence in treatment. Unfortunately, child therapists can easily adopt a negative perception of parents. This usually arises from the fact that they both use very different conceptual systems concerning the child, and this difference easily leads to misunderstandings. Sometimes therapists need to remind themselves that parents love their children and are just as, or more, concerned about the child's therapy as the therapist. We also need to remember that parents initiate and maintain children in treatment, and a therapist will create therapeutic obstacles by having a negative attitude toward a child's parents. The bottom line is that except for court-ordered treatment, children are in psychotherapy by permission of their parents, and denigrating a parent is not a useful therapeutic strategy. With these cautions in mind, we now need to learn the ways in which parents do interfere with therapeutic progress.

Some parents tend to view the therapist as an extension of themselves or their desires for their child. In other words, whether they are aware or unaware of their behavior, they see the therapist as their agent, someone who will change the child to be the way they want. This creates problems for a number reasons. First, a child will usually resist a therapist who she believes is trying to enforce the parents' wishes. This is true even if the child does not have any particular aversion to what the parents' want. Children do not like to feel they are being manipulated. Second, what the parents want may not be what the child wants and trying to find another manipulative agent, the therapist, usually does not work. Third, and most important, what the parents want may not be what is best for the child. That is something that needs to be decided by parents, therapist, and child. Not only are parents often wrong in what they want, but even when they are right, the child may not be capable of the desired change.

One obvious consequences of this situation is that the child may dislike therapy altogether, and resist coming to sessions. Certainly developing a close therapist-child relationship will be difficult under these conditions. As a result, the child will not be free to question her own feelings and behaviors because most of the energy will be used in detecting and resisting the manipulation by the parents. Another consequence is that the therapist will feel pressured by the parents, and therapy is not effective under such pressures.

Sometimes parents retard therapeutic change by reinforcing dysfunctional behaviors which either maintains existing emotional problems or stops a child from developing more appropriate behaviors. Often, they are not aware of what they are doing, but at other times they are and simply cannot help themselves.

> One mother maintained her son's emotionally based stomach problems by only giving him attention when he was sick. His older sister was suffering from a chronic disabling disease which required all the mother's time and attention. Her younger son was in treatment because his nausea and ulcer-like symptoms were psychogenic in origin. Needless to say, the stomach problems were a good way to get his mother's attention because she could not ignore them, yet they allowed him a way to protest her lack of attention without seeming to complain about his disabled sister. The boy was not able to give up his psychogenic illness because his mother reinforced these symptoms with her attention and concern. Initially, the mother was unaware of how she was rewarding her son's symptoms, but she was able to stop when the therapist made her aware of her actions.
>
> I treated an immature and fearful high school freshman who was afraid to ride his bicycle farther than his immediate street. After some time he was ready to venture further and looked forward to riding to school and local malls. However, his mother thwarted this plan by forbidding him to leave the street and giving him automobile rides wherever he needed to go. Although she was aware of what she was doing, she continued because she could not overcome her worry about his getting hit by a car. This rewarded his dependence and confirmed his own fears about riding farther than his street. Although he was ready for a therapeutic change, she could not tolerate that, and it took a number of sessions with her before she was able to stop reinforcing his own fears.

A more serious therapeutic problem occurs when a parent disagrees with the therapist's methods. Generally, parents do not have a problem with the theoretical approach used by a therapist since they are not well-versed in psychotherapeutic theory and are content to leave that to the professional. Disagreements are more likely around specific issues, such as when a child should be punished, how to stop sadistic anger at siblings, or whether they should search an adolescent's room for beer or drugs.

Obviously, therapists are not always right and a parent's views must be considered. Actually, the issue is not one of right or wrong, but whether or not there is a respectful sense of cooperation. Therapists and parents can have disagreements, but when there are constant or irrational disagreements, this will create a therapeutic obstacle.

There are many reasons for such disagreements and these usually come about because the parents want to get rid of the annoying symptoms. However, they may not want their child to find a better adjustment if it threatens the family homeostasis or conflicts with a comfortable neurotic parent-child relationship. In other words, certain parents may want the child to change, but not to a normal adjustment. In other situations the parents may want to get rid of the problematic symptoms, but not at the cost of uncovering issues that are embarrassing or difficult for other family members.

In addition to disagreements on the way in which treatment is carried out, parents and therapists can disagree on the goals of treatment. Most parents want some version of a healthy development for their child, but the dysfunctional needs and irrational thinking of some disturbed parents color the goals they want for their child. Often, these parents will say they want appropriate goals, but then thwart their child's efforts in this direction. This especially comes up around issues of independence and control. Parents may know their youngster needs to become independent, yet they will fight age-appropriate behaviors with which they disagree. One common example occurs with friends. Children have to learn how to choose appropriate friends and in this normal process they will make mistakes. Parents might agree with this, but still try to choose their child's friends, forbid them from seeing certain kids, or put pressure on the therapist to force the child to change their friends.

There are some parents who are very inappropriate around certain issues, and no amount of intervention by the therapist can change them. In those cases, the therapist has the uncomfortable task of helping the child understand the inappropriate aspects of their parents' attitudes without having the child reject the parent. This is done in many ways, according to the idiosyncracies of the parent and child issues.

> The father of one patient was so controlling that he tried to interfere in every part of his son's life, telling him he should take more science courses, what books he should read, which friends were no good, and just about anything else about which he had an opinion. He believed he wanted his son to become an independent adult, but actually wanted his son to be like him. At times he tried to control his son's therapist. This boy grew up enraged at his father and oversensitive to anyone he thought might be trying to control him. As a result, he became explosively angry at anyone close to him and at normal authority figures. An important part of treatment was getting him to understand his father's problems and why his father could not change. He remained angry at

his father for a long time, but eventually was able to understand him. He still became furious when his father tried to control him, but his anger no longer intruded into all other areas of his life.

When there are disagreements about methods and goals in treatment, parents usually thwart therapeutic progress by consciously or unconsciously placing limits on what a child may bring up. For example, the child may be allowed to talk about certain topics, but not others, especially those that include the parents. Discouraging certain topics cripples treatment. How can a child engage in a heuristic questioning if certain questions are off-limits?

When treatment becomes too threatening, parents sometimes begin to skip appointments or even terminate treatment. In rare cases, parents will find quiet ways to sabotage treatment, sometimes encouraging their youngster to be noncooperative or subtly ridiculing the therapist or deriding the therapist's interventions. Some very insecure parents may quietly sabotage treatment because they are threatened by the close child-therapist relationship, and they need to reassure themselves that the child's therapist is not a better parent than they are. They may need to do this to avoid feeling they have failed and had to resort to help.

Dealing with parental obstacles to treatment is one of the most important and vexing problems facing a child therapist, and as always, there are no universal solutions. Each situation must be dealt with according to the particular idiosyncracies of the parent, child, and therapist. Certainly, the best way to avoid these difficulties is to establish and maintain a good parent-therapist relationship. This should be started during the initial meetings, and at this point the therapist can prepare the groundwork for handling problems.

I like to tell parents about the child-therapist relationship, adding that as treatment goes on, I may sometimes seem to side with their child. I do this because the child needs to feel important and because she is less powerful than the parents and usually needs such support more than they do. I also explain that what the child tells me is confidential. This also conveys the idea that I am not their agent and that the child's thoughts and feelings will be respected. Doing this at the beginning of treatment orients the parents and helps prevent problems from arising. When appropriate, I will remind them during later sessions, especially if I am going to have a joint meeting with child and parents.

When parental difficulties do arise, a therapist must think of it as another aspect of psychotherapy in that the parents' fears, insecurities, jealousies, and illogical thinking must be treated. The intervention will vary according to the situation, but one way or another the parents must be helped. Obviously, a therapist must try to avoid letting his own emotions intrude. Unfortunately, the therapist does not have the same close therapeutic relationship and that limits therapeutic effectiveness. The obvious solution is to try to build that relationship. Sometimes the therapist needs to schedule parent sessions to do this, while at other times family sessions may be needed. Whatever the format, the therapist cannot allow an adversarial relationship to develop and such sessions should not deteriorate into a polite struggle with each side trying to sway the other. Neither should such sessions become a negotiation. Like every other therapeutic endeavour, emotional issues need to be aired and dealt with and the focus must be the long-term development of the child. To do this effectively, a therapist will need to model cooperation and nonemotional reasoning for the parents, but if such parent sessions are treated as another form of psychotherapy and the therapist works within the limitations of the parents, then many parent related treatment problems can be resolved.

Therapeutic Obstacles Created by Schools

Because schools are such a crucial part of any child or adolescent's life, the attitudes and policies of teachers and administrators not only have an important impact on the child, they also can create difficulties in therapy. Of course, most schools do not create therapeutic obstacles but are cooperative and helpful in facilitating treatment. Over the last few decades, schools have begun to use psychologists as consultants and to hire school psychologists which has made schools more aware of psychological difficulties and how to help treat them. In fact, all schools do what they think is best for the child from their point of view, but that is the crux of the problem. Schools often have very different ways of understanding children than do therapists, and although both are trying to help children, differences and disagreements arise.

One of the most important differences arises from the fact that a teacher spends a great deal of time with a child, usually six or seven hours a day, five days a week, and they are very task oriented in their approach. Such actions as inattentiveness in reading group, bothering other kids in math, skipping class, or even smoking pot in the parking lot cannot be tolerated since it interferes with the purpose of school, namely learning. As a result, teachers tend to demand short-term behavioral changes. Compared to therapists, they are more concerned with the concrete outcome of an intervention, and this difference has been increased over the last decade with the emphasis on criterion-based teaching. This is in contrast to most psychodynamic therapists who, realizing that psychological changes can take a long time, focus on change in all aspects of a child's personality not just increased self-control. Therapists also tend to emphasize the process of any treatment intervention as well as the outcome.

Another clear difference is that teachers and school staff tend to be concerned with obvious emotional problems rather than more subtle emotional difficulties. Generally, they are sensitive to emotional difficulties that result in any form of underachievement, inappropriate aggression, and injury to other students. Due to their bureaucratic institutional nature, school staff and teachers are ultrasensitive to violations of authority and the destruction of school property. As a result, they overfocus on these problems and tend to be less concerned with children who are acquiescent and quietly unhappy. They often overlook students who are socially isolated or have subtle fears and depression that do not have a direct impact on their school functioning.

I knew of one high school student who was in therapy because of his social isolation and his borderline illogical reasoning. Even though he was a scapegoat to the tougher kids, the school did not identify him as a problem because his grades, though far below his capabilities, were average. The school took little interest until he was caught riding on the top of the school elevator. With this violation of school rules, they became active in helping with his treatment.

This difference in perception of emotional difficulties can cause problems to therapists. Since teachers and other school staff tend not to notice those children who have subtle problems, they may not see the need for a treatment intervention and be less cooperative in an overall educational-therapeutic plan. Often, this lack of cooperation can be overcome at therapist-school meetings during which the therapist can enlist the needed cooperation by explaining the child's needs and how the school can help. School personnel almost always want to help. When given reasons and told what to do, they usually become cooperative.

More serious therapeutic obstacles arise with those children the school personnel are concerned about, and again the crux of the problem is the differing needs and orientations of the parties. When a student becomes a problem for a school, especially an aggressive or disruptive student, the child's therapist is likely to feel some pressure to resolve the problem either from the school directly or from the parents who have been contacted by a teacher or principal. Of course, therapists need feedback from a school since this is not only helpful, but often essential. However, feedback is quite different from demands for the therapist to solve their problem. That can be detrimental. In some situations, the school can place pressures on the child directly in a way that thwarts the process of treatment.

> I had been treating an electively mute third-grader who had never spoken to any teacher or child in school. After seven months of treatment, he began to speak to me, but still did not talk to anyone at his school. At the first school meeting, both his teacher and the school nurse told me that we needed to be very firm and force him to talk. I discussed the fact that this approach had not worked in kindergarten, first, or second grade and explained my therapeutic approach. After politely listening, the teacher said she was worried about his passing because she was not sure how much he was learning. The nurse volunteered that perhaps he should not be in school because he did not talk. This youngster was

doing above-average work on all his written assignments and was even popular with his classmates. Clearly, this was an attempt to put pressure on me to somehow change him immediately, or, at the least, soon.

My approach was the opposite. I did not put any pressure on him to speak, but wanted him to understand why he did not talk, and this approach was beginning to be successful. I did not hear from the school for a few months, but the next message was from his teacher who wrote that she was going to recommend he be retained because he was failing oral reading. Obviously, a child who did not speak could not do well in oral reading, so this seemed another attempt to pressure both him and me. I scheduled another meeting with the school, and they agreed not to retain him. By the beginning of the next year, he was talking normally to teachers and students.

The pressure that a school can bring to bear on a therapist can take many forms. They might disagree with a treatment plan or seem to go along with it, but in fact sabotage any intervention. Sometimes they may say something cannot be done because of school rules. There are even times when a rivalry develops between school staff and therapist over who is more effective. Wise therapists will avoid this situation as it will only harm the child in the long run.

In some situations, schools, through their rules, attitudes, and expectations, will create problems that need to be dealt with in treatment. To the extent that this interferes with ongoing treatment, it presents a therapeutic obstacle. For example, some school systems with a highly academic orientation focus their efforts on educating talented children, and children with average ability are not as well-respected or given the same attention. Children who cannot cope with such expectations, or who are average in ability, usually have a difficult time and feel a sense of worthlessness. Often they become anxious, feeling they must learn faster or more than they are able. They do not fit in that school and these difficulties must be addressed in treatment. When a school creates a crisis, this can even shift the entire focus of treatment.

A high school sophomore who was being treated for his aggressive outbursts and lack of school motivation set off a firecracker in the school. It did minor damage to a desk, but the school felt it was dangerous to other students and a flagrant violation of school rules. The student was immediately suspended from school. The matter was then taken to the local school board and for a month and a half he and his parents waited for the board to make a final decision. Finally, they decided to expell him from classes and prohibited him from setting foot on school property for one calender year.

Rather than allow their son to go without any education for a year, the parents tried to find an alternative school placement, but two months went by before they could find another school for him. Needless to say, the content of therapy switched from understanding and controlling his aggression to how he would cope with this expulsion and where he would now go to school. For these months, the focus was on his constant worries concerning the school's decision and then the realistic anxiety of whether he could find another school to attend. Not only was the needed discussion of his poor school motivation and anger put aside, but later he was more resistent to trying to deal with these issues because of the fears they raised.

In certain situations, schools do not support or respond to changes made in treatment. Naturally, this will retard therapeutic progress. Robert Rosenthal (1973) documents this phenomenon in his work on the "Pygmalion Effect." He and other researchers found children who made noticeable improvements in intellectual level and achievement, but their teachers did not recognize these changes because they did not fit their prior expectations of the children. In some cases, the teachers' attitude toward the child became even more negative. Although this phenomenon is not widespread, and most teachers will be pleased and support therapeutic progress, it does occur and can be a problem with disruptive children.

I can remember one eighth grade boy who had made excellent progress controlling his disrespectful and disruptive school behavior. All of his teachers could see the progress except one, who could not give up her previous opinion. She continued in her attempts at heavy discipline no matter what he did, and the two of them fought throughout the year in spite of the fact that he had become a very well-behaved student in his other classes. Of course, this confused and vexed the boy, and we spent a good bit of time talking about the situation. In some ways, he learned a good bit about coping with disappointment and irrational perceptions of adults, but this was not crucial to his central personality problems.

There are times when schools can even create problems for child and therapist through their best attempts at helping a child. This can occur in many ways. I am familiar with many situations where a school instituted a behavior-modification program to modify different problem behaviors in school, but this failed because the behavior-modification plan was inappropriate for that child and his symptoms. The intervention was initiated with the best of intentions and required a good bit of effort, but the only result was an increase in anger and frustration on the part of teachers and student, and it caused more problems for the therapist who now had to deal with these new school-created emotional resentments.

Sometimes schools will insist on giving a child increased services or educational help when this is not wanted and inappropriate at that time. A friend treated a very bright youngster who was doing poorly in school because of a lack of motivation due to an imminent family disintegration. The school tried to help him with his poor grades by insisting he attend resource room classes. This only made matters worse. Being seen as different and a dummy by his friends allowed him even less motivation for school, and he did worse. Unfortunately, this took us away from discussing his family difficulties. The school would have been better advised to just simply wait, since he was a bright youngster who would easily make up the work when he had the motivation.

Peer Relationships and Therapeutic Obstacles

All children, even socially isolated ones, are deeply affected by their peers for the simple reason that peer relationships are important determinants of social status and self-esteem. Rejection by other children, whether it takes the form of being ignored, teased, excluded, or even physically beaten, has a very powerful influence on children, and a child will resist treatment if it brings the risk of peer rejection. This resistance or outright rejection of treatment can be a serious therapeutic obstacle because usually a child's fear of losing social status far outweighs his or her desire for treatment.

Age Determinants of Peer Obstacles

Sensitivity to the opinion of peers is roughly related to the age of the child and the peer group's perception of treatment. Generally, younger children up to the age of nine or ten are not dependent on peer group opinion, so they present less of a therapeutic problem. Latency age children between nine and twelve are the most difficult because they have a strong need for group approval. However, groups at this age are not known for their excessive loyalty to their individual members, and so latency age children often have a normal insecurity about their group of friends. In addition, the values of groups at this age emphasize competence, toughness, and conformity, and these are seen as antithetical to psychotherapy. The most serious violation of these values concerns competence. Many children view treatment as an admission that they have problems, and this is the opposite of the competence demanded by peers. They feel that to admit any weakness is to be a "wimp," and "wimps" become scapegoats in latency age groups.

Most forms of treatment emphasize a sensitivity to emotions because, as part of treatment, they emphasize recognition of feelings. However, latency age youngsters, especially boys, tend to ignore feelings, and it is not a common topic with their peers. Male groups are caught up with physical or mental competence. A boy who tried to talk about feelings would be teased or worse. Another common focus of many psychotherapies is the questioning of conformity, but this, too, goes against typical latency group values.

Adolescents present less peer-related treatment difficulties because important changes have occurred during the years that separates the two groups. The most important is that adolescent groups have taken on society's acceptance of psychological treatment, and they usually do not see it as an indication of weakness. To the contrary, many adolescents in treatment will discuss troubled friends, saying it is too bad they do not have the courage to face their emotional problems. Another factor is the greater acceptance of nonconformity. Although group allegiance is still very high and exclusion still a serious threat, adolescent groups tolerate and even encourage certain types of nonconformity. Except for certain male subgroups, most teenagers have begun to accept and value emotional sensitivity because individually they have experienced the adolescent upsurge of emotions and have learned to help friends cope with the multitude of both painful and pleasant emotions.

Generally, peer-related problems are exacerbated with children who are social isolates or have tenuous relationships with other children. Even though they seem to have nothing to lose because they do not have many friends, they are more insecure and especially sensitive to the idea that they will lose the little social status they have.

Individual Differences and Peer Obstacles

There are many peer-related treatment problems that are not associated with age, but are reflective of individual idiosyncracies. Most children with aggressive or acting-out difficulties seek peer support for their behavior. Friends often give their support for skipping classes, stealing, sexual promiscuity, and alcohol and drug use. Since therapists try to decrease such dysfunctional behavior, this puts them at odds with the child's peer group or peer sub-group. The same is true of rebellion against authority figures, which peers usually support (provided it does not overstep even their tolerant bounds), but therapists do not. Actually, therapists may tolerate and even accept such behavior as a therapeutic strategy, but they seldom encourage serious authority violations. In addition, therapists are usually perceived as authority figures and so a child will often reject the therapist and treatment as a way of following the dictates of his friends.

Children also may become concerned that their treatment will cause them to lose their friends. This has some basis in fact. As children change in treatment, their interests, values, and activities change, and they may lose interest in their old friends. Even worse, they may begin to question and criticize the values, attitudes, and behaviors of their present friends, and they may feel disloyal as the result of such an evaluation. A transition from one peer group to another is not easy, and many children can sense that they may have to face this problem if they change during treatment. Giving up old friends who are familiar and safe is difficult enough, but even harder is trying to become part of a new group. Children, especially adolescents, already have social positions and reputations which may make acceptance difficult. Also, some of the new group members may feel threatened, believing they will be displaced, and so they will make acceptance difficult.

A similar phenomenon is true of socially isolated children, because if they make interpersonal changes as the result of treatment, they may have to form friendships and become part of normal peer groups. In reality, this is not too difficult once the child develops the needed social skills, but during therapy the idea of such social contact may be overwhelming. The fears of rejection and embarrassment will be so anxiety-provoking that usually this will need to be addressed as part of treatment.

Therapeutic Obstacles or Therapeutic Opportunities

A chapter such as this has a somewhat pessimistic tone because it focuses on the many obstacles to treatment. But psychotherapy by its very nature is an optimistic endeavour. In reality, there is a bright side to this chapter because every obstacle to treatment presents a therapist with another opportunity for treatment. If we look upon therapeutic obstacles as another manifestation of the child's problem, then the obstacles provide the therapist with therapeutic material. As the therapist works to treat the obstacles, she is also treating the child's other problems. Therapeutic obstacles are only problems when they stop or interfere with the therapeutic process. But psychotherapy is so flexible a method that good therapists can usually turn a therapeutic resistance to their advantage.

> An excellent example of this process occurred with a thirteen-year old boy who had a very poor self-concept, was doing poorly in school, had only a few casual friendships, and was mildly depressed. Acquiescing to his parents wishes, he came willingly to his first three or four therapy sessions, but was only minimally cooperative. Near the end of one session he said he did not want to continue and did not see why his parents brought him in the first place. His therapist replied that what he mentioned was very important and they needed to discuss that at the beginning of his next appointment.
>
> The therapist knew he was sensitive about the social stigma his peers put on treatment and coming to therapy sessions exacerbated his already poor self-esteem. The next session the therapist brought up the

topic by telling him why he thought his parents had brought him to treatment, and then asked if there were any reasons he thought he needed therapeutic help. In a nonconfrontive way that valued his patient's opinion, he initiated a questioning process that tried to get the boy to question his situation and his dislike of therapy. Initially, he denied he needed help and told the therapist that everything was fine; that he was not depressed and had friends. As they spoke further, the therapist asked if he felt upset that his older brother was not only attending a fine college but was the star of the basketball team. His older sister was attending a top private school and was also a good athlete. This led to questions about why his parents had kept him in public school, and this in turn led to talking about how he was not an academic or an athletic star. He became more depressed as the session continued, focusing on the differences between him and his brother and sister. He seemed determined to talk anyway. By the end of the session, his therapist said they ought to talk more about whether he was as good as his brother and sister, and he readily agreed. In this situation, the boy was reluctant to continue treatment because therapy was a blow to his personal and social esteem, but his therapist saw this obstacle as an opportunity to reach the central problem of therapy.

Minority Children and Emotional Difficulties

The Effect of Minority Status on Children

Every therapist is aware that a child's emotional difficulties can have varied and diverse origins, but an increasingly common set of circumstances is associated with the children of minority groups. The United States has had a long history of immigration and the assimilation of foreign people; indeed almost all of us were immigrants at one time or another except for Native Americans. Ironically, they, too, have become a minority group. Since the arrival of the Pilgrims in the early 1600s, we have been the haven for many immigrant groups. In spite of this generally proud history of acceptance, our government and the established culture have often been insensitive to the difficulties of minorities and at times, outright rejecting. With the exception of Blacks, who were carried here against their wishes, most other immigrant groups sought out the United States. They usually faced very difficult problems maintaining their own culture and unique values in the face of an inexorable pressure to become "Americans" (Borstein, 1987).

Often, minority groups isolated themselves or were isolated in their own neighborhoods. This isolation was not only geographic, but vocational, social, and in hundreds of ways that reflected disenfranchisement. At various times in our history, the "melting pot" concept of America carried a positive connotation which helped children and their parents to accept the difficulties of existing in dual cultures. At other times, the political and social climate of the United States was explicitly rejecting. This was especially true for minority groups who were obviously different in terms of color, language, family style, or religious beliefs.

One exception to this pattern of minority rejection was the American educational system. Since the establishment of the first towns of our Pilgrim ancestors, we have insisted upon public education for all children, and this has been the primary means by which we have incorporated our minority groups (Leve, 1980). In spite of the unquestionably beneficial results of this system, it has and continues to create special problems for minority children. Because public schools as an institution reflect and promote the established culture, they often are at variance with the religious, social, and moral values of our minorities. This can have a profoundly disturbing effect on our minority children. Basically, they are asked to conform to two different cultures, and, as children, they are usually ill-equipped to understand their dilemma or the resulting confusion. As a result children often feel different from others and mismatched to their environment.

Schools are powerful institutions in the lives of children, and they are likely the strongest agents of societal conformity. Schools usually ignore the subculture of the minority children in attendance, and in both subtle and direct ways force assimilation through a middle-class curriculum and teaching style. Although schools are the most direct agents for cultural conformity, other day-to-day experiences, such as advertising, television, friends, athletic teams, also exert an inexorable pressure toward assimilation.

"Fitting in" for the minority child comes with great emotional costs. In effect, our minority children suffer a "differentness syndrome" in which the child is alienated from the important individual, groups, and institutions in his or her life. (Ramirez, 1991). Having to choose between cultures forces children to reject crucial parts of themselves. In choosing, they can "fit in," but they lose part of what Manuel Ramirez calls their "true selves." The end result is a loss of individuality, feelings of isolation, loneliness, self-rejection and anger or depression. Often the child is mismatched with both cultures and feels alone and misunderstood.

The greater the difference between the dominant culture and the minority culture, the greater the risk that a child will suffer a "differentness syndrome" and concomitant emotional problems. Manuel Ramirez (1991) has identified some of the common differences between modern American and traditional cultures.

1. Gender role definition: Traditional environments tend to emphasize strict distinctions between gender roles; modern environments encourage more flexible boundaries between these roles.

2. Family identity: Traditional environments foster strong family identities; modern environments emphasize individual identities.
3. Sense of community; Traditional cultural styles encourage a strong sense of community, modern environments emphasize individualism.
4. Family identification: Family loyalty and identification are emphasized in traditional communities while individual identities are more valued in modern societies.
5. Time orientation: People reared in traditional communities have a stronger past and present time orientation while people who are more modernistic are oriented toward the future.
6. Age status: Traditional societies associate increasing age with increasing wisdom; modern societies value the vitality of youth.
7. Importance of tradition: Traditional environments value traditional ceremonies as a reinforcement of history whereas modern value orientations tend to view tradition as a potential barrier to progress.
8. Subservience to conventional authority: In traditional societies people are socialized to follow norms and conventions and to respect authority; in modern societies people are encouraged to question authority.
9. Spirituality and religion: Traditional societies emphasize the importance of spirituality and religion in life events; modern societies are characterized by an emphasis on science and secularism.

The preceding list shows how pervasive the differences between traditional and modern societies are in the United States and give some indication of how profound the effects can be for a child. They literally touch every important aspect of the child's emotional life. Coping with such competing demands is a difficult task for many minority children, and a minority child, like any youngster, seldom has the flexibility to accept and integrate the demands of both cultures. Of course, negative experiences such as criticism from parents and family members or from teachers or other representatives of the established culture will decrease a child's flexibility and adaptability and increase the risk of emotional difficulties. Such negative experiences can come in many forms. The child may be called a "gook", a "nigger", a "dago" or some other racial slur. He may be criticized by his parents for wanting to hang out with his "American" friends rather than going with them to church. Conversely, he may be criticized by a teacher for missing school on a religious or ethnic holiday. He may realize the police are more suspicious of him than of his friends. Of course, he may feel a sense of shame because of his skin color, hair, or physical size.

The Treatment of Minority Children

The treatment of minority children is something of a paradox. It requires a unique and specialized approach especially sensitive to the needs of minority children and yet also relies on traditional therapeutic techniques and utilizes the concepts of traditional personality theories. In this sense, the treatment of minority children is unique. In addition, the therapist must accept special assumptions to meet the special difficulties with which minority children must cope. (Ramirez, 1991).

First, we must assume every child has the capacity for multicultural development and that full participation in a multicultural environment is an enriching experience. Second, the therapist must respect the child's multicultural origins and unique cognitive style. Third, we must assume the therapist also has preferred cultural styles and needs to become aware of this cultural style. Finally, treatment should include opportunities for multicultural growth and should encourage the child to take advantage of positive diversity challenges.

The treatment of minority children also includes special goals in addition to the therapeutic goals appropriate to that individual child. These are as follows:

1. Children need to recognize that they are victims of the pressure to conform and that this is not a problem of their own making.
2. Children need to overcome the feelings of "differentness" which are thrust upon them when they cannot or will not conform.
3. Children need to abandon the false self they have developed and become aware of their unique self.
4. Children should become aware of the individuals and forces in their life which have prevented them from enjoying their diversity and isolated them from many beneficial experiences in their life.
5. Children should try out new values and cognitive styles in the safe environment of therapy so that they can extend these new behaviors into their overall environment.

As in any therapy the first step is to bring the child to an awareness of the problem, and here the child must become aware of his feelings of differentness and mismatch. Such feelings are painful and children will tend to avoid or repress them, so the therapist must provide an atmosphere of security. The child must sense that with the therapist's help he is strong enough to confront such painful feelings and situations. A crucial aspect of this process is the attitude of the therapist. The therapist must be free of her own prejudices. These cannot be hidden or disguised because the child will recognize such biases and sense them as a threat. If the therapist cannot feel and communicate open respect for the child's culture, the child will not feel respected. Of course, the child needs a sense of safety and protection from the therapist rather than a subtle threat.

The key criteria here is whether or not the therapist finds value in the morals, religion, social patterns, and overall way of life of the minority group. If you cannot give an unequivocal "yes" to this question, then you should not take on the case. Being aware of one's prejudicial feelings is not a simple matter. Many prejudicial feelings can go unrecognized because we are so immersed in our own culture that we may not be sensitive to the issues of those from another culture. The very definition of what is a prejudicial attitude is likely to differ from one person to another. A therapist may feel secure thinking she has only enlightened and accepting attitudes toward her patients minority group, yet the patient or his family may see subtle aspects of prejudice in the therapist's attitudes. The real issue isn't whether or not the therapist is prejudiced, but whether the child and his parents feel their culture is respected. Because this is such a crucial aspect of treatment, Ramirez (1991) recommends therapists consult with multiculturally sensitive colleagues so they can be aware of any negative attitudes that might result in countertransference problems. Any such issues should be discussed openly with the child and the child's parents.

As the child begins to feel secure with the therapist, the therapist can begin to make the child aware of his feelings of cultural mismatch and differentness. This is often a difficult kind of confrontation because many of the issues will be sensitive and anxiety-provoking. For example, a child who is striving to be accepted by his nonminority classmates may not want to recognize the internal strain caused by his rejection of his cultural values. Such recognition may make the youngster aware of the still-powerful ties to his own culture, an awareness that will not only threaten his desire to be accepted by his nonminority friends but also may make the child aware of repressed guilt feelings for rejecting his own culture. Obviously, children do not want to face such complex feelings. They are more likely to prefer a simpler situation in which they wholly accept or reject. Nevertheless, the task of the therapist is to bring the child to a realization of the complexity of both their multicultural situation and feelings. This is a point when the heuristic process may help the child to question his feelings, emotional reactions, and behaviors, thus making the child aware of the cultural strain.

The next step in treatment is to help the child realize what is causing this cultural strain. Now the multicultural conflicts in the child's overall social, familial, and interpersonal environment becomes the subject matter of therapy. For example, a group of friends may be going to a baseball card store at the same time as an aunt and uncle are coming over for their usual Sunday visit. The child wants to go with his friends and be part of their group, while the parents expect the child to stay home and be part of the family. This situation provides a direct confrontation between the values of the minority family and that of the established culture. In therapy, the pressures on the child need to be discussed. The child will obviously want to go with his friends, but agreeing with the child misses the crux of the problem. The central issue is that the child is caught between two cultures, and he needs to realize that as well as identify the source of conformity pressures both within the minority family and the modern peer culture. The child may be buffeted by such thoughts as, "I'm letting my uncle down . . . I hope my friends don't see how old-fashioned my father is . . . I'm being too rebellious . . . I'm bad . . . If I don't go with my friends, they'll know I'm different . . . If I buy that rookie card my friend told me about, my father will think it's a waste of money."

When these thoughts and others like them can be exposed in therapy, the child can identify the sources of his emotional conflicts. Now the therapist can introduce the general concept of cultural mismatch so that the child can recognize other emotional conflicts caused by trying to satisfy the demands of two different cultures. This follows a somewhat cognitive-behavioral approach in that it provides the child with a cognitive understanding, an overall conceptual framework to use in recognizing and understanding mismatch situations. Generally, the concept of mismatch should not be introduced until the youngster has some sense of security in therapy and has begun to feel a sense of self-pride. In addition, the child should have overcome most strong feelings of anger, anxiety, and alienation.

The next stage in this process is making the child aware of the false self that has developed in an attempt to cope with cultural mismatch and the overwhelming sense of being different. Usually children will develop a false self in an attempt to cope with the many conformity pressures they are facing. For example, in an attempt to conform to perceived pressure from his modern peer culture, the child may reject all aspects of his culture of origin. Perhaps the child may object to his father's "old-fashioned" ideas or refuse to invite friends home because he lives in a two-family house and his grandparents live upstairs. In this way the child's false self rejects all aspects of his culture and accepts all aspects of the established culture, obviously a false and artificial discrimination. This leads to arguments with family members and an indiscriminate acceptance of people and things the child may not in fact like or want. Ultimately, such a false identity leads to unhappiness with aspects of the child 's life that cannot be changed.

When the child comes to recognize the false self that has developed he can then begin to let the real self emerge. The real self is the core personality that reflects the unique personal likes and dislikes of the child. The realistic personality is not determined by outside pressures to conform, either perceived or realistic. Now the child is free to accept or reject aspects of either culture based on his own desires, needs, and wishes. At this point the child can find value in cultural diversity which not only frees the child from emotional conflicts, but allows for an enriched and fuller life.

Children seldom enter treatment solely because of difficulties originating from cultural mismatch, however, these problems are often important aspects of the overall treatment of many children, especially as psychotherapeutic treatment becomes increasing available to our minority children. Our culture is still afflicted by such cultural stereotypes as men are better than women in science and math; tall, thin people are better than short, heavy people; light-skinned, blond-haired people are smarter than dark-skinned, dark-haired people. These and other myths fuel the emotional problems of culturally diverse children. In truth, few of us are able to fit these ideals, and to the extent that we allow such myths to determine the identities of our children, they will suffer the pain and anguish of an unsatisfied life.

Section III

The Content of Child Psychotherapy

At the very beginning of this book I said that for ease of learning and improved understanding we would divide psychotherapy into three aspects: process, content, and sequence. The chapters in this section deal with the second aspect of psychotherapy, content.

If process refers to "how" change occurs, content refers to "what" is done during treatment. In respect to child treatment, a therapist must decide what emotional and behavioral problems are to be treated and what techniques will be utilized. Content is a crucial aspect of treatment since it determines the focus of treatment, and each therapist and child must either directly or indirectly decide on this focus.

There are many ways for a therapist to identify a child or family's dysfunctional behaviors and emotional conflicts, and we will discuss how a therapist identifies these issues in chapter nine. Unfortunately, this is not a simple process and any therapist can be and often is easily misled into missing crucial problems. All therapists must rely on information reported by others and then must analyze and interpret this information correctly, avoiding intentional or unintentional biases and distortions. This is not an easy process. It is further complicated by the fact that the therapist receives information from many sources, parents, child, school staff, etc., each reflecting an egocentric view. The time dimension complicates the situation even further because the therapist must also decide on whether to focus treatment on present problems and issues or those from the past.

Chapter ten discusses play as a therapeutic technique which is an important determinant of therapeutic content. Depending on the child's age, play often is an important form of communication between child and therapist, especially because almost all emotional difficulties will show up as a distortion in play. In that sense, play is a means of communication, a medium of change, and an indicator of emotional difficulties.

There is little doubt that chapter eleven, which discusses the therapeutic relationship, is the most important chapter in this section. In most forms of treatment, the child-therapist relationship is the main motivating force for change. Without the security and trust inherent in a close therapeutic relationship, a child is unlikely to question his feelings and actions. Of course, the relational aspects of treatment are very complex and multifaceted, and these must be understood by any competent therapist.

9

The Identification of Emotional Conflicts

Obviously, therapists must understand the emotional difficulties of the children they are treating if they are to be effective. This seemingly simple process is rather complex in that it requires both the gathering of information from many different sources with very different perspectives, and the analysis and evaluation of this information. I suppose any and all information about a child is potentially useful, but for efficiencies' sake, therapists must be somewhat selective or they will be wasting their time, and sometimes too much information about a child can be overwhelming and confusing.

Gathering Therapeutic Information

In adult treatment (although I am hard pressed to give an exact dividing line between children and adults), we tend to seek out meaningful information from the individual adult and only to a peripheral degree do we look to outside sources. When working with children, the situation is different. We look to parents and other responsible adults as important information sources, sources that may provide information as important or more important than what we might learn from the child. Without going into a long discussion on social ethics, we need to realize that the key to this situation is the word "responsible." Our society, as do almost all others, dictates that parents are responsible for their children and, hence, they define their child's difficulties. Of course this varies with the age of the child: The older the child the more responsibility he assumes, and the more we allow the child to define his problems and trust the information that child provides.

Since parents or teachers usually decide whether or not a child has emotional problems and needs treatment, they are normally the first sources of information about a child. Only after these important adults have defined the problems, and in the process provided their information, do we then look to the child. This situation, of course, changes with age, and many therapists, myself included, reverse this procedure with older children and routinely ask to see teenagers before they meet with their parents.

We must be aware that the first information a therapist receives will usually give her an initial orientation or perspective, and a wise therapist should be aware of the possible distorting effects of such initial information, whether this comes from parent, child, or teacher.

Although a competent therapist continually gathers information throughout treatment, the information gained from initial meetings is crucial as it provides a therapist with her first orientation to the child and the family. Although the sequence of the initial assessment can be done in any order, it usually includes the following procedures.

1. Preparation by obtaining and reviewing initial information.
2. Meet with parents to obtain history, reason for referral, and assess parental characteristics.
3. Meet with child to assess child characteristics and establish rapport.
4. Feedback meeting with parents to describe findings and recommendations.

During the evaluation procedures there are many categories of information and many ways to obtain the information. In the remainder of this section we will discuss the more important aspects of the evaluation procedures.

Family Information

Because each source of information is different in terms of the perspective and the type of information provided, we need to discuss this issue to fully understand it. To reiterate, the first information about a child is usually provided by parents. They are a very useful source in that most (but not all) parents are competent reporters who provide relatively accurate information. Parental information is reasonably easy for a therapist to assimilate because they converse at a similar verbal level and the thought processes are also similar. Of course, they usually spend more time with their child, are likely to see a greater sample of behavior, and will know the child better than any other person. Children are likely to exhibit greater extremes of emotional behavior with their parents.

Inherent in these advantages of parental information are also disadvantages. The obvious disadvantage is that parents are emotionally involved in their child's difficulties, and they will distort their descriptions. Often, parents are part of the problem in that they are a partial or fundamental cause of their child's troubles. In some situations, parents are oblivious to their own part in their child's emotional problems, and such parents are likely to unconsciously introduce distortions by leaving out important information or overemphasizing irrelevant events. Other parents who are aware of their own inadequacies are likely to distort their account of their child because of guilt or fear of exposure to the therapist. This is such a common situation that an experienced therapist will automatically look for such distortions as it is valuable information and will be important in any course of treatment. I know of one mother who continually minimized her son's dysfunctional behavior with other boys. This ended months later when she confessed to the therapist that she felt responsible because she had dropped him when he was an infant, and she burst into sobs of relief when the therapist reassured her that symptoms such as his were unlikely to result from such a minor trauma during infancy.

Therapists must always be aware that to a great extent parents define a child's problem. In our society, parents have almost total control of what happens to their child, and despite advice from teachers, school psychologists, and administrators, they decide whether or not their child's problems are serious enough to warrant treatment. A therapist must understand that for practical purposes mental illness in children is defined according to parents, and she must work within those parameters. A therapist can and should try to educate parents when she believes the parental perceptions and decisions are in error, but the fact remains that the behaviors a parent reports as problematic will be filtered through their own concept of "mental illness." Obviously, the therapist needs to understand the way a parent defines emotional problems if that therapist is to be sensitive to the deletions and distortions of that parent's report.

Even inexperienced therapists quickly learn to see the differences between parents in their reports about a child. A father may emphasize certain behaviors and situations while the mother may dismiss these. Often they both agree on an event or circumstance, but one parent will see great significance in it while the other will have little reaction. Seeing such differences between parents is important for later treatment, and in itself is vital information in understanding etiological factors in the development of the child's emotional difficulties. This is especially true because whatever the treatment format, individual, family, group, or some variant or combination of these, a therapist must use such differences in her work with the parents and in the understanding of the child. In many cases, the distortions of information and differences among parents may be much more important that the original information. This is especially true because whatever the therapeutic mode, parents are directly or indirectly part of treatment. In the end, it is the parents that control therapeutic access to their child, so knowledge of a child may be useless unless a therapist understands the parents and can help them to support and continue treatment.

Another source of information is from siblings or the extended family. Many individual therapists tend to overlook such seemingly peripheral people, but family therapists are quite used to gleaning information from grandparents, aunts and uncles, or anyone who has close contact with the child. Certainly, anyone who lives in the same home can provide important data, and often from a new and useful perspective.

Sometimes people who do not live in the home, but have an important influence on the family or have a close relationship with the child, will be valuable resources. The uncle of one high school sophomore I treated was an important figure, even though he lived an hour away from the child. He was important because the child's father had died, and he became the primary person to help his older sister (the child's mother) make decisions. In fact, he accompanied the child's mother to all of our meetings and was a much more accurate and unemotional source of information about his nephew.

In a similar situation, a friend had been treating a seemingly autistic kindergartener for over a month when he became aware of a first generation immigrant grandmother who lived upstairs from the family. Upon further inquiry, he learned that she took care of the boy while the mother and father worked, which was the greater part of the child's day. When he had her come in for a session, he found that she was blatantly schizophrenic in her thinking and provided a terribly confusing and chaotic caretaker for the child. What appeared to be autistic behavior in the youngster was really total cognitive and emotional disintegration in response to his grandmother's distorted behavior. When she was removed as his primary caretaker, and he was enrolled in a structured day-care setting, most of his autistic-appearing behavior spontaneously disappeared.

An initial family session is often very useful and is especially valuable when it comes to the therapist's first contact with siblings. This introduction gives the therapist an opportunity to think about the emotional differences between children raised in the same home under a similar set of environmental conditions. Also, the therapist can see for herself the interactions between the children and the differences in the parents' response to each child.

Information from the Child

Utilizing information from children is a much more difficult task. Obviously, they do not have the verbal ability of an adult and, therefore, may be less able to communicate their thoughts. More importantly, children are more egocentric and lack the ability to step back from themselves and see themselves from another person's perspective. They are not able to abstract information and come out with generalized ideas about themselves and express these deductive ideas, as can adults. Thus, they do not give accurate or general self-reports, and in the case of young children, they do not even think about observing their own behavior. As a result, therapists must observe the behavior of children and do the abstraction and deduction. This observation of behavior, and subsequent analysis, is the crux of a therapist's diagnostic work and will be the subject of many later sections in this chapter.

As with parents, there are characteristic distortions and omissions in obtaining information from children. The primary one is that children seldom see themselves as facing emotional conflicts. This comes from their inherent egocentrism and the fact that they usually do not understand the idea of "mental illness." In addition, they are so oriented in the present that they do not really think of how things might be different because that requires a future orientation. Of course, older children are better able to comprehend this than younger ones. In younger children their problems are part of them and so well integrated into their identity that they naturally accept them. For the most part, they cannot and do not conceive of things being different.

Another factor to be considered is that children, like adults, may try to hide problems they are aware of. Whether through fear, guilt or embarrassment, they may not want their therapist to find out certain things about them, and they may do this purposely or without their conscious awareness. Avoiding or hiding problems is one of the more common therapeutic difficulties. Most therapist both expect it and have many ways to therapeutically cope with it.

Environmental Information

Every child lives in an extended environment which includes school, friends, and a complex community system. Every environment will be different according to geographic area, subculture, culture of origin, religion, and socioeconomic factors. Since each environment is unique, a therapist must know the child's environment well and understand how it affects the children she treats.

School is usually the most important aspect of a child's environment, and in almost all situations the therapist needs to know about the child's school life. The importance of school in every child's life can hardly be overestimated. By the time they are in kindergarten, or earlier if in nursery school, children spend a large portion of their day within this setting. More importantly, school should be looked upon as the "work" of children, and to the extent that they are successful or fail in school will have a great impact on their present and future adjustment. Certainly, it has an immense impact on a child's feelings of self-esteem and self-confidence, and rarely will you see a child doing poorly in school who does not have poor self-image.

The most common and clearly identified school difficulties are some form of discipline problems. In whatever form it occurs, whether fighting with other children, disobedience to the teacher, refusal to do work, or destroying school property, a school quickly moves to deal with this problem, and they have usually put their own disciplinary procedures in place before they turn to psychological help. Academic failure, whether through refusing to do schoolwork or due to learning difficulties, is also easily identified, since most schools have their own procedures and specialized staff to deal with the problem. A less commonly identified problem is the child who quietly withdraws from school life. There are many other typical problems and conflicts that arise in school, and a therapist must have this information in order to fully understand and treat a child's emotional difficulties.

When therapists are part of the school staff, they have little trouble obtaining this kind of information since it usually comes out in both formal staff meetings and the typical everyday teacher-therapist interactions. The more difficult situation involves outside therapists consulting with school staff members. I find that there is an inertia about such communication, perhaps due to a combination of the usual heavy time pressures of busy professionals and the institutional bureaucracy and formality of a school system. Usually therapists cannot be disturbed during their sessions and teachers cannot leave their classrooms, so even telephone contact can be difficult. Face-to-face meetings are complicated by the formal procedures and notifications that schools often must follow concerning Planning and Placement Team (PPT) procedures. As a result, school-therapist contacts are often overlooked, especially if school difficulties are not a direct focus of treatment. Of course, the optimal situation would provide for frequent school-therapist communication.

Generally, therapists are better off if they can establish direct nonbureaucratic communication with a child's teacher, since she is the person who knows the child best. A teacher knows the child's everyday behavior, and this is very valuable information for a therapist. If the child has more than one teacher, then the therapist needs to meet will all the teachers, usually in a group. That way the therapist can get more than one perspective. The difference in the child's behavior with different teachers is often instructive information.

Another benefit of direct contact with teachers occurs when the therapist wants to implement changes in the classroom. Usually, the teacher almost always implements any changes. If the therapist and teacher have had direct contact, there is less chance of miscommunication, and knowing the teacher the therapist will be able to tailor any interventions in accordance with the individual strengths and weaknesses of that teacher. Similarly, the teacher will be better able to give the therapist feedback on what will or will not work.

I personally prefer informal meetings with teachers to the bureaucratic PPT meetings, which include administrators, guidance people, and ancillary school staff. Although talented and knowledgeable people are always helpful, school administrators can sometimes inhibit openness in teachers, and the more people at a meeting, the more the information seems to become diluted and less specific. Face-to-face meetings with teachers allow for a useful kind of feedback and a more in-depth exchange of information about the child. Sometimes therapists may find it easier to talk with school psychologists because we tend to use the same language and conceptual framework, but they do not have the same intense contact with a child. Besides a good therapist ought to be flexible enough to modify her thinking and language to assure useful communication with teachers or any nonmental health professional.

Another area of important information concerns peers. I dislike the formality of the word "peers" since it makes me wonder if the child aspires to England's House of Lords, and I would rather think in terms of friends, best friends, and no friends. Obviously, the degree to which children have friends tells us a great deal about so many things: their happiness, their ability to communicate, their interests, their ability to share, and the way they are perceived by classmates. Knowing that a child has no friends, or is constantly rejected by others, will automatically identify certain crucial topics of treatment. Therapists need to know the quality of the friendships. Does the child have one or a few "best friends?" Children who have "best friends" usually are better able to share, have more open communication, and seek out and tolerate greater closeness than children who only have class or neighborhood acquaintances. A therapist needs to know other details, such as how long have they been best friends? What is the prestige level of the friend? Is he or she reasonably well-liked or a social isolate? Equally important is how a youngster gets on with friends. Are friendships marked by constant eruptions of aggression, and is the fighting a form of minor verbal bickering or sudden explosive physical attacks?

Unfortunately, a therapist seldom gets direct information about friends and the quality of friendships. Therapists rarely have access to a child's friends, and so they usually gather such information by asking parents, teachers, or their patient. Obviously, these sources are subjective and cannot always be relied upon. I remember one twelve-year-old telling me that he had many friends, and when I questioned him further, he proceeded to name off all the children in his classroom. Certainly, he did not even have the concept of what a friend was to include every child he knew. I later found out that he had no friends and was rejected by his classmates. Another very dysfunctional seventeen-year-old named his many friends, but I later found out they were all adults, such as his family physician, school guidance counselor, and some of the office staff at his part-time job.

Better and more direct access to such information is obtained if the therapist is part of the children's overall environment. Therapists who are staff members of the child's school or residential facility will be able to make their own observations of the number and quality of friendships and also have quicker and more detailed feedback from other staff. An easy way to learn about a child's friends and prestige is to obtain a class sociogram. To do this, the child's teacher asks each child in the class to secretly write down the two children they would like to invite home to play or talk to during lunch. A quick analysis of who chooses the child and whether or not those children have been chosen by others will provide the therapist with important therapeutic information about the prestige level and friendship patterns of his or her patient.

The extent of a child's participation in physical sports can provide useful therapeutic information. Generally, this kind of activity is a positive indication of psychological functioning. It indicates self-motivation, robust and socially appropriate interest patterns, the ability to cope with the frustration of losing, and, in the case of team sports, an ability to cooperate and handle the complexities of group interactions. Of course these are rather generalized concepts, but knowing the details of sport participation will be helpful therapeutic information. The area of athletics also can be a source of problems for some children because it demands that an individual hold together under stress and adversity. For example, issues such as lack of self-esteem easily can be identified in the context of athletics. In addition, coping with realistic difficulties, such as "win at all costs" Little League coaches and team cliques that exclude certain members, can be difficult but useful therapeutic issues.

Structured Evaluation Techniques

Another way of obtaining therapeutic information is through the use of structured methods, such as projective testing, self-report questionnaires, structured child interviews, and historical inventories. These are useful and efficient methods and have the advantage of gathering a wide spectrum of information. One possible difficulty in using these techniques is that they are directive. Usually, there are specific directions telling the child or parent what to do with little room for individual flexibility and self-expression. This may generate expectations that treatment itself will be similarly structured and inflexible, and a therapist may have a difficult time changing this "mind set." Such expectations are not a problem if the treatment chosen is similarly structured, but is more problematic if the therapist attempts to use any of the more flexible, client-directed forms of therapy. Often this problem can be circumvented by directly explaining that although completing this questionnaire or that test is quite different from the usual way of doing things, it will be helpful to the therapist. If the therapist gains the child's and parent's understanding, there should be little problem.

Projective Testing

Using tests like the Rorschach, TAT, CAT, Draw-A-Person, or one of the sentence completion tests, has been a traditional way for therapists to evaluate a child. Usually, these are given as part of a complete testing battery, but they must be administered by a skilled clinical psychologist since their value depends on a knowledgeable interpretation. Although there is a serious controversy about their reliability and validity within clinical psychology, tests are popular and well accepted. Projective testing has not been used as frequently during the past ten years because many therapists believe that eventually they can obtain the same information during their therapy sessions without the waste of time and increased expense. However, projective testing can generate valuable information, and is very useful in many situations.

Testing is often done by the therapist providing that he or she has the clinical testing skills. Many psychologists, however, believe any testing should be done by someone other than the therapist. If the therapist does the testing, the patient is more likely to expect treatment to be more structured and evaluative in nature, and, as I mentioned earlier this may become a problem for later treatment.

Historical Inventories

Historical inventories are ways of efficiently collecting historical and demographic information about a child and his or her family. These can be filled out by one or both parents and the child, if he or she is old enough to do that much writing. The therapist can also fill them out by asking the questions on the form and recording the responses. Although the latter way is more work, I prefer it as it allows the therapist to deviate from the "canned" questions to follow up on an unusual or clinically important response. Appendices C and D are good examples of typical historical inventories. Appendix C is completed by the therapist asking and recording the questions, and Appendix D is completed independently by the parents.

Structured Child Interviews

The structured child interview is an alternative to the more traditional nonverbal play interview which uses a spontaneous and experiential format. In a structured interview, the child is asked specific questions from a standardized interview form. The objective is to make a specific diagnosis. Although therapists need a wider range of information and are not primarily concerned with a simple diagnostic description, this kind of interview can be useful both in the information obtained and the fact that since the interview is the same for all children, a therapist can make comparisons between different children. A number of such techniques exist. The most flexible of these is the Child Assessment Schedule (CAS)(Hodges, Kline, Stern, Cytryn & McKnew, 1982), which has both semi-structured and structured forms. It contains approximately one hundred fifty yes-no questions and takes forty-five to seventy minutes to administer. The Diagnostic Interview Schedule for Children (DISC)(Costello, Edelbrock, Dulcan, Kalas & Klaric, 1984) and the Diagnostic Interview for Children and Adolescents (DICA)(Welnner, Reich, Herjanic, Jung & Amado, 1987) are two highly structured measures which have more than two hundred sixty questions in a yes-no format and take more than an hour to administer. There also are parental versions of these three techniques.

Self-Report Questionnaires

Self-report questionnaires are similar to structured child interviews, but they are completed by the child. In that sense, they look similar to traditional tests, but the needed language and reading skills obviously have been modified to be appropriate to children. Children can either read the questions themselves or have the items read to them. Usually these self-report measures focus on specific psychological issues, problems or diagnoses. One of the best known of these self-reports is the Child Depression Inventory (CDI)(Kovacs, 1985). This is a twenty-seven-item test derived from the adult Beck Depression Inventory. The child is asked statements concerning depression and then indicates whether or not they apply using a simple rating scale. This is only one of many depression-rating scales. Other self-report measures focus on problems such as childhood fears, trait anxiety, social anxiety, social relationships, self-esteem. A comprehensive survey of these is contained in Annette LaGreca's book, *Through the Eyes of the Child* (LaGreca, 1990).

Organizing and Analyzing Therapeutic Information

Now that we have discussed how therapists go about gathering the information they need in psychotherapy, we need to look at the second and more difficult part of this process: organizing and analyzing the information. For the most part, information is organized in levels ranging from specific facts to general concepts. Perhaps the simplest level is that of specific symptoms, which describe a child's problems in terms of actual behaviors. This is the level at which we see the most immediate and dangerous problems. These are the difficulties that, when severe, must be dealt with without delay. For example, I treated a sixteen-year-old anorectic youngster who was purging and refusing to eat. She had lost more than thirty pounds and was coming close to a life-threatening crisis. Obviously, I decided that the first intervention had to deal with her starvation, and later I would worry about the underlying conflicts that had contributed to this dangerous situation. In this case, the symptoms of the eating disorder represented an obvious, but crucial, level of therapeutic information, and one which could not be ignored.

At the next level of information gathering the therapist looks beyond the immediate behaviors to seek out localized conflicts within the youngster's immediate environment. This level of information reflects fairly recent emotional conflicts that cause the symptoms. Such causal conflicts might be conflicts with parents, siblings, friends, teachers, and members of the extended family. For example, my anorexic patient was extremely sensitive to the opinion of her boyfriend, believing that he would break up with her because she was too fat. She also felt that her friends were thinner and better-looking than she was and her anorexia was a form of competition with them. Obviously, her anorectic symptoms were a way of reassuring herself that her boyfriend would not leave her and that she was as thin and beautiful as her girlfriends. Anything that threatened her self-image would be defended against. These social conflicts were basic to her symptoms and provided me with another, more causal level of information. Because these conflicts were a serious problem in their own right and an important factor in her anorexia, they required serious exploration in our psychotherapy sessions. Usually, children are reluctant to recognize these kinds of conflicts, so we often see defenses and resistances at this level of analysis.

Deeper conflicts are those reflecting general and stable personality characteristics. On this level we tend not to define an interpersonal conflict in terms of specific behaviors, but we use words like aggressive tendencies, depression, and social anxieties. On this level, therapists are almost always using some sort of theoretical framework to sift and sort their ideas about a child. In the case of my anorexic patient, she was a very insecure girl whose poor self-concept stemmed from disappointments early in her life. The effect of this poor self-concept waxed or waned depending on what her friends and her mother said. Her poor self-concept is a good example of a deeper level of emotional conflict because it has become an entrenched personality characteristic resulting from difficulties early in her development. On this level, the theoretical orientation of the therapist is important because most personality theories postulate different aspects of early development to explain such problems as poor self-concept. In turn, the theoretical orientation of the therapist will affect the analysis and therapeutic use of this level of information.

Theories and Therapeutic Information

We have already discussed the fact that theories are useful because they help therapists analyze and put meaning to the huge number of discrete facts they gather during the evaluation procedure. Of course, evaluation is not limited to the beginning phases of treatment, but is an ongoing process. Theories provide a framework within which therapists can organize their thoughts which might otherwise deteriorate into confusion given the complexity and multidimensionality of a child's life. Of course, there are many, many theories, each providing a different framework for organizing information and each tending to focus on and highlight a particular area or aspect of functioning. Most personality theories emphasize some aspect of development. For example, Daniel Stern's theory emphasizes the developmental processes during infancy. Classical psychoanalysis focuses on psychosexual development during childhood. Erik Erikson's theory emphasizes the adjustment tasks of ego development through different stages across the entire life span.

Other theories tend to ignore the developmental process and focus on behavioral or social interactions. Thus, operant behavior therapy highlights environmental contingencies and how they determine behavior. Person-centered theory focuses a therapist on the self-corrective tendencies of a patient. Certain cognitive theories focus on defects in the logical thinking of a child.

Each theory tends to have a specific time orientation and inherently directs therapists to organize their information in accordance with that time focus. Freud and most of the classical psychoanalytic theorists focus on the past in that they look for personality determinants in the early years of life. Daniel Stern and other object relations theorists go even further back and orient a therapist toward the psychosocial interactions of infancy. Karen Horney and others seem to go as far back as possible by emphasizing the traumatic experience of birth. Actually, some of Carl Jung's ideas go beyond birth and focus a therapist on the archetypal ancestors of their patients. Most other psychodynamic theories also have a past-time orientation, but a limited past in that they concern themselves with recent child-parent interactions and interpersonal conflicts. For example, the psychodynamic conflicts arising from a child's reaction to his alcoholic father are relatively recent difficulties in that the problems may be a few years old. Similarly, the causes of a child being isolated by his classmates are likely to be only a few years old.

Behavior therapies, both operant and respondent, are oriented toward the present. They deal with contemporary problems and sometimes purposefully ignore past developmental information as a distraction. For example, behavioral contracts which attempt to control aggressive classroom behavior are concerned with current dysfunctional activity and do not attempt to target last year's or even last month's behavior. Most cognitive theories are also present-oriented, but because they deal with maladaptive interactions, they include some events from the recent past so long as they are relevant to present difficulties.

No theories deal directly with the future, since a therapist would have to be a wizard to obtain and organize information about events that have not yet occurred. However, some therapies have a future orientation in that the way they analyze and organize therapeutic information reflects a direct concern with future behavior. Gestalt, and to a limited extent existential, theories reflect this approach.

Examples of How Theories Organize Information

Each theory is different in the way it integrates therapeutic information, and we cannot hope to cover the workings of each with appropriate examples. However, a sampling of this process with a few theories hopefully will give the reader a general understanding of how theories provide a useful framework for the organization of therapeutic material. Our first example will utilize Alfred Adler's theory of "Individual Psychology."

> Scott was referred to a clinic due to chronic mild depression and underachievement in school in spite of the fact that he had an IQ of over 120 and no detectable learning difficulties. During the first session his therapist found Scott to be a tall, unusually handsome 12-year-old who was impeccably dressed. He was quiet, but not shy, and always cooperative, following his therapist's suggestions as to what they should do or talk about. He admitted his school deficiencies, but was uncomfortable talking about them. Much of their conversation dealt with how "great" his male classmates were and how "lame" the girls were. One session, when the conversation turned to a current congressional election between a male and female candidate, Scott not only said he wanted the man to win, but that he would die if the woman was elected.
>
> Using this and other similar information, the therapist hypothesized that Scott was a "discouraged" youngster who felt a generalized sense of inferiority. Scott felt powerless to deal with any strong individual, and especially strong females. He handled these feelings by seeking and accepting defeat in his schoolwork and other difficult tasks, and obtained a temporary and unsatisfying sense of adequacy through his well-groomed and good-looking appearance. Interestingly, this could also be seen symbolically in his model-building activity where Scott insisted on having his therapist do the difficult structural parts of a car model while he only worked on the easier cosmetic features.
>
> The family evaluation revealed that Scott's father was an extremely passive man and his mother was the dominant parental figure. She made most important family decisions, such as how money was spent, where and when they went on vacations, and how the children would be disciplined. Early in therapy, Scott told how he hated his mother's dominance and was angry at his father for not standing up to her. He even told of how his mother chased him around the house threatening

> to cut his long hair with a household scissors while his father did nothing to protect him. This and many of his early recollections told of his anger and frustration with his own inability to stand up to his mother.
>
> Adlerian theory postulates that people often try to "save face" by avoiding their failures, and there were many instances of these self-protective acts in Scott's life. In one instance, he confessed to purposely having poor handwriting because then his teachers could not read his exams and see how little he knew.

This example illustrates how Scott's problems were integrated into Adler's theories on inferiority, and it provided his therapist with the necessary conceptual framework to guide treatment. It showed the idiosyncratic nature of Scott's discouragement, especially when confronted by any strong female personality. It also showed that confronting his feelings of anger and discouragement toward his father were crucial to overcoming his poor self-esteem. Unfortunately, it does not show the detailed process by which Adlerian theory guided the therapists's interpretation of his every word, gesture, and reaction into a comprehensive understanding of Scott's difficulties, an understanding that would direct the process of treatment. That can only be accomplished through a time-consuming and detailed analysis of each evaluation session.

Our next example describes how Daniel Stern's theory on the development of self can be used to organize patient information.

> Ashley, a fourteen-year-old student at a boarding school, was referred as an emergency because of severe panic symptoms in which she suffered heart palpitations, hyperventilation, and hysterical crying. During these phobic attacks, she pleaded that she be allowed to return home. Ashley and her parents had chosen the school in spite of the fact that it was more than a thousand miles from her home. She had been at the school only about two weeks when the panic attacks began. The choice of such a distant school was surprising because Ashley had previous panic reactions during summer camp.
>
> Her therapist believed that Ashley's problems had their roots in her infancy and could be explained by Stern's theory which merges infant development and psychoanalysis. As a result, she focused a great deal of her evaluation on Ashley's mother's description of their mother-infant interaction.
>
> Ashley was an only child who was born when her parents were in their mid-thirties. Her father seemed a quiet man who readily admitted he was insecure around young children. His love for his daughter was obvious, but he wished they had a closer relationship. By contrast, Ashley and her mother were alternately very close and very angry at

one another. At times Ashley seemed childishly dependent on her mother, but at other times she would fly into violent temper tantrums, breaking things and cursing at her mother.

Although pregnancy and birth were uneventful, Ashley was a colicky baby, and her mother felt tense, frustrated, and confused by her new infant. She remembered being constantly afraid that Ashley might hurt herself falling, eating something harmful, or hitting her head on a sharp corner. In retrospect, she described Ashley's infancy as the worst time of her life. Evaluating the details of the mother-infant interaction in terms of Stern's four crucial self-invariants, her therapist realized that Ashley had difficulties in the integration of her core self during her first year and a half. Although feeding was not a problem, her mother recalled that Ashley never cuddled and so she felt rejected, as if she were doing something wrong. Many of her descriptions of this period indicated that she and Ashley were out of tactile synchronization in that her attempts to engage her through touching were ignored or made her cry. Other recollections indicated that she was so concerned with Ashley's response that she could not enjoy the usual mother-infant games. When Ashley did respond to the usual infant stimulation games, like tickling or touching her nose or toes, her mother could not regulate her arousal level, being either too stimulating or too tentative. Ashley's mother related how she felt excited whenever Ashley looked at her, and very disappointed when she did not make eye contact. This oversensitivity to her infant resulted in an unregulated arousal level in the baby in that she was either too aroused and needed to shut out her mother's overstimulation or she was underaroused and provided insufficient feedback to her mother.

This pattern of mother-infant interaction indicated that although Ashley's sense of self-agency and self-history had evolved with little difficulty, she had deficits in self-coherence and self-affectivity. The symptomatic effects of their early symbiotic relationship and extreme interaffectivity resulted in various mother-daughter difficulties during her childhood years. Later, as she came into the normal separation experiences of late childhood and adolescence, she began to experience separation anxiety. When faced with the severe separation of a boarding school, she panicked and become overwhelmed by the unresolved problems of her infancy.

These two examples illustrate the advantages to using a theoretical system to organize therapeutic integration, but there are disadvantages as well. Unfortunately, all theories emphasize certain aspects of personality and development over others, and so they tend to overfocus a therapist toward certain types of information. This means that they also direct a therapist away from any information that is not relevant to the theory, causing the therapist to ignore important information or critical emotional conflicts.

Many personality theories not only attempt to explain the causes of emotional disturbance, but also specify treatment methods to deal with the emotional problems. Some are very directive and the treatment process is a distinct part of the overall theory, such as in psychoanalysis and gestalt therapy. Others are not as specific, but by the very nature of the theory imply a certain focus in treatment or influence a therapist toward a certain type of intervention. For example, existential psychotherapy inclines toward psychodynamic treatment techniques, but does not specify a particular treatment process. In most cases the information generated by a theory is clearly inappropriate to another treatment process. The information on past mother-infant relations is clearly inappropriate for an operant behavior therapist because such a therapist is interested in present target behaviors, behavioral contingencies, and effective reinforcements.

Heuristic Treatment and Evaluation

The process of evaluation is somewhat different with heuristic psychotherapy in that the process of questioning is uniquely suited to information gathering. Since the primary goal of treatment is to bring about a questioning attitude in the child, there is little difference between treatment and evaluation because by helping the child to wonder about his behavior and feelings, the therapist can simply listen and thus gather the needed information. Actually, the technique of questioning, when properly carried out, inherently pushes a child to discover conflicts and dysfunctional behaviors. At the beginning of treatment the therapist has little information about a child and will need to ask more direct informational questions to start the process. This questioning should only occur in the first few sessions, at most.

Perhaps the biggest difference is in the use of theories. Because this treatment approach is so flexible and not tied to any personality or developmental theory, a therapist can use whatever theory seems to best describe the child. Of course this means the therapist must be familiar with a broad number of theories and be flexible enough to utilize them.

Alternatively, a therapist need not choose any theoretical approach to organize his therapeutic information. As already stated, this has the advantage of not limiting a therapist's perspective. The heuristic process usually will organize and integrate evaluative information from the child's own perspective. This allows a therapist to generate an idiosyncratic theory for that particular patient. In other words, a unique personality theory is developed for each child based on the information provided by that child. As the therapist listens to the information provided by the child, she also hears the emotional intensity of that information and is aware of the temporal sequence in which the information is presented. This allows a therapist to see the connection between events, the relative importance of behaviors, and a comparison of emotional reactions. Ultimately, this begins to form a theory specific to that child which focuses on developmental deficits, how these deficits affected the child, and how the emotional conflicts produced by such developmental difficulties are related. Such a theory will be inherently tied to the treatment process because the evaluation has been generated as part of treatment.

In developing this idiosyncratic theory of a child, a therapist can borrow useful concepts from one or more theories that are helpful in understanding the youngster. So long as the concept fits the child, any concept from any personality theory can be used. The danger is in trying to make the child fit into the theoretical concept.

A thorough knowledge of normal development is essential in developing an idiosyncratic theory of a child. Anyone who works with children ought to be familiar with the normal process of cognitive and emotional development. This is the least biased and most flexible starting point. A comparison between the child's history and normal developmental processes will show us the developmental deviations and what life events underlie these deviations. By looking at the relationships and similarities between these deviations, we can begin to develop an idiosyncratic theory for that particular child. The advantage to such a theory is that it identifies the significant individuals and events responsible for the child's emotional conflicts in addition to the particular stage in which they occurred.

Using a heuristic type of evaluation to develop an idiosyncratic theory for a particular child is a valuable, but difficult task. As in almost any type of evaluation, the first step is to obtain a history from parents, teachers, or other important adults. This almost always includes a general description of the child's symptoms. Sometimes, but not always, particular symptoms can be a guide to particular emotional conflicts. As already mentioned, seeing the similarities between different conflicts will help identify personality patterns.

The heuristic process begins with the child sessions, and the following guidelines may be helpful in providing the needed structure for these initial therapist-child meetings. There are five general areas that need to be covered, and these will generate different kinds of information. These areas are:

1. Affectual quality
2. Communication abilities
3. Social interactions
4. Family interactions
5. Physical problems

Generating questions in these areas will provide a great deal of information. The areas of affect and communication help a therapist identify the overall constellation of problems. Distortions in affect tell a therapist how a child's emotions are affecting functioning in other areas of life. Knowing which situations, events, and relationships result in inappropriate, rigid, or rapidly changing affects can provide important cues toward identifying the causes of such distortions. Similarly, distorted communications are a sign of emotional conflict and confused or regressive communications will also help identify the particular areas of emotional conflicts. The last three topics—social interactions, family interactions, and physical problems—are the areas within which psychological problems occur, thus difficulties in these areas will identify the particular conflicts underlying the child's symptoms. These are the areas that identify the nature of the child's difficulties and provide the information that child and therapist will need in the course of treatment. Heuristic questioning motivates the child to analyze these areas of his life and discover the source of the emotional troubles.

If the above explanation of a heuristic evaluation and development of an idiosyncratic child theory seems a bit vague, it is because we have been attempting to discuss a complex therapist-child interaction in the abstract. Having a real-life child and family situation is always more illustrative and, hopefully, the following example will provide a better understanding of the process. Rather than attempt to describe every aspect of this girl's emotional situation, this example will just illustrate the process the therapist uses in generating a cohesive individualized description of her personality.

> Becca, a senior at a boarding school, asked to see a therapist because she was depressed and had no close friends. Her teachers and mother agreed that she was unhappy in spite of the fact that she was a good student and seemed to get along well with other students and was especially liked by the school staff. They also felt she lacked confidence. Because she was seventeen-years-old, her therapist decided to see her before seeing her mother. Her father, who was an alcoholic, was not available, as Becca's mother had recently asked him to leave the family home and he was living with a relative in another state. During their first two sessions, her therapist directed their conversation toward what she felt was wrong with her life. These sessions were more descriptive than questioning, although the main question underlying most of their conversations was, "What's wrong?" Like her teachers, he found her to be a very likable young woman, but her affect was characterized by a pervasive sadness and lack of spontaneity. She communicated quite well with the therapist, but reported that she seemed to have little in common with other students and regretted that she had not formed at least one close friendship during the past three-and-a-half years of school.

Reflecting on her affect and communication skills, he realized that though she was moderately depressed she could control her sadness, and generally it did not interfere with her overall functioning and did not overwhelm her. She was able to communicate well with adults, but did not seem to have the interests or spontaneity of other teenagers. These conversations identified what her problems were, but not what had caused or maintained them.

The first area of psychological conflict to emerge was her father's chronic alcoholism and his resulting life-threatening medical problems. Except for two half-hearted attempts at treatment in a residential treatment facility, he had been alcoholic for as long as she could remember. Becca's mother was a shy and passive woman whose social activities depended on her husband. For most of the marriage, she could not recognize her husband's problems directly. Indirectly she and her two daughters coped with the father's drinking by forming an emotionally close threesome and excluded the father. After her husband's last failed treatment attempt and with help from a local Al-Anon group, she forced him to leave the house, saying he could not return until he no longer abused alcohol. The father remained alcoholic.

Becca's home was in a resort area where there were almost no activities for teenagers aside from partying and going to bars. Her sister fit into this social life, but Becca did not, perhaps because it was too reminiscent of her father's problem.

This thumbnail sketch of Becca's family gives some insight into the source of Becca's depression. Becca loved her father and in her own adolescent way had made repeated attempts to help him, to no avail. As a result, she felt powerless to stop his drinking but still worried about the serious damage he was doing to his kidneys and liver. She also had noticed that he was beginning to show signs of memory loss and other cognitive damage. In spite of her worries, Becca was very angry at her father's inability to stop drinking and for all the hurt he had caused her through her childhood. At the same time, she felt guilty for not being able to save him from his ultimate untimely death. This combination of guilt, anger, and powerlessness was behind her depression and lack of spontaneity.

Becca's difficulty with making close friendships seemed related to both her mother's personality and her father's alcoholism. She closely identified with her mother's shyness and probably protected her mother by staying home to provide companionship and take the place of the emotionally absent father. As a child she had one close friend, but since, like her mother, she was shy, she tended to avoid many of the usual child activities. When she became a teenager, the alternative of leaving her mother and making close friends was difficult because the popular peer activity was drinking and that meant she risked becoming like her father. This not only would worry her mother, but also raised her own fears about becoming alcoholic. As a result, she stayed at home, giving up a social life and feeling isolated and inhibited with other teenagers. This allowed her no opportunity to develop the skills needed for close friendships.

Although this brief description leaves out many important details and other aspects of her situation, it illustrates how an idiosyncratic theory for a patient is developed through a heuristic evaluation.

10

Play as a Therapeutic Medium

What Is Play?

Play is a difficult word to define because it covers such a wide range of behaviors and activities that almost anything an individual does can be play. Nevertheless, everyone seems to know what it is and can usually recognize a child at play. Play can be identified by the obvious enjoyment of the activity: In a word, it is fun. Children typically have a relaxed attitude in their play, even if they are concentrating and intently involved in the activity. Often play involves some kind of challenge for a child because if the activity is too easy, the child will lose interest and stop. Similarly, it must not be too difficult or the child will become frustrated and give up. Play has a lack of goal-directedness in that the process is more important than the outcome. In other words, children play for play's sake and not for what they achieve as a result of their efforts. In that sense, play is a break from reality and the demands of life. In spite of its seeming unimportance, most child developmentalists believe it is the core process of human development and learning and as such is crucial to emotional and cognitive growth (Chance, 1979).

Even if experts have a difficult time providing a definitive definition of play, they can identify certain attributes that describe this crucial early activity. Play is intrinsic in that it is done for its own sake and not a means to an end. It is usually spontaneous in that children will begin to play on the spur of the moment with little or no planning. Certainly, it is a voluntary activity in that they choose it over more serious and organized types of learning, such as school. Of course, the most obvious characteristic of a child at play is the happiness and enjoyment he or she experiences.

The Value of Play

There are many ways in which the process of play fosters overall development. Most forms of play are physical and children learn to enjoy the action and movement of activities like wrestling, hide and seek, tag, hopscotch, cowboys and Indians, or just running and jumping. Aside from being a way of practicing muscular skills and refining body coordination, children find an intrinsic joy in these spontaneous bursts of activity. Physical play is a crucial activity because unless even simple skills such as walking, grasping, and running are practiced, children can never progress to higher skills such as climbing on monkey bars, swinging high on a swing, or, eventually, the more demanding sports such as bike riding, tennis, soccer, or baseball.

Play is crucial to cognitive development in so many ways that it is probably the central process through which children learn about the world around them. Most of the preoperational and concrete operational mental structures, as well as language and an understanding of rules, come through some form of play. Play may even contribute to the development of concentration and an adequate attention span.

Play is crucial to the social and emotional development of children. This has important implications for psychological treatment. Generally, the most popular children are those who are best at initiating and maintaining play (Chance, 1979). Also, play enables children to take on and try out different social roles, which gives them a better ability to understand the feelings of others. Activities such as games involve rules which teach the concepts of fairness, sharing, controlled competition, and social reciprocity, all crucial to socialization.

In play, children can test fantasies, and this process contributes to reality-testing in that children can learn what is real and what is pretend. A child can pretend that a cardboard box is a spaceship, but as the child learns about astronauts and blast-offs he or she also learns that a cardboard box has serious limitations that make it a very poor spaceship because it will always remain earthbound and it just does not have the look of a NASA rocket.

This process of pretend-play enables a child to try out the world of adults without fear of serious consequences. Boys can play war, but when they are shot they do not really die. When they pretend they are dead, they can undo the process and come back to life and to another pretend game.

Play often helps children develop an adequate self-concept because they learn to master things through the safe process of play. This sense of mastering one's environment is crucial to a sense of self-worth and adequacy. The outside world is a fascinating, but overwhelming place, and when the child learns to control part of it through symbolic play she cannot help but gain a sense of control over that confusing world which eventually grows into a generalized notion of self-competence and self-esteem.

Play is also crucial in the development of social skills since most early peer interactions take place within play activities. Even adult-child interactions involve a great deal of reciprocal play above and beyond the necessary caretaking activities. Actually, many caretaking tasks include some form of play, such as a mother playing "This little Piggy" with an infant's toes as part of the diapering process.

Many of the most crucial social skills are developed through play. Even something as basic as eye contact has its origins in simple mother-infant play games. Games such as "house," "school," or even cowboys and Indians give children a chance to take on other roles, which in turn helps them learn the feelings and reactions of other people. This kind of activity is crucial in the learning of empathy. Almost any kind of play, especially that involving turn-taking, will teach cooperation, another crucial skill for later social relationships. Children not only learn positive social skills, but also how to cope with rejection. For example, when a child invites another child to play school, but is ignored, that child has the opportunity to learn alternative responses. She may entice the second child saying, "I'll let you be teacher" or "You can use my dolls if you play." She might even suggest another game more to the second child's liking, ask their friend what they want to do, or even turn to another child. Whatever their reaction, they are actively engaged in learning social flexibility, and, just as importantly, learning how to cope with their own hurt and rejection, all of which are necessary social skills.

Play and Psychotherapy

Play is an important part of child psychotherapy for many reasons, and, as a general rule, the younger the child, the more likely that play techniques will be utilized. However, play is only a tool of psychotherapy, a technique which facilitates emotional expression and allows communication between therapist and child. In this way, play is crucial as a means of communication between therapist and child since children do not have the precision of language or even the verbal labels to communicate their emotions to a therapist. In the process of normal cognitive development, children first express their emotions through action. Later fantasy becomes the predominant mode of emotional expression, but not until late in childhood do children master the verbal skills needed to accurately express their emotions.

Most children of six or seven are still in the preoperational stage of development, and so they are learning to use words, but the abstract nature of feelings and desires is still beyond their ability. If children at this age are facing serious emotional conflicts of any kind, the stress, frustration, and unhappiness creates an emotional disequilibrium which usually seeks expression. Adults will talk to others as one means of relieving their feelings, but action-oriented children are likely to act out these emotions in some way, usually through play. This is a very normal process used by all children. For example, a child may admire a particular adult or even an adult role such as that of astronaut or jet pilot and, as a way of expressing these positive feelings, they may pretend to be these people during play. In a similar way, emotionally disturbed children will vent their fears, anger, and frustrations through their play. For example, Daniel was a five-year-old child I treated who, among other problems, was soiling himself and afraid of using the toilet. His parents had become very upset with his constant soiling, and had began to punish him. In therapy, he played a repetitive game of using blocks and model furniture to build houses which had one room, the bathroom. This room was constantly destroyed and rearranged, while he took dolls and had them argue and fight. He became very excited and often nervous as he played out this repetitive game, and this was an obvious attempt to relieve the stress he felt over his soiling and his parents punitive reaction.

Most play of this sort is imprecise and often distorted because of the child's fears and frustrations. Directly playing out an accurate recapitulation of the traumatic events might be too threatening, even overpowering, and so the child often has a need to distort the accuracy of their play. For example, Daniel never included parental dolls in his play as that might have been too close to his own situation.

Often a child's play will seem distorted because, although the play is accurate according to the child's inaccurate reality, it is not understood by the more sophisticated and logical mind of the therapist. A child's reality is quite different from that of an adult in many ways because of her limited life experiences and typical childish egocentric distortions. Of course, therapists must develop the flexibility and therapeutic skill to decipher the child's play reality and use this in helping a child come to recognize and understand her emotional disequilibrium. When play is used in this way, it becomes an indispensable part of therapist-child communication; with young children it is usually the only means of communication.

Play is also useful in that it relaxes a child, and physical play activities are especially relaxing. There are many advantages to this. Relaxing activities make a child more comfortable and that child is more likely to enjoy the therapy session which will contribute to a more positive therapeutic relationship. A relaxed child will be more expressive and in general open in all forms of communication. Also, such a youngster will be less frightened by her own emotions, and hence less likely to be defensive. In addition, when a child is more relaxed her behavior will be more natural rather than artificial and so the therapist will get a better and more accurate sample of the child's behavior and emotional conflicts.

Play as a Therapeutic Device

We have discussed psychotherapy as a special form of communication, and using this analogy to understand play therapy is useful in that it demonstrates the unique features of this form of treatment. Of course, play therapy or some variation of it is used because a child does not have the language sophistication needed for a concept-oriented verbal psychotherapy. However, even if a child does have a language level that permits verbal communication, play therapy may be more advantageous. Communication through play may be more meaningful and easier for a child to understand. Although play therapy is used across the entire range of symptoms and conflicts, it is especially useful for children with internal conflicts such as fears, guilt, poor self-esteem, grief, and depression. Communication about these problems requires a great deal of verbal sophistication, and since most young children cannot express themselves in this fashion, they find such problems expressed easiest through actions and activities. Another advantage to play as the better medium for emotional communication is because the play itself may create emotional reactions and make such emotional reactions more powerful.

Play therapy may be a better treatment choice because it is the more familiar activity for children, hence a child will be more comfortable and relaxed. Also many children who are able to utilize verbal communication are uncomfortable talking face to face with an adult, and play activities make for a comfortable barrier between child and therapist. Although play activities may be appropriate at any age if they facilitate communication (I have even found them useful with adults), the general rule is that the older the child's developmental age, the more a therapist can utilize verbal methods. A therapist has to be careful not to inflict play activities on a mature child who might feel insulted by being brought into a playroom, but this is seldom a problem when the child is given a choice of mode of communication.

Usually, play therapy is more indirect in that the focus is on the particular play activity and not directly on the emotional conflict, as it is in a verbal adult psychotherapy. Because it is indirect, play therapy is sometimes a slower process or at least seems like a slower form of treatment. I am not sure that matters because if it is the most appropriate choice of treatment, nothing else would bring quicker results. Also, the rate of change in treatment always depends on the child, and play therapy can result in quite rapid social and emotional changes.

> A good example of this was a six-year-old girl who amazed me by how quickly she resolved a phobic reaction. About three months before, she had been in an automobile accident in which her father's auto was sideswiped by another car and ran off the road into a ditch. Although

the car was totaled, no one was hurt, but shortly afterwards she began to panic and cry when she had to ride with her parents. Eventually, she refused to even get in a car unless she kept her eyes closed and sat on the floor in the rear. At that point she came to see me. After talking with her parents, I spent the next half-hour with the little girl. We spent our time playing with cars and blocks building garages and houses and sometimes having the cars crash into things. During some of the crashes, she told me what was happening to the people in the cars, when they were hurt, and which ones died.

I saw her a week later and as she walked in she looked at me and in a loud voice asked, "How did you do that?" Dumbfounded, I asked, "Do what?" She replied, "How did you make me not scared of cars?" She then told me that after leaving our last session she was not afraid anymore and decided to not keep her eyes closed and to sit on the seat. By the next day she told her parents that she did not mind riding in the car, and thereafter showed no signs of being anxious. Unable to give her an answer (I was as befuddled as she), we spent the rest of our session playing with other toys, and I then terminated treatment.

Therapist Behaviors in Play Therapy

Obviously, the behaviors of a therapist in a play-therapy session will differ according to the particular theory with which the therapist subscribes. For example, a psychoanalytic therapist will emphasize interpretation, while a nondirective therapist will emphasize empathic responding. However, in this book I have taken the view that a therapist should not adhere to one theoretical system but needs to use and blend theoretical approaches so that they fit the individual needs of each child. Accordingly, there are a common set of therapist behaviors that need to be utilized, whatever the approach chosen.

Therapist Involvement

Play is an active process, which means that the child is doing something. It is an interaction between the child and a play object, the child and the therapist, or usually both. This means the therapist must be involved to the extent that play is maintained. Different theories advocate different degrees of therapist involvement. Many theorists, such as Anna Freud, Melanie Klein, and Haim Ginott, recommend the therapist not become actively involved in the child's play but remain a nonplaying observer. Other theorists, such as Louise Guerney, see the therapist as an active participant.

The issue is not which rule one agrees with, but which approach is best for the child according to the therapist's goals and the child's needs. If the child can maintain play activities that lead to cathartic experiences and emotional and cognitive understanding without the therapist's involvement, then the therapist can take a more passive role. Often though, a child needs the therapist's participation in order to maintain the play activity. Usually, a child will be more active and interested in a play activity when another person is involved. Without such reciprocal interaction, the child may become bored and lose interest. Another advantage to active play participation is that the therapist can help guide the play. In this way the therapist can better focus play around activities that reflect relevant emotional issues.

Therapists differ on how they physically position themselves in relation to the child. Should they sit at a desk or does that seem too distant? Should they lay on the floor or does that compromise their adult status? I do not think there should be any hard-and-fast rules because decisions are dependent on such considerations as the personal comfort of the therapist, the age of the child, the play activity, and the physical limitations of the therapy room. I have carried out therapy session in rooms that were literally little more than large closets because that was all the school had available. My patients and I had little choice but to sit in chairs because there was not enough room to play a game on the floor.

Generally, a therapist ought not to invade the physical, usually three-foot personal space comfortable to our culture, but this is not a hard-and-fast rule. They may sit (or slouch) in chairs or the floor so long as they are comfortable, and at times I will put my feet up on my desk without concern that I am compromising my therapeutic role. Usually, but not always, the therapist ought to be at the same vertical level as a child. If the child is seated, the therapist usually does the same, and if the child is on the floor, the therapist may find that position more favorable. Usually, the play activities of younger children, especially preschool children, are centered around the floor and so the therapist may have to sit or lay on the floor, but this is not likely to compromise his or her status in the slightest. (One therapist friend, who had acute back problems, even saw his adult patients laying flat on the floor.)

Structuring

The therapist must orient a child to play therapy so that the child understands what is expected. Most of this is done in the first session, when the therapist tells the child where and how often they will meet and what they will be doing. Of course, such structuring needs to be done at a level appropriate to the child's age and cognitive ability. Certainly, the therapist ought to introduce the child to the play material by showing the child some of the toys and games available and invite the child to choose one for them to play. In other ways, structuring continues throughout treatment as the therapist is constantly, usually nonverbally, telling what the child can do and what the therapist will do. Throughout therapy, the therapist may introduce new toys and activities or remove objects from the room in order to facilitate treatment. This, too, is a form of structuring.

Limit-Setting

Setting limits is an important therapist behavior because it is necessary for controlling the therapy session, and, in itself, is an important therapeutic intervention. Some typical limits are the following:

1. The child cannot physically attack the therapist.
2. The child cannot purposely destroy nonconsumable property.
3. The child has to remain in the therapy room.
4. The child cannot stay beyond the allotted therapy time.
5. All toys and play material must be left in the playroom.
6. Nothing can be thrown out the window.

Although most therapists set these limits, there are other personal limits that each therapist may decide upon. For example, depending on the age and abilities of children, I often ask them to help me set up activities and put them away when we are finished. Therapists have a great deal of flexibility in how and when they tell children about therapy rules. Some therapists prefer to set limits at the beginning of treatment, while others impose limits at the time a rule is broken. Most therapists decide on their own set of limits, but others allow the child to participate in the choice of therapy rules.

Therapists should tell the child about therapy rules in a friendly, informal, and low-key way and try not to appear authoritarian or challenging to a child. They ought to avoid presenting the child with a long list of "things you can't do," since any list seems long to a child and will be hard to remember. Also, a long list may be intimidating to a shy or fearful youngster and make the child even more inhibited. A noncompliant child may see such a list as a challenge and try to defy the therapist—hardly a positive way to begin treatment.

Obviously, therapists need to be very clear and explicit in relating limits to be certain the child understands what is required. For example, children need to be told, "You must not run your crayon along the wall," rather than, "You are not allowed to destroy my office." Once a limit is established, the therapist must be consistent in applying the rule, unless there are extenuating circumstances. Using a rule on one occasion and ignoring it another time will be confusing and nontherapeutic for any child.

Enforcement of limits is a difficult problem and one in which therapists often differ. Obviously, limits need to be enforced or they are meaningless, and therapists should never issue limits that are unenforceable. The problem is that limits are designed to be helpful and protective for children, but the enforcement will often be perceived as punitive and will result in an angry and/or defiant reaction. The enforcement for violation of limits must be done in an idiosyncratic that way reflects the emotional conflicts and needs of each child. Most therapists prefer a gradually sequenced system as follows:

1. The first time the child violates a limit the therapist tells the child about the rule. "You aren't allowed to break my pencils, otherwise we won't have any when we want to use them."
2. The second time the rule is restated. "Remember what I told you about breaking the pencils? You're not allowed to do that."
3. For a third violation the rule is restated with a consequence. "If you break another pencil I will have to take them away, and you won't be able to use them."
4. For the fourth violation the therapist issues another reminder and takes the pencils away.

Up to this point, things are relatively clear-cut, but when children persist in breaking limits, therapists must face some difficult decisions, and they often disagree in how to deal with the child. Some therapists continue talking with the child, trying to use reason to change the child's behavior. Others will stop the child by removing any objects he or she is breaking. Still others will terminate the therapy session, and, in some situations, a therapist will physically restrain the child, grasping the child's hands or holding the child in a chair.

How far to go in enforcing limits brings out a great deal of emotional debate among therapists. Many reject the idea of any kind of physical restraint, while others believe that terminating a therapy session is an unwarranted rejection of the child. Everyone must choose his or her own way of handling such situations, but the choice should depend on the severity of the violation and not on the therapist's emotional reaction to the transgression. Breaking a toy may cost money, but is not as serious a transgression as a physical attack in which the child throws a heavy toy at the therapist or begins to bang his or her head on the floor during a temper tantrum. In the first situation, the therapist can use less intrusive means and for a longer period of time, whereas the second situation is more serious, both for the physical safety of the therapist and the child. The therapist also must protect the child from the serious guilt that might result from being able to hurt the therapist or the debilitating fear resulting from the loss of control manifested by such an intense temper tantrum. Obviously, limit violations that deal with the safety of the child and therapist are the most serious and need to be quickly and stringently enforced using whatever means the therapist feels is appropriate. In extreme cases, the parents might have to be brought in to control the child and might have to be present in future sessions, at least until the child develops greater self-control.

The most important factor in setting limits is avoiding a "battle of wills" with a child. Setting limits should not be an opportunity for child and therapist to engage in a power struggle which will only give the child a confusing and possible destructive example of adult behavior. Limit-setting is a useful way of demonstrating that having certain rules helps people get along. Appropriate rules that are logical and fair facilitates closeness, warmth, trust, and safety in a relationship. Battling the child for personal control obscures this very important lesson.

Consistency is another important aspect of limit-setting. Never set a limit with a child and not follow through; that is, almost never. Obviously, a therapist who sets a firm rule and then violates it is confusing the child and probably causing the child or adolescent to wonder whether the therapist can be relied on. However, there are extenuating circumstances and individual situations that require flexibility on the part of the therapist. So long as such exceptions are explained and understood by the child, there should be little difficulty suspending a limit or modifying it to fit a new situation. I usually follow a rule mandating that children should not leave the therapy room during our time. I will violate this if a child has to go to the bathroom or if we go to a field adjoining my office building because we need more room for some sports activity like throwing a football around or flying a newly built paper airplane. These are easily explained and understood changes, although if a child needs to go to the bathroom too often I ask that she try to go just before our therapy hour begins.

Limit-setting has long been an important part of play therapy and some theorists such as Bixler and Ginott feet limit-setting should be the primary vehicle of change in play therapy. They believe setting limits actually gives the child a sense of security and children eventually respond to this seemingly paradoxical kind of protection. Limits give a child a clear definition of what they can and cannot do, and this lack of ambiguity is reassuring to the child, especially to a child who has had to cope with chaotic adults who have been unable to provide a structured environment. Certainly, children realize that some limits are for their own protection, and, ultimately, they come to appreciate that fact. When the therapist does not allow a child to put scissors in an electric socket or break a window, the child will come to understand that he or she can get a nasty shock or be cut by broken glass.

Children benefit from all limits, not only those that specifically protect them. Breaking property or hurting the therapist is an expression of unacceptable anger, and such inappropriate outbursts can be frightening to a child and are likely to raise strong feelings of guilt. Even inappropriate expressions of affection such as a twelve-year-old boy wanting to kiss his therapist or a thirteen-year-old girl wanting to sit on her therapist's lap is likely to raise troublesome emotions. Limits protect a child from these impulses, and show the child that the therapist will protect her from being overwhelmed by her own feelings.

Setting limits can often help children, especially impulsive children, learn better self-control. As children continue to obey therapy limits, they realize they are able to tolerate these new demands and inhibit their emotional impulses with the help of the therapeutic structure. In time, they may become able to follow these limits without the therapist's help. Hopefully, this will extend to other situations outside the therapy session. Limits also help children learn to use verbal means to express their needs rather than their past impulsive attempts at immediate gratification. This is learned through modeling their therapist since the therapist uses predominantly verbal means to control the child's impulsive attempts to break the therapeutic rules.

Therapists are also protected by the imposition of therapeutic limits. Protecting the therapist's physical well-being as well as the toys and personal property in the playroom takes a good bit of pressure off the therapist, and allows him to focus the full attention on the child and the therapeutic process. This also minimizes any negative transference feelings which might become an added impediment to treatment, since it is difficult to develop a positive relationship with a child when continually threatened and angry. Therapists who are not able to impose and maintain proper limits are bound to feel frustrated and dissatisfied, both with the child, for constantly challenging them, and with themselves for their inept therapeutic activities.

Therapist Involvement in Play

Play therapy can be a difficult process to learn because most adults have lost the spontaneous enjoyment of play through their own maturation and have learned to see play as a frivolous activity, inappropriate for adults. Many parents of patients contribute to this negative attitude because they see therapy as an expensive, important, and very serious endeavour, and they do not understand how silly games can be an integral part of the therapeutic process. Since play does not come naturally to most adults, they must relearn this skill and, even more importantly, dispel the commonly held adult attitudes about the unimportance of play. A good child therapist must learn to be comfortable and enjoy playing with his patients. To achieve that, the therapist must allow himself to regress to an earlier behavioral and communication level while still maintaining the adult levels of cognition and analysis required of a competent therapist.

Play therapy necessitates many therapeutic decisions on many aspects of the therapist's behavior, and as usual there are many differences of opinion depending on theoretical orientation, personal preference, and style. One of the most basic issues concerns the activity level of the therapist during the play-therapy session. Does the therapist function best as an active participant in the play activity or as a passive observer who allows the child to play alone? Theorists like Haim Ginott believe the therapist should not become part of the child's play activities to assure that the therapy hour belongs strictly to the child, and because that would compromise the therapist's adult role. Certainly, not being part of ongoing play activities allows the therapist to concentrate solely on the child's emotional difficulties as they are manifested through play without any distractions.

Other theorists believe the therapist needs to engage in the child's play activities, and they support this belief for a number of reasons. The most obvious is that playing with an adult is more interesting than playing alone, and as a result most children will better engage in treatment. Also, shared experiences usually brings about a closer relationship between therapist and child. Most importantly, participating in play gives the therapist more control over the session. The therapist's choice of reactions and responses in the play activity can direct treatment into areas of relevant emotional conflicts. In many situations, the therapist can create feelings and reactions in the child and make these difficulties more accessible for treatment. This can be done in many ways depending on the skill and creativity of the therapist. Also, it can be done verbally or nonverbally, directly or subtly, whatever is most meaningful, understandable, and cathartic for the particular child. For example, in treating a defensively arrogant youngster who could not face his unrecognized feelings of poor self-esteem, I guided him into choosing a very difficult activity in which he was likely to fail. His reaction to the failure was so obvious and dramatic that he had little difficulty recognizing his defensive reaction.

Some therapists follow the child's lead in deciding whether or not they should be part of play. Obviously, if the child chooses a solitary activity, he or she is telling the therapist to stay out of the play. However, there are very few activities that cannot include the therapist because even if the therapist is not directly involved he or she can be indirectly involved. For example, drawing and painting is a solitary activity, but the therapist can help the child set up and clean up the paints, and the child may ask the therapist for suggestions on what to draw. Some of my patients like to shoot a toy gun that fires rubber bullets, but I often help set up targets and load the gun. One child I have been treating insists I participate by having a competitive shooting match to see who can knock down the most dominoes, which we use as our target.

For the most part, the therapist needs to follow the patient's lead in deciding whether or not to take a direct part in the child's play. More often than not, the child invites, and often insists that the therapist play, and in these situations the therapist should participate. Obviously, the type of activity will dictate the extent of therapeutic participation. Most games such as, "Connect Four," "Sorry," or "Candyland," require two people, but other activities may necessitate therapeutic involvement as part of helping the child. For example, a therapist friend was discussing a case in which her eight-year-old learning-disabled patient choose to build a car model, but was too young and inexperienced to do the difficult parts. As a result, she proceeded to construct the hard parts while he watched. At these times they talked about building the model with the discussion focusing initially on how he felt about not being able to do the difficult parts and later on his not being able to complete difficult school work.

I saw one eleven-year-old boy who liked to build models and we cooperated by my building the model while he painted it. This allowed us lots of time for talking. Usually, our conversation focused directly on the model, but indirectly it dealt with many other emotional concerns. In another situation, a child and I cooperated by my reading the directions while he glued the model together. This kind of intimate cooperation was a wonderful corrective emotional experience since a major emotional conflict centered on his father's lack of interest in his son's activities and his lack of demonstrable warmth.

Therapeutic Communication during Play Sessions

Play therapy is a form of communication, and, as in any form of communication, it depends on the developmental level of the child both for its sophistication and content. Young children are likely to select simple play material and activities reflective of an early level of emotional functioning. They will prefer games requiring little skill, such as "Candyland," and activities like bottle-feeding a doll, building with blocks, or using finger paints or crayons. They also will tend to focus on the play activity rather than talk, and when they do talk, they are likely to talk to themselves rather than the therapist. Children of a higher developmental level will select more complex materials and talk more with their therapist. Obviously, the therapist needs to recognize and communicate with the child in accordance with her developmental level. Thus, a therapist will use more actual play interactions to communicate with a younger child. For example, a preschool child might show her fear of being hurt by first feeding a doll, then hitting it with the bottle. If the child is not able to understand a verbal clarification like, "The dolly must be hurt," the therapist might pick up the doll and rock it gently and pat its head, or even put a Band-aid on the spot where it had been hit. With developmentally older children, the therapist can begin to rely more on verbal interactions and often the play activity becomes an adjunct to the verbal conversation. Of course, nonverbal play communication can be appropriate at any age.

Play therapy does present the therapist with some unique difficulties, especially if the therapist becomes involved in the child's play activities. The most obvious one is that the therapist has to interpret the meaning of the child's play within a conceptual framework that allows him to understand the child's emotional conflicts. Trying to tease out the complexity of a youngster's emotional difficulties by watching that child at play can be difficult. Even more difficult is the fact that the therapist needs to communicate therapeutic interventions back to the child via play activity, and this is an unfamiliar form of communication for adults. Fortunately, this skill can be learned through good training, skillful supervision, and experience, and learning such skills becomes the continual work of a competent child therapist.

Therapeutic communication through play is made even more difficult by the fact that the therapist has to do many things at one time. If the therapist is playing with the child, he must observe and analyze the child's behavior, interpret emotional meanings, remain empathic, and communicate with the child either verbally or through corrective emotional experiences while also being a spontaneous, involved partner in the play. In other words, the therapist must be sufficiently attentive to the activity to be a realistic playmate, and, while so distracted, remain a thoughtful therapist. Sometimes this may seem like a juggler trying to keep ten balls in the air at one time, but this, too, is a skill developed slowly through years of experience.

A competent therapist often shifts the intensity of his play involvement in a very natural and spontaneous way to fit the particular situation. For example, a therapist wanting a child to experience the warmth of cooperation and the sharing of a common goal in addition to bringing out other relevant emotional conflicts might suggest they build a simple plastic car model because the instructions to such models are straightforward and construction does not demand a great deal of thought. As a result, the therapist has time to be attentive to the child, helpful with the model, and can still concentrate on therapeutic issues.

Too intense an involvement in a play activity may tend to shut both child and therapist off from meaningful communication. For example, the complex gluing and cutting required by a more advanced balsa wood model often demands all the attention of both therapist and child, leaving little time available for personal attention to the child or for therapeutic interventions. I find that the popular computer games, such as Nintendo or Game Boy, are useless therapeutic tools for this reason. Even when they are used as two-person games they are too demanding of attention and leave no room for therapist-child interactions. Of course, there are many situations where using complex play materials is beneficial for one reason or another—the child may be bored by a simple model or the therapist may feel that a difficult task will provide a needed challenge. Therapists need not always steer a child toward simple tasks. Any game or activity can be used so long as the therapist can be sure the inherent complexities do not interfere with the therapeutic process.

In certain situations and with certain children, an intense play involvement may be desireable because of the strong emotional reactions that are generated. The power of such reactions may be useful because it gives the therapist needed material to use in treatment and because such emotional displays cannot help but make the child aware of her feelings. Certainly it will make denying such emotions more difficult. Often this is a very effective way to lead the child into the questioning process, and this can be done in a verbal or nonverbal fashion. Perhaps the most obvious example I can think of is a card game called "Spit," taught to me by one of my patients. It involves direct and intense competition between two players who have to attend to nine different stacks of cards at one time and slap their cards down on the correct pile before their opponent does. I cannot think of any game that raises competitive feelings so quickly, or more intense anger and frustration in losing. Children are likely to "blow up" or "explode" in a very open way, and may provide the therapist with just the kind of emotional material needed for a helpful therapeutic intervention. The therapist may verbally reflect on the child's emotional outburst, ask the child to think about what caused such a violent reaction, or simply say nothing, leaving the child to wonder about the "explosion." Whatever the chosen intervention, simply using an intense activity to bring about the reaction can be a useful form of treatment.

Cheating

Whenever any kind of competitive play activities are used with a child, whether it be a complex game like "Monopoly," "Clue," or "Mastermind," or a simple game of marbles or tic-tac-toe, some children will cheat, and a therapist will be forced to deal with this situation. Overt cheating cannot be ignored because it gives the child a signal that such behavior is acceptable or that the therapist does not care enough to deal with a behavior that almost every child knows is unacceptable. Of course, a therapist must be sure a child is cheating before confronting the situation.

The essence of any cheating is an overbearing need to win that overrides other more important aspects of the activity, such as personal relationships, a sense of fairness, and adherence to rules. In some way, this is almost always related to some form of personal sense of insecurity in the child, but insecurity is too general a description to be therapeutically useful. A therapist is most effective if he knows something about the origins of these feelings, what present experiences maintain the feelings, and how such feelings surface. One severely learning-disabled child, who was continually ridiculed by his classmates, repeatedly cheated his therapist as a way of gaining a success, even if a flawed success. He cheated openly, his need to win overriding any thought of disguising his dishonesty. His angry reaction to the ridicule of his classmates was to gloat over his win and ridicule his therapist, telling him how incompetent he was.

A different youngster was embarrassed by a loss in a game, believing he was incompetent. He was afraid he would lose his therapist's respect and his therapist would no longer like him. His method of cheating was subtle and disguised. He needed to win in order to convince his therapist he was a competent player, but not at the risk of being detected and having his therapist become angry with him.

Dealing with cheating is an important part of treatment, but must be dealt with in a sensitive way or it can damage crucial aspects of the therapist-child relationship. Once the therapist is sure the child is cheating, the behavior must be brought into the open. In most instances, a child will try to avoid such direct exposure. A therapist needs to avoid acting angry or authoritarian. A direct, but matter-of-fact attitude is useful as it presents the cheating as simply another emotional problem that needs to be dealt with.

Once the cheating is exposed, there will be a tendency to deal with the cheating directly, but a competent therapist will avoid this. Trying to explain fairness and the eventual futility of cheating should come later. At this point, the therapist needs to treat the cheating as any other therapeutic issue and try to determine what emotions motivate and maintain the behavior. Using the heuristic process, the therapist should try to bring the child to question what kinds of thoughts and feelings are behind the cheating. As we have said, there are many reasons for cheating, which will differ from child to child, and the therapist's task is to bring the child to question and become aware of these reasons in the idiosyncratic fashion that brings about a self-understanding. As with all treatment issues, each understanding should lead to new questions, which lead to new understandings. Since the issue of cheating comes from a lack of self-esteem, most of the heuristic questions will initially focus on this area.

Only after the therapist has dealt with the emotional conflicts and motivations underlying the cheating should the therapist attend to the behavior itself. Giving the child a lecture on morality is usually not very helpful because children hate lectures and may not have the cognitive level to be able to understand adult morality. Usually, the best approach is to focus on the immediate game or activity and show how cheating may make the child feel better in the short term, but eventually will destroy the fun of the game. A game is only fun if no one knows who will win in the end, and so if one person wins continually the game will become boring. Also, cheating makes a game too easy, and easy games, too, become boring. This kind of interaction, which shows the child the implications and consequences of cheating, is much better than a discussion of what is fair and unfair, and why the child should be fair.

Another approach is to focus on the feelings of the cheater and the person cheated. Explaining that the child will feel better and enjoy winning more when she has "really" won is understandable to most children. Also, asking the child to imagine what she would feel like if she were being cheated is helpful. The child can easily imagine feeling deceived and angry, and how she would want to quit, especially if she knew at the start that she could not win. In the end, the game would come to an angry end, and the fun would be over.

Should a therapist purposefully lose at a game? This is a difficult question, a somewhat risky thing to do, and always depends on the circumstance and the needs of the particular child. I must confess that at times I have purposely lost to a child in a game if I felt it was therapeutic. There are many reasons for "throwing" a game, some better than others. The therapist may want to avoid an angry outburst, build the child's self-esteem, reward the child for trying, or a host of other reasons. Usually, "throwing" a game should be a last resort after the therapist has decided that other means of coping with the situation would be unsuccessful. For example, I prefer to deal directly with the anger a child experiences at losing rather than avoid such a situation, because the emotions generated by that kind of experience can be turned to good therapeutic use.

There is little doubt in my mind that purposefully losing is a definite deception and such behavior is generally inconsistent with the role of a therapist. However, when the therapist is sure that losing is in the best therapeutic interest of the child, then it becomes an acceptable and useful behavior. If a therapist does decide to purposefully lose, it should be done subtly so that the child is unaware of the therapist's motivation. That means the therapist must be familiar enough and competent enough with the game or activity to not be detected. Otherwise the deception will be undone, the therapist exposed, and some sensitive explanations will be needed to maintain the child's trust.

Often there are alternatives to purposefully losing that can be used to achieve the therapist's purpose. When worried that a game is so difficult that the child is doomed to lose, the therapist might modify the rules of the game. For example, in playing checkers with a child I often take only eight men on my side instead of the normal twelve. If the child objects that this is unfair I say that I am older and have played checkers lots more than she has so it really is fair. Besides, once she begins to win all the time then we can go back to the regular rules and I will begin to play with all the checkers. With some creativity, the rules of almost any game can be modified so it helps the child. Another alternative is to select games or activities that rely on chance and not sophisticated cognitive strategies which put the older (and hopefully smarter) therapist at an advantage. If the child insists on a game that favors the therapist, I sometimes allow the child to lose a game or two and then point out that winning all the time is boring for me and losing continually is unfair to my patient. We would be better off choosing a game that makes us equal. Then I will suggest a few chance-determined games and ask the child to select one. Modifying games can be effective strategies in avoiding undesired angry outbursts or damaging a child's self-esteem.

Physical and Material Aspects of Play Therapy

Play therapy is such a flexible technique that almost any room (I have even used a large closet) and play activity can be utilized. The actual materials used in play therapy are limited only by the personal preference and creativity of the therapist. Therefore, this section will provide some basic guidelines and reflect some of the many kinds of material used by child psychotherapists.

As already mentioned, almost any room is suitable for play therapy as long as it has space enough for the therapist and child and play material. There are, or course, advantages to having a reasonably large room with shelves or a cabinet for games, models, and other play supplies. A good playroom will not contain breakable items and certainly no dangerous items. Tools such as X-acto knives and sharp scissors should be in a drawer or shelf controlled by the therapist. The therapist's personal items should be out of the way or removed from the room so they cannot be broken. Obviously, the room should be private and reasonably soundproof so confidentiality will not be compromised. I prefer a room with a rug or carpet so both the child and I can be comfortable sitting or lying on the floor. I also have large pillows which can be used as floor cushions and back rests. I find that having all play material in one place, such as a cabinet, is useful so the child can readily select the particular game or activity she wants for that session.

The play therapy room should have an adequate number of games and supplies to give a child a reasonable selection of activities, and it should cover the full cognitive-developmental ages appropriate to the patients being treated. As already mentioned, almost any game or activity can be used although Eileen Nickerson (1980) recommend the following three criteria in the selection of appropriate games:

1. "The game should be either familiar or easy to learn."
2. "The game should be appropriate for the individual or group in terms of age level or development."
3. "The game should have clear, inherent properties which are related to the therapeutic outcomes desired."

While these are reasonable guidelines, they may not always be appropriate. In some situations, the therapist may need a game that is unfamiliar or difficult to learn as a challenge to the child or to provide a useful therapeutic frustration. Many games may not have a clear and inherent relation to a therapeutic outcome, but this may be brought about through the creative efforts of the therapist.

Probably every game and activity invented or sold has been used in play therapy at one time or another, which is a testimony to the flexibility of child psychotherapists. Whatever game is used it must interact with the interest and personality of the therapist. For example, I am comfortable building models of all kinds with my patients, while some friends tend to avoid using models. One friend makes great use of finger paints, but I have had little success using that medium.

Many therapists find that physical activities are helpful with both individual children and groups, and they use such games as dodgeball, red light/green light, giant steps, or just catch with a football or baseball. While physical games are usually played outside, they can be used inside with some modifications. A patient and I developed an indoor baseball game using a wad of paper covered with Scotch tape and a three-sided bat made out of cardboard. We made up rules that fit the size of my office. The game was a wonderful one for this nonathletic youngster because after seeing that he was good at this game, he was secure enough to deal with his feelings of being rejected because he was not athletic. Another physical two-person game that can be played indoors is what I call, "Hit the Penny." Putting a penny on the floor, each person stands on opposite sides about four feet away and tries to hit the penny using an ordinary rubber ball. As one person throws the ball at the penny, the ball bounces up so that the other catches it, and then it becomes his or her turn to throw the ball. If you hit the penny you get one point, and if it flips over you get two points. This tends to be a fair game because if one person hits the penny more than the other, the penny tends to move toward the other person making it easier to hit.

Needless to say, physical activities can be useful in a number of ways besides utilizing the direct emotional content inherent in the activity. Many children are more comfortable when their bodies are in motion, and when they are relaxed they may be more accessible for therapy. Attempting some kind of simple physical activity with one's therapist is relatively safe. The therapist does not pose the same sort of threat to an athletically incompetent child's self-esteem as does a peer, and so could be a way of starting a youngster toward exploring and possibly enjoying these activities. Physical activities with very active (or especially hyperactive) children is beneficial since it serves to siphon off some of their excess energy and makes them better able to participate in more passive therapeutic activities. It is also useful whenever a child is under stress or in a crisis. The physical activity can be used to release energy. Under the right circumstances, it helps build and solidify the relationship between child and therapist.

I learned this early in my training while working in a residential treatment program. At the time, I was treating a thirteen-year-old boy who had serious difficulties with his masculine identity, in part because he felt abandoned by his father. On our way to a snack machine, we passed another therapist (my supervisor) shooting baskets with one of his patients. My patient looked interested, and we began playing a game, the two of us against my supervisor and his patient. We had a fun time, and as therapists even managed to end the game in a tie score (being protective of our patients' self-esteem). The game had quite an effect on my patient and for five or six sessions afterwards he kept talking about what a great team we were, and how well we had set each other up for shots. There was little doubt in my mind that our team cooperation was a wonderful corrective emotional experience which not only put a new perspective on his estrangement from his father, but subsequently raised many questions about their relationship.

Therapists often find games of skill useful, and since there are many of these games available, a therapist can easily pick one that matches the developmental and emotional level of the child. Some of the simpler ones are "Sorry," "Stratego," double dominoes, or card games like Go Fish. Others, such as chess, "Mastermind," "Quibic," or "Pente" require a great deal of experience and cleverness to figure out a winning strategy. Skill games can be used for many purposes. They can be used to challenge a child, teach a youngster that with effort she can master a seemingly impossible situation, or almost any other relevant issue with which a creative therapist needs to deal. They also can raise emotional reactions by frustrating a youngster, bringing out blatantly angry reactions, or a depressive response to losing.

We have already mentioned that games of chance are useful in putting the therapist and child on an equal footing in a competition, despite the differences in their intellectual ability in games and strategies. They are also useful because they are easy games that are not likely to be a challenge. They may provide a more relaxed atmosphere than skill games. Unfortunately, they tend to become boring over time. Games that I have found useful are "Chutes and Ladders," dominoes, and card games such as War, Steal the Old Man's Bundle, Old Maid, and Uno.

Some play activities are useful because they help bring out feelings of anger or overt aggression. Almost any competitive game can be used in this way because many children have an aggressive reaction to losing in any circumstance. Usually, the more intense the game, the greater the emotional reaction. Often, games that require a great deal of self-control can result in an explosive outburst when a child loses. Chess is a good example. It requires a high level of thinking and concentration, and sitting still in front of a chessboard inhibits physical movement. In such a situation, a youngster has little opportunity to let off steam, and more than once I have seen children suddenly toss board and pieces in the air as the prelude to a full-blown temper tantrum when they realized they were going to lose.

Obviously, some toys, such as guns, are symbolically aggressive in their very nature, and these can be useful in play therapy. I have two kinds of toy guns that shoot rubber bullets, and both boys and girls find these attractive toys. The rubber bullets are harmless, but they have enough speed to knock down targets made of piled up dominoes. Often, making targets is a therapeutic activity. I have had children draw pictures of hated classmates, out-of-favor friends, irritating siblings, and sometimes parents which were then used as targets and fired at with great vehemence.

Art activities are a standby of play therapy because they allow children to give visual expression to their problems and conflicts. Also, art activities are flexible, are appropriate with any age group, and often allow children to express emotions with more openness and greater ease than they find possible through verbal communication. Many therapists find that having a child draw or paint is an excellent way to obtain useful therapeutic information in addition to giving the therapist a valuable nonverbal way to interact with a youngster. An easel containing many large sheets of paper, simple water paints, and a brush provides a child with an enjoyable way to express herself. The same can be done with a box of crayons and a pad of blank art paper although, in my experience, crayons seem to be more inhibiting than a brush and paints.

There are many types of art activities that are useful in play therapy. Perhaps the simplest is the serial drawing approach (Allan, 1978). The therapist asks the child to draw any picture the child wishes, then the therapist discusses the picture with the child, asking questions such as, "What's going on in the picture?", "What happens next?", "Can you give it a title?" Another creative activity is the game of squiggles (Nickerson, 1973)(Nickerson, 1983) in which the therapist makes a simple squiggle design which can be any variation of a straight, curved, or wavy line, and the child has to finish it, making a completed picture. The goal is to allow the child to communicate her inner thoughts and emotions through pictures. This game can be varied so that the child alternately gives the therapist a squiggle to finish.

The great advantage of art activities is that because they are symbolic in nature, they give children the opportunity to express what may be troubling them, and provides the therapist with a symbolic way of responding. Often, they can be useful in overcoming a youngster's reluctance to share embarrassing or frightening conflicts. Art therapy is not only a technique of play therapy, but often is seen as a separate treatment modality carried out by specialized art therapists. In this chapter on play therapy we can only touch on some of the aspects of art techniques, but more information can be obtained from the many books written on this topic.

Play Techniques and the Therapist's Personality

Although I have only mentioned some of the many games, activities, and play techniques that can be used in child treatment, one can see there is almost no end to useful play activities. Which ones are selected mainly depend on the child's interests, but such selections are also guided by the therapist. Therapists have their own affinities for certain play materials and are likely more skilled and comfortable in the use of one technique. This is a natural phenomenon and therapists often develop their own repertoire of toys and games. Some of us are not skilled or dislike using one technique or another and that fact needs to be recognized so that a therapist can find the materials and activities that are more useful.

Certainly, therapists should feel free to be innovative and find any new materials they believe will be useful. I often go through toy or art supply stores on the lookout for such new materials. One recent find is a package of very sophisticated paper airplanes called "Whitewings." These are easily built by most children, appeal to both boys and girls from seven to fourteen, and children are excited because they fly so well when completed. I find them useful as an activity that highlights issues around self-confidence and allows the child and I to talk easily while working on the airplanes. Packages of Popsicle sticks (unused) and white glue is another material that allows for easy therapeutic discussions while the child is busily engaged in building various objects. These materials appeal to me, but everyone must find what is useful in their own mode of treatment.

11

The Therapeutic Relationship

The Importance of the Therapeutic Relationship across Treatments

Most experienced therapists would agree that the relationship between child and therapist is the most crucial aspect of any psychodynamic psychotherapy. It is the delicate instrument upon which the warmth, conflicts, and emotions of treatment are played out, and most psychotherapies would seem vapid and ineffective in the absence of such a relationship. However, the importance of the therapeutic relationship often goes unrecognized in cognitive and behavioral treatments. Perhaps this is because those therapies emphasize other treatment variables focusing on reinforcement, behavioral contingencies, and environmental consequences, all of which seem unrelated to personal closeness. In reality, all therapies require some balance between personal intimacy and social distance in a proportion that is optimal for both the type of treatment and the needs of the particular child and therapist. For example, psychoanalytic or psychoanalytically oriented psychotherapies encourage a child to develop a close and trusting relationship with a therapist, and this becomes a crucial part of treatment. However, this type of closeness is very different from that of a parent or friend, because the therapist must also maintain a separateness which allows for objectivity and therapeutic reflection. Of course, the object of a parental or friend's relationship is simply closeness and love, while the object of a therapeutic relationship is that of helping the child overcome problems, and this necessitates a very different kind of closeness.

Just as a dynamic therapist must balance closeness and distance, so must a behavioral or cognitive therapist. An operant behavior therapist needs to maintain some degree of cooperative relationship in order for a child to participate in a behavioral intervention and not attempt to thwart it. I suppose that behavior modification is likely to be more successful if the child has some trust in the therapist, and a sense that the therapist has the child's best interests at heart. However, a behavioral therapist should not strive for intimacy because that is likely to interfere with treatment. The successful completion of a behavioral treatment requires that the child senses the therapist will not be swayed by such intimacy or friendship, but will continue to insist on following behavioral consequences. Too close a relationship is likely to confuse children, perhaps leading them to believe that behavior therapy is no different than the nonrigorous, flexible, and imprecise relationships with which they are accustomed. However, a proper therapeutic distance will alert the child to the fact that behavior therapy requires a relationship very different from that of a parent or peer. By recognizing this, he will be better able to understand and go along with the behavioral paradigm.

Successfully generating and carrying out a behavioral contract with a child provides a good example of the complexity and balance needed in such a therapeutic relationship. Establishing a behavioral contract requires that the child be cooperative and motivated to write and agree to a contract. Eliciting such cooperation is best done through a trusting relationship which leaves the child secure in the belief that the therapist is suggesting a behavioral contract because that is in the child's best interests. The relationship should also be positive, which is more likely to make the child enthusiastic about the contract and want to successfully complete it. However, positive aspects of the therapeutic relationship need to be tempered by a serious and purposeful attitude on the part of the therapist which communicates a demand that the contract be carried out fully. Of necessity, that puts constraints on developing any degree of therapeutic intimacy since the child may then feel that violating the contract would be overlooked by a forgiving therapist. This delicate balance between friendship and purposefulness must be maintained throughout the intervention since if and when the child does not carry out some aspect of the contract the relationship will be an important factor in bringing the child back on task and regaining the motivation and enthusiasm needed to complete the contract.

The therapeutic relationship is similarly critical in the cognitive therapies. Here, the therapist and child are in closer and more frequent personal contact so they are likely to become more intimate, especially as the child will need to share and discuss his emotional conflicts. Such closeness needs to be facilitated. However, the main role of the therapist lies with other tasks, such as helping the child understand the reality of a situation and prescribing tasks and exercises designed to overcome a symptom such as depression or unreasonable fearfulness. In carrying out such cognitive tasks, the therapist often needs to establish a teaching role, perhaps even a somewhat authoritative teaching role, in helping a child. If the therapeutic relationship has overemphasized closeness and intimacy, a child may have expectations of dependence which are counterproductive to the task-oriented demands of cognitive therapy. Again, a therapist must strive for a sensitive balance in the therapeutic relationship, and this balance will differ for each therapist and child.

> This was brought home to me when I was supervising one of our graduate students who presented a case of a socially fearful medical student he was treating with cognitive behavioral techniques. His patient, Mark, had such severe social anxieties that he had few friends, dated infrequently, and even had difficulty talking with other students. Class presentations were a nightmare and as early as five days before, Mark would experience shortness of breath, a tight chest, hyperventilation, and a pounding tachycardia. Even answering questions in class or on medical rounds was frightening. The student therapist had been very successful in alleviating almost all of these anxiety reactions over the course of fourteen sessions using Beck and Emery's AWARE model and SPA exercises. These procedures allowed Mark to expose himself to social situations gradually and substitute adaptive thoughts for the self-defeating ones. And although the therapist believed any success was predominantly due to the cognitive procedures, he utilized the therapeutic relationship in a very beneficial fashion. When Mark stated during the first session that he did not think anything would help him, his therapist confessed that he too had suffered these social anxieties, and that therapy had helped him overcome these problems. Mark seemed comforted by hearing this.
>
> Analyzing his own feelings, the therapist realized that he felt a special closeness to his patient because they were both graduate students, and he believed his patient shared that feeling. Also, because of his own past difficulties, he felt he had a unique understanding of the pain Mark was experienced. He believed Mark understood his empathic feelings and appreciated this.
>
> There were many advantages to this shared closeness. Certainly, it increased Mark's trust in the therapist, gave him a firm belief that therapy would be successful, and increased his motivation to carry out the cognitive tasks. Thus, while the closeness of their relationship was beneficial to therapy, it did not foster a detrimental therapeutic dependence, nor did it distract attention from developing a cognitive understanding of the social anxiety or interfere with carrying out in vivo cognitive tasks. Rather, the therapist used the closeness to increase the patient's cooperation without allowing it to change the orientation of the treatment, and the teaching role often necessitated by cognitive therapy was

not compromised. Initially, they practiced role-playing, oral presentations and conversations with other people. Together, they worked on "homework assignments" in which the behavior of talking to someone was broken down into stages of greeting, greeting plus topical discussions, and greeting plus small talk. As Mark completed these assignments, he found his "anxiety" changed into "excitement," he began to make friends, and then began to go out with them. Mark became so motivated in treatment that without being asked by his therapist he began to keep a daily log of his social successes and brought this into his sessions. There was little doubt in his therapist's mind that the therapeutic relationship between them was instrumental in the success of the treatment.

The Uniqueness of a Therapeutic Relationship

In earlier chapters we have mentioned the fact that children experience many aspects of psychological treatment as unusual, but this is especially true in terms of the relationship that develops between therapist and child. Child-therapist relationships are so out of the ordinary expectations of children that many children are likely to be quite confused by this new situation. There are a number of reasons for this. First, adults do not usually spend a great deal of time listening to children, and when they do interact, the adults usually do the talking. In fact, most adults, such as parents and teachers, spend a great deal of time telling children what to do and how they should do it. They may listen to a child's complaints, and caring adults may even listen to a child's ordinary conversation, but usually that is boring to adults, and they seldom do it for any great length of time. By contrast, therapists tend to give a child a great deal of attention and listen to them for long periods of time, perhaps almost as long as the child wants to talk. Most children find this pleasing, but it certainly is outside of the usual kinds of child-adult contact.

Another difference is that strange adults seldom become emotionally close to children, yet this is exactly what happens in psychotherapy, and this unusual adult (the therapist) seems to actually seek out this closeness. The therapist does this by paying attention to what the child says, and little problems usually dismissed by other adults are taken seriously. Rather than giving the child a quick solution or ignoring a problem, the therapist seems to care about how the child feels. Perhaps the most unusual aspect of this closeness and interest is that it is maintained over a long period of time, usually on a weekly basis. This is very unusual behavior for a stranger or any adult who is not a close relative.

Adults seldom like to do the same things as children, and early on, children learn that while most familiar adults will play with them, adults either tolerate the activities or are bored by them. Children can often persuade parents to play with them, but this seems more of a favor, and few children would easily approach a stranger and expect them to play with the same enthusiasm as another child. Again, children find a therapist different in this respect. The therapist not only seems interested in children's games and activities, but often seems to like to do these things. Children are not used to this at all.

There is one last aspect of a therapeutic relationship that children find very unusual. Children are almost never told that what they say to an adult will be held in strict confidence and never be told to another adult. This indicates that the therapist respects the child in a way they have never before experienced, and it is a signal that the child's thoughts and actions are important, probably in a way they never dreamed possible. As a result, children sense that therapy is an experience very different from other adult relationships and that it will have an unusual importance in their life.

Of course, confidentiality is a complex legal and ethical issue and its limitations must be explained to a child in a way that can be understood. For example, in many states therapists are required to violate confidentiality in the case of physical or sexual abuse, and parents may have access to records kept by a child therapist. I usually explain this by saying, "I will not tell your parents or anyone else what we talk about unless it is not very important or you give me permission to talk about something. But, if we talk about something that is going to hurt you or if you are going to do something that will seriously hurt you or someone else, then I might have to tell someone. If I have to do that, I will always tell you first." Since I am very careful and circumspect about what goes into a child's records, I seldom have to worry about a court-ordered release of information that would violate the promise I have made to a child. I usually find that taking the time to explain the limitations of confidentiality increases rather than diminishes the child's appreciation of the therapist's respect, and enhances the uniqueness of psychotherapy.

In the beginning of psychotherapeutic treatment, these unusual aspects of the child-therapist relationship subtly inform the child that therapy is different from any other relationship they may have had, and it is different in a number of ways. First, there is a definite purpose to this kind of friendship, and the ultimate purpose is to change the child's behavior in a positive way. Eventually, most children recognize this fact even if they are not aware of it at first. Second, while a therapeutic relationship has some of the qualities of parenting and friendship, it also has some important differences, and these differences will contribute to behavioral and emotional changes. Last, there are important limits to the relationship, and these limits will also be quite different from the more common type of relationships that they have encountered in their lives to date.

The Therapeutic Role

As we have already seen, the type of therapeutic relationship that is established is important in all forms of treatment, but it is especially crucial in psychodynamic treatments because it determines how the child will react to the therapist. Therapeutic relationships can vary in many ways, but a therapist must create the kind of relationship that will facilitate the behaviors, reactions, and activities that are congruent to the form of treatment being employed and that will be helpful to the child. There are many different types of relationships, but there is no one that is best since that depends on the personality and characteristics of both child and therapist. A therapist must also differentiate between the child's attitudes toward therapy as opposed to attitudes toward the therapist. Usually, these are related, but often a child may dislike the idea of treatment and still like the therapist. Perhaps the child senses that therapy may expose a terrible secret, force a frightening confrontation, or threaten an unsteady self-confidence. Whatever the particular issue, most children sense that therapy may involve painful changes and interfer with the status quo of their life. Of course, the opposite may also occur: The child may dislike the therapist. However, the most common situation is that the child objects to treatment and, as a result, also dislikes the therapist. The important thing is that the therapist be aware of the child's negative feelings and try to deal with them, otherwise they cannot help but interfere with the development of any therapeutic relationship. How this is done will depend on particulars of the individual therapeutic situation.

Generally, a positive therapeutic relationship is more desireable, but this is only a general rule. Successful treatment can also occur when the relationship is negative. Affection between therapist and client is usually helpful to any therapeutic process, but the success of treatment does not depend on the expression of affection.

The crucial aspect is not whether a child likes the therapist, but the extent of involvement and degree of intensity in the relationship. Of course terms like positive and negative are too global to really describe something as complex as a therapeutic relationship. Negative feelings such as anger and fear can easily coexist with positive feelings, and this is usually the case. Being liked by the child is not an important part of any psychotherapy, although an inexperienced therapist may inadvertently spend a good deal of effort trying to get the patient to like him. Therapeutic relationships are better based on such things as respect for the therapist, a belief that the therapist cares, or that the therapist has the power to help and heal. Often, a feeling that the therapist will protect the child is more crucial than whether or not the therapist is liked. Almost all therapeutic relationships will also change over time according to the stage of therapy and the issues and conflicts being dealt with. Positive relationships are easier because they introduce fewer extraneous problems to deal with and allow therapist and child to struggle directly with conflicts stemming from the child's life.

Therapeutic Alliances and Therapeutic Relationships

There are many dimensions and degrees of intensity that characterize a therapeutic relationship, and knowing the kind and quality of a therapeutic relationship is crucial in directing treatment. To a great extent, this will determine what the therapist does and when he does it. Understanding the difference between concepts such as a therapeutic alliance and therapeutic relationship is helpful therapeutic information.

The Therapeutic Alliance

A therapeutic alliance between therapist and child occurs when the child decides to cooperate with the therapist in trying to overcome his emotional difficulties. This usually develops early in therapy, well before the establishment of a therapeutic relationship. At this time the child understands his particular emotional and behavioral difficulties are maladaptive and need to be changed or certainly modified, and that the therapist is an important person in helping him bring about such a change. In a sense the relationship, is a sort of unspoken agreement that the child and therapist have similar goals and a shared task. Usually, a therapeutic alliance indicates that the child identifies with the therapist and generally looks to the therapist to direct the treatment process. This is possible even with oppositional or recalcitrant children because, although they may fight therapy and therapist, deny that therapy is helpful and say how much they hate it, they usually know why they are coming to their sessions and what is expected of them. Such children may try to avoid the alliance; nevertheless, they understand it, and even their resistance can become an unacknowledged engagement in treatment.

The practical consequences of a therapeutic alliances are many and beneficial for the progress of treatment. For the most part it indicates that at least on a cognitive level the child is open to interventions and suggestions from the therapist. More importantly, it means the child is cooperative and participates in sessions. There are still many therapeutic tasks that are beyond the child because they are too angry to try to understand the reality of a situation or too frightened to confront a traumatic event. However, those therapeutic tasks that are within his ability will, over time, be attempted. Perhaps attempted is the wrong word because the child may not consciously or enthusiastically confront a therapeutic task. The process is usually more subtle and drawn out, but, irrespective of the nature of the problem or intervention, the child will on some level cooperate with the therapist's activities. This may be through play activities or more direct verbal interactions—the actual means are irrelevant. This level of relationship characterizes many child therapy cases and therapeutic interactions, and this level of engagement can result in excellent therapeutic progress.

The following case example of Matt, a fourteen-year-old boy attending a private school, illustrates a therapeutic alliance. Matt's alliance with his therapist characterized the first two months of his weekly psychodynamic therapy sessions. Although he entered treatment at his parents' request as a result of a minor plagiarizing incident which resulted in his being suspended from school for a week, he and his therapist established a solid therapeutic alliance which enabled him to cooperate with his therapist on the many upsetting aspects of the plagiarism incident and his subsequent suspension. Realizing he needed to confront his feelings around this incident, he followed his therapist's lead in expressing the terrible fear of being caught and the embarrassment when the incident was made public to other students. Matt spent a great deal of these early sessions remembering small incidents, such as waiting alone in the library while the student-faculty committee decided his fate, and calling home to his parents to confess what had happened.

Although his therapist was able to use their therapeutic alliance to deal with this issue, Matt showed much less enthusiasm about confronting other, more painful issues. Matt suffered a serious genetic problem in consequence of which he was shorter than other boys, not as athletic, and had an unusual body stature. Perhaps because of these problems, he was isolated from the mainstream of social life and had no close friends. His physical abnormalities and social inadequacies were embarrassing to him, and although he and his therapist were able to talk about these problems, such discussions were superficial and resulted in little progress. These were painful topics that required more than the therapeutic alliance established between them; it needed the trust and protection characteristic of a deep therapeutic relationship.

The Therapeutic Relationship

Psychotherapy acquires a deeper intensity and more robust flexibility when the therapeutic alliance evolves into a therapeutic relationship. This, of course, requires more time and is characteristic of long-term treatment, since deep therapeutic relationships cannot develop quickly. A therapeutic relationship has all the attributes of a therapeutic alliance—the realization that there are emotional problems and that these need to be changed, the identification with the therapist and the openness to therapeutic interventions, and the unspoken agreement between therapist and child. However, a therapeutic relationship implies a great deal more than this. It indicates that child and therapist have developed a deep emotional bond, one so deep that the child now projects many of his feelings onto the therapist and looks to the therapist for emotional support. The crux of the relationship, and the part that is most useful in treatment, is the sense of safety and security provided by the therapist. This feeling is what makes a therapeutic relationship different from the therapeutic alliance and, in fact, quite different from almost all other relationships. Feeling protected allows the child to trust the therapist so that secret feelings, thoughts, and memories that are usually hidden can be exposed and changed. Exposing such sensitive feelings, thoughts, and memories is very difficult, as these have usually been repressed and the child is almost always resistent to having such potentially painful or frightening emotions brought out, either to someone else or himself. A child is likely to consciously or unconsciously resist such openness because he sees it as a serious threat.

Establishing a sound therapeutic relationship is the key to overcoming such resistances, and while creating such a therapeutic relationship is often difficult in practice, it is simple in theory. As the first therapy sessions unfold, the child learns that the therapist is concerned about his hurts and problems. The therapist is also attentive, either through listening to the child or providing and sharing enjoyable play activities. The child senses the warmth of the therapist and such warmth is comforting to an emotionally upset child. The pain, fears, and anxieties he feels make him vulnerable and insecure, and he will naturally gravitate toward someone who can provide the warmth that will alleviate and dispel these unpleasant feelings. Sometimes the attention and warmth of the therapist temporarily distract the child from his difficulties; at other times the problems seem to temporarily dissipate. The result is that the child begins to form a bond to the therapist. It is a special bond in that it is closely related to overcoming his emotional problems. At first this takes the form of a therapeutic alliance in which the child will accept the purpose of treatment and cooperate with the therapist in the shared task. However, the growing emotional bond between therapist and child results in far greater significance because it provides the child with a sense of security so powerful that it has the potential to overcome years of emotional conflicts.

Therapeutic confidentiality provides a small first step in this process. It tells the child that he is special to the therapist and what he says will be respected. It also tells the child that the therapist can be trusted. However, since a therapist informs a child of confidentiality during their first session, it only provides the child with a cognitive sense of security; a belief that is expressed in words. When a child accepts the offer of confidentiality, he in essence is accepting a stated promise from a relative stranger. The child is likely to believe the promise because of the authority of the therapist and nature of the situation rather than any deeply established personal trust. At this point in treatment, the therapist is little more than a strange adult and the child has not had time to develop such a deep personal trust.

The stated confidentiality reassures the child that whatever he is guilty of or embarrassed about will not be told to others, whether they be parents, teachers, friends, or even strangers. In this way, confidentiality protects the child from others, but it does not protect the child from himself, his own sense of shame or the terror of his anxieties. That can only occur when the child has a solid sense of trust in the therapist, and this can only emerge out of a close emotional bond developed over a period of time. In order for a child to feel secure that the therapist will protect him from these feelings, the child must have an unspoken emotional sense of security. The child must believe that whatever he tells to the therapist, no matter how shameful, such information will not destroy, damage or change the therapist-child bond. Not only will it not affect the therapist's opinion or feelings toward the child, it will not affect the therapist's dedication to helping the child. It means that the bond between therapist and child cannot be destroyed. In such a relationship, issues of protection and confidentiality need not be stated. On an emotional level, the child knows that the therapist will always try to do what is best. In this way the therapist intuitively tries to protect the child from feelings, thoughts, and memories that will overwhelm. In this case, the word "protection" means more than simply coddling a child and not allowing that child to experience any emotional pain. Similarly, it does not mean the therapist will not confront the child with maladaptive or antisocial behaviors. Rather, the child instinctively relies on the knowledge that the therapist will carry out any confrontations, indeed any therapeutic move, in a way tolerable to the child and ultimately in his own best interest.

Developing a Therapeutic Relationship

Because children are so different, there is no definitive plan for engaging a child in a therapeutic relationship. However, there are general guidelines and concepts that are helpful for a therapist to keep in mind. Most of these come under the rubric of positive behaviors and are well know to anyone who works with children. Certainly, the most important for a therapist is to listen carefully and attentively to what the child says. This simple human behavior can go a long way in developing a strong relationship because it tells the child he is important, even special, and that positive feelings will naturally be returned.

The child must also feel that the therapist understands. This can take many forms. Perhaps the therapist indicates that he believes what the child says, even when other adults do not. Even if what the child says is not believed, it should be accepted. As always, a therapist needs to be careful when challenging anything a child says. Even when distorting the truth or telling an outright lie, a child always has some strong reason that underlies what he is saying, and the therapist needs to respect that reason. One way to handle such a situation is to respond to the feeling behind the lie rather than the words themselves.

For example, a severely learning-disabled child who had a terrible sense of self-esteem continually told me rather wild tales of how he was the star player on his junior high school basketball team, and each session he would provide me with an inflated report of how many points he had scored. In fact, he was not the star of the team, he seldom scored any points, and ultimately ended up quitting the team because he was so discouraged by his poor performance. Rather than challenge his distortions, I attended to his wish to be a star player and enjoy the acclaim and self-satisfaction that go along with being a star. In response I would say things like, "Jim, I think it would be wonderful to score 40 points in a game. Scoring that many points would make anyone feel real great," or "It must be great to believe you are such a good shot. Any coach would really want a player like you." By answering him in this way I was not agreeing that I believed what he had told me, but was confirming that he really needed to be a star athlete and I understood that need.

For now, we will ignore the strategic dangers of such a response and concentrate on how it affects the relationship. Obviously, these kinds of responses are sensitive to the child's emotional inadequacies. The child senses you understand how badly he feels, and that you understand and support the feelings behind the fantasy that the child so desperately needs. Without confirming the child's distortions and lies, the therapist tells the child that his hurts are understood. In addition, the therapist shows a sense of kindness in not confronting the child and taking away even a false kind of happiness. Most children know that they are lying, and while they realize the therapist does not accept the lie, they also appreciate the fact that it is also not challenged.

Another example of how allying oneself with a child helps build a strong therapeutic relationship was told to me by a close friend who had had a troubled childhood. He told how as a student in a therapeutic boarding school, he was suspected of stealing a ring from another boy (he had stolen it). After being caught, he was accused by everyone on the staff except his therapist. The therapist knew he had stolen the ring, but did not accuse him, and when my friend insisted on his innocence, his therapist offered to buy another ring to replace the missing one and did so. My friend was terribly impressed by the fact that even knowing he was being lied to, the therapist still sided with him and tried to help him. The intensity of the therapeutic bond between them was so strong that even forty years later he remembered the incident and told me about it. He also credits that therapist as the most important individual in his life and the one who turned him away from being a delinquent adolescent.

Children easily develop a liking for adults who are interested in them so long as the adult is reasonably cheerful and has a good sense of humor. They usually do not develop an affinity for adults who are depressed or overly serious, so therapists need to avoid inflicting such behaviors on their child patients if they expect the child to bond to them. If a therapist is sensitive to the subtleties of feelings of children, then that too will make them attractive to children.

Another important aspect of building a therapeutic relationship is simply liking a child. Children sense when they are liked, and their natural response is to like their therapist in return. In this way a reciprocal bond is formed. Being fond of a child is very easy because most child therapists enter the field because they already like children and want to spend their careers helping them. For most therapists, just being involved with a child on a regular basis is circumstance enough for the development of such positive feelings.

The Value of a Therapeutic Relationship

The emergence of a therapeutic relationship opens up new opportunities in treatment, and becomes one of the most important tools at a therapist's disposal. A therapeutic relationship brings about three primary changes in a child and each allows the therapist new treatment possibilities.

Therapeutic Openness and Therapeutic Security

We have already discussed the deep sense of safety that a child feels and how that allows the child to tolerate more emotional pain, embarrassment, and anxiety than he ever could under other circumstances. This increased tolerance for emotional pain allows for the emergence of psychological conflicts and traumas which had previously been repressed or consciously avoided. The new sense of safety and basic trust in the therapist will greatly increase the amount of therapeutic material available in treatment. More importantly, it allows for the emergence in treatment of intensely emotionally laden and therefore important therapeutic material.

> A good example of this was a high school junior who had become very close to one of her teachers. In the course of doing joint extra-school projects over the summer, she lived with his family in his house, and in a short period of time they became emotionally involved although they avoided serious sexual involvement. Being extremely guilty over her own perceived initiation of the relationship, she was unable to unburden herself with anyone or even think about how to cope with her conflicting feelings. As a result, she became depressed and increasingly withdrew from any social contact. Because of her deep depression, she began to see a therapist twice a week, initially focusing on her lack of friends and her depression. Over the course of treatment, she and her

therapist formed a close therapeutic relationship, and after four months she felt sufficiently secure to tell her therapist about the relationship and asked his help in ending it. As they worked through the situation, she said she was unable to bring it up before because she thought everyone including her therapist would hate her when they learned of what she had done. Now she knew that no matter what she did her therapist would not hate her, and even if he did not approve of what she had done, she could count on him to help her, no matter what. Needless to say, she was immensely relieved to unburden herself of the guilt, and together they were able to end this potentially devastating situation in a way that enabled her to realistically see not only her responsibility for what had happened, but also where she had been victimized.

Another example that I am presently dealing with involves a high school senior whose mother has been suffering with a potentially fatal illness for the last seven months. At present she has no choice but to face a dangerous surgical procedure. My patient is very close, even dependent on his mother and has no relationship with his divorced father who long ago abandoned his family. The thought of losing his mother is so traumatic that he had been unable to discuss the possibility other than to tell me that if she dies he will kill himself. I believe this is a very serious threat. In past sessions my direct attempts to deal with this situation have been rejected because even thinking about her death is exceedingly painful, and openly discussing any aspect of their situation is intolerable.

I have been seeing this boy for over a year and we have established a close therapeutic relationship which has allowed him to deal with other less traumatic issues, such as his lack of school motivation or performance, his lack of friends, and his insecurity with girls. I felt that getting him to confront the traumatic situation concerning his mother would be best accomplished by directly using and intensifying our relationship, as opposed to directly trying to force him to confront something he was unable to face. This started by my reassuring him that no matter what happened, I would always be available to meet with him, and that our sessions would not end irrespective of what happened to his mother. Gradually, over the past three sessions we have begun to tentatively talk about the implications of her condition, but not the reality that she may die. Slowly, he has begun to talk about her trips to the hospital and his meetings with her physicians; and reluctantly telling me of her poor prognosis. He has also mentioned the possibility of her death, although this is dealt with only briefly. As soon as he begins to get emotional, he changes the subject. I plan to continue intensifying our therapeutic relationship so he can feel therapy is a safe place where he has someone who will help and comfort him no matter what happens. I feel this is the way I can best help him cope with his mother's illness and stop him from trying to take his own life if she does not survive her surgery.

Medical Traumas and Therapeutic Openness

There are certain exceptional situations where very traumatic material can be dealt with in treatment without the emergence of a true therapeutic relationship. This occurs when children are faced with a terminal illness or some similar devastating trauma and as a result they are forced into developing an immediate deep therapeutic trust. Such children are so fearful and so traumatized they suspend their usual social reticence and ignore obstacles to intimacy. Likely, the overwhelming fear impels such children to reach out to anyone who can give them warmth and protection. In this way they quickly form a bond and react to a helping stranger as they would toward a parent or some other familiar caretaker. This rapid therapist-child bonding is intensified because in such situations the parents are often absent—both physically absent when the child is actually undergoing a medical or surgical procedure and emotionally absent because their own fear and grief cause them to be less responsive to the child's needs. Being part of the treatment team from the beginning, the pediatric psychologist or social worker is there to provide help. Unlike the child's parents, the therapist is not devastated by the illness but is emotionally available to the child.

In such situations, children do not have a chance to repress their emotions because they are immediately faced with needles, spinal taps, bone marrow extractions and the like. Normally, children would want to avoid remembering such traumas, but facing the reality of additional medical procedures, they feel a need to share their anxieties. Sensing the pain and emotional absence of their parents, they may be afraid that if they unburden themselves they will cause their parents to withdraw even further. In a reversal of roles they may feel a need to protect their devastated parents. In such a situation, a pediatric psychologist or social worker reaching out to the child is crucial because the child is likely to respond. With this caring adult, the child can feel safe enough to unburden himself knowing that the therapist is strong enough to listen. In such situations, a therapist working with a terminally ill child is able to help him or her face not only their death, but equally terrible experiences such as losing their hair as a result of chemotherapy treatments, being wheelchair-bound, and enduring painful surgical procedures.

A close friend and colleague works with terminally ill children. This kind of treatment requires a special therapist and special therapeutic skills. But these children are also special, and with help, can endure terrible experiences. I have seen my friend, Joe, tell a twelve-year-old boy that his cancer treatments were unsuccessful, and he will die within two months, Nevertheless, the bond between them was so strong the child was able to calmly listen to him say what no one else could. After sobbing in Joe's arms, the boy asked if together they could decide on what he wanted to do before he died. When that was done, he asked Joe's help in planning out his funeral. I cannot think of a more poignant example of bonding or a clearer case of a child bravely facing his most terrible fears.

Transference

Transference is an old and rather imprecise psychoanalytic term. It describes a situation where children transfer the emotional feelings and reactions from parents or other familiar adults onto their therapist. According to psychoanalytic theory, such feelings are powerful and are the underlying determinants of most of our emotional reactions. Even if we do not fully accept this aspect of psychoanalytic theory, most personality theories agree that early child-parent interactions are very significant. There is a good bit of controversy between psychodynamic therapists about whether early parent-child relationships are the most significant cause of an individual's intense feelings in psychotherapy or whether such feelings also reflect other important aspects of the child's life. Most present-day therapists take the broader view that both past and more contemporaneous emotional reactions can become an important part of therapy. Whatever the theoretical belief, there is little doubt that intense feelings between therapist and child are generated as a natural consequence of the therapeutic relationship, and many other aspects of the child's emotional life will be symbolically played out in the therapeutic relationship. These transference feelings are an important part of psychodynamic treatment and can be effectively used as a therapeutic technique.

Transference reactions are especially important for two reasons. First, because when they emerge in a therapy session the therapist can deal with them in the here and now. This is far more powerful to the child than an abstract discussion of a past incident. Secondly, feelings that emerge within the therapy session are usually much more powerful than remembered feelings that were generated from outside incidents. Perhaps this is one of the major differences between adult and child psychotherapy. Most of the therapeutic material in an adult session is brought in from extra-therapeutic incidents in the individual's life, whereas as a result of play and the contemporaneous orientation of child psychotherapy, most child therapeutic material originates within the session. Sometimes these are dealt with directly by talking about the feelings, and other times symbolically. The important factor is that dealing with transference feelings gives them an immediacy far greater than simply talking about them in the abstract as a historical incident.

The essential aspect of using transference reactions is that the therapist must create a split between the child's egocentric emotional reaction and the child's ability to understand and assess the reaction in a reasonable way. A wise supervisor of mine once said, "You are trying to get the good parts of the child working on the bad parts."

The sequence of the intervention is as follows. First, the child is upset by some older, perhaps longstanding emotional reaction to a parent or other important individual. That reaction is carried into the therapy session and projected onto the therapist. As a result, the child reacts as if the therapist is part of the original emotional reaction or incident. Because the intensity of the emotional reaction is out of proportion to whatever has gone on between the child and the therapist, the therapist now has the opportunity, in an obvious or subtle way, to make the child aware of the discrepant reaction. While this may sound logical and simple, it is not. Remember that a therapist is dealing with emotions which do not follow any of the rules of cognitive logic.

As in other therapeutic issues, the crux of the intervention is in helping the child become aware of what he is doing and feeling, and this is done through some form of heuristic questioning. Either through the therapist's questions, the therapist's own emotional reactions, corrective emotional experiences, or therapeutic clarifications, the child is helped to attain a new perspective on the transference reaction. The advantage of transference interventions is that they tend to be more powerful and pervasive, affecting many areas of the child's life.

Within the therapy session there are certain behaviors that usually alert a therapist to the emergence of transference issues, and these can be either positive or negative. Negative transferences are easier to detect because they are usually marked departures from commonplace human interactions. Perhaps the most common indirect indication of a negative transference is a consistent pattern of missed or late appointments or a lack of involvement in the therapy session. Of course, children express their negative feelings more directly, often by rejecting the therapist and denying they have any need for treatment. Any kind of open hostility toward the therapist is a strong indication of transference because most therapists do not act in a way that would provoke such a contentious reaction, so the origin of these feelings is likely in relationships outside of therapy.

Overt fear of the therapist is a less commonly seen transference behavior since most children try to hide such feelings, often behind a facade of trying to please their therapist. However, rarely do therapists give children any reason to fear them so this, too, usually indicates a transference problem. Another indirect transference signal is when a child continually changes the subject or quietly rejects what the therapist has said. Sometimes children develop a fear of being rejected by the therapist, although this is not as easy to detect because it is usually well hidden and usually denied by the child.

Obviously, therapists do not often engender such behaviors, and so these feelings, too, are projections of other extra-therapeutic adult relationships.

Positive transference behaviors are less easily detected because they are similar to ordinary pleasant child-adult interactions, and in general we are all more sensitive to negative behaviors than positive ones. Sometimes children bring little gifts for their therapist, and this is one of the most obvious signs of transference feelings. They may bring candy, a postcard from a family trip, a school drawing, or the loan of a favorite book. Sometimes the child gives the therapist a steady stream of compliments, but this, too, is a more subtle version of gift-giving. Some children will bring things to the session to show the therapist, and this is often an attempt to please. At the very least, it may indicate the child feels that he is not good enough and an interesting object will overcome a perceived lack of worth. These behaviors also commonly represent disguised emotions whose origin is outside of therapy but are being played out within the session between therapist and child.

Therapists need to be aware of what role they are cast in by the child. Perhaps they are seen as the morally good father, the loving mother, the cruel teacher, or even a needed "buddy." Of course, as the therapist comes to understand the role she is expected to play and the reasons behind that role, the therapist is in a much better position to use such information in therapy. Excessive dependence on the therapist for help in play activities or other therapy activities is a sign of transference feelings as is crying. Actually, crying is a form of trust in the therapist since children need to feel close to someone before they can allow themselves such an open display of emotion. All of these behaviors reflect problematic feelings outside of therapy that are brought into the session and put upon the therapist.

Countertransference

The other side of transference is countertransference, which relates to feelings the therapist has concerning a child. Obviously, children raise feelings in their therapist. Some of these feelings arise as a result of treatment; others originate in the therapist's personal and developmental history. All therapists need to be aware of countertransference feelings, but those therapists who do intensive psychotherapeutic work with children need to be especially concerned. Obviously, the therapist's feelings can be detrimental to the therapeutic process by clouding a therapist's judgment and generating nontherapeutic emotional reactions. However, countertransference feelings can also be an aid in treatment in that they alert the therapist to what the child may be doing to create those feelings. In that sense, they provide the therapist with valuable information that will help in understanding the child.

Good therapists always try to be alert to their own emotional reactions, but countertransference feelings are often difficult to detect within oneself. Psychoanalytic and other psychodynamically oriented therapists often enter their own therapy as part of their training in order to be better aware of their own emotions and how these emotions might affect their therapy. Perhaps the best way to detect and understand such feelings is through good supervision in training and, later, through consultation with one's colleagues.

By their very nature, countertransference issues are complex and highly idiosyncratic, and this means there are no hard and fast rules to follow. Because therapists are so different, countertransference behaviors will be different. Dealing with such matters is probably best learned through sound individual supervision, and a detailed discussion of this topic is beyond the scope of this chapter.

Unfortunately, in spite of the importance of countertransference the topic, has tended to be neglected in recent years. However, it is an important aspect of most psychodynamic treatments.

Testing New Behaviors within the Therapeutic Relationship

As children develop an emotional understanding of their difficulties through psychotherapy, they begin to confront their fears and accept the finality of hurts they cannot change. As a result, they begin to see the futility of their existing dysfunctional reactions. At this point, they start to explore the possibility of finding alternative behaviors, thoughts, and emotional reactions to replace these older and less adaptive responses. Often, these unfamiliar responses will seem frightening or foreign compared to their older, more familiar reactions, and children are likely to be reluctant to risk testing out these new responses. To do this, they need to feel a sense of security, a feeling that they will be protected if their attempts at change fail. The closeness of a therapeutic relationship can provide this sense of security because the child knows that however frightened he feels and however great the risk, the relationship with the therapist can be relied on. This produces two important implications. First, the child can try out these new behaviors, thoughts, and emotional reactions with the therapist knowing that with the therapist, he is safe. Secondly, the child can risk these new behaviors with other adults or peers and know that whatever the reaction, he still has the security of the therapist to rely on. This symbolic security is terribly important and will carry over to people and situations outside of therapy.

Realistically, children may try out new behaviors that are not adaptive, and, as a result, will have negative consequences. A common example is when overanxious children begin to become more confident and then go overboard, becoming defiant to parents and acting out in the classroom. This reaction to their new-found confidence is certain to result in a negative response from these adults. Similarly, they may be disappointed to find that even though they feel more confident and assertive, their friends will not tolerate being bossed around. In both these situations, the child will have to modify and change the new behaviors to ones that are more palatable to others.

Using the therapeutic relationship to help a child try out alternative responses can be accomplished in a number of ways. The easiest is for the therapist to encourage the child to try out new ways of behaving and reacting within the therapy session. The child can then receive either direct or indirect feedback from the therapist without feeling rejected, abandoned, or becoming the object of punishing anger. This kind of feedback may be verbal or occur within the context of play activities. For example, an anxious, overcontrolled child may begin to become overly aggressive in play as a result of new insights in treatment. In such a situation, the therapist can let the child know through his own reactions that such overly aggressive behaviors are not likely to be tolerated or accepted by others and will bring on rejection or anger. Thus, rather than feeling the feared rejection or anger in reality and withdrawing into old responses, the child has the security to continue to search for alternative behaviors that will be better accepted.

In addition to trying out new behaviors within the session, children can use fantasy to imagine what would happen if they behaved differently with parents and peers. The therapist can help them imagine situations and symbolically face such situations within the security of the therapeutic relationship. In this way they have the benefit of the therapist's feedback, but this is much less threatening than the fear of the actual consequences. Through such fantasy experiences the therapist can also help the child explore and prepare for the negative consequences of his or her behavior changes.

In one form or another, there is little doubt that the relationship between child and therapist is important for all forms of treatment. Unfortunately, its importance in behavioral and cognitive treatments has probably been neglected. Hopefully, as treatments are blended and used together, this situation may be rectified. Certainly, its importance in psychodynamic treatments is crucial and has been best studied and used in this context. With the development of a therapeutic alliance, both therapist and child know he or she has accepted the same treatment goals and both will work together toward finding beneficial changes in the child's emotional life. If this deepens over time into a therapeutic relationship, then the therapist has an important instrument for therapeutic change. With such a relationship, the child has the safety to open up issues that might be too frightening to face in any other circumstance. Although the formation of a deep therapeutic relationship takes time and will not occur with most children, the advantages of this kind of transference cannot be overemphasized.

Section IV

The Sequence of Psychotherapy

This section deals with the sequence by which the therapeutic process unfolds. Because each child's treatment is unique and different, the timing of psychotherapy has to be a very flexible process. Nevertheless, it still follows a progression that has a beginning, middle, and end, and a therapist must be aware of this sequence and the structure that this imposes on therapy. This structure dictates that particular issues and problems must be dealt with in a certain order. For example, certain issues arise during the first sessions that are unique to that initial contact. These issues set these sessions apart as quite different from other sessions, and if these issues are ignored or put off to later sessions, the child will be confused and the progress of therapy will be impeded. The first few sessions in therapy are different in that they set the attitudes and expectations of the child, and put a greater emphasis on the gathering of information. The setting of expectations is crucial to the success of treatment, and in that sense the beginning of treatment is a preparation for the sessions that follow. Initial sessions ought to prepare the child so that the remainder of therapy is followed in an orderly, efficient, way. Of course, there is no sharp demarcation between the beginning of therapy and later sessions, and there is often a good bit of overlap in therapeutic tasks. For example, issues such as confidentiality, which are usually associated with the initial sessions, may carry over or reappear in the middle stages of therapy. Similarly, the kind of therapeutic interventions that usually characterize the middle of treatment can often start on the very first session. Nevertheless, sessions in the beginning of therapy have a different quality and a particular focus that set them off from other sessions.

The middle sessions, too, have a very different focus. These usually constitute the bulk of treatment and concentrate on personal problems, everyday life issues, and the intensification of the therapeutic relationship. This is the time in which the major work of therapy occurs.

Termination is another unique time, in that the focus of termination is the beneficial breaking of the therapeutic bonds and preparing the child for reactions to termination. This overview identifies some of the many sequence issues involved in psychotherapy. We will cover these in detail in the following chapters.

12

Special Considerations in Beginning Psychotherapy

Establishing a Therapeutic Atmosphere: Initial Sessions

Many years ago a very wise therapy supervisor told me that "the most important goal of the first session is simply to get the child to come back for another session." If this seems an excessively pragmatic way to begin therapy, it certainly captures the essence of what needs to occur in that first session. Unless the child returns, there can be no psychotherapy, and much of the therapist's task in these early sessions centers around involving the child in treatment. We have already discussed how and why psychotherapy is a strange and even disconcerting event for a child. During the first sessions, the therapist must try to overcome any of the child's negative reactions and show the child that therapy is a positive (if not always pleasant) experience. Secondly, the initial sessions usually determine the tone of therapy and thus establish the communication patterns for later sessions. Lastly, these sessions determine the child's expectations of what therapy will be like, and this too sets a pattern for later sessions.

I suppose the main way the correct pattern is set is by making the first session an enjoyable experience. To this end, although the therapist must gather information and begin the therapeutic process, he should purposely avoid intently delving into embarrassing issues and traumatic emotions that will characterize later sessions. Children are not ready for such emotional digging when they are unfamiliar with the therapeutic process and the strange adult therapist; time must elapse before a therapist can ask that of a child. Aside from focusing on what a therapist must avoid, we need to look at what he must do to bring about an enjoyable initial experience, and these activities will be the major part of the next section.

Establishing the Tone of the First Session

Overall, a therapist should strive to put a child at ease in these initial sessions. Children will likely be somewhat anxious coming to the first session, and a friendly demeanor on the part of the therapist will greatly alleviate their anxiety. In spite of the seriousness of psychotherapy, therapists need to be cheerful and show they are pleased to meet a child during the first session. Hopefully, this will be a natural response because anyone who chooses to be a therapist will look forward to meeting a new child patient. This means the therapist should smile and seem happy to meet the child.

When appropriate, a therapist can be humorous, but one should not tell lots of jokes in an effort to entertain. Children will see through such attempts to win their favor, and besides running the risk of turning them off, it will give them an erroneous expectation of therapy. Obviously, a therapist should never be teasing or sarcastic as that provides a poor model and children will detect the hostility behind such behavior. Eventually, this will alienate the child. Since children are likely to be self-conscious in the early sessions, a therapist ought to avoid staring at the child. Appropriate eye contact is all that is needed.

First Contact Between Child and Therapist

The initial contact between therapist and child is an indirect one and is usually done by the parents under the therapist's instructions. Since the therapist typically meets first with the parents in a diagnostic and history-taking session, the therapist needs to tell the parents what they should say before bringing their youngster to the first session. These instructions should be simple and to the point. I usually instruct parents to tell the child the following: "Tell Brian what I'm like and what I look like [I have a beard]. Also say that when Brian and I get together, we'll talk and maybe play some games, and I think he will have fun. Be sure to answer any questions he has about me, and explain why he is going to see a therapist." Through these simple instructions or other similar ones, the therapist hopefully prepares the child for the new experience. Using the parents, who the child is likely to trust, helps give the needed reassurance.

Many parents need more than these simple directions because they are apprehensive about telling the child she needs treatment. In those situations it is useful to spend a good bit of time discussing the situation in detail. Often a therapist needs to reassure and support a nervous parent when he or she is afraid of the youngster's reaction.

There are many ways to initiate contact with a child. Some therapists prefer to meet with the child and his parents together for the first session. This allows the therapist the advantage of observing family interactions directly and usually avoids any separation problems as the child is still with his parents. This would certainly be the method of choice for therapists with a family-therapy orientation.

The next step is meeting the child for the first session. After the therapist comes into the waiting room to meet the family, he should greet the parent, then pause and allow the parent time to introduce the child. If the parent does not do this, then the therapist should make the introductions, saying something like, "You must be Lisa, I'm Dr. Leve. We're going to spend some time talking [and depending on the age of the child] and maybe play with some of my toys. Why don't we go to my office while your mother waits out here for us?"

This simple introduction accomplishes a number of things. First, by using the child's name you are indicating that you know who the child is and probably have some knowledge about her. Secondly, in using a title like Dr., or Mr. or Ms., you are indicating this is an important and somewhat formal relationship. Finally, in telling the child what you both are going to do, you are indicating that you are not a medical doctor or teacher and you will not give them a physical exam or a test.

At this point the therapist should say, "Let's go to my office now," and lead the way to the therapy room. Unless the child is very young, I do not try to take their hand. I feel such early physical contact may be disconcerting to the child. Since children are seldom talkative in the walk to the office, I do not try to engage them in conversation until we enter the office. Children do not find this silence disturbing. Of course, if they do initiate a conversation, the therapist should respond with warmth and enthusiasm.

Observing Waiting Room Interactions

The therapist can learn a great deal that will be useful in the first session from observing the child and parent in the waiting room. Obviously, the first thing to notice is physical proximity. Are parent and child sitting together or apart? If sitting together are they in physical contact and seemingly dependently tied to each other? If apart, does this indicate a lack of emotional contact, a healthy independence, or simply a lack of available chairs? The child's activity level should also be observed. Is the child actively moving around the waiting room, perhaps disturbing other people and out of the parent's control? Is the parent making an effort to try to control the child? Does the child sitting passively with the parent seem to want to be protected from the strange place and people? Of course, the parents' reaction to their child's behavior should also be noticed. Perhaps the most useful information comes from observing what parent and child are doing. Are parent and child simply sitting in the waiting room doing nothing, or is each engaged in a book or magazine of their own? It is useful to find out if the parent brought some book or toy for the child to read or play with while they are waiting. Are they engaged in a joint activity, such as looking at a magazine together or talking? Are they both truly engaged in the activity, or is the parent simply reading something to the child while the child ignores the parent? Often the child's reaction to the therapist can be predicted from watching waiting-room behavior and that gives the therapist a chance to deal with any expected difficulties.

Another useful bit of information is the reaction of parent and child when the therapist arrives. Is the parent relaxed and pleased to see the therapist, or nervous and ill at ease? Does the child stare at the therapist in a fearful way, or does she seem curious and interested, as if assessing this new adult? More obvious reactions are when the child moves closer to the parent, perhaps hiding her face in the parent's lap, or when older children stare at the therapist with open hostility. These cues are not only valuable in preparing the therapist for any difficulties in getting the child into the therapy room, but are also valuable information for later sessions.

Explaining the Structure of Therapy

The first session is the time for structuring therapy by telling the child what to expect. Obviously, the therapist needs to introduce himself by telling the child his name. This should be done in the waiting room or at first contact between child and therapist. This may need to be repeated, as young or overly anxious children may not remember the therapist's name the first time they hear it. Since younger children are not familiar with psychotherapy, and this is an unusual experience, the therapist needs to explain himself and psychotherapy. This often needs to be done with older children and adolescents, even those who seem knowledgeable, because they often have misconceptions and wide gaps in their understanding. The best way to do this is to explain what you will be doing in practical terms, and how it will help the child. I personally do not like long, involved explanations as children will see what therapy is about soon enough, and the actual experience is the best explanation. I usually tell a child some variation of the following: "When we get together we will talk about many things, including your problems, and sometimes we may want to play with games or toys. In this way I can learn about you and help you feel better about the things that bother you, especially if you're unhappy or scared".

Without going into a long explanation, you want to tell the child that you can help her. In doing this, you are basically trying to instill an expectation of hope about treatment. However, do not overdo this and run the risk of raising unrealistic expectations. One way to do this is to ask the child to tell you about something that bothers her, and then tell the child you will try to help her with that problem. For example, if a nine-year-old boy says that fighting with his parents is a problem, you can tell him you will try to get the parents to see his side and understand his anger at them. This does not raise an unrealistic expectation but lets the child know you are fair, that you take his feelings seriously, and will try to help. This kind of early interaction sets a tone that hopefully will carry through all remaining sessions.

A very important task of the initial sessions is to correct erroneous perceptions the child may have about treatment. For example, with very young children I often tell them I am sort of like a doctor, but a different kind of doctor than the one who gives them shots or listens to their heart. With adolescents and older, seemingly more sophisticated children, after introducing myself I usually ask them if they know why they have come to see me. I also say that I imagine they have questions about what we will be doing, and I will try to answer them. A good way to get at such misperceptions is to try to explore the child's fantasies by asking what they know about this place and do they know what therapists do. Another important fantasy to explore is the child's fear of being crazy; this is especially important for therapists who work in a hospital or institutional setting. Try to find out what "crazy" means to the child without simply applying your own definition. This is important to do with any affect-laden word the child uses. This is also the time to explain how long and how frequently you will be meeting with them.

At some point in the first session, the therapist should ask the child why she is coming, since this is another way to get at the child's fantasies about treatment. If the child says "I don't know," then ask her to guess. The answer to this question will give the therapist an indication of where the child may want to start. If the child cannot respond to either question, you can say something like, "Well, your parents told me . . ." and then see how the child reacts. Whatever the process, the therapist needs to explore the child's initial concept about treatment and then reassure the child by correcting any misperceptions.

Some children will be anxious and the therapist needs to try to put these children at ease. Talking is often too difficult for such children, as it is too passive and too adult an activity. A helpful alternative is suggesting some game or play activity. This takes the attention off the child and onto an activity. Offering a snack also can be helpful in relaxing a child since eating is intrinsically relaxing, gives the child something to do, and interposes an activity between therapist and child. (But only offer snacks if this is something you plan to continue throughout treatment.)

Even if a child is comfortable with a talking type of interaction, be careful not to focus too directly on the child's symptoms, especially embarrassing symptoms like bedwetting or stealing. During the first session, these are best mentioned in a matter-of-fact fashion to let the child know you are aware of the problems but are sensitive enough to avoid making the youngster self-conscious. If the child seems eager to talk, that is fine, but this is too early to push a possibly distressing discussion. With problems that are painful, a therapist should express genuine concern. Needless to say, you should avoid placing any kind of blame on the child, and do not take sides in parent-child disagreements. If either child or parent tries to put you in that situation, you need to say something like, "I don't really know you very well yet or enough about this situation, but I certainly want to hear your side of things".

A good approach in the initial session is to let the child do "reality talk." In other words, let the child talk about everyday things or whatever she feels like talking about because this will allow the child to feel more at ease. The therapist should respond at the level of the child and avoid attempting to generalize, comment on, or explain what the child is "really" saying. The best thing to do is just listen and be interested. If the child does bring up her problems, the therapist should be alert to the child's becoming uncomfortable, and in that case be flexible enough to switch to another topic. Generally, the first session is a time when the therapist tries to promote the child's self-esteem and self-worth by pointing out the child's assets.

The first session is the time when confidentiality is usually explained to the child. As we have already mentioned, this concept is unique for children. They usually find it not only fascinating, but they like the fact that what they say and feel are being given a special kind of respect. There are two important reasons confidentiality should be explained in the initial session. First, the child is likely to feel more positive toward therapy and therapist as a result of being made to feel special, and this is an important goal of the first session. Secondly, the child needs the protection of confidentiality in order to be open with his therapist, and the earlier this starts the better. By telling the child about confidentiality, the therapist is also telling the child that this kind of openness is desired and expected as part of treatment. This expectation needs to be inculcated from the very beginning of therapy.

Understanding the Initial Feelings of the Child toward the Therapist

We have already discussed the importance of the first session in establishing expectations and patterns that will carry through to the remainder of psychotherapy. This is especially important in the therapist-child relationship. Whatever feelings the child brings to the first session, she will be focused on the therapist as the most obvious and important feature of the experience.

There are many aspects of psychotherapy that are anxiety provoking to a child, such as the strange locale, the unfamiliar adult, and the fact that the child may sense a confused and perhaps anxious attitude on the part of the parents. However, many children bring their own emotional reactions to the therapeutic setting, and these also will make them ill at ease. For example, some children have a strong sense of guilt about things they did and believe the therapist will find out that they have done something terrible. Most children feel guilty about even relatively normal transgressions, such as stealing some loose change, hitting a younger sibling, or some sexual activity, and they fear this will be exposed. Although the first session is much too early for the therapist to be aware of the particular fears of the child, he should be alert for such nervous signs and be ready to reassure the child.

Since the child is dealing with a new situation and a strange adult, some degree of anxiety will almost always be present in the first therapy session. This is true no matter what other emotions the child shows. Children often try to disguise their anxiety with other emotions and behaviors. For example, a child may feel and act emotionally distant from the therapist. In this way, she hides her fearfulness and protectively places a social barrier between her and closeness to the therapist. In some cases the child will try to disguise her fearfulness by becoming overly pleasing or emotionally distant because such behaviors give the youngster some control over her interaction with the therapist and allow some protection from this strange adult.

With other children, the natural apprehension the child feels is likely to exacerbate characteristic emotional behaviors. For example, a child who characteristically responds in an angry fashion may become enraged, arguing that she does not like the therapist and does not need to come to these sessions. In reality, the child's anger may in fact be fueled by her worry and apprehension. A secondary benefit is that the angry outburst serves to maintain distance from the therapist, and it provides the youngster with an emotional release. In these early sessions, the therapist should not be fooled by such diverse emotional reactions but instead be alert for signs of anxiety. In that way, the therapist can act to help the child feel more at ease.

Perhaps the most common and easily seen fear is that of separation from a parent. The younger the child the more likely this will be a serious problem. Obviously, preschool and early grade school children are more likely threatened when they are asked to separate from their mother and go off with a strange adult. However, do not overlook the fact that this reaction may be common in children up to adolescence. In rare instances teenagers may also be frightened by the prospect of separation, but the social embarrassment involved in admitting this is so intense that such teenagers will usually disguise their reaction and are more likely to display anger or isolation.

Dealing with Separation Problems

There are many ways to deal with separation fears in the first session, and what is done will depend on the severity of the reaction. A child will usually show some kind of reaction upon meeting the therapist in the waiting room. Perhaps the child will cling to the parent, hide behind her, or refuse to look at the therapist. This is not the time to physically force the child into the office, because it will not only frighten the child but likely cause a rather instant resentment. In addition, the therapist is demonstrating that the child has little say in the therapy process and that the therapist's decisions will prevail. This is likely to make the child feel relatively powerless, thus creating false expectations about her role in future sessions. In addition, physical force is likely to create an embarrassing scene in a waiting room which will not improve the self-esteem or public image of the therapist.

As I mentioned earlier, the best approach to a child with separation fears is to have the parents prepare the child before bringing her. When the therapist suspects that separation may be a problem, parents need to be coached on how to introduce the idea of psychotherapy to the child. I make sure the parents tell the child about me; for example, what I look like, how I act, or anything else they think the child might like to know. Be sure the parents let the child know what will happen ahead of time by telling her that we will spend most of our time playing games and talking, and I think she will enjoy our time together. Providing this kind of preventative information is probably the best and easiest way of handling separation fears. As you might expect, it will not work with all children.

When a child refuses to go with the therapist on the first session, there are a number of approaches from which to choose, depending on the orientation and assertiveness of the therapist, the personality of the child, and the extent to which parents can assist. Some therapists believe that children should not be forced or coerced in any way. If they refuse to go with the therapist, their wishes should be respected (Axline, 1947). In this case, the therapist should talk with the child briefly in the waiting room, asking that she come back next week when they can try again. I personally do not favor this laissez-faire approach because if a child is in need of treatment, it should not be postponed. Also, the therapist may be providing the child with an unrealistic sense of control for later sessions. Parents, too, may be confused since they have gone to the trouble and expense of bringing the child to therapy only to have the therapist seem to undo their decision.

At this point, the therapist can decide to talk with the child in the waiting room so long as it is not too crowded and there is a modicum of privacy. This is easier to do in a private waiting room where no one else is present. In this situation, the only difference between the therapy room and the waiting room is the physical location since therapist, parent, and child are already together.

This approach may seem awkward and embarrassing for the therapist, but it often works. It is more difficult to carry out in a typical clinic waiting room since other children and parents will be watching the proceedings, and, in the case of children, they may try to intrude into the situation. However, if the therapist is not overly self-conscious or upset by having his freedom curtailed, this can even be a useful procedure in the public waiting room typical to most clinics.

A more comfortable approach is to tell the child that his parent can come up to the therapy room with him, and the first therapy session can begin with the parent present. In this situation I ask the parent to bring a magazine or book so she can sit and read. In this way the parent is present in the therapy room but does not interact with the child, thus leaving the child free to be engaged with the therapist. If the child tries to cling to or talk to the parent, I say, "Bob, your mom is busy reading and since we have things to do and play with, you shouldn't disturb her." Parents usually are quick to take the hint, and if the child persists, they say they are busy reading and then ignore the child. If the parent does not take the hint, then in front of the child I tell the parent she should continue reading and not interact with her youngster. When the child seems relaxed and comfortable with therapy room and therapist, I suggest the parent will be more comfortable in the waiting room. If the child agrees, the parent can leave. At this point the therapist might say, "Why don't we go and see your mom in the waiting room after she leaves because that way you can be sure she is still there. We can go anytime you want." This gives the child some sense of control over what is happening and reassures the child she has not been left.

Another approach is to ask the child to go with you, but promise that you will take her back to the waiting room in ten minutes to check on the parent. Often this provides the child with enough reassurance to separate from the parent. When I have used this approach, I find that once the child becomes engaged in a therapy activity, she forgets about checking on her parent or does not want to interrupt the activity. I often have to remind the child that we need to return to the waiting room to check on her parent, but I am scrupulous about doing this because I want to demonstrate to the child that I will always keep my promises.

The worst situation is when the child absolutely refuses under any circumstances to go with the therapist. Since the child is in need of treatment, there is no choice but to force the issue. However, any physical force should always be done by the parents, never the therapist. At this point the therapist can suggest that the parent walk or even carry the child to the therapy room. I also ask the parent to stay until I feel the child will not try to bolt out the door. I do not want to be in a situation of having to physically bar the door. Some therapists prefer not to have parents in the session; after they bring the child to the office, they ask them to leave. In this situation the child may try to push the therapist out of the way, but usually children do not directly attack the therapist.

Do not try to force an adolescent into therapy with physical means. At that age it will not work because they are too big and have too much control over their own life. Besides, the risk of a physical fight with either parent or therapist is dangerous and likely to result in a permanent rejection of therapy and therapist. If an adolescent is serious about rejecting treatment, there is little anyone can do about it, and at that age she has too many ways to thwart the process. The best thing to do is wait and let the adolescent know you are available if and when she changes her mind.

Understanding Initial Feelings of the Therapist toward the Child

Just as the child develops early feelings toward the therapist, so, too, the therapist has reactions to the child. A therapist needs to be aware of such feelings both because they will affect interactions with the youngster and because they are an important source of information. Of course, every therapist has his own personality and characteristic emotional reactions, and any reactions to the child's behavior must be viewed against this background. Fortunately, although therapists differ from one another, each of us has a stable way in which we emotionally respond to a child in the first session. Since we know relatively little about a child in the first session, chances are good that therapists begin these sessions relatively consistently from one child to another. Therefore, differences in our emotional reactions are in response to the child. It is the awareness of these personal feelings that provides as much or more valuable therapeutic information as we might receive from a more objective analysis.

The most important question to ask during and after the first session (indeed, it is a useful question all through treatment) is, "How did the child make me feel?" This is usually not a difficult question to answer as it only requires the therapist to reflect on his overall emotional reaction toward the child at the end of the session (although a thorough review of the session is likely to show that the child generated differing feelings at various times). Most therapists have positive feelings toward a new child patient at the end of the first session, but such a global assessment is too simplistic. Aside from knowing whether or not you like or dislike the child, you need to ask yourself questions such as, "Did I feel sorry for him?", "Was I feeling apprehensive that she might break something?", or "Was I becoming irritable, but being careful not to show that?" Such questions force the therapist to go into greater detail in understanding his feelings toward the child.

Once a therapist is aware of what feelings the child has created, the next question is, "How did the child do it?" This is a useful question because it will give a therapist valuable insights into the child's mode of functioning. If the therapist felt uncomfortable, even anxious in the therapy session, perhaps it was because the child seemed to be constantly exploring drawers and cabinets without permission and the therapist was always one step behind and worried that the child might break something or see private papers. Maybe the child often ignored what the therapist was saying and only partially responding to the therapist's attempts to engage the child.

Perhaps the session ended with the therapist feeling especially pleased and having a special fondness for the child. Was this because the child was being overly ingratiating toward the therapist, openly saying how much she liked the therapist and all the fun things in the office? In the case of an adolescent patient, was she being overly cooperative, trying hard to be a good patient by answering anything the therapist asked and being very open about her emotional problems? Often children can create an initial fondness in the therapist by acting dependent and looking to the therapist for help.

The most important question and the one most difficult to answer is, "Why did the child need to create these feelings?" This question gets at the motivation behind the actual behavior and identifies the causal factors that underlie the child's emotional problems. It is a crucial question because the answer to this is the key to what the therapist should do in therapy. Knowing a child's conscious and unconscious needs directs the therapist to what issues are important. Of course, there are so many different motivations and causal factors—as many as there are children. An example or two cannot give a comprehensive picture of the many reasons why and how children create emotional reactions in their therapist, but hopefully the following example can serve as an illustration of how a therapist goes about understanding and using his own emotional reactions to a child.

> Ben was an eight-year-old I was seeing for the first time. After our time together I tried to reflect on how I felt during the session. My first reaction was to realize I felt somewhat exhausted by our time together, as if I had been constantly one step behind Ben throughout the session. In spite of this, I found Ben to be very likable; more so than the majority of children I had seen for a first session. Thinking about my sense of fatigue and always being one step behind, I realized that during the session Ben was in constant motion. I remembered him always moving around my office, looking into drawers and cabinets, and constantly asking me questions. Although the pace of his conversation was not rushed and he was very polite in listening to my answers, he talked a great deal for a first session. The constancy of his talking made listening to what he was saying an effort, because he no sooner finished one thought than he was rambling on about something else.

When I tried to understand why he seemed so likable I realized he had made an unusual effort to please me. As part of his constant talk he told me how much he liked my office and the neat toys and games I had. He also said he had been scared when his mother told him he was going to see a psychologist, but now that he knew me, he was not scared any more. In fact, he wanted to come again. I also realized that many of his questions were about me, especially what I liked to do. He seemed pleased by what I told him and acted as if he were impressed. Knowing how Ben went about making me feel the way I did toward him, I began to understand why he was so active during our time together and why he needed to be so ingratiating to me. This was a youngster who was very frightened by being in the presence of a large and strange man. His constant talking was a way of releasing the anxiety he felt. His exploration of my office was likely an effort to reassure himself that it was a safe place. His ingratiating behavior toward me was his attempt to make sure I was safe. By doing everything he could to make me like him, he made sure that he would not be in any danger from me. I, as a strange male adult, was an unknown quantity to him at this first meeting. I might become angry or aggressive, but now that I liked him, everything was all right.

This observation was confirmed when I learned more about his traumatic background and an especially traumatic experience he had recently undergone. Although his new stepfather seemed to be a caring individual who Ben liked, his natural father had been a very angry man who often exploded at both his wife and son. Although he had not physically abused Ben, he constantly shouted at him for the slightest transgressions and, at times, did hit him. There were often horrible scenes in which he would physically beat Ben's mother in front of Ben. When Ben was six his mother divorced her husband, and there had been no contact between Ben and his father since that time. Three months before our therapy session, Ben had been left in the care of a male relative for a week. During that time he had been repeatedly sexually abused; the abuse was both emotionally and physically painful. Throughout the week he was threatened with a number of terrible punishments if he ever mentioned to anyone what was happening. Among other things, the male abuser promised he would come back and kill him, and burn down his house and kill his family.

Obviously, the emotional reactions I felt toward Ben during our first session were a direct consequence of the traumatic experiences he had suffered. Ben was potentially frightened by any male adult, but he was especially frightened by a therapeutic situation in which he had to be alone in a room with an adult man. I seemed to be someone who was nice and who would not harm him, but as a result of his past experi-

> ences, he could never be sure. In consequence, Ben was very anxious in my presence and his anxiety came out in his constant motion and exploration of my office. The frantic movement served as a physical release for some of his tension, and the accompanying exploration of my office was probably an unconscious way to learn about me to see if I really were someone who was dangerous and might hurt him. Certainly, his interest in my personal life served this purpose. Finding nothing to indicate that I was dangerous was reassuring, but he still needed to protect himself. Ben did that by being especially pleasant, at times even ingratiating. In a sense, his defense was to be overly nice to me because then I could not get angry with him or physically hurt him. In this way Ben was unconsciously protecting himself as best he could from this unknown adult whom he sensed was potentially a serious danger. Obviously, knowing my own emotional reaction to Ben also led me to how he caused such a reaction and what was behind such behavior. Knowing this not only told me his characteristic style of behaving under stress, but also what issues I would expect to emerge and need to work at in later sessions.

I hope this example demonstrates the importance of the therapist's own reaction to a child and how much information can be gleaned from such self-awareness. It is a crucial therapeutic skill to use in the beginning of treatment.

13

The Termination of Psychotherapy

Just as the beginning sessions of psychotherapy demand special treatment techniques and theoretical considerations, so, too, are the final sessions special. The ending of psychotherapy has a unique quality and brings up many new issues that need to be dealt with before a satisfactory termination can occur. Although we will discuss many of the complex aspects of termination, there is essentially one overriding issue to the termination process: the loss of a relationship. Loss is not unique to the therapeutic process, but, sadly, is a part of every individual's life. Some of the children we see in treatment have suffered some traumatic loss such as the death of a parent, grandparent, sibling, or close friend. Even those children who are fortunate enough to avoid experiencing such an actual loss still face the usual fears of maternal separation and abandonment. Thus loss can occur in many symbolic forms and still be a serious and traumatic issue for children. The ending of therapy reawakens this common issue, and so it not only becomes a problem to overcome, but also a therapeutic opportunity for emotional growth.

Deciding When to Terminate Treatment

Depending on the needs of the child and the theoretical orientation of the therapist, psychological treatments differ in their time orientation. Some are relatively short-term while others may go on for years. Nevertheless, all psychotherapy has an end point, and the therapist, child, and parents must decide on when treatment will end. This is not an easy decision because, like all other aspects of psychotherapy, there are a multitude of variables to consider. However, there are certain identifiable criteria for making this decision. In this section we will discuss these criteria.

Symptom Remission

Perhaps the most obvious and specific criteria for ending psychotherapy is the remission of the child's symptoms. Every child begins therapy with a particular complex of symptoms, and when these symptoms are significantly modified or no longer exist, the therapist may decide that an end to treatment is warranted. For example, the child who began therapy having anxiety attacks and stomachaches every morning before school and is now able to tolerate a normal classroom for the entire day might be ready to end treatment. The electively mute youngster who refused to speak to anyone outside his immediate family and is now able to talk appropriately to neighbors, teachers, and friends also may be ready to terminate. Similarly, an end to treatment might be appropriate for the bulimic teenage girl who started treatment with eating binges and self-purging and now is able to eat normal meals and stop the impulse to throw up after every meal. These indications of termination are objective and easily identified, but the simplicity of symptom remission can be deceiving. Few children are completely free of all their symptoms, so the question becomes one of severity. What is an acceptable level of symptom remission? There is also the question of symptom substitution. Has the child given up his initial symptoms, but developed new ones? Are these new ones serious enough to extend treatment? Are they really related to the original difficulties or are they minor problems, part of normal developmental difficulties that will arise and then disappear over time?

Certainly, evaluating symptom remission depends on who is evaluating the situation. The school-phobic child who no longer has overt anxiety attacks and stomachaches may seem to be symptom-free to his parent who has already left for work before school begins, but if the child is still fearful of his classroom and uneasy in the morning, the child is not symptom-free. The parent, who has the responsibility of getting the child to the school bus and worries about being late for his or her own work, may have yet another perspective. The therapist, knowing that these residual symptoms are to be expected, may feel that from a long-term perspective the child is symptom-free. Obviously, this commonplace example shows the seeming simplicity of using symptom remission as a criteria for termination is quite useful, but not as clear cut as might be expected.

Parental Criteria for Termination

Obviously, parents have a strong voice in the termination of treatment; in fact, they have the ultimate decision. Parents must be an integral part of the process from the beginning, not only because they must concur with the decision, but also because after treatment has ended they must help their child maintain the therapeutic gains. Because the parental role is quite different from that of the therapist, they are sensitive to different aspects of their child and often have a different set of criteria for termination. Although parents can understand and be sensitive to the entire range of emotional difficulties, generally they look toward symptom remission as the primary indication that treatment should be ended, and they especially focus on here and now symptoms that impact directly on them. This means they are particularly sensitive to problems in parent-child interactions, such as temper tantrums, arguments, stealing, lying, or running away from home. Of course, dangerous symptoms such as anorexia or suicidal depression are difficult to ignore, and only the most insensitive of parents would be oblivious to such life-threatening problems. School difficulties are attended to if only because poor report cards, calls from teachers, and parent-school conferences are difficult to ignore. Many parents are sensitive to other, more subtle emotional difficulties, but this often varies with parental personality, socio-economic level, education, and psychological knowledge and sophistication.

As a general rule psychotherapists are future-oriented and give more importance to abstract factors in deciding on termination. They attend to such issues as peer interactional skills, ability to trust, and whether or not the child can express and accept warmth. Generally, parents are more likely to terminate treatment sooner than a therapist because of this difference in time orientation as symptoms are likely to change sooner than the more future oriented, subtle factors important to the therapist.

Financial burdens and other pragmatic considerations also make parents likely to terminate sooner than most therapists. As a general rule, the closer the socio-economic and educational level of parents and therapist, the more likely they will consider similar factors in termination. However, the usual excessive concern with symptoms and "here and now" orientation of parents can be modified by the therapist. During parental sessions the therapist can educate parents as to the importance of the more subtle aspects of their child's behavior, and expand the scope of the parent's evaluation of their child.

Parents exercise their influence on the termination process in another important way. Not only are they involved in the decision to end treatment, but they must also be able to support termination, and this means they must be capable of maintaining and promoting the gains made by their child. Whether a five-year-old or a high school senior, parents are a powerful influence in a child's life and through their conscious and unconscious encouragement can help their child continue the treatment gains. However, parents can also either consciously or unconsciously thwart a child's progress in many ways, but most often this centers around issues of assertiveness or independence. Many parents are threatened by children who challenge them, form their own opinions, or refuse to do everything they say. Others want, even need, their child to be dependent on them. In spite of wanting their son or daughter to overcome emotional problems, they may have a difficult time tolerating the new-found independence and assertiveness that underlies such positive changes. Hopefully, a therapist will be able to see these difficulties before termination and help the parents cope. This can occur by suggesting parents receive treatment of their own, either with the child's therapist, through family sessions or by arranging for them to seek their own therapy.

Unfortunately, such changes are likely to become obvious only near the end of treatment because that is when the child will begin to try out any new behaviors. At this point, the therapist is often facing a deadline in her attempts to deal with the situation. A brief treatment approach, using either a cognitive or reality-oriented approach, can help the parents support the child's therapeutic changes. When time is not as critical a factor the therapist can use a psychodynamic approach. This helps parents become aware of the psychological issues that underlie their reluctance to accept the changes in their child. Whatever the chosen mode of intervention, the therapist must make a serious attempt to help parents accept the situation.

Parents, like their child, also must be prepared for termination, although the process is less critical because they are not breaking an intense therapeutic relationship and will not experience the same degree of loss. However, in some situations, the parents will have developed strong emotional ties or become dependent on the therapist, and the therapist may need to help one or both parents cope with a serious emotional loss. Commonly, parents miss the advice, support, and reassurance of the therapist, and the therapist will need to help them develop a new self-confidence toward their child. Of course, they should be reassured that they can always get in touch with the therapist if they need to.

The most difficult situation is when the child is ready for termination but the therapist knows that because of their own difficulties, the parents cannot support the child's progress. After the therapist has done as much as can be done to help the parent or parents directly, there is little choice but to try to help the child deal with the situation, and this task becomes an important part of psychotherapy. This presents the therapist with a delicate situation. Usually the child realizes the parents are having difficulty accepting the new behaviors, so the therapist must give the child insight into why the parents cannot do this without blaming them. Simply siding with the child against the parents is not helpful at this stage. Hopefully, the child has enough perspective as a result of treatment that he or she can understand the reasons behind the parents' inability to accept new independent behaviors. In this situation, the therapist can help the child work out ways to deal with parents' problems.

Surprisingly, children, even learning disabled or borderline children, can do this. I have poignant memories of one particular parent-child session that illustrates this. I was beginning to terminate treatment with Darin, a fifteen-year-old borderline boy I had seen in weekly sessions for two years. A central problem was Darin's overbearing dependence on his widowed mother. He stayed around the house, following her from room to room, talking, and expecting her to do everything for him. Often when she went to the bathroom, he would wait outside the door still talking to her. Over the two years we worked together, he began to spend time away from the house enjoying school activities and making friends. At this point, his mother no longer complained that she felt smothered by him, but began to do everything she could to thwart Darin's independence. Although she had her own therapist, she was unable to make much progress in letting her son go. I tried holding joint sessions to discuss the problem, but with little success. During one particular session, she became more and more resistent and complained constantly about Darin not being around and not being helpful to her. Darin tried time and again to argue with her, at times pleading that he was trying to be helpful but he did not want to stay around the house; he also wanted to be with his new friends. As his mother became more agitated, Darin realized she was not able to hear what he was saying, and in desperation turned to me and shrugged, as if to say, "Can you see what she's like? What can I do?" At this point I realized that further joint sessions would be fruitless, and I needed to help Darin cope with his mother's distress. We spent the next few sessions talking about her difficulties, and why she was unable to allow him his independence. I reassured Darin that his attempts at becoming independent were appropriate and needed to continue, adding that he was already a sophomore in high school and, in spite, of her efforts, his mother could not really hold him back. If nothing else, time would soon take care of the problem.

School Criteria for Termination

Like parents, teachers tend to be attentive to "here and now" problems. In a school context, these include classroom disruptions, hitting or bothering classmates, disobeying teachers, lack of motivation, and poor school performance. As these problems are ameliorated, teachers and other school staff look toward termination of treatment, whether this means moving a child back into a mainstream classroom or ending therapy sessions with a school psychologist. Generally, school personnel have an indirect effect on termination because they are not part of the decision-making process and are seldom asked whether a child can end treatment either in a clinical setting or with a private therapist. However, they can provide crucial information to both parents and therapist as to how a child is doing, and in that way they do have a voice in termination.

Unfortunately, such information varies with the attitudes and requirements of a school system as well as with the personality of the particular teacher. Some teachers seem to have little difficulty with an emotionally disturbed youngster while others are driven to distraction, so a therapist must try to evaluate the tolerance and endurance of the teacher when using such information. Since the primary objective of school is learning, a teacher's opinions are often skewed by a child's achievement. Therefore, the emotional problems of children who are earning good grades are likely to be underestimated while the opposite will be true for children with poor grades. Robert Rosenthal's studies on the "Pygmalion effect" document the powerful distortions that can occur due to a teacher's expectations (Rosenthal, 1973)(Rosenthal & Jacobson, 1966). A therapist considering termination must be aware of these distortions when utilizing school information. Of course, school is only a part of a child's life. Teachers see only a limited aspect of a child's total life, a fact that must be taken into account.

Children who have made significant therapeutic progress in many areas often do not show a corresponding change in their school grades. In my personal experience, school grades are one of the last factors to show improvement after treatment, and I have at times terminated therapy feeling confident that the child's grades would improve within six months to a year. Fortunately, my belief has usually been substantiated.

Child Consideration for Termination

Young children almost never directly ask to terminate treatment, probably because they do not have the intellectual sophistication to understand that psychotherapy is a sequential process in which the alleviation of their emotional difficulties results in the end of their treatment. Actually, young children only vaguely understand the connection between their emotional problems and therapy because that requires they see their behavior from another person's perspective. They are far too egocentric for that. Usually, they just like or dislike therapy, and seldom think beyond this simplistic assessment. Thus, rather than deciding whether the time is right for termination, they may want to end their sessions because they are bored, want to spend more time with friends, or become unhappy with their therapist. If they also dislike therapy, they usually want to end their sessions as soon as possible. Compliant and dependent children will usually follow the wishes of parents and therapist and continue the sessions regardless of their feelings.

As children get older, they become increasingly able to understand that therapy has an end point, and they are more likely to request an end to treatment. By the time they reach adolescence, they have definite feelings about termination and will voice their opinions. Their request needs to be taken seriously.

Whatever the age of the child, his behavior both in and out of psychotherapy is likely to indicate whether the child is ready for termination. In therapy, play becomes more constructive and less impulsive and disorganized. The child begins to interact with the therapist in a less emotionally chaotic and mutually respectful way. He may seem more self-confident, have made meaningful friendships, and made significant progress in school. These kinds of changes in the child's behavior indicate the therapist can consider termination and need not wait for the child to bring up the subject.

Peer Criteria for Termination

The opinion of the child's friends and classmates are almost never used in determining termination, primarily because they are considered too young to be taken seriously, and they occupy a very different part of the child's life from parents and therapist. I have already mentioned that an increase in peer interactions is a good indicator of termination, but this is usually judged indirectly either through teacher and parent observations or by the therapist listening to the child's conversation during therapy sessions. Actually, direct peer judgments have been found to be very reliable and valid, and it is too bad that such a useful perspective is largely ignored. Objective measures such as peer sociograms have been used in research situations, but these measures have not found their way into common therapeutic usage. This is especially unfortunate because the judgment of classmates and friends, even as young as the primary grades, are not only unbiased, they tap some of the most important social and emotional skills of a child. When a child has begun to develop sound friendships, this indicates that he has developed some crucial skills. At least to some extent the child has learned to control his impulsive emotional reactions. Basically, normal kids do not tolerate much emotional grief from other kids. Those children are quickly rejected and become social isolates. Friendships require tolerating emotional closeness, expressing warmth, sharing interests and possessions, compromising on activities, and generally being loyal to one another. These form the basis of good emotional adjustment and indicate that termination is appropriate. Assessing peer reactions will indicate the extent to which a child has developed these skills. My own opinion is that developing good social relationships is the single most important criteria for termination and future prognosis.

General Termination Criteria

If we look beyond the simple alleviation of symptoms as the criteria for termination, there are a number of other factors that should guide this decision. Perhaps the most important is whether the child can maintain and promote the gains made in treatment. This is a difficult judgment to make and is usually made solely by the therapist because a therapist not only has more of a concern for emotional issues likely to arise in the future, but also has the knowledge of child development and personality theory to make such predictions. However, all the theory in the world cannot ensure that predictions about a child's emotional functioning one, three, or five years in the future will be accurate. In addition to theoretical expertise, such assessments must be made with an intimate knowledge of the child gained over many therapy sessions, and the deeper the therapist's understanding of his patient, the more accurate such assessments will be.

To make these predictions, however tentative, the therapist must look beyond symptomatic changes and focus on what changes have occurred in a child's basic emotional functioning. Perhaps the following questions and guidelines will be helpful.

1. *Are the child's emotional problems under control?* For termination, a child need not be symptom free, but any difficulties should be a lingering phenomenon and not significantly affect the child's life. The following example will illustrate this question. David, a fourteen-year-old, began treatment as a result of violent temper outbursts toward his parents and teachers. After forty sessions, his therapist decided to terminate treatment in spite of the fact that David still tended to argue with these adults. However, David now understood why he fought with them, the arguments did not escalate into the previous inappropriate swearing and hurling objects, and he was able to accept not always getting his own way. Although the situation was not perfect, David's control over his anger was continually improving and so this was an acceptable time for termination.

2. *Has the child learned to control his or her impulsive behaviors?* Most children, depending on their age, will show some impulsiveness, but this should be age-appropriate and have definite limits so that it does not interfere with the child's overall functioning. The key criteria is whether the child can control his impulsiveness and regain behavioral control. A ten-year-old who continues to play with friends after being called home for supper should come in after a couple reminders. Even if he remains angry at his mother, the confrontation should not escalate into a temper tantrum during dinner, and any anger should be forgotten in a short time.

3. *Is the child's thinking level appropriate to his or her age?* Children need to have a good grasp of cause and effect, be realistic in judging situations, and be able to discriminate important from unimportant details in their life. These skills are basic to normal adjustment and indicate that a child has at least the rudimentary cognitive skills needed for normal emotional functioning. These are signs that termination may be considered.

There are some exceptions in applying this guideline with children who are intellectually impaired or schizophrenic. Intellectually impaired youngsters usually have difficulty with cause-and-effect reasoning and may not be able to discriminate important from unimportant life issues. But these are cognitive limitations that cannot be surmounted by psychotherapy. In this case, there is no sense in delaying termination when the therapist and parents feel the child has come as far as he can.

I recently terminated treatment with a nineteen-year-old slightly retarded patient who had made excellent progress in a cognitively oriented therapy. Among other gains, he had established some social contact with other students, no longer inappropriately followed girls for whom he had developed an unrealistic infatuation, learned appropriate topics of social conversation, and was able to control his bizarre sexual behaviors. In spite of the fact that he still functioned at a ten-year-old social level and had great difficulty with understanding social relationships, I felt he had made as many gains as he could at that point, and we ended treatment.

Schizophrenic children also have limits to their cognitive abilities, and in spite of the fact that they may have made important gains in treatment, these children will likely still have important deficits in their thinking. At some point, a therapist must question whether further treatment is worth the effort. Hopefully, therapy has brought them to the point where they can function adequately on some level. Perhaps the youngster will need further supports, such as a self-contained class, a therapeutic summer camp, a specialized living situation, or additional treatment, at a later date.

> A good example of such a situation was Jason, a fifteen-year-old I had treated for two years in weekly sessions. He was a very dysfunctional boy who became violently car sick in any bus, subway, or automobile. In high school he was a complete social isolate who had no interest in or knowledge of typical teenage affairs. After two years of treatment, he was no longer car sick, had obtained and held a summer job, and although he still had no friends, he was trying to participate in age-appropriate activities by joining the yearbook staff and becoming assistant manager of the track team. Although his impulsive and illogical thinking had improved, he still functioned on a preadolescent level in his interactions with other high school sophomores. We terminated treatment at this point because I felt that in terms of contemporaneous problems, we had accomplished all we could and the basic developmental difficulties underlying his distorted thinking would not be helped by additional sessions. I also knew that, as he faced future life issues such as a career and the intimacy of a male-female relationship, he would again need additional treatment.

4. *Is the child's fantasy level appropriate for termination?* A youngster's fantasies and daydreams are a good indicator of emotional growth, and the therapist is in a unique position to evaluate such fantasies through play, therapeutic conversation, or projective material. Age-appropriate fantasies often indicate creativity, are a natural way of working through conflicts, and in general are a sign of good emotional adjustment. The expansiveness and extent to which a fantasy departs from reality is not a poor prognostic sign so long as the child recognizes the difference between fantasy and reality. Fantasies should make psychological sense in that they serve a purpose, attempt to master a fear, or express a conscious or unconscious wish. These kinds of fantasies are positive indications for termination. Of course, fantasies that are disorganized, bizarre, or disconnected are poor prognostic indicators.

5. *Does the child have the ability to learn from emotional experiences?* One of the most important therapeutic changes to indicate termination is the ability to learn from emotional experiences. A successful treatment experience hopefully produces a robust series of changes in overall functioning, and not just in the child's present adjustment. Children's lives change constantly in many ways, large and small. They gain and lose friends, change teachers, classes or even schools each year, and, depending on family stability, may have to cope with personality changes in their family members. If a parent loses a job, there will be changes in the family's financial circumstances. Children have to adjust to such changes. One of the reasons emotionally disturbed children need treatment is because they are unable to weather such disruptions. Seeing a child's emotional reaction to these disruptions provides a therapist with important information, and can tell the therapist if the youngster has developed the emotional skills to handle ongoing life changes. This can be done by comparing how a child adjusts to changes that occurred early in therapy compared to how they are handling similar changes at the present time. When a child can tolerate such changes, and even benefit from them, that child has learned new and more adaptive emotional reactions which are a positive prognosis for the future.

6. *Can the child recover from emotional traumas?* Every child's life is rife with emotional upsets, but normal children have the ability to suffer through these experiences and return to a normal emotional equilibrium. The ability to recover emotionally is a very important prognostic sign for termination. The degree to which a child falls apart as the result of an emotional trauma is not always an accurate indicator of therapeutic progress because it depends not only on the child's personality, but also on the stresses and traumas inherent in that child's environment. While we expect a normal child to maintain a general emotional balance, the more important factor is the child's ability to recover from the emotional trauma. That ability shows the youngster will tolerate future emotional upheavals, a crucial consideration for termination of treatment.

7. *Never terminate psychotherapy in the midst of a crisis.* Termination can be a difficult time for a child for many reasons, and it presents its own unique problems that center around separation, the loss of an important relationship and self-reliance. Trying to deal with these issues and a crisis at the same time is difficult. Even if the child is ready to end therapy, a therapist is better off helping the child cope with the crisis first and delay termination to a later time. This more conservative approach is easier for the child and avoids the risk of termination becoming prolonged or even interrupted.

Premature Termination

Ideally, every child should end treatment symptom-free and with all his or her emotional conflicts laid to rest, but this is not always the way things happen. Many times treatment must be ended before the child is ready or the therapist feels that termination is appropriate. There are many reasons for this. Families move away, therapists take new career positions in other states, student therapists must rotate to new training sites, insurance runs out, parents lose their motivation to continue treatment, or families can no longer afford treatment (I personally feel the latter should never be a reason for termination because an ethical therapist has a responsibility to continue therapy once a relationship has been established. Unfortunately, this ethic has too often been lost to the bureaucracy of third-party payments and the accepted selfishness of modern capitalism). Termination of psychotherapy in these situations presents a therapist with additional difficulties and these will be discussed in a later section of this chapter.

There are three unique situations when a therapist will decide to prematurely end treatment. The first is when the initial problems and present emotional difficulties have been successfully dealt with, yet there is little doubt that the child does not have the emotional skills to cope with new developmental tasks at different ages. In other words, the emotional tasks of a future developmental stage may be too difficult. For example, a child who after therapy is able to cope with the more benign social relationships common at ages nine and ten may not be able to deal with the more complex social and sexual relationships of adolescence. The therapist may anticipate that the child's present emotional skills will be inadequate for a later developmental age, yet if the child cannot make any further therapeutic progress at that time, termination is indicated. The therapist can prepare the child for this situation, saying something like, "As you get older you may face new problems in high school and college and you might need to see a therapist again. I hope that you will remember how helpful therapy can be and will not hesitate to see me or another therapist." Of course this needs to be said many times and in many different ways. Usually a therapist can not predict exactly what new problems a child will face because that depends on the unknown meanders of the child's life; however, this kind of preparation for both child and parents will be helpful.

Another situation involving premature termination can occur when the present emotional issues have been successfully treated, but the therapist knows they will reemerge at a later time due to new stresses and life traumas. Some learning-disabled children exemplify this situation. As a result of treatment, these children may have successfully dealt with their feelings of inadequacy and lack of self-confidence in the context of school and classmates. At this point treatment would be terminated because there are no serious problems to deal with and hence no further motivation for treatment. However, these problems in self-esteem and lack of confidence can still emerge later in life.

A colleague reported a vivid example of exactly this situation with one of her adult patients. This thirty-four-year old man had been seen in psychotherapy as a child and had resolved many of the emotional difficulties stemming from his severe reading difficulties. For many years he was not only symptom free, but had a successful career in his own plumbing business. However, he became severely depressed when his business suffered a moderate financial setback due to a downturn in the local economy. As a result, he was unable to work and began to isolate himself from his family and friends. The basis for his depression was the reemergence of his lack of confidence and self-esteem, which caused him to question his competence in all areas of his life, including his career. Although he had resolved his emotional problems in the context of his childhood environment, these same problems had reemerged in a new context after more than twenty years.

The last situation in which a therapist should elect premature termination is when treatment is unsuccessful. All treatment research indicates that there are some children who do not benefit from psychological treatment. There can be many reasons for this: a patient-therapist mismatch, a child who cannot form a relationship, lack of support for treatment by parent, or a host of other difficulties. Whatever the reason, once the therapist is satisfied additional treatment is futile, therapy should be terminated. Of course, the usual attention to termination issues should be observed because the youngster may still be dealing with a difficult separation and loss.

Reactions to Termination

Children can react in many ways to termination, but all will likely experience some emotional reaction. Perhaps the child will feel frightened and insecure without the support of the weekly psychotherapy sessions. Perhaps he will feel a sense of loss as a result of leaving the familiar therapist with whom he has shared many aspects of his life. The loss of the child's therapist may be an isolated experience, or it may be one of many losses experienced in his life.

The particular reaction will depend on the child's history, the course of therapy, and the intensity of the therapeutic relationship. Whatever the reaction or absence of reaction, a therapist cannot assume the child does not need to be prepared for this final stage of treatment, and a therapist should attend to termination issues with every child. However, the way the therapist deals with termination will depend on the type of reaction the child experiences.

Reality Reactions

Many children, having come to a sound resolution of their emotional difficulties, are ready to leave treatment and the dependence of psychotherapy. Such children want to be independent and perhaps, sensing they have successfully dealt with their problems, have already started to pull back from their therapist. Perhaps "pulling back" does not accurately describe the situation. More accurately, they now have a different perception of the therapist: they have begun to view their therapist as an adult friend rather than as a helper, and they are able to understand and respond to the reality of termination issues without emotional distortions.

Of course, this does not imply that the youngster will have no reaction to the ending of psychotherapy. Likely, he will miss therapy and the therapist and may feel frightened. Such a reaction is to be expected and is a healthy response to any loss. The main point is that since the child understands the reality of the situation, the therapist can deal with termination in a realistic way. Likely, the therapist will reassure the child that any fears about leaving therapy are normal and to be expected. Similarly, the therapist needs to give the child permission to feel sad about the ending of their relationship. Often children are reluctant to voice these intimate feelings openly and the therapist may want to help the child through modeling her own feelings, saying "We have been together for quite some time and I'm going to miss you." Whatever the technique, the therapist needs to help the child express such feelings and accept them as a normal part of termination.

When children have done well in treatment and successfully dealt with termination, the therapist may find that the last session is a good time for review and self-evaluation. This should be a positive way of saying good-bye in that the therapist can help the child see all the beneficial changes that have been made and how much has been accomplished as a result of the child's efforts. This is not so much a pat on the back as a realistic recognition of the child's accomplishments. This is best accomplished by not just telling the child how well he has done, but by helping the child discover this on his own, because that will have more meaning.

Grief Reactions

Most children who have experienced previous losses are likely to suffer grief reactions in response to termination because the loss of their therapist will bring up the same feelings they experienced in the earlier loss. The reemergence of these feelings will occur even if the issues around earlier losses have been dealt with in therapy since termination will make the child feel vulnerable. This reaction can occur whatever the nature of the actual loss. It is likely to occur if a parent or close relative has died or even if the child has lost a pet they loved. I know a friend who still is sad thinking about a puppy who was taken from him when he was five-years-old and had only had the puppy for a week.

A common childhood loss occurs as a result of divorce. In this situation the child may lose the parent completely if the parent moves away, or the loss may be partial if the noncustodial parent only sees the child on a limited visitation schedule. The main thing to remember is that loss can be actual or symbolic, and there may be little difference in the emotional response.

In this situation the therapist has an excellent opportunity to help the child deal with the grief, whatever the source. Sometimes the child may associate the grief with the loss of the therapist or sometimes with a significant earlier loss. The object of the grief reaction is irrelevant. The main point is that the emotional reaction is now accessible and the therapist has a wonderful opportunity using whatever therapeutic approach is needed to help the child overcome the grief. If the child has made good therapeutic progress, an existential approach is often useful in helping the child realize there are and will continue to be many traumatic situations that cannot be avoided or changed, but only endured.

Once the child has dealt with the pathological elements of the grief reaction, the therapist can then focus on the realistic part. In spite of the sadness of parting, therapy is no longer needed. The child has made wonderful gains, and therapy has to end. The therapist can explain that the child now has a part of therapy and his therapist within him in the form of skills he will always use. Also, they will remember each other and still have contact in their thoughts. In many cases, the therapist may want to reassure the child that, if necessary, they can still see each other on occasion, and the child can always return if once again he needs the therapist's help. The therapist might even schedule another session a month or two down the road as a way of demonstrating that the child is not being abandoned. If the child is still having difficulty, especially when he is anxious about termination, the therapist might elect a gradual termination, cutting back to every other week or every third week at first, then once a month, and finally complete termination.

Pathological Reactions

Pathological reactions are usually experienced in children with impaired thinking, borderline personalities, or conduct disorders. They will often respond to termination with anger or serious distortions of reality, depending on the particular content of their emotional problems. A child will become angry if that is his characteristic emotional response, although the child usually will deny he is angry over termination but will get angry at the therapist over other things. The important point is to be aware of any increase in the child's anger at this time.

Distortions in reality around termination can take many forms. A good example was a teenager with borderline reasoning abilities whom I treated. He had lost his mother to cancer when he was young. Even though we had dealt with this trauma in therapy, it reemerged on termination. When I told him at the beginning of one session that he was ready to end treatment, he seemed to accept this and agreed, but as the session progressed, he became quiet and sad. Finally, unable to contain his fear, he blurted out, "You're not sick are you? Are you going to die?" This gave us another opportunity to talk about death and his mother's death.

Dealing with pathological reactions is difficult because of the defects in reasoning, but the therapist has already been dealing with this over the course of the child's treatment and so should know how to relate to the youngster. If the reality distortions can usefully be dealt with, then that is the first step. Of course, children who respond with anger will have some sort of hidden distortion of reality fueling the anger, but may refuse to deal with that. After attempting to make the child aware of the reality distortion, the therapist needs to try to correct it by trying to point out what is reality and what are fantasy distortions. Usually a cognitive approach is most useful in stressing the realistic aspects of termination, and that is what the therapist must do. In addition, the therapist must be reassuring to the child. The therapist should tell the youngster how well he has done, and because it was done so well, it is time for therapy to end. He should also say that he feels sure the child will be able to handle problems by himself now. If the therapist was not sure of this, they would not be terminating. As always, the therapist should tell the child what is going to happen, allowing sufficient time for discussion and reactions.

Appendix A

Summary of Child Treatments

Behavioral Treatments

Behavior therapies are based on learning theory. There are many kinds of learning theories, but all attempt to explain behavior changes as an individual's reaction to changes in his or her environment. These changes follow certain learning principles which both control and predict a person's behavior. Behavioral treatments, which were developed through experimental work with animals, tend to focus on relatively specific problems. The methods tend to be structured and overall treatment time is brief.

Operant Behavior Therapy

This type of treatment is a pragmatic application of operant learning theory as espoused by B. F. Skinner. The focus is on the consequences of the child's behavior and the therapist attempts to modify behavior through techniques of positive reinforcement, extinction, punishment, response cost, and token economies. In this treatment, the therapist or behavior modifier attempts to take control of certain aspects of the child's life or, acting as a teacher, instructs other adults to take on this control. This treatment has found popular application in schools and other institutions as a way of decreasing undesired behavior and increasing positive behaviors. Many therapists find that this is a useful technique to teach to parents even when they are engaged in another type of psychotherapy with the child.

Respondent Behavior Therapy

This treatment is based on the Pavlovian theory of classical conditioning which involves the pairing of conditioned and unconditioned stimuli and responses. At present there are a number of separate techniques that fall under this category. In systematic desensitization, anxiety reactions are treated by first teaching the child relaxation techniques, then constructing a hierarchy of the feared situations and teaching the child to relax while imagining those situations. In emotive imagery, usually used with young children, the therapist relaxes the child through pleasant stories, then he presents the fearful events to the relaxed child through a therapist-generated hierarchy. Using a related procedure, in vivo desensitization, the child experiences the feared situation directly under the therapist's supervision and protection. In implosion therapy, the therapist has the child experience unrealistically high intensities of the fearful objects or events so that they will be better able to tolerate their fears in normal situations. Throughout all of these techniques, the therapist structures the course of therapy and directs the child's activities.

Modeling

Modeling is the use of the well-known learning technique by which children observe and imitate the behavior of others. In modeling, children watch a model carry out behaviors that they are unable or unwilling to do. The model may be seen live, on film, or video, or in covert modeling where the model is pictured in imagery. In participant modeling, the imitation procedure is combined with guided reinforced practice. As in other behavioral treatments, the therapist decides on how the therapy is carried out and what symptoms will be treated.

Cognitive Treatments

Cognitive therapy developed out of behavior therapy, but here the focus is not on modifying behavior per se. Rather, the therapist tries to change the cognitions or thought patterns of the individual. Cognitive therapists believe thoughts and cognitive patterns mediate changes in emotions and behavior, so their methods are aimed at changing dysfunctional ways of thinking. Usually this is done in a direct and confrontive fashion. Like behavior therapy, the treatment tends to be very structured and brief and diagnosis is not an important part of the therapeutic process.

Rational-Emotive Therapy

Developed by Albert Ellis, RET assumes that emotional problems arise from faulty reasoning and the task of the therapist is to correct this by modifying the self-verbalizations of the individual. This is done by forcefully challenging irrational beliefs and using basic logic to show the individual his self-defeating ways. In addition, imagery is used by asking the client to imagine certain upsetting situations. This is done to help the client understand the relationship between irrational thoughts and pathological behavior. Often the therapist directs the client to carry out various cognitive exercises as homework. The therapist controls and structures the overall course of treatment and his role is direct and forceful. Treatment is usually relatively brief.

Beck's Cognitive Learning Therapy

Developed by a psychiatrist, Aaron Beck, this treatment also assumes that disturbed behavior is usually the result of faulty reasoning. It further assumes the client has developed personal rules that are illogical, arbitrary, or too absolute. In therapy the client is helped to label their failures and challenge irrational rules. Beck's methods are often used with depressed individuals and a salient feature of treatment is getting the individual to gain a sense of competence. To do this, the therapist directly helps the client master some positive act, no matter how small. As part of treatment, the client is given homework which consists of graded task assignments. This, too, is a structured treatment in which the therapist is very directive.

Michenbaum's Self-Speech

Michenbaum's method is based on the belief that what a child says mediates his or her behavior. In order to change the behavior, the therapist teaches the child self-statements. These are words or phrases which the child uses to guide or control himself. In addition to learning to use the phrases, the child is taught to use them at appropriate times. In this treatment, the therapist functions much like a classroom teacher, often modeling what he wants the child to do and guiding the child through verbal and written exercises.

Self-Instruction Training

Philip Kendell has developed a treatment technique that is similar to Michenbaum's self-speech and this method has been used extensively with impulsive and hyperactive children. This very structured treatment consists of a progressive series of lessons which teach a child rigid techniques to control behavior. When faced with a problem, the child is taught to carry out certain prescribed steps which will allow them to cope with the problem in a controlled fashion. As the child learns these steps through the series of lessons, he or she is rewarded for successful performance. Kendell's methods rely on extensive teaching material in the form of lesson plans and directed exercises which the child completes. In both Kendell's and Michenbaum's methods, the therapist controls the course of treatment. The range of behaviors treated also tends to be narrow and specific.

Psychodynamic Treatments

The category of psychodynamic treatments is somewhat difficult to define because it covers such a wide range of ideas and theories. In spite of the theoretical differences, these treatments are similar in that they emphasize the relationship between the child and other people as a crucial part of treatment. Most therapists believe children go through distinct stages in their development, and they believe that a child's past development is crucial to treatment. Whatever their differences, these psychotherapies comprise a category of treatment that is separate from those previously discussed. At the present time, these are probably the most widely used treatments.

Classical Child Psychoanalysis

Melanie Klein, Anna Freud, and others originated this form of treatment by modifying Sigmund Freud's psychoanalytic methods for child treatment. Problems are seen as a result of unresolved conflicts at an earlier psychosexual level which results in an imbalance of the id, ego, and superego. This method relies on free association, play, dream analysis, and analytic interpretations to help the child achieve insight. The therapist is passive and nondirective, and this allows the child to develop a transference neurosis which is used to help the child gain insight into his or her emotional difficulties. In its traditional form, the child sees the therapist twice a week or more, and therapy often continues for years. This is very time-consuming, expensive, and serious intrusion into the child's life.

Ego Psychology

A refinement of psychoanalysis developed by Heinz Hartmann, Erik Erikson, David Rappaport, and others, this treatment assumes that the ego, not the id, is the prime mover in personality development. Ego psychologists believe that individuals continue to go through stages of development from birth to death as a result of the Ego's attempt to adapt to external reality and an Ego Analytic therapist needs to be concerned with all stages, not just those that occur in the early years. Thus the content of the treatment differs from that of classical psychoanalysis, however, the therapeutic techniques such as free association, play, transference, and interpretations are similar.

Adlerian Therapy

Alfred Adler was one of Sigmund Freud's original students. He broke from Freud's emphasis on sexuality and formulated his own theory of personality development based on strivings of superiority. Adler did not necessarily see this striving for superiority as a banal impulse, but in many cases it reflected a need to live a more perfect life. The need for superiority arose from natural and inevitable feelings of inferiority which arise from physiological weakness and the inferiority inherent in being a child among competent elders. Psychopathology is based on individual reactions to inferiority and can take many forms. In therapy, Adlerian therapists rely heavily on interpretations that connect the past and present with the future. They also give a child feedback about both their mistakes and their strengths. Dream analysis is also used to help the child toward a more fulfilling social existence. Adler was instrumental in establishing many of the first clinics for children and, in addition to the psychotherapy he developed, his ideas are often used as the basis for parent workshops on child rearing. The course of treatment is usually short and often time limited.

Object Relations Theory

This treatment developed by Ronald Fairbairn, Otto Kernberg, Heinz Kohut, and others differs from classical psychoanalysis in that it emphasizes the relationship between the self and objects as the major motivation in personality development ("object" is Sigmund Freud's original term for other people since they are seen as "objects" of gratification). In many ways, object relations theory is a marriage of psychoanalysis and developmental theory, According to these theorists, children go through different stages, from normal autism, in which the infant is undifferentiated in respect to others, to normal symbiosis, in which there is confusion between self and others, to differentiation, in which the child can now separate and individualize himself from others, to integration, when the child not only separates himself from others, but can also begin to understand relationships. Object relations theorists believe that emotional difficulties are related to identity confusion and narcissism. Techniques known as mirroring and transference are an integral part of treatment. Treatment is intensive in that children often come once a week or more, and treatment often lasts well over a year.

Psychoanalytically Oriented Psychotherapy

This is a very commonly used type of treatment which incorporates the basic ideas of psychoanalysis but in a much more flexible form. There is less reliance on establishing a transference neurosis, and regression is not encouraged. For the most part, conversation centers on current issues and is reality-oriented. Changes in behavior are carried out through corrective emotional experiences and intellectual insights. In general, this kind of treatment requires a greater amount of planning on the part of the therapist. Therapy lasts a shorter amount of time than classical psychoanalysis and in some cases is brief, often requiring less than fifteen sessions. The therapist usually does not take a very directive role, although he or she does passively guide the content and makes interpretations.

Gestalt Therapy

Fritz Perls was one of the main innovators of this kind of treatment. In Gestalt therapy, problems are seen as disorders of growth and interruptions in social development. Because of this, children remain stuck on childhood fantasies and future-oriented thinking. Therapy is an attempt at consciousness-raising rather than ameliorating symptoms, and this is done through cathartic experiences and trying to move the child to a sensory awareness of the present. Therapy is active and confrontative and utilizes many "Gestalt exercises." The therapist avoids any attempts to control the child; in fact, one goal of treatment is to have the child discover that he never really needed therapy. This type of treatment usually lasts a year or more.

Existential Psychotherapy

This treatment, based on the concepts of existential philosophy, was proposed by theorists such as Ludwig Binswanger, Medard Boss, Ernst Keen, and Rollo May. Existential theorists believe individuals must face and find meaning in the darker experiences of life. The crux of this treatment is to find meaning in the way the child sees life and accept the child's freedom to choose his own solution. Although existential therapists use varying techniques, they all try to be authentic in the way they respond to the child. They foster the child's openness to meet the world and not lie or hide from it. The source of psychopathology is lying and avoidance which then leads to neurotic anxiety and meaninglessness. Treatment consists of confronting the child, being authentic in responses to the child and not letting the child hide or lie. In this the therapist does not control treatment, but does confront the child.

Another type of existential psychotherapy is William Glaser's reality therapy. This treatment is present-centered and based on encouraging a child to accept responsibility for his actions. Much of the therapist's work centers on the child's emotional strength and what the child does to maintain his pathological symptoms. Existential psychotherapies are not short-term and may last a year or more.

Client-Centered Therapy

In the 1940s, Carl Rogers presented his first ideas on what is now called client-centered therapy. This treatment is more concerned with the process of therapy rather than espousing a theory of personality development. In that respect, it is a very pragmatic treatment which centers on the relationship between child and therapist. Carl Rogers believed the therapeutic relationship encompasses all the conditions necessary for beneficial change. The task of the therapist is to empathically understand the child's feelings and mirror these feelings back to the child. In this way the child can see the distortions in his emotions and behaviors, and this initiates the change process.

The general theory underlying this form of psychotherapy is that all people have a basic motivation for self-actualization, which Roger's defines as an inherent tendency of people to develop capacities which enhance life. People also have a need for positive regard from others, and often this need to be liked and loved by others becomes so strong that we give up our need for self-actualization in the expectation of receiving love. The ultimate goal of client-centered therapy is enhanced self-actualization, but intermediate goals focus on the alleviation of the problems caused by the overdependence on positive regard from others. In this form of treatment, the therapist allows the child to control many important decisions in the therapeutic process. This treatment is long-term and can last more than a year.

Appendix B

Family Therapies

Behavioral Family Therapy

This approach to family therapy is based on principles drawn mainly from behavior modification and social learning theory. The task of the behavioral family therapist is to train parents to modify the child's behavior through effective contingency management. Typically, parents are seen by themselves without their children, but older children and adolescents are usually introduced in the sessions. Parents are first taught to define, record, and monitor their child's behavior. They then intervene to accelerate positive behavior with reinforcements and to decelerate negative behaviors through extinction, appropriate punishment, and time-outs. Parents also use behavioral contracts. These are written agreements in which the child agrees to modify behaviors according to a certain criterion and receives specified reinforcement contingencies. This type of family treatment focuses on present behaviors and is designed to be a short-term treatment.

Structural Family Therapy

This form of family treatment developed by Salvador Minuchin attempts to restructure the family organization and change the dysfunctional transactional patterns. The therapist acts as a director who manipulates the family in order to expose inappropriate coalitions, subsystems and boundaries. The therapist strives primarily for actions that change the family system; achieving insight among family members is not an important part of treatment. The main focus is on present family patterns, although the therapist deals with past dysfunctional transactional patterns as they affect the current family functioning. The length of treatment depends on the particular family and its problem.

Psychodynamic Family Therapy

Most of the early innovators of psychodynamic family therapy, such as Nathan Ackerman, Ivan Boszormenyi-Nagy, John Bell, and James Framo, came from a psychoanalytic background and, as a result, psychoanalysis is the major theoretical basis for this treatment. Psychodynamically oriented family therapists deal with family conflicts and distorted relationships that arise from intrapsychic problems of individual family members. Thus the focus is on the individual as well as the family. In this type of treatment, the therapist attempts to uncover unresolved conflicts from the past in an attempt to lead both individuals and family to meaningful insights. To do this, the therapist remains neutral and unintrusive compared to most other forms of family therapy and therapy is usually long-term. By leading family members to better self-insights, they are better able to understand each other and change the family interactions in a positive way.

Communicative Family Therapy

The three major innovators of this approach are Jay Haley, Virginia Satir, and Don Jackson. They believe that problem families have dysfunctional rules of communication among family members. The goal of family treatment is to have the family discover and modify these rules. Communicative family therapists are action-oriented, present-oriented, and directive, and they openly manipulate the family rather than rely on insight and interpretations. This is done through such techniques as: 1.) prescribing the symptom, in which the therapist instructs the family to exaggerate a problem which alters its meaning to the family since it now comes from the therapist, and 2.) relabeling, in which the therapist redefines the problem so that it has different meaning to the family. Using these and other techniques, the therapist interrupts maladaptive feedback loops "games," and the overall homeostatic balance of the family, forcing it into other more adaptive ways of relating.

Appendix C

Parent Questionnaire

1. Headaches
   - *If yes,* is child ever sick with them?
   - Does it affect sight at all?
2. What about stomachaches?
   - *If yes,* does child vomit?
3. Does child ever wet bed?
   - *If yes,* how often?
   - Has child always wet bed, or when did it start?
   - Does he/she wet when away from home?
4. Does child wet pants or are there daytime accidents?
   - *If yes,* how often?
   - Has child always wet pants; when did it start?
   - Does child wet when away from home?
5. Does child soil himself/herself?
   - *If yes,* how often?
   - Has child always; when did it start?
   - Does child soil when away from home?
6. Has child ever had staring spells, or periods of being out of touch?
   - *If yes,* is there eye blinking, or lip smacking or any repetitive movements during staring spells?
   - Are the spells preceded by any unusual sensations, e.g., feelings of panic or odd tastes or smells or stomach upset or getting pale?
   - Does child fall down during spells or lose control of bowel or bladder?
   - Is child alert afterwards, or drowsy and confused?
   - Are there headaches afterwards?
7. Does the child fall down a lot?
   - *If yes,* is it because child trips over something or does child just seem to fall over?

- Is falling down usually preceded by unusual sensations, e.g., feelings of panic, odd tastes, smells, stomach upset or getting pale?
- Any loss of bowel or bladder control?
- Is child alert afterwards, or drowsy and confused?
- Are there headaches afterwards?
- Is there any repetitive movements of arms or legs during these spells?

8. Does child have any mannerisms or tics, such as twitches of face or shoulders, or a habit of blinking?
   - Any other habits, such as picking at his clothes, rocking, smacking his lips or other repetitive movements?
   - *If yes,* can you get the child's attention, or is the child "out of touch" while performing these movements?
   - Is there any falling down associated with these movements?
   - Or headaches, or wetting or soiling self?
   - Are these movements preceeded by any peculiar sensations, e.g., feelings of panic, or upset stomach, or odd taste in mouth, or anything else?
9. Does child stutter or stammer?
   - *If yes,* what is it like?
   - How often?
   - When did it start?
10. Does the child have any other difficulty with speech?
    - *If yes,* what is it like?
    - How often?
    - When did it start?
11. Was talking delayed compared to your other children?
12. Was it intelligible, or was there a long period when you were the only one who could understand your child?
13. Has child ever had speech therapy?
14. Did you ever think that your child could not hear well?
15. Has child ever seemed to have trouble understanding you, like saying "Huh?" or "What?" frequently, or having you repeat directions?
16. When child is telling you about a story or experience, does the child make sense, or do you have trouble understanding what the child is talking about?
17. How active is child? Restless? Always up and on the go?
18. About how many minutes can the child sit still?
    - At supper?
    - In a car?
    - Reading?
    - Making something?
19. Is the child easily frustrated, giving up too quickly in his/her efforts?
20. Is distractibility or attention span a problem?
21. Is he/she a fidgety child—always moving some part of body, handling things, squirming?

22. Does the child fail to finish things he/she starts?
23. How is child doing in school?
    Failing Below average Average Above average
    - Reading
    - Spelling
    - Arithmetic
    - Handwriting
24. Has the child ever repeated a grade?
    - *If yes,* which grades and why?
25. Has the child ever had special help in school?
    - *If yes,* how often per week?
    - Since when?
    - Is it helping?
26. Would you say child losses his/her train of thought? His/her mind drifts from one thing to another?
27. How is your child remembering things, e.g., how to dress self in right way, bedtime routine, or how to get a job done?
    - Can you leave your child to do things by himself/herself, or do you have to supervise a lot?
28. How is your child at following a long series of directions?
    - If you send your child to get three things from another room, does he/she always forget one or two things?
29. Does your child have trouble recalling your directions if asked to repeat them?
30. Does child think very slowly? Child seems to be in a fog?
31. Does child seem to have trouble remembering things he/she really cares about?
    - Does he/she lose his/her things a lot?
    - Does he/she forget to bring what he/she needs for school?
32. Write down the sports child most likes to take part in.
    - For each sport, compared to other children of same age, how well does child do in each sport? (i.e., below average, average, above average)
33. Would you say your child is clumsy or uncoordinated?
34. How often does child get hurt, have accidents?
35. Is discipline a constant thing? Is child always "getting into things?"
36. How does child respond to discipline?
    - Does it seem to help or is child doing the same thing five minutes later?
    - Repeats same behavior over and over again?
37. Does child deny mistakes or blame others?
38. Childish or immature? Acting like a much younger child?
39. Wants help doing things he/she can do alone?
40. Clings to parents or other adults; needs constant reassurance?
41. Is child excitable and impulsive? Acts without thinking?

42. Does child have unpredictable mood swings; mood changes quickly or drastically?
43. Is child the sort who has trouble getting along with brothers and/or sisters?
44. Trouble getting along with other children?
    - Not much liked by other children?
45. Tends to do things on his/her own? Solitary?
46. Does child have difficulty with his/her vision?
    - *If yes,* what type of difficulty?
    - When did it start?
    - Has child ever had vision training?
    - *If yes,* when?
    - With whom?
    - For how long?
47. Does child have problems with sleep?
    - *If yes,* what type of problem?
    - How often?
    - When did it start?
48. Does child have eating problems?
    - *If yes,* what types of problems?
    - How often?
    - When did it start?
49. Does child take vitamin supplements?
    - *If yes,* what kinds?
    - How often?
50. Does the child have any special problems, experiences, or worries about sexual issues?
    - *If yes,* please explain.
51. Is child unable to stop a repetitive activity?
    - *If yes,* what types of activities?
    - When did it start?
    - How often?
52. Is child destructive?
    - *If yes,* what does he/she destroy?
    - When did it start?
    - How often?
53. Is child cruel to animals or others?
54. What special interests does the child have, such as hobbies or special activities?
55. What are your child's strengths, and what makes him/her special to you?
56. List three adjectives that best describe your child.

Please make any other comments you wish– . . .

Appendix D

Therapist-Parent Inventory Interview

Face Sheet Information
Name of child:
Name of parent being interviewed:
Age of all family members:
Religious affiliation:
Address:
Home and work phone numbers:

I. *Child's History*
   a. Presenting symptom(s)
   b. Course of symptoms
   c. Past developmental information, medical information, social and psychological history
   d. Child's relationships with parents and siblings

II. *Parent's Marital History*
   a. Ages of parents at marriage
   b. Time span between marriage and birth of first child
   c. Marital conflicts
   d. Conflicts over children
   e. Current marital status: married, separated, divorced, widow

III. *Parent's Personal History*
   a. Primary family, past and present
   b. School and vocational
   c. Social and avocational
   d. Medical and psychological problems

IV. *Other Problems*
   a. Previous marriage(s)
   b. Other children
   c. In-laws
   d. Neighbors

V. Parent's Opinion of Causes of Emotional Problems and Their Ideas about Treatment.

Bibliography

Achenbach, T. M., (1992) *Developmental Psychopathology*. In Bornstein, M. H., & Lamb], M. E. (Eds.) Developmental Psychology, 3rd Edition. Hillsdale, N.J.: Lawrence Erlbaum

Achenbach, T. M. & Edelbrock, C. S., (1978) The classification of child psychopathology: A review and analysis of empirical efforts. Psychological Bulletin, 85, 1275–1301

Allan, J. A. B., (1978) "Serial Drawing": A therapeutic approach with young children. Canadian Counselor, 12,(4) 223–228.

American Psychiatric Association (1952). *Diagnostic and Statistical Manual of Mental Disorders, 1st Edition*. Washington, D.C.: American Psychiatric Association.

American Psychiatric Association (1968). *Diagnostic and Statistical Manual of Mental Disorders, 2nd Edition*. Washington, D.C.: American Psychiatric Association.

American Psychiatric Association (1980). *Diagnostic and Statistical Manual of Mental Disorders, 3rd Edition.*: Washington, D.C.: American Psychiatric Association.

American Psychiatric Association (1987). *Diagnostic and Statistical Manual of Mental Disorders, 3rd Edition, Revised*. Washington, D.C.: American Psychiatric Association.

Axline, V., (1947) *Play Therapy: The inner dynamics of the childhood*. Houghton Mifflin Co: New York.

Beitman, B. (1987) *The structure of individual psychotherapy*. The Guilford Press, New York.

Beutler, L. E., (1986) Systematic eclectic psychotherapy. In J. C. Norcross (Ed.), *Handbook of eclectic psychotherapy,*. New York: Brunner/Mazel.

Boorstin, D. J., (1987) *Hidden History*, Vintage Books: New York.

Chance, P., (1979) *Learning Through Play: Summary of a Pediatric Round Table Cochaired by Brian Sutton-Smith, Ph.D.*, and Richard Chase, M.D., The Company, Piscataway, New Jersey.

Chatwin, B., (1987) *The Songlines*. Viking Books, New York.

Costello, A. J., Edelbrock, L., Dulcan, M., Kalas, R., & Klaric, S. (1984) Report on the NIMH Diagnostic Interview Schedule for Children (DIS-C) Washington, D.C.: National Institute of Mental Health.

KlarFrank, J. & Marmor, J., (1978) *Effective Ingredients of Successful Psychotherapy.* Brunner/Mazel, New York.

Freeman, R., & Hunt, P. (1982) *Tried and True: Games for children's activity therapy groups.* College Park, MD: University of Maryland.

Garfield, S. L. (1986) An eclectic psychotherapy. In J. C. Norcross (Ed.) *Handbook of Eclectic Psychotherapy.* New York: Brunner/Mazel.

Glicklich, L. B., (1951) A historical account of enuresis. Pediatrics, 8, 859–876.

Greenberg, L. S. and Safran, J. D., (1987) *Emotion in Psychotherapy,* Guilford Press, New York.

Greencavage, L. M. & Norcross, J. C., (1990) Where are the commonalities among the therapeutic common factors? Professional Psychology: Research and Practice, 21, 372–378.

Group for the Advancement of Psychiatry. (1966) Psychopathological disorders in childhood: Theoretical considerations and a proposed classification, (Report No. 62). New York: Group for the Advancement of Psychiatry.

Hartmann, D. P., Roper, B. L., & Gelfand, D. M. (1977). An evaluation of alternative modes of child psychotherapy. In B. Lahey & A. E. Kazden (Eds.) *Advances in Clinical Child Psychology (Vol. 1).* New York: Plenum Press.

Hodges. K., McKnew, D., Cytryn, L., Stern, L., & Kline, J. (1982). The Child Assessment Schedule (CAS) diagnostic interview: A report on reliability and validity. Journal of the American Academy of Child Psychiatry, 21, 468–473.

Johnson, J., Rasbury, W. C., & Siegal, L. J., (1986) *Approaches to child treatment: Introduction to theory, research, and practice.* Pergamon Press, New York.

Kovacs, M., & Beck, A. T. (1977) An empirical approach toward a definition of childhood depression. In J. G. Schulterbrantt & A. Raskin (Eds.) *Depression in Childhood: Diagnosis, treatment and conceptual models.* New York: Raven Press.

Kovacs, M. (1985) The childhood depression inventory. Psychopharmacology Bulletin, 21, 995–998.

LaGreca, A. M., (1990) *Through the Eyes of the Child.* Allyn and Bacon, Boston.

Leve, R. M., (1980) *Childhood: The study of development.* New York: Random House.

Luborsky, L., McLellan, A. T., Woody, G. E., & O'Brian, C. P. (1983, July) Therapist's success rates and their determinants. Paper presented at the meeting of the Society for Psychotherapy Research, Sheffield, England.

Matison, R., Cantwell, D., & Russell, A. T. (1979) A comparison of the DSM II & DSM III in the diagnosis of childhood psychiatric disorders II: Interrater agreement, Archives of General Psychiatry, 36, 1217–1222.

Nickerson, E. T., (1973) The use of art as a play therapeutic medium in the classroom. *Art Psychotherapy,* 1, 293–297.

Nickerson, E. T. & O'Laughlin, K. S. (1978) *Action therapies.* Lexington, Mass.: College Xerox Publishing.

Nickerson, E. T. (1980) It's fun—but will it work? The use of games as a therapeutic medium for children and adolescents. Journal of Clinical Child Psychology; 9, 78–81.

Nierenberg, B., (1988) Personal Communication.

Norcross, J. C., (1986) Eclectic psychotherapy: An introduction and overview. In J. C. Norcross (Ed.) *Handbook of Eclectic Psychotherapy.* New York: Brunner/Mazel.

Norcross, J. C. & Guy, J. D. (1989) Ten therapists: The process of becoming and being. In W. Dryden & L. Spurling (Eds.) *On Becoming a Psychotherapist.* London: Tavistock/Routledge.

Ollendick, T. H. & Hersen, M. (1993) *Handook of Child and Adolescent Assessment.* Boston: Allyn & Bacon.

Piaget, J. & Inhelder, B., (1969) *The Psychology of the Child.* New York: Basic Books.

Piaget, J., (1969) *Judgement and Reasoning in the Child.* London: Routledge and Kegan Paul.

Piaget, J., (1969) *The Mechanisms of Perception.* New York: Basic Books.

Prochaska, J. O., (1984) *Systems of Psychotherapy.* Dorsey Press, Homewood, Ill.

Prochaska, J. O. & DiClemente, C. C., (1984) *The Transtheoretical Approach: Crossing the traditional boundaries of therapy.* Homewood, Ill.: Dow Jones/Irwin.

Prochaska, J. O. & DiClemente, C. C., (1986) The transtheoretical approach. In J.C. Norcross (Ed.) *Handbook of Eclectic Psychotherapy.* New York: Brunner/Mazel.

Quay, H. C., Classification. (1979) In H. C. Quay & J. S. Wherry (Eds.). *Psychopathological Disorders of Childhood (2nd Ed.).* New York: Wiley.

Ramirez, M., (1991) *Psychotherapy and Counseling with Minorities: A cognitive approach to individual and cultural differences.* Pergamon Press, New York.

Ramirez, M. & Castaneda, A., (1974) *Cultural Democracy, Biocognitive Development and Education.* New York: Academic Press.

Rappoport, J. L. & Ismond, D. R. (1990) *DSM III-R Training Guide of Childhood Disorders.* New York: Brunner/Mazel.

Rosenthal, R., (1973) The pygmalion effect lives. Psychology Today, 7,4, 56–66.

Rosenthal, R. & Jacobson, L. (1968) *Pygmalion in the Classroom; Teacher expectation and pupils intellectual development.* New York: Holt, Rinehart and Winston.

Rutter, M., Lebovici, S., Eisebberg, L., Sneznevskij, A. V., Sadoun, R., Brooke, E., & Lin, T. Y. (1969) A tri-axial classification of mental disorder in children. Journal of Child Psychology and Psychiatry, 10, 41–61.

Rutter, M., Shaffer, D., & Shepard, M. (1975) A multiaxial classification of child psychiatric disorders: An evaluation of a proposal. Geneva, Switzerland: World Health Organization.

Rutter, M. & Shaffer, D. (1980). DSM III: A step forward or back in terms of the classification of child psychiatric disorders? Journal of the American Academy of Child Psychiatry, 19, 371–394.

Shaw, B. F., (1983, July) Training therapists for the treatment of depression: Collaborative study. Paper presented at the meeting of the Society for Psychotherapy Research. Sheffield, England.

Schetky, D. H. & Benedek, E. P. (1992) *Clinical Handbook of Child Psychiatry and the Law.* Baltimore: Williams & Wilkins.

Strupp, H. H., (1981) Toward the refinement of time limited dynamic psychotherapy. In S. H. Budman, (Ed.), *Forms of Brief Therapy, New York, Guilford Press.*

Sugarman, S. (1986) Individual and family therapy: an overview of the interface. In S. Sugarman, (Ed.), *The Interface of Individual and Family Therapy.* Aspen Publishers, Rockville, Maryland.

Weiner, I. B., (1975) *Principles of Psychotherapy,* John Wiley & Sons, New York.

Welner, Z., Reich, W., Herjanic, B., and Jung, K. (1987). Reliability, validity, & parent-child agreement studies of the Diagnostic Interview for Children and Adolescents (DICA). Journal of the American Academy of Child Psychiatry, 26, 649–653.

Winnicott, D. W., (1971) *Playing and Reality*, Basic Books, New York.

Wolberg, L. R. (1982) *The Practice of Psychotherapy*. New York: Brunner/Mazel.

Zeig, J. K., (1987) The evolution of psychotherapy-fundamental issues. In J. K. Zeig, (Ed.), *The Evolution of Psychotherapy*, Bruner/Mazel, Inc., New York.

Index